Biomass, Biorefineries and Bioeconomy

Edited by Mohamed Samer

Published in London, United Kingdom

Biomass, Biorefineries and Bioeconomy
http://dx.doi.org/10.5772/intechopen.97968
Edited by Mohamed Samer

Contributors
Jean-Philippe Terreaux, Rakesh Govind, Jack Baltzersen, Shiva Charan, Dulce María Diaz-Montaño, Nkosikhona Madolo, Francis B. Lewu, Mohamed Samer, Prince Nana Amaniampong, Martina Francisca Baidoo, Nana Yaw Asiedu, Lawrence Darkwah, David Dodoo-Arhin, Jun Zhao, Francois Jerome, Guilherme Moscato Malavazi, Alireza Shafizadeh, Payam Danesh, Grimaldo Quispe Santivañez, Henry Juan Javier Ninahuaman, Sholahuddin Sholahuddin, Chikako Asada, Yoshitoshi Nakamura, A. B. M. Abdul Malek, Rona Joyce B. Landoy, Rex B. Demafelis, Bernadette T. Magadia, Anna Elaine D. Matanguihan, Ifeanyi Michael Smarte Anekwe, Edward Kwaku Armah, Emmanuel Kweinor Tetteh, Gabriela E. Moeller-Chavez, Rosa Angélica Guillén, Cristina Lizama-Bahena, Luis Gerardo Trevino-Quintanilla, Martin Barragan-Trinidad, Victoria Bustos, Nina Štirmer, Ivana Carević, Johan Werkelin, Meheretu Jaleta Dirbeba, Meegalla R. Chandraratne, Asfaw Gezae Daful

First published in London, United Kingdom, 2022 by IntechOpen
IntechOpen is the global imprint of INTECHOPEN LIMITED, registered in England and Wales, registration number: 11086078, 5 Princes Gate Court, London, SW7 2QJ, United Kingdom

British Library Cataloguing-in-Publication Data
A catalogue record for this book is available from the British Library

Additional hard and PDF copies can be obtained from orders@intechopen.com

Biomass, Biorefineries and Bioeconomy
Edited by Mohamed Samer
p. cm.
Print ISBN 978-1-80355-720-5
Online ISBN 978-1-80355-721-2
eBook (PDF) ISBN 978-1-80355-722-9

Meet the editor

Prof. Dr. Mohamed Samer is a laureate of the 2019 Cairo University Scientific Excellence Award. He is also the recipient of the 2017 Privilege Medal of First Class issued by the Egyptian President and laureate of the 2016 State Encouragement Award conferred by the Egyptian Government. He obtained his Ph.D. from the University of Hohenheim, Germany. He has led seventeen research projects and established five research laboratories. Dr. Samer has 120 publications, 70 of which are peer-reviewed articles published in high-impact journals, and 20 patents to his credit. He is a member of thirteen scientific societies and a peer reviewer for thirty scientific journals. He is also a reviewer for seven research funding agencies.

Contents

Preface

This book provides useful information on biomass (i.e., biological wastes or biowastes) generated from agriculture and forestry, food industry, and wastewater treatment.

Biomass is a largely untapped source for the production of value-added bioproducts and bioenergy. Their recovery utilizes biological and chemical processes that provide alternative sources for biochemical feedstocks in the production of different bioproducts. For instance, high-value biochemicals can be recovered from biomass using biorefineries. Similarly, many opportunities exist for alternative bioenergy and biofuels that can be produced from biomass through utilizing biorefineries. Resource biorecovery thus supports sustainability goals by reinjecting products into the circular bioeconomy.

This book is a helpful resource for NGOs, universities, research institutes and centers, experimentalists, academics, scientists, scholars, researchers, as well as undergraduate and graduate students worldwide specializing in energy engineering, environmental engineering, bioresource engineering, biosystems engineering, microbiology, biochemistry, and biotechnology.

Dr. Mohamed Samer
Professor,
Faculty of Agriculture,
Department of Agricultural Engineering,
Cairo University,
Giza, Egypt

Section 1

Biomass and Bioeconomy

Chapter 1

An Approach to Modify the Current Agricultural and Agro-Industrial Systems into Integrated Bioindustrial Systems and Biorefineries to Develop Sustainable Bioeconomy

Mohamed Samer

Abstract

The existing agricultural and agro-industrial systems are not economically, environmentally, and socially sustainable as they implement the linear mode of production, which should be amended to the cyclic mode of production to promote sustainability. Therefore, this study aims at providing an approach to transform the present agricultural systems (beef, dairy, and poultry farms as well as cereals and vegetable crops production) and agro-industrial systems (ethanol industry and fish industry) into integrated bioindustrial systems and biorefineries by altering their linear mode of production into a circular mode of production to create a coherent bioeconomy, where the bioeconomy includes the conversion of renewable bioresources and waste streams into value-added bioproducts, such as food, feed, pharmaceuticals, nutraceuticals, biomaterials, biochemicals, biofuels, and bioenergy. Whereas the integrated bioindustrial systems allow designing cyclic production and consumption systems to maximize the resources and energy use efficiencies, forming a further ecologically sound and healthy environment through conversion of biowaste into value-added bioproducts, and emphasizing the socio-economic development through creating new employment opportunities and ground-breaking technologies and novel bioproducts. An important key issue is that digitalization is essential to the development of the bioeconomy, where digitalization supports practices innovation by boosting both supply and value chains in the circular bio-based economy.

Keywords: bioeconomy, biomass valorization, bioprocessing, bioproducts, biorefinery

1. Introduction

Current agricultural and agro-industrial systems apply the linear mode of production and, therefore, the majority of today agricultural and agro-industrial production and consumption systems are unsustainable. In other words, current agricultural and agro-industrial systems are economically, environmentally, and socially not sustainable. Precisely, the problems associated with nowadays agricultural, and agro-industries are (1) inefficient use of resources, (2) inefficient use of energy, (3) high production costs, (4) high environmental risks, and (5) massive wealth gap between the poor and the rich. Therefore, sustainability is a key issue in this context, where sustainable development encompasses the integration of social and environmental issues with economic development to convene the pressing needs of the population at present without undercutting the requirements of future generations. One key issue is to mimic the sustainable models provided by natural ecosystems. Precisely, turning the linear mode of production (linear economy) into the cyclic mode of production (circular economy). The current farming and agro-industrial processes have two main problems, which are the inefficient use of energy and wastes are not utilized within the production processes, which leads to the degradation of the surrounding environment. In contrast, natural ecosystem -which should be mimicked- allows the efficient use of energy, and all wastes are bioremediated and utilized by the system. Hence, the current farming and agro-industrial processes (linear) should be amended to mimic the natural ecosystem (circular), where this leads to the concept of industrial ecology, which fills the gap between the farming and agro-industrial processes on the one hand, and the ecologically sustainable natural system on the other hand.

2. Bioeconomy

According to the EU, "the bioeconomy encompasses the production of renewable biological resources and the conversion of these resources and waste streams into value-added products, such as food, feed, bio-based products, and bioenergy" [1]. Furthermore, "the transition to a more circular economy, where the value of products, materials, and resources is maintained in the economy for as long as possible, and the generation of waste minimized, is an essential contribution to the EU's efforts to develop a sustainable, low carbon, resource-efficient, and competitive economy. Such transition is the opportunity to transform the economy and generate new and sustainable competitive advantages" [2]. Consequently, the bioeconomy is broader and deeper than a circular economy. On the other hand, biomass is defined as "the biodegradable fraction of products, waste, and residues from biological origin from agriculture (including vegetal and animal substances), forestry and related industries including fisheries and aquaculture, as well as the biodegradable fraction of industrial and municipal waste" [3]. In other words, biomass types are agricultural biomass (crops residues and animal wastes), fisheries biomass, algae biomass, and forest biomass.

Circular bio-based economy aims at reaching a net zero-carbon community by creating sustainable technologies and efficient resource use approaches to substitute the fossil-based economy. The circular bioeconomy primarily depends on biomass as a building block, while social, economic, and environmental are the principal factors. The technologies that are projected to be industrialized under circular bioeconomy must guarantee that the value of product carbon is preserved to decrease the wastewater production, greenhouse gas (GHG) emissions, and impairment to the ecosystems. In the context of circular bioeconomy growth, the biomass production, process advancements, and reuse approaches ought to be well defined to meet the global supply chain and demand. This urges conducting techno-economic assessment (TEA) and life cycle analysis (LCA) of every product and process.

3. Bioprocesses and bioproducts

Bioproducts or bio-based products are biomaterials, biochemicals, and bioenergy derived from renewable biological resources. The biological resources include agriculture, forestry, and biologically derived waste. One of the renewable bioresources is lignocellulose. Cellulose-based materials and lignocellulosic tissues are biologically derived natural resources.

Conventional bioproducts and emerging bioproducts are two broad categories used to categorize bioproducts. Examples of conventional bioproducts include building materials, pulp and paper, and forest products. Examples of emerging bioproducts include biofuels, bioenergy, starch-based, and cellulose-based ethanol or bioethanol, bio-based adhesives, biochemicals, bioplastics, etc. Bioproducts derived from bioresources can replace much of the fuels, chemicals, plastics, etc. that are currently derived from petroleum. As a result, the emerging bioproducts are environmentally friendly products and independent of fossil sources.

Bioprocessing and bioproducts production include the use of engineered microbiological systems for generating biofuels, bioelectricity, and new high-value bioproducts. Additionally, scientists are investigating the utilization of forestry products in untraditional applications, including industrial foams and flame-retardant materials. This needs to combine a conglomerate of mathematics, biology, and industrial design, and consists of numerous varieties of biotechnological processes, which pertain to the design, development, and implementation of processes, technologies for the sustainable manufacture of biomaterials, biochemicals, and bioenergy from renewable bioresources. Bioprocessing deals with the design and development of equipment and processes for making bioproducts such as food, feed, pharmaceuticals, nutraceuticals, biochemicals, biopolymers, and paper from biological materials (i.e., biomaterials). Practically, bioprocessing takes place in devices called bioreactors.

Bioreactors are categorized, based on the mode of operation, as a batch, semi-continuous or continuous bioreactors. Microorganisms growing in bioreactors may be submerged in a liquid medium or may be attached to the surface of a solid medium. The bioenvironmental conditions inside the bioreactor, such as temperature, nutrient concentrations, pH, and dissolved gases (especially oxygen for aerobic processes) affect the growth and productivity of the microorganisms.

4. Value-added bioprocessing of biowastes

Biological wastes i.e., biowastes, generated from agriculture, wastewater treatment, or industry are a largely untapped source for the production of value-added bioproducts or bioenergy. Their recovery utilizes biological and chemical processes that provide alternative sources for chemical feedstocks to produce different products e.g., bioplastics or other biopolymers, high-value biochemicals, protein for animal feed, and enzymes. For example, nutrients, cellulose, volatile fatty acids, extracellular polymeric substances, or proteins can be recovered from biowastes. Similarly, many opportunities exist for alternative energy products, e.g., bioethanol, biobutanol, biogas, biohydrogen, or bioelectricity. Resource biorecovery thus supports sustainability goals by reinjecting products into the circular economy.

For instance, the value-added bioprocessing of fish waste produces numerous bioproducts, which are: (1) pharmaceuticals such as proteins, jadomycin, collagen, lactic acid, glycerol, proteases, lipases, and collagenases; (2) nutraceuticals such as omega-3, amino acids, fish oil, fatty acids, carotenoids, isoflavones, and lutein; (3) chemicals such as 1,2-propanediol and 1,3-propanediol, dihydroxy-acetone, and methanol; (4) biofuels such as biodiesel, bioethanol, and biohydrogen; and (5) further products such as fish meal and fish silage. On the other hand, the value-added bioprocessing of slaughtering waste produces the same above-mentioned products except that the intermediate product, in this case, is the tallow compared to fish oil as an intermediate product in the bioprocessing of fish waste.

Furthermore, there are several potential uses of fish waste in the production of further pharmaceuticals such as chymotrypsin, pepsin, enzyme inhibitors, anticoagulants, insulin, nucleic acid, nucleotides, protamine, and proteolytic enzymes. Besides, several biochemicals can be produced such as bile salts, glue, gelatin, leather, and pearl essence.

5. Industrial ecology and eco-efficiency

The industrial ecology is the design of industrial infrastructures as a series of interlocking manufactured ecosystems in order to maximize the energy use efficiency, reduce the costs, reduce the environmental problems, identify new value-added products, and maximize the resources use efficiency, which leads to the sustainability. An important key issue is the interpretation of the insinuation of employing the ecological models to restore the agro-industrial systems, through applying the concepts of eco-design and eco-efficiency leading to a cleaner production allowing to reach a zero-waste and zero-emission system. This requires inevitably conducting environmental impact assessment and life cycle analysis of the agro-industrial processes and products. On the other hand, the aim of eco-efficiency is to boost the values of products by optimizing the utilization of resources and minimizing the negative environmental impacts by incorporating both efficiency and innovation into the industrial process without expensive pollution control techniques.

6. Cleaner production

The cleaner production procedure is the first step in the implementation of the concept of industrial ecology. The procedure includes: (1) the examination of production systems in terms of the efficient use of natural resources and the efficient use of energy, and (2) the utilization of life cycle analyses method to evaluate the products and the agro-industrial processes in order to minimize waste and pollution as well as reduce costs and identify new prospects such as new products and employment opportunities.

Regarding the products, the procedure aims at reducing the negative impacts throughout the entire life cycle of the product from cradle to grave, i.e., from design to final disposal. Regarding the agro-industrial processes, cleaner production aims at (1) efficient use of raw materials, (2) efficient use of energy, and (3) reduction of emissions and wastes. An important key issue is to incorporate environmental concerns into designing processes and delivering the products.

7. Integrated bioindustrial systems and biorefinery

The concept of integrated bioindustrial systems aims at (a) designing circular production and consumption systems leading to maximize the efficiencies of resources and energy uses and to allow the required energy and resources for forthcoming development, (2) forming a further ecologically sound and healthy environment through less waste is generated at each level of production and the conversion of waste into value-added products, and (3) emphasizing the socio-economic development through creating new employment opportunities and ground-breaking technologies and new products.

The biorefinery is the cornerstone of the integrated bioindustrial systems, where a biorefinery is a production plant that combines bioconversion processes biomass and devices such as bioreactors to generate biofuels, electrical energy, heat energy, and value-added biochemicals from biomass. The International Energy Agency, Bioenergy Task 42 on Biorefineries, has defined biorefining as the sustainable processing of biomass into a spectrum of bio-based products (food, feed, chemicals, materials) and bioenergy (biofuels, power, and/or heat). Considering that biomass is all organic matters -except fossil fuels- such as forest materials, agricultural crops residues, livestock manure, organic fraction of municipal solid wastes, fish processing wastes, and food processing wastes [4].

The concept of biorefinery has several objectives: (1) maximizing energy use efficiency, (2) maximizing resource use efficiency, (3) minimizing environmental problems, (4) creating new value-added products, and (5) creating new employment opportunities. However, there are some critical concerns such as the competing uses of materials, market demands, and production costs.

The biorefinery has several advantages: (1) through producing numerous products, a biorefinery takes advantage of the numerous components in biomass and their intermediates then intensifying the value derived from the biomass, and (2) through producing various low-volume, nevertheless high-value, chemical products such as nutraceuticals and pharmaceuticals and a low-value, nonetheless high-volume liquid transportation fuel such as biodiesel and bioethanol, (3) meanwhile generating electrical energy and heat, through combined heat and power (CHP) plant, and (4) creating new high value-added products maximizes the feasibility, where the high-volume fuel's production meet the energy demands, and the electricity and heat production minimizes the energy costs and decreases the greenhouse gas (GHG) emissions.

However, the subsequent concerns should be considered: (1) risk of excessive consumption of edible crops, (2) risk of deterioration of organic and mineral content of soils, (3) risk of excessive utilization of chemical fertilizers and pesticides to advance the production levels, (4) risk of competition between food and biorefinery, and (5) risk of deforestation.

The following is an approach to transform the present agricultural systems (beef, dairy, and poultry farms as well as cereals and vegetable crops production) and agro-industrial systems (ethanol industry and fish industry) into integrated bioindustrial systems by altering their linear mode of production into a circular mode of production to create a coherent bioeconomy, where the bioeconomy includes the conversion of renewable bioresources and waste streams into value-added bioproducts, such as food, feed, pharmaceuticals, nutraceuticals, biomaterials, biochemicals, biofuels, and bioenergy.

Cereal and vegetable production encompasses the utilization of several inputs such as water, fertilizers, pesticides, seeds, and energy. The products are grains, fruits, and tuber/roots. However, the waste is agricultural crops residues (**Figure 1**). The concept of bioeconomy is to use the output i.e., waste, of an industry or production system as an input i.e., feedstock, in another new industry. Therefore, this waste is planned to be used as feedstock for a new forage industry, where the produced forages are used

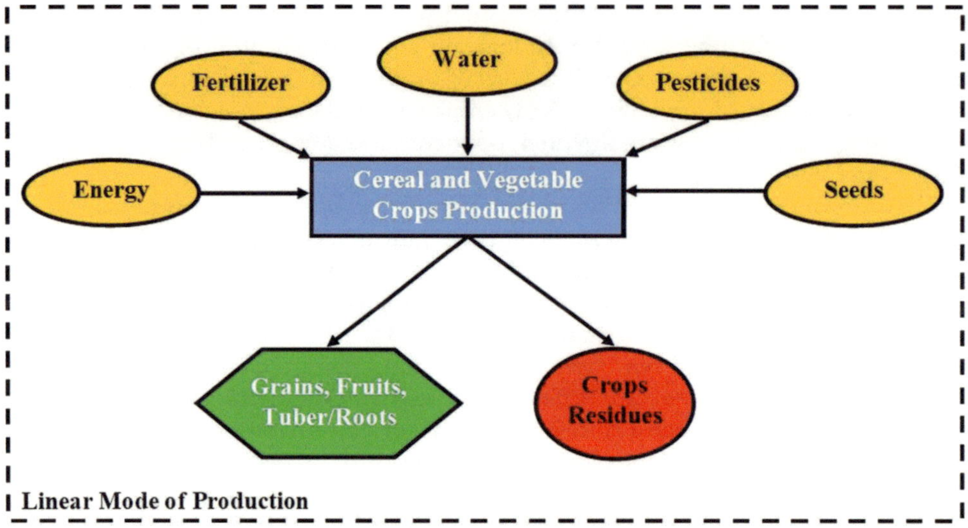

Figure 1.
Linear mode of cereal and vegetable crops production (the orange oval designates the input, the blue rectangle designates the industry, the green hexagon designates the product, and the red circle designates the waste).

for feeding livestock in a new livestock production system that produces milk and meat. However, this industry generates animal waste i.e., manure, which is planned to be used as feedstock for a new biogas plant that produces biogas that fuels the cereal and vegetable crops production system. Besides, the generated sludge is used as a biofertilizer within the crops production system. Part of the generated sludge is used in a new compost facility and the produced compost is used within the crops production system as a biofertilizer. An important key issue is that 4 new industries were established and, therefore, 5 new products were produced, which are considered as economic development. It should be noticed that the core of all these newly planned industries and facilities, which were integrated with the crops production system, is creating new employment opportunities, which is considered as social development. Furthermore, these integrated bioindustrial systems have zero-waste, zero-emission, and efficient resources and energy use, which are considered as environmental development (**Figure 2**).

Beef and dairy production encompass the utilization of several inputs such as water, forages, and energy. The products are milk and meat. However, the wastes are slaughter waste, manure, and whey (**Figure 3**). The concept of bioeconomy is to use the output i.e., waste, of an industry or production system as an input i.e., feedstock, in another new industry. Therefore, the slaughter waste is used as feedstock in a biorefinery to produce biofuels, biochemicals, pharmaceuticals, and nutraceuticals. Additionally, manure and whey are planned to be used as feedstock for a new biogas plant, where the produced biogas is used for fueling the beef and dairy production system. The biogas plant generates sludge, which is used as biofertilizer for a new crops production system that produces grains and tuber/roots. Besides, the generated crop residues are used as feedstock for the forage industry, which produces forages for beef and dairy production. Part of the generated crops residues is used in a new compost facility and the produced compost is used in fertilizing the crops production as biofertilizer. An important key issue is that 5 new industries were established and, therefore, 9 new products were produced, which are considered as economic development. It should be noticed that the

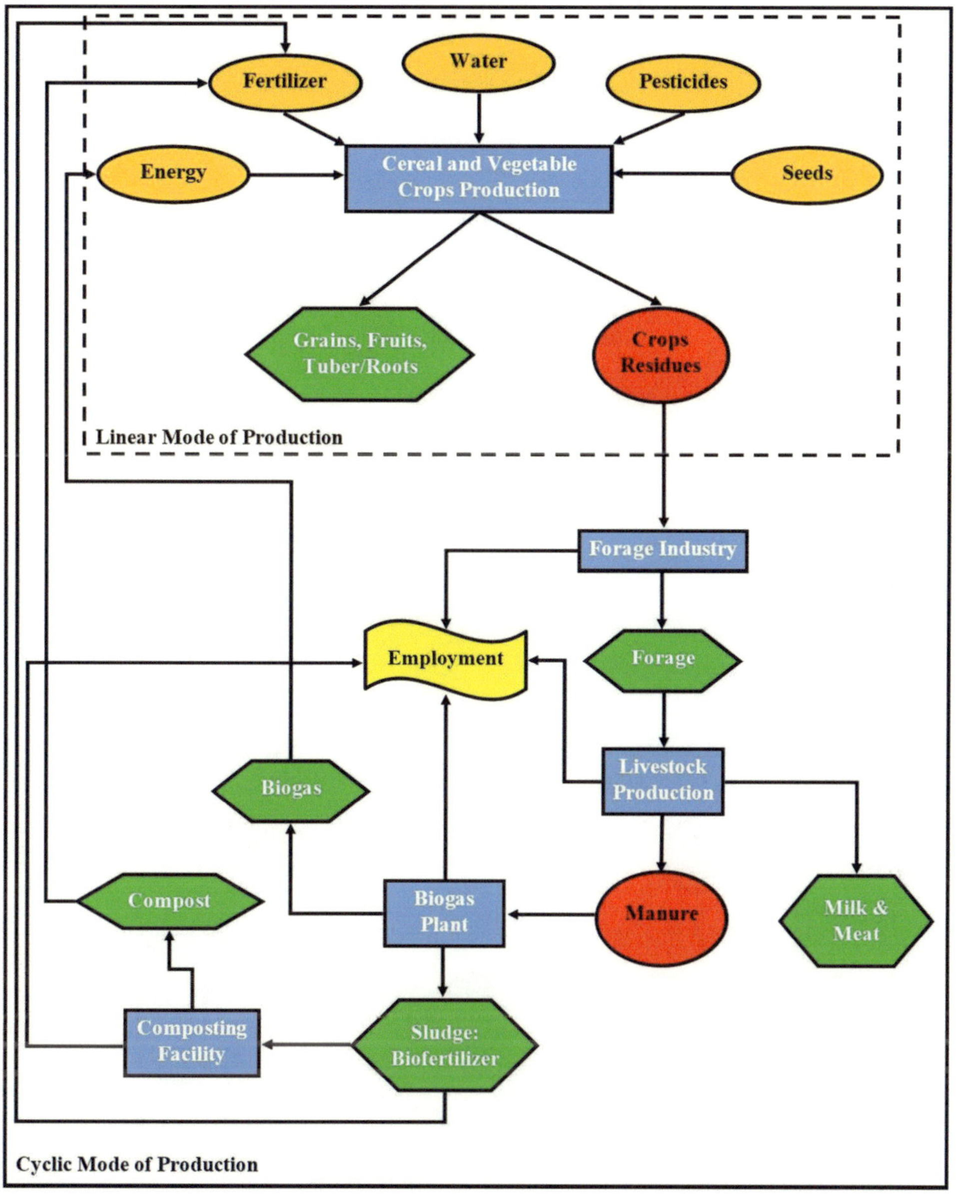

Figure 2.
Cyclic mode of cereal and vegetable crops production through integrated bioindustrial systems (the orange oval designates the input, the blue rectangle designates the industry, the green hexagon designates the product, the red circle designates the waste, and the yellow wave designates the employment opportunity).

core of all these newly planned industries and facilities, which were integrated with the beef and dairy production system, is creating new employment opportunities, which is considered as social development. Furthermore, these integrated bioindustrial systems have zero-waste, zero-emission, and efficient resources and energy use, which are considered as environmental development (**Figure 4**).

The poultry industry encompasses the utilization of several inputs such as water, forages, and energy. The products are meat and eggs. However, the wastes

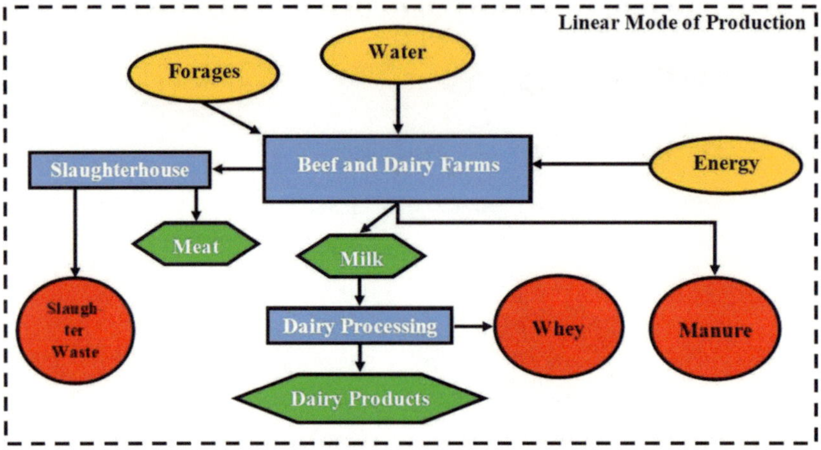

Figure 3.
Linear mode of beef and dairy production (the orange oval designates the input, the blue rectangle designates the industry, the green hexagon designates the product, and the red circle designates the waste).

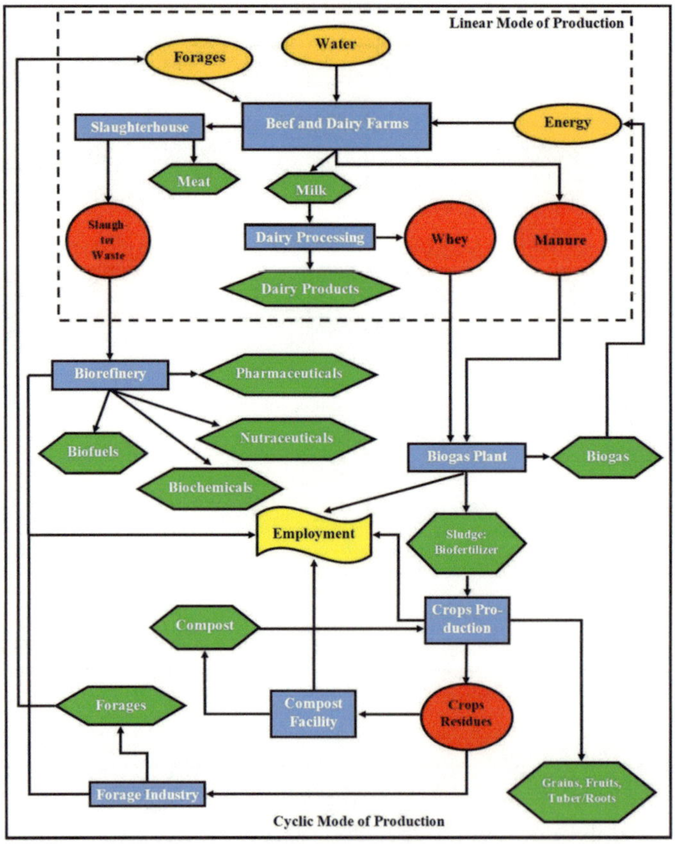

Figure 4.
Cyclic mode of beef and dairy production through integrated bioindustrial systems (the orange oval designates the input, the blue rectangle designates the industry, the green hexagon designates the product, the red circle designates the waste, and the yellow wave designates the employment opportunity).

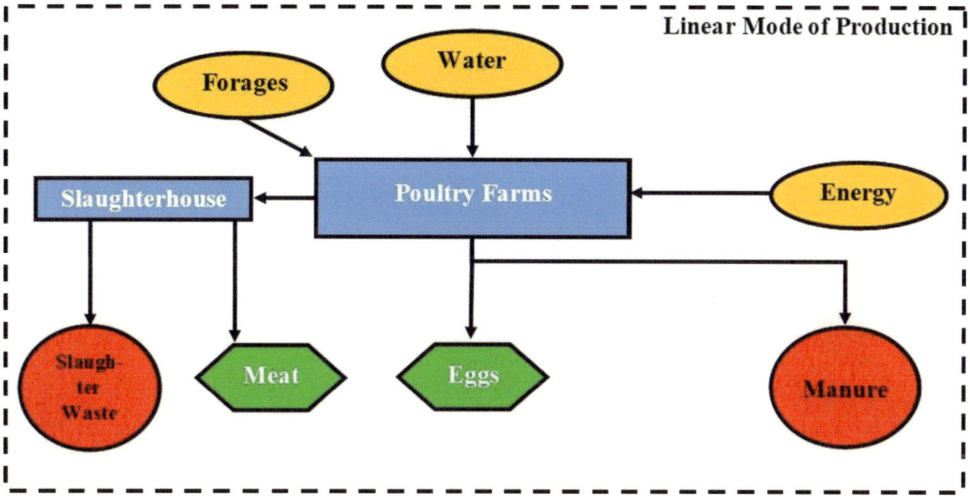

Figure 5.
Linear mode of poultry production (the orange oval designates the input, the blue rectangle designates the industry, the green hexagon designates the product, and the red circle designates the waste).

are slaughter waste and manure (**Figure 5**). The concept of bioeconomy is to use the output i.e., waste, of an industry or production system as an input i.e., feedstock, in another new industry. Therefore, the slaughter waste is used as feedstock in a biorefinery to produce biofuels, biochemicals, pharmaceuticals, and nutraceuticals. Additionally, poultry manure is planned to be used as feedstock for a new biogas plant, where the produced biogas is used for fueling the poultry production system. The biogas plant generates sludge, which is used as biofertilizer for a new crops production system that produces grains and tuber/roots. Besides, the generated crop residues are used as feedstock for the forage industry which produces forages for the poultry farms. Part of the generated crops residues is used in a new compost facility and the produced compost is used in fertilizing the crops production as biofertilizer. An important key issue is that 5 new industries were established and, therefore, 9 new products were produced, which are considered as economic development. It should be noticed that the core of all these newly planned industries and facilities, which were integrated with the poultry production system, is creating new employment opportunities which is considered as social development. Furthermore, these integrated bioindustrial systems have zero-waste, zero-emission, and efficient resources and energy use, which are considered as environmental development (**Figure 6**).

The fish processing industry encompasses the utilization of several inputs such as water, feed, and energy. The product is canned fish. However, the wastes are a large amount of fish waste and a large amount of wastewater (**Figure 7**). The concept of bioeconomy is to use the output i.e., waste, of an industry or production system as an input i.e., feedstock, in another new industry. Therefore, a large amount of wastewater is planned to be used as feedstock for a new wastewater treatment plant, where the treated water is used as input water in the fish processing industry. Further, this plant generates sludge, which is planned to be used as feedstock for a new biogas plant that produces biogas that fuels the finish processing industry. Besides, the generated sludge is considered a new product as biofertilizer. On the other hand, the large amount of fish waste is used as feedstock for a new biorefinery that produces fish meal and fish silage, pharmaceuticals (proteins, jadomycin, collagen, lactic acid,

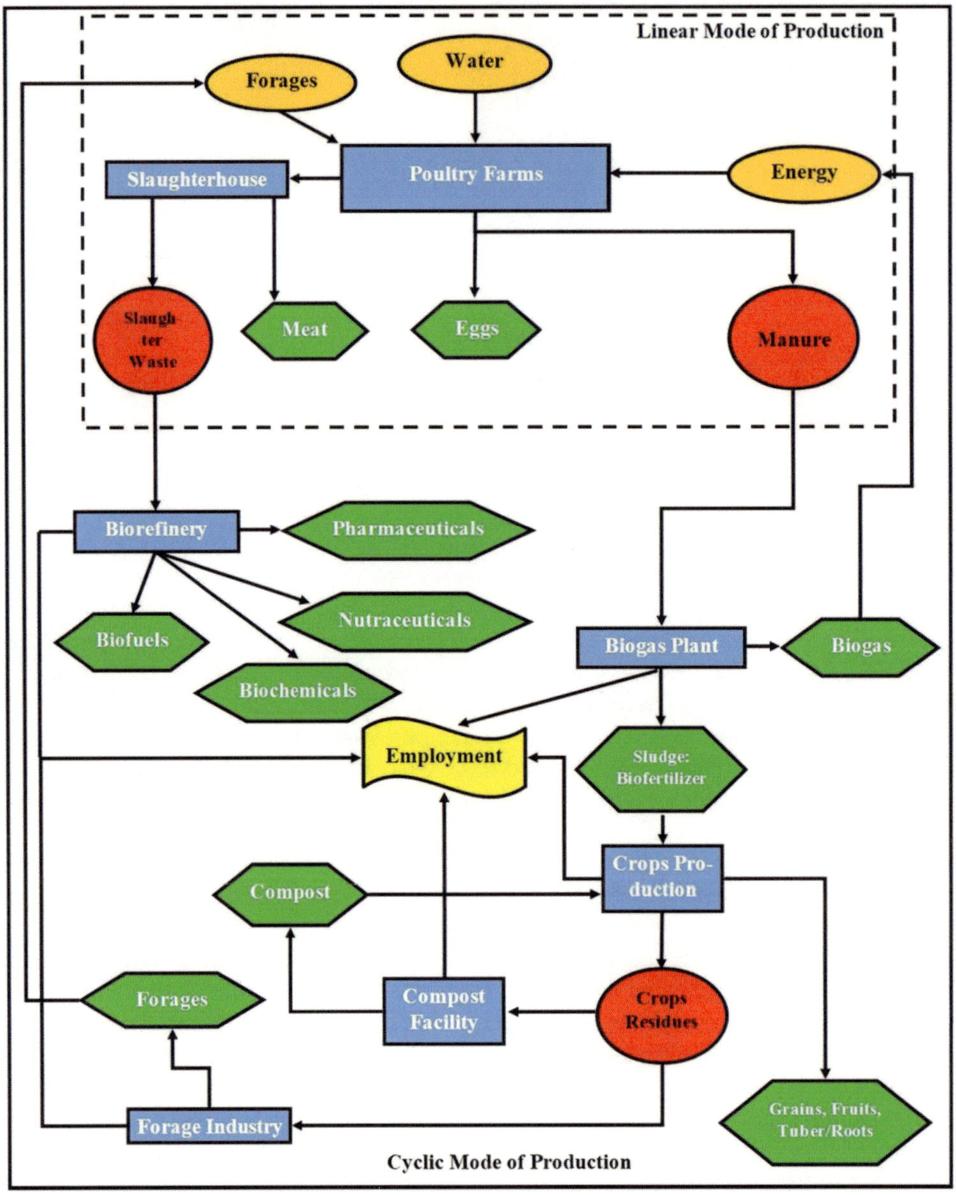

Figure 6.
Cyclic mode of poultry production through integrated bioindustrial systems (the orange oval designates the input, the blue rectangle designates the industry, the green hexagon designates the product, the red circle designates the waste, and the yellow wave designates the employment opportunity).

glycerol, proteases, lipases, and collagenases), nutraceuticals (omega-3, amino acids, fish oil, fatty acids, carotenoids, isoflavones, and lutein), chemicals (1,2-propanediol and 1,3-propanediol, dihydroxy-acetone, and methanol), biofuels (biodiesel, bioethanol, and biohydrogen). An important key issue is that 6 new industries were established and, therefore, a multitude of new products were produced, which are considered as economic development. It should be noticed that the core of all these

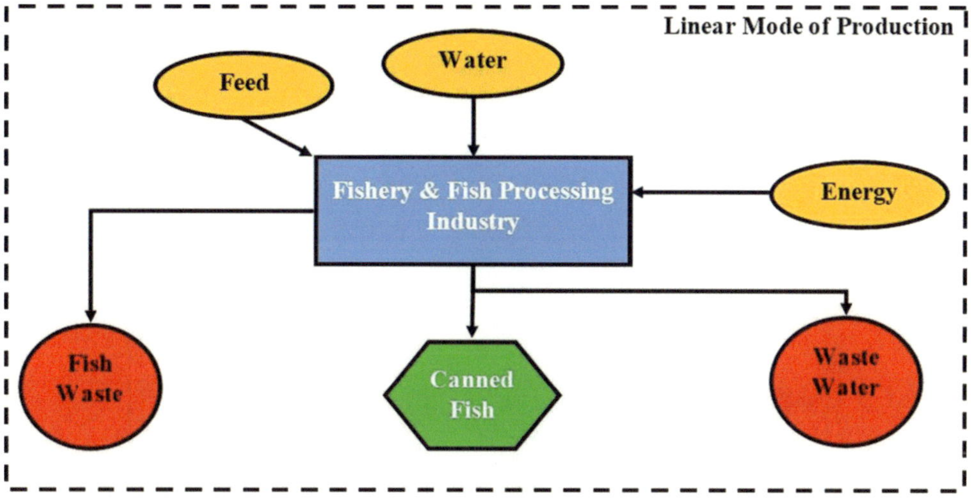

Figure 7.
Linear mode of fish industry (the orange oval designates the input, the blue rectangle designates the industry, the green hexagon designates the product, and the red circle designates the waste).

newly planned industries and facilities, which were integrated with the fish processing industry, is creating new employment opportunities, which is considered as social development. Furthermore, these integrated bioindustrial systems have zero-waste, zero-emission, and efficient resources and energy use, which are considered as environmental development (**Figure 8**).

The bioethanol industry encompasses the utilization of inputs such as energy and raw cellulosic materials. The product is bioethanol. However, the waste is broth (**Figure 9**). The concept of bioeconomy is to use the output i.e., waste, of an industry or production system as an input i.e., feedstock, in another new industry. Therefore, this waste is planned to be used as feedstock for a new processing industry that produces wastewater and biofertilizer, where these products are used in a new hydroponics system that produces biowastes (crops residues). These wastes i.e., crop residues, are planned to be used as feedstock for a new forage industry that produces forages for a new livestock production system. However, this industry generates animal waste i.e., manure, which is planned to be as feedstock for a new biogas plant, which produces biogas that fuels the bioethanol industry. Besides, the generated sludge is used as biofertilizer for a new crops production system. Part of the generated sludge is used in a new compost facility and the produced compost is used within the crops production system as biofertilizer. The produced crops residues from the new crops production system as feedstock in a new compost industry, which produces a biofertilizer. An important key issue is that 6 new industries were established and, therefore, 7 new products were produced which are considered as economic development. It should be noticed that the core of all these newly planned industries and facilities, which were integrated with the bioethanol industry, is creating new employment opportunities, which is considered as social development. Furthermore, these integrated bioindustrial systems have zero-waste, zero-emission, and efficient resources and energy use, which are considered as environmental development (**Figure 10**).

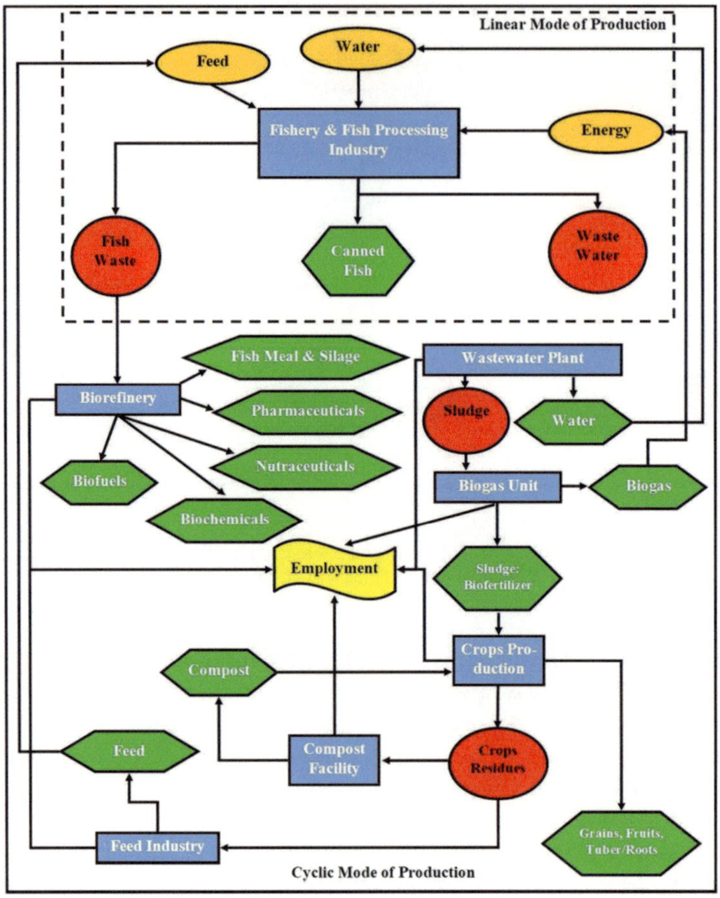

Figure 8.
Cyclic mode of fish industry through integrated bioindustrial systems (the orange oval designates the input, the blue rectangle designates the industry, the green hexagon designates the product, the red circle designates the waste, and the yellow wave designates the employment opportunity).

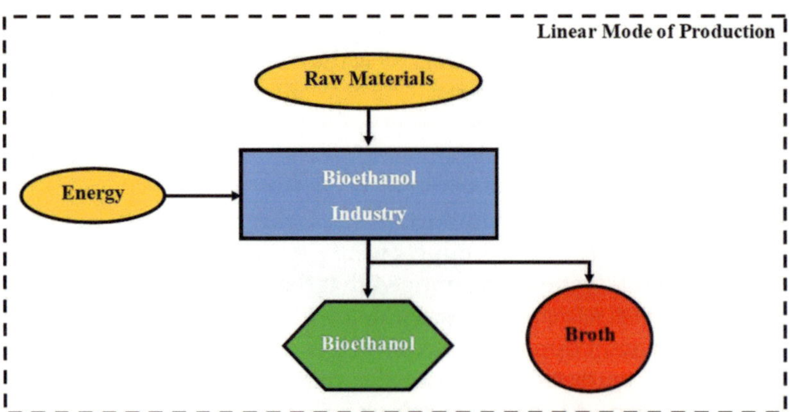

Figure 9.
Linear mode of bioethanol industry (the orange oval designates the input, the blue rectangle designates the industry, the green hexagon designates the product, and the red circle designates the waste).

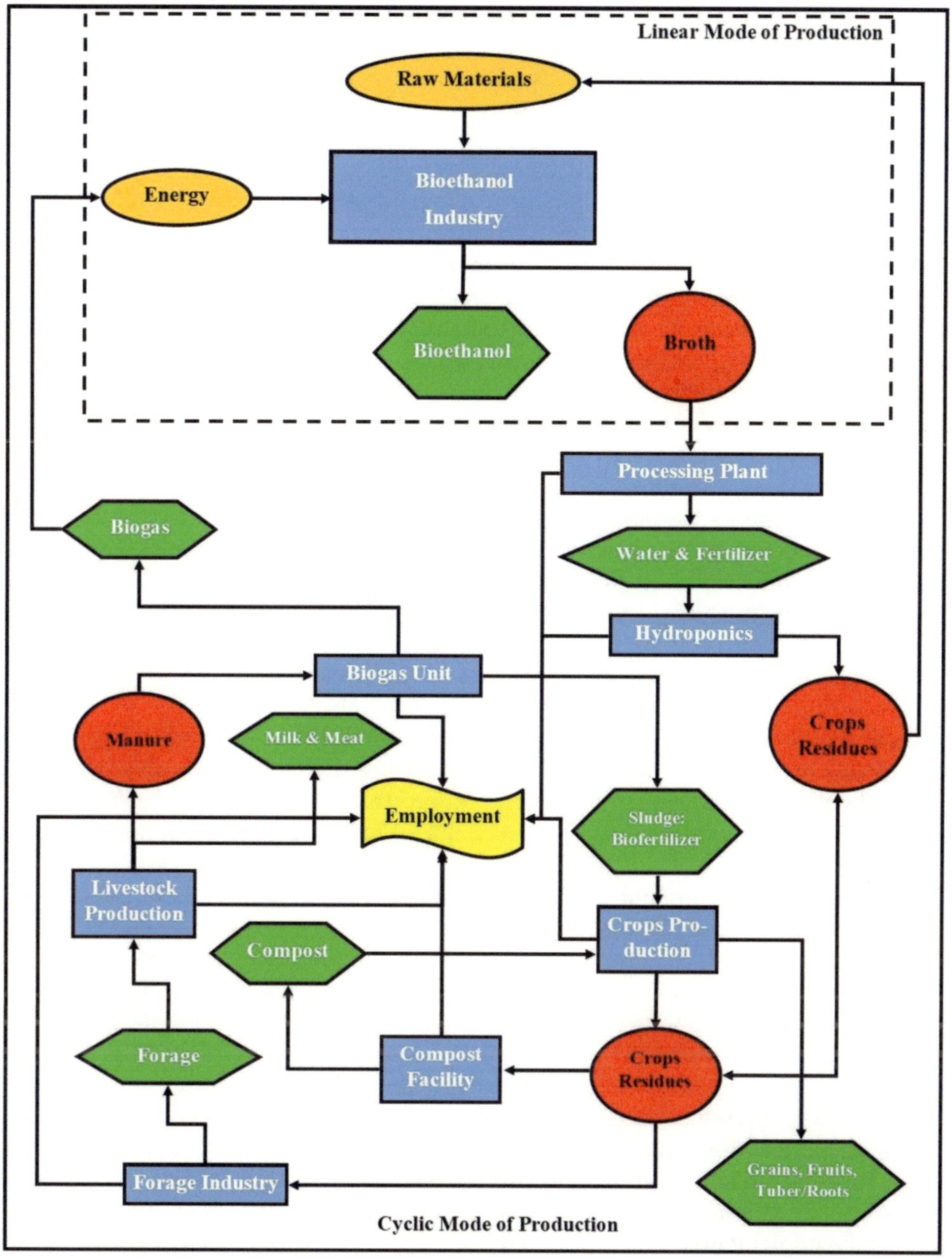

Figure 10.
Cyclic mode of bioethanol industry through integrated bioindustrial systems (the orange oval designates the input, the blue rectangle designates the industry, the green hexagon designates the product, the red circle designates the waste, and the yellow wave designates the employment).

8. Digitalization in the bioeconomy

Digitalization is essential to the advancement of the bioeconomy. Digitalization is promoting intelligibility throughout the value chains and facilitates to scrutinize the conformity with afforded standards. Digitalization modifies the route for expanding traditional bioeconomy and is converting the bioeconomy into a progressively multi and interdisciplinary proficient sector.

The digital revolution in the bioeconomy has 3 unique aspects: (1) the utilization of digital tools as a tool for monitoring. For instance, real-time monitoring of farming operations such as crops, and livestock can provide timely and feasibly added value. Likewise, in forestry, monitoring provides added value by processing data, optimizing the conservation and use of forest products, (2) data aid the development of value chains in terms of reusing, recycling, and repairing. Digitalization provides data analysis for biorefineries or bioindustry can assist in identifying new products evolving from what was formerly considered as biowaste, and (3) data-driven at its core, biosciences are growing precipitously owing to the expanding repository of information. Its application can be observed through a wide range of products and services such as the usage of genomes for therapeutics, personalized medicine, and pharmaceuticals. It can be noticed as well in the advancement of biochemicals as alternatives for petrochemicals.

Digital tools offer a variety of prospects within the traditional bioeconomy sectors such as farming, fisheries, and forestry. For farmers, the ability to track and monitor their livestock and crops boosts daily operations and grants for accurate development. There are also prospects for improved precision, as data is pooled promptly throughout the value chain from forage to dairies, slaughterhouses, products manufacturing, marketing, and consumption. Within the forestry industry, digital tools can be used for monitoring, forecasting, and management of forests.

Digitalization is encouraging practices innovation by boosting both supply and value chains in the circular bio-based economy. Thus, digitalization is able to play a role as a facilitator of circular bioeconomy procedures by for instance altering business patterns. Manipulating data to detect gaps for improving manufacture, or even to pinpoint how to help obtain value from both current production lines and bio-based waste streams are components of this development. At this point, streams of the circular bio-based economy, for instance, biowaste streams, are employed in different approaches since the data-driven procedures are strengthening the bioeconomy.

Digitalization is a component of the circular bioeconomy, where the bioindustrial systems are aiming at applying the circular economy standards that broaden the lifecycle of biowaste by recycling them as feedstock for bioenergy generation. Digitalization, smart algorithms, and advanced computer modeling guarantee resource boosting in the bioindustrial systems, raise the value of green production and are a factor in energy trade-off. Applications include open innovation platforms providing data access, which is open for research and development (R&D) as well as business. Digitalization can be used to create higher-value products in the circular bio-based economy. Digital tools can be implemented for making new value-added bioproducts. For instance, the production of novel and high-value bioproducts using existing bioresources.

Big data is cornerstone in developing biosciences. In the health sector, for instance, big data is accelerating encouraging results in biomedical research. At this point, the quick leap of data-driven analysis is anticipated to reach a higher level of personalized medicine and pharmaceuticals. High levels of digitalization such as blockchain and artificial intelligence coupled with its application in, for instance, agriculture, aquaculture, and forestry, brand-new bioproducts, and recycling of by-products are projected to occur. The intersecting role of data for R&D as well as an invention in bioeconomy is applied in contemporary waste management such as the use of bacteria in biowaste degradation.

Data analysis is crucial for a profitable green transition. Numerous biorefineries implement data in fostering the applications of biosciences in utilizing, for instance, forest by-products. Biomaterials such as lignin were found to be valuable feedstock in the production of food, feed, and adhesives. Technologies such as pyrolysis use biological but inedible feedstock and produce liquid bio-oils. The bio-oil is consistent with the current fossil oil infrastructure, and thus fills one of the gaps arising between the bio-based economy and the petroleum-based economy. The rapid leap of data analysis is able to accelerate finding solutions for global challenges.

A digital transformation is in progress in the circular bio-based economy. Guaranteeing that rural communities realize the profits of this transformation necessitates a re-outlining of the discussion to emphasize not only the digitalization itself but the growth potential it offers. This prospective is comprehensive and involves the formation of innovative bioproducts, services, and bioindustries. While based on rural resources, these opportunities necessitate additional collaboration that reinforces rural–urban relationships. The digital revolution of the circular bio-based economy likewise retains the capability to carry out businesses in conventional circular bio-based economy sectors attracting a wider cross-section of communities. This leads to create new employment opportunities for rural communities.

Generally, the applications of digital tools include prototyping electronic boards, internet of things (IoT) platforms, software, and cellphone applications to control the operation of the bioproducts production systems as well as compute the input materials and energy on the one hand and the output materials and energy on the other hand. Similar applications include livestock farming, for example detecting the activity and health of the animals and informing the animal owner. Further applications include operating the cooling/heating systems based on detected indoor conditions in greenhouses and livestock barns. Another application is in precision farming to control the farming operations conducted by agricultural machinery connected to satellites. Further application is that digital tools can control the interoperability of agricultural systems e.g., control the soil-based sensors to be consistent with the tractor. Additionally, the role of mechatronics is highly foreseen in these applications. Finally, a further application is the use of QR-codes (Quick Response code) to boost comprehensibility across the value chain. For instance, QR-codes are used to track livestock, allowing consumers to trace the food they consume from its source through the route to the retailer. Several applications in this context were developed as cell phone applications [5] and desktop software [6–9].

9. Recent advancements

Nanotechnology and laser radiation have been implemented in the production process of several bioproducts [10–16]. Besides, the implementation of life cycle analysis (LCA) and environmental impact assessment (EIA) methodologies are of high importance to analyze the life cycle of bioproducts and to determine the environmental impact of the production processes [17–21]. A key issue is to conduct a techno-economic assessment (TEA) of the used technologies in the production process [22].

10. Summary and conclusions

This study provides an approach to convert the present agricultural systems (beef, dairy, and poultry farms as well as cereals and vegetable crops production)

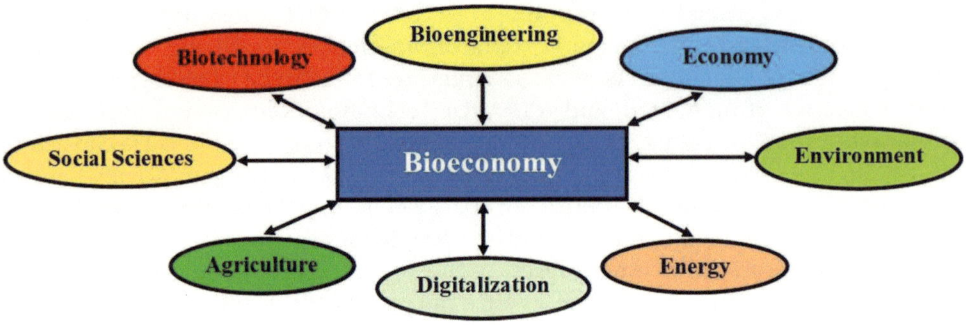

Figure 11.
The fields of science related to bioeconomy.

and agro-industrial systems (ethanol industry and fish industry) into integrated bioindustrial systems and biorefineries through amending their linear mode of production into a circular mode of production to develop a sustainable bioeconomy. This development includes the bioconversion of biowaste streams from the existing agricultural and agro-industrial systems into value-added bioproducts, such as food, feed, pharmaceuticals, nutraceuticals, biomaterials, biochemicals, biofuels, and bioenergy where these novel bioproducts are considered as economic development. Whereas the core of the planned bioindustries is creating new employment opportunities, which is considered as social development. Furthermore, these integrated bioindustrial systems have zero-waste, zero-emission, and efficient resources and energy use, which are considered as environmental development. An important key issue is that digitalization guarantees resource boosting in the bioindustrial systems, where applications include the development of electronic boards, internet of things (IoT) platforms, software, and cellphone applications for monitoring and controlling the operations, computing input and output materials, and energy, and fostering comprehensibility across the value chain. **Figure 11** summarizes the fields of science related to bioeconomy.

Author details

Mohamed Samer
Faculty of Agriculture, Department of Agricultural Engineering, Biosystems Engineering Group, Cairo University, Giza, Egypt

*Address all correspondence to: msamer@agr.cu.edu.eg

References

[1] Ronzon T, Lusser M, Landa L, M'Barek R, Klinkenberg M, Sanchez Lopez J, et al. Bioeconomy Report 2016. JRC Scientific and Policy Report. EUR 28468 EN. Publications Office of the European Union, Luxembourg; 2017

[2] Available from: https://eur-lex.europa.eu/legal-content/EN/TXT/HTML/?uri=CELEX:52015DC0614&from=ES

[3] Available from: https://eur-lex.europa.eu/legal-content/en/ALL/?uri=CELEX:32009L0028

[4] International Energy Agency. 2009. Biorefineries: Adding Value to the Sustainable Utilisation of Biomass. Bioenergy Task 42 on Biorefineries

[5] Samer M, Helmy K, Morsy S, Assal T, Amin Y, Mohamed S, et al. Cellphone application for computing biogas, methane and electrical energy production from different agricultural wastes. Computers and Electronics in Agriculture. 2019;**163**:104873

[6] Samer M, Hatem M, Grimm H, Doluschitz R, Jungbluth T. A software for planning loose yards and designing concrete constructions for dairy farms in arid and semi-arid zones. Emirates Journal of Food and Agriculture. 2013;**25**(3):238-249

[7] Samer M, Hatem M, Grimm H, Doluschitz R, Jungbluth T. An expert system for planning and designing dairy farms in hot climates. Agricultural Engineering International: CIGR Journal. 2012;**14**(1):1-15

[8] Samer M, Loebsin C, von Bobrutzki K, Fiedler M, Ammon C, Berg W, et al. A computer program for monitoring and controlling ultrasonic anemometers for aerodynamic measurements in animal buildings. Computers and Electronics in Agriculture. 2011;**79**(1):1-12

[9] Samer M. A software program for planning and designing biogas plants. Transactions of the ASABE. 2010;**53**(4):1277-1285

[10] Attia YA, Samer M, Moselhy MA, Arisha AH, Abdelqader AA, Abdelsalam E. Influence of laser photoactivated graphitic carbon nitride nanosheets and nickel nanoparticles on purple non-sulfur bacteria for biohydrogen production from biomass. Journal of Cleaner Production. 2021;**299**:126898. DOI: 10.1016/j.jclepro.2021.126898

[11] Abdelsalam EM, El-Hussein A, Samer M. Photobiostimulation of anaerobic digestion by laser irradiation and photocatalytic effects of trace metals and nanomaterials on biogas production. International Journal of Energy Research. 2021;**45**:141-150

[12] Samer M, Abdelsalam EM, Mohamed S, Elsayed H, Attia YA. Impact of photoactivated cobalt oxide nanoparticles addition on manure and whey for biogas production through dry anaerobic co-digestion. Environment, Development and Sustainability. 2021;**23**:14683-14696

[13] Abdelsalam EM, Samer M. Biostimulation of anaerobic digestion using nanomaterials for increasing biogas production. Reviews in Environmental Science and Bio/Technology. 2019;**18**(3):525-541

[14] Abdelsalam E, Samer M, Attia Y, Abdel-Hadi MA, Hassan HE, Badr Y. Effects of laser irradiation and

Ni nanoparticles on biogas production from anaerobic digestion of slurry. Waste and Biomass Valorization. 2019;**10**(11):3251-3262

[15] Abdelsalam E, Samer M, Abdel-Hadi MA, Hassan HE, Badr Y. Influence of laser irradiation on rumen fluid for biogas production from dairy manure. Energy. 2018;**163**:404-415

[16] Attia YA, Kobeasy MI, Samer M. Evaluation of magnetic nanoparticles influence on hyaluronic acid production from Streptococcus equi. Carbohydrate Polymers. 2018;**192**:135-142

[17] Samer M, Hijazi O, Abdelsalam EM, El-Hussein A, Attia YA, Yacoub IH, et al. Life cycle assessment of using laser treatment and nanomaterials to produce biogas through anaerobic digestion of slurry. Environment, Development and Sustainability. 2021. DOI: 10.1007/s10668-021-01264-9

[18] Ioannou-Ttofa L, Foteinis S, Moustafa AS, Abdelsalam E, Samer M, Fatta-Kassinos D. Life cycle assessment of household biogas production in Egypt: Influence of digester volume, biogas leakages, and digestate valorization as biofertilizer. Journal of Cleaner Production. 2021;**286**:125468

[19] Hijazi O, Abdelsalam E, Samer M, Attia YA, Amer BMA, Amer MA, et al. Life cycle assessment of the use of nanomaterials in biogas production from anaerobic digestion of manure. Renewable Energy. 2020;**148**:417-424

[20] Hijazi O, Abdelsalam E, Samer M, Amer BMA, Yacoub IH, Moselhy MA, et al. Environmental impacts concerning the addition of trace metals in the process of biogas production from anaerobic digestion of slurry. Journal of Cleaner Production. 2020;**243**:118593

[21] Abdelsalam E, Hijazi O, Samer M, Yacoub IH, Ali AS, Ahmed RH, et al. Life cycle assessment of the use of laser radiation in biogas production from anaerobic digestion of manure. Renewable Energy. 2019;**142**:130-136

[22] Samer M, Abdelaziz S, Refai M, Abdelsalam E. Techno-economic assessment of dry fermentation in household biogas units through co-digestion of manure and agricultural crop residues in Egypt. Renewable Energy. 2020;**149**:226-234

Chapter 2

Economic Assessment of Biomass Based Power Generation

A.B.M. Abdul Malek

Abstract

Biomass based power generation systems can play a significant role to alleviate energy crisis and reduce fossil fuel dependency in the countries that possess abundance of agricultural and forest biomass resources. Particularly the countries to go for biomass energy in a large scale must know power and energy potential for biomass based commercial production with proper economic assessment of the possibilities. In-depth knowledge is must to assess the profitability and sustainability of the projects. Profitability measures how the investment in the project can be secured to have an ensured surplus to be shared by the stake holders and sustainability ensures the long-term existence in the business with a positive trend of gaining market share day by day or simply to be in the business. This chapter will present the details of the economic assessment of biomass- based energy projects in terms of net present value (NPV), internal rate of return (IRR), discounted payback period (DPB), and cost of energy. The economic profitability measure is a must before advancing to a venture whether it is self-financed or loan financed. So, it is hoped that readers of the chapter should develop a proper evaluation capability and know how to analyze the biomass-based energy projects.

Keywords: economic assessment, discounted cashflow, life cycle cost, net present value, internal rate of return, payback period

1. Introduction

Biomass based energy generation systems impart low environmental impact. To be specific, these systems produce a very low level of CO_2 or other toxic gases or radioactive materials, unlike the ones that are produced by the fossil fuel energy systems. But we are very much reluctant to establish these traditional systems (i.e., coal, natural gas, oil -based power plants) for producing our final energy forms in power plants or vehicles [1, 2]. The estimated average price of 6.9 c/kWh from biomass-based power generation is not yet cost effective comparing to fossil fuel technologies can offer a price in the range of 4.2–4.8 c/kWh [3]. Investment cost for the biomass-based power generation technologies generally take a higher scale compared to other technologies due to diverse fuel characteristics, collection and pre-treatment of the fuel needed

Densification process	Type of biomass	Bulk density (kg/m^3)
Without densification	Sawdust	47.7
	Wood Chips	209–273
	Straw	40–60
Palletization	Wood Saw Dust	606
	Straw	360–500
Briquetting	Wood Saw Dust	505
	husk	410
	Fruit Fiber	250

Table 1.
Comparison of bulk density with different processes [5].

prior to introducing to the generation system [4]. The fuel handling requires extra installation and maneuvering cost involvement. **Table 1** shows some of the established fuel densification processes used in biomass- based power generation systems.

Thus, a detailed economic feasibility study must be done prior to jumping into a project.

2. Basics of economic assessment of a biomass based power generation system

The practical outcomes of a biomass-based energy system can be evaluated mainly from two aspects. Number one is from energy content of the biomass in a desired form and number two is economic justification of the specific power generation systems. The evaluation process follows some steps like [6]:

1. evaluation of costs and benefits over the years of operation. Costs involved are investment costs, fuel cost, cost of fuel collection and pre-treatment, costs for operation and maintenance, servicing and insurance against damage etc. On the other hand, benefits may be direct revenue earning or savings for replaceable energy i.e., the avoided bill costs, the incentives received from CER, or revenue earning from the selling of energy to the utility companies under certain tariff rates;

2. analysis of cash inflows and outflows;

3. evaluation of the economically effective space otherwise would have been left empty;

4. estimation of the energy recovery factor pertaining to the analysis done;

5. Sensitivity analysis for the most significant parameters.

2.1 Economic analysis and use of discounted cash flow

The discounted cash flow concept can be presented in a simple equation. The total earning from the project in its life span is represented by, G. Overall return from the project activities is R with the cost incurred C. The simple relation then looks like the following Eq.

$$G = R - C \tag{1}$$

As the initial investment and the subsequent cash flows occurs in different time frames, so a time value effect is imparted to this simple equation. This time value is included in the relation using some correlation coefficients which equalize the time value of the money or the future payments of receipts are discounted. So, discounted cash flow (DCF) tries to figure out the value of an investment on the base year and highlights on how much money it will generate in the future.

Each of the future cash flows must be "deflated" first to go back to base year. So, future cash flows must be multiplied by the discount factor:

$$\frac{1}{(1+r)^j} \tag{2}$$

Where, r is the discount rate and j is the year index.

Thus, discounted cash flow is used to get Net Present Value (NPV) of an investment following the equation:

$$NPV = \sum_{j=1}^{n} \frac{CF_j}{(1+r)^j} - Io \tag{3}$$

Where.

Io - initial investment.

n = years of duration of the investment.

When the net present value (NPV) results to a positive figure, it means at the end of life of investment the discounted cash flows produced throgh out the entire life possess higher inflow than the cost of the initial investment, and other associated costs and therefore, the erection of a plant is justified from a financial point of view; vice versa when the NPV is negative.

Details of net present value and other indicators that uses discounted cashflow like internal rate of return (IRR), and discounted pay back period will be discussed in details in later sections.

2.2 Tools used for economic performance analysis

Economic performance is better understood with the value a product or service provides to the willing customers. A higher value means a higher price customer willingly pays for the product or service. Economic value that a customer is willing to pay for tradable goods, may be greater than the actual market price (thus creating an economic surplus) but it is not usually less [7]. Otherwise, customer would not buy the product replacing the available one. Economic performance must be justified with proper tools, so that the user of the product put their preferences over other available alternatives.

The following tools are commonly used for economic assessment of biomass-based energy projects:

- Life Cycle Cost (LCC)
- Net Present Value (NPV)
- Internal Rate of Return (IRR)
- Discounted Payback (DPB)
- Levelized Cost of Energy
- Profitability Index (PI)
- Sensitivity Analysis

2.3 Life cycle cost analysis

Life cycle cost (LCC) gives a basis for comparing bioenergy technologies to conventional energy technologies. This method accounts the total system cost during a specified time period (life of the project). It comprises the initial investment and operational cost during the useful life. LCC is the sum of total cost that includes not only initial investment but also costs directly related to repair, operation, maintenance, transportation to the site, and fuel used to run the system. All of these costs are discounted with a MARR to the present value (PV). An LCC analysis allows the designer to study the effect of using different components with different reliabilities and lifetimes. It is also helpful for comparing costs of different designs and/or determining whether a hybrid system would be cost – effective option.

The equation of life cycle cost analysis is [8].

$$LCC = C + M_{wp} + E_{wp} + R_{wp} - S_{wp} \tag{4}$$

LCC = Life cycle cost.

C = initial cost of installation- the present value of the cost on capital resources.

M_{WP}= Aggregation of all yearly operation and maintenance costs- includes wage of the operators, site access, guarantees paid, and all other regular maintenance costs.

E_{WP}= Aggregation of all yearly energy cost including fuel cost and its transportation to the plant site.

R_{wp}= Aggregation of all yearly replacement costs.

S_{wp}= Salvage value.

2.4 Net present value (NPV) analysis

The net future earnings are discounted to the base year with the rate selected to justify minimum attractive rate of return (MARR). The investment is deducted from the present sum of benefits. This value is called NPV [9].

$$NPV = -S + \frac{CF_1}{(1+r)^1} + \frac{CF_2}{(1+r)^2} + \dots + \frac{CF_T}{(1+r)^T} = -S + \sum_{j=1}^{T} \frac{CF_j}{(1+r)^j} \tag{5}$$

Net present value shows the following advantages for project assessment:

- Time value of money is included in net present value analysis
- This method considers cash flows disregarding the accounting profits. All cash flows are considered but non-cash flow benefits are not taken into consideration.
- Net present value method is consistent with the objective of profit maximization.

But net present value (NPV) has the following limitations for evaluating a project:

- The calculation is complex and hence requires skill handling.
- It is particularly difficult to quantify the return on investment in an economy where inflation varies year to year and hence necessitates year to year adjustment
- Net present value method does not consider hidden costs or incomes not shown as cash flow.
- Misleading results are probable when the projects are mutually exclusive. In that case profitability index is a more suitable method for summarizing the output.

2.5 Internal rate of return analysis

Internal rate of return discounts all the cash back, providing zero NPV throughout the investment life of the project [9].

$$NPV = -S + \sum_{J=1}^{T} \frac{CF_J}{(1 + IRR)^j} = 0 \tag{6}$$

This method uses a widely understood percentage rate as the decision variable to compare mutually exclusive investments or individual investments whether public or private. Incremental internal rate of return analysis is preferred to individual analysis by analysts.

Internal rate of return method for project economic analysis has the following merits:

- Time value of money is taken in to account
- Negative values can be used
- No need to have a precise calculation of discount rate, only a guess is supplied for assessment.
- The output of IRR method is a rate, which can directly measure of project profitability.

In analyzing the economic performance of a bioenergy project, the use of internal rate of return method got the following limitations:

- The calculation of IRR is to go through a trial-and-error method so it is difficult to attain the final point if done manually.
- It is assumed that cash flows generated by the project can be reinvested at its internal rate of return. This is quite unrealistic.
- IRR can have a negative value. Moreover, there is a possibility of having multiple internal rates of return to be produce for the same project.

There exists a huge theoretical preference for NPV analysis for project appraisal and investigations suggests that corporate executives prefer internal rate of return (IRR) analysis over net present value analysis. Actually, managers like to compare projects of varying sizes in terms of predictive performance, using IRR as a decision metric put a summary value of the firm performance rather NPV returns a value of merit figure not a rate. IRR method is an obviously a shortcut of assessing the economic viability of a project.

2.6 Discounted payback period

Discounted payback period is a modified version of the payback period that accounts for the time value of money. This is the time period when the project cash inflows reach a 'break even' or to get the point where the net cash flows generated is equal to the initial cost of the project. Discounted payback period can be used to evaluate the profitability and feasibility of a project [10]. DPP can be calculated by solving the following Equation [11].

$$\sum_{1}^{DPP} \frac{CF_n}{(1+r)^n} = 0 \tag{7}$$

Where, CF_n is the cash flow related to the n-th year and r is the discount rate.
Discounted payback period (DPP) has the following limitations

- No track is kept for the cash flows in the project life after the recovery period is achieved.
- This method may not be consistent with the goals of profit maximizing for the business owners. And, the cash flows occur after the DPP attained are generally becomes insignificant but practically all the cash flows through out the span of economic life contribute the project outcome.
- Discounted payback period method plays a minor role in mutually exclusive project selection.
- Discount rate is considered fix for the whole span of project. But in practical, the rate must be adjusted for inflation in a regular interval.

2.7 Levelized cost of energy (LCOE)

Table 2 shows a sample Microsoft excel worksheet to evaluate NPV, IRR, and Payback Period for a biomass- based energy project. Levelized cost of energy is a uniform equivalent rate that is calculated from the revenue stream of an energy project. The revenue generated is discounted at IRR to yield an NPV. The calculated NPV is converted to annual payments and then divided by the project's annual energy output. The unit stands at $/kWh. This LCOE is a first order parameter to evaluate projects attractiveness. The LCOE should be at a comparable level to defend the competitor's price. LCOE analysis of power generation plant is a price estimation

Year	Generation (kWh)	Revenue Earning (MYR)	Cost of sales (MYR)	Gross Profit (MYR)	Operating Expenses (MYR)	CER/Tax (MYR)	EAT (MYR)	Cumulative Earning (MYR)
0							−54,576,000	−54,576,000
1	65,700,000	13,797,000	7,450,366	6,346,634	586,146	2,436,500	8,196,988	−46,379,012
2	70,080,000	14,716,800	7,972,960	6,743,840	606,827	2,601,500	8,738,513	−37,640,499
3	79,978,800	16,795,548	8,889,223	7,906,325	628,282	2,976,215	10,254,258	−27,386,241
4	79,978,800	16,795,548	9,172,407	7,623,141	650,544	2,976,215	9,948,812	−17,437,429
5	**79,978,800**	**16,795,548**	**9,464,912**	**7,330,636**	**673,644**	**2,976,215**	**9,633,207**	**−7,804,222**
6	79,978,800	16,795,548	9,767,059	7,028,489	697,617	2,976,215	9,307,087	1,502,865
7	79,978,800	16,795,548	10,079,180	6,716,368	722,497	2,976,215	8,970,086	10,472,951
8	79,978,800	16,795,548	10,401,620	6,393,928	748,321	2,976,215	8,621,822	19,094,773
9	79,978,800	16,795,548	10,734,737	6,060,811	775,127	2,976,215	8,261,899	27,356,672
10	79,978,800	16,795,548	10,734,737	6,060,811	802,955	2,976,215	8,234,071	35,590,743
11	79,978,800	16,795,548	11,800,419	4,995,129	831,847	1,040,821	3122461.5	38,713,205
12	79,978,800	16,795,548	11,538,820	5,256,728	861,845	1,098,721	3296162.25	42,009,367
13	79,978,800	16,795,548	11,910,593	4,884,955	892,996	997,990	2993969.25	45,003,336
14	79,978,800	16,795,548	12,294,800	4,500,748	925,346	893,851	2681551.5	47,684,888
15	79,978,800	16,795,548	12,691,877	4,103,671	958,944	786,182	2358545.25	50,043,433
16	79,978,800	16,795,548	13,102,279	3,693,269	993,842	674,857	2024570.25	52,068,003
17	79,978,800	16,795,548	13,526,474	3,269,074	1,030,094	559,745	1,679,235	53,747,238
18	79,978,800	16,795,548	13,964,952	2,830,596	1,067,755	440,710	1322130.75	55,069,369
19	79,978,800	16,795,548	14,418,218	2,377,330	1,106,884	317,612	952,835	56,022,203
20	79,978,800	16,795,548	14,886,798	1,908,750	1,147,541	190,302	570,907	56,593,110
21	79,978,800	16,795,548	15,333,402	1,462,146	1,181,967	70,045	210,134	56,803,244
						IRR	12.40%	
						PV	61274142.67	
						NPV	6698142.67	
						PBP	5.84	

Table 2.
Sample Microsoft excel worksheet to evaluate NPV, IRR, and PBP [12].

based on specific assumptions. The assumptions are made for the simplification of calculations. A standard form used by most of the industries worldwide is as below:

$$LCOE(T) = \frac{\sum_{n=0}^{T} \frac{TIC(n)+OM(n)+FC(n)}{(1+r)^n}}{\sum_{n=0}^{T} \frac{EP(n)}{(1+r)^n}} \tag{8}$$

where TIC, is the total investment cost in the year, OM is the annual operation and maintenance cost, FC is the annual fuel cost, EP is the estimated annual generation and T is life span of the project in years. **Table 3** shows a comparison of LCOE values of different renewable energy sources at different areas. Biomass based energy can be seen as an attractive mode of energy source in the range 0.03–0.07 $/kWh which is much lower margin than solar PV [13].

Country	Biomass	Geothermal	Hydro	Solar PV	Onshore wind	Offshore wind
China	0.03	na	0.03	0.10	0.05	0.14
Europe	0.07	0.12	0.08	0.15	0.065	0.15
Middle East	0.07	na	0.07	0.14	0.09	na
India	0.04	na	0.04	0.09	0.07	na
USA	0.07	0.09	0.05	0.13	0.05	0.12

Table 3.
Average LCOE from renewable energy source in 2017 ($/kWh) [13].

2.8 Profitability index (PI)

Profitability index is the ratio of the future cash flows to initial investment. If the value is 1 than the project is at breakeven point and greater than one means project is profitable. If mutually exclusive projects are ranked based on PI than it eases the decision making. If an individual project shows to have a PI ratio less than 1 then, it indicative that the future cash inflows cannot cover the expenditures.

The simple relation of profitability index in terms of NPV and I_0 can be written as,

$$PI = \frac{NPV}{I_0} + 1 \tag{9}$$

The present value of a single payment made in the future can be written as, [8].

$$PV = FV(1+i)^{-n} \tag{10}$$

Profitability Index (PI) is a relative parameter. It shows how much present value of cash inflows generated for each dollar invested. It is a ratio not having unit unlike NPV.

Decisions for using the Profitability Index:

Accept the investment project proposal if index is greater than 1.0.

Reject the project proposal if index is smaller than 1.0.

When the index equals 1.0, it makes it indifferent whether accept or reject.

So, the investment alternatives should be ranked from highest index to lowest one.

Sample problem on profitability analysis:

Three mutually exclusive projects are under consideration for decision making. The economic attributes are as follows:

Project	A	B	C
Initial investment	$40,000	$42,000	$55,000
Year 1 profit	$ 12,500	$ 13,000	$ 13,500
Year 2 profit	$ 12,000	$ 12,000	$ 12,500
Year 3 profit	$ 11,500	$ 11,000	$ 11,500
Year 4 profit	$ 11,000	$ 10,000	$ 10,500
Year 5 profit	—	$ 9000	$ 9500
Year 6 profit	—	—	$ 8500
Economic life	4 years	5 years	6 years
Salvage value	$7000	$8500	$10,000

The opportunity cost of capital is 10%. Identify the best alternative among those three using profitability index.

Solution: Profitability index for the three mutually exclusive projects can be calculated as:

Profitability Index of Project A:

$$PI_A = \frac{\frac{\$12,500}{(1+0.1)} + \frac{\$12,000}{(1+0.1)^2} + \frac{\$11,500}{(1+0.1)^3} + \frac{\$11,000}{(1+0.1)^4} + \frac{\$7000}{(1+0.1)^4}}{\$40,000} = 1.05.$$

Profitability Index of Project B:

$$PI_B = \frac{\frac{\$13,000}{(1+0.1)} + \frac{\$12,000}{(1+0.1)^2} + \frac{\$11,000}{(1+0.1)^3} + \frac{\$10,000}{(1+0.1)^4} + \frac{\$9,000}{(1+0.1)^5} + \frac{\$8,500}{(1+0.1)^5}}{\$42,000} = 1.14$$

Profitability Index of Project C:

$$PI_C = \frac{\frac{\$13,500}{(1+0.1)} + \frac{\$12,500}{(1+0.1)^2} + \frac{\$11,500}{(1+0.1)^3} + \frac{\$10,500}{(1+0.1)^4} + \frac{\$9,500}{(1+0.1)^5} + \frac{\$8,500}{(1+0.1)^6} + \frac{\$10,000}{(1+0.1)^6}}{\$55,000} = 0.99$$

Since project B has the highest profitability index, it should be chosen among the three alternatives.

2.9 Sensitivity analysis

A sensitivity analysis illustrates how much the merit figures will change in response to a given change in an input variable. There always exist some critical parameters which have significant impact on the final sought parameters like Net present value or internal rate of return, IRR). For example, the estimate of energy produced from a biomass-based energy project is often a major factor. Cost of the project, and estimated operation and maintenance cost are other factors generally considered to have greater impact in a sensitivity analysis.

A sensitivity analysis done for the operation of a power generation plant with revenue earning, costs of generation, and operational expenses as the parameters to have significant impact on IRR and Payback period, PBP. These parameters are plotted with ±10% change from the business-as-usual scenario. **Table 4** below gives the sensitivity analysis done in the three parameters, revenue earning; the cost of goods sold and operational cost and the resulted changes in IRR and payback period. When all other parameters are fixed and revenue earning is declined by 10% then the

	−10%		−5%		0%		+5%		+10%	
	IRR	PBP	IRR	PBP	IRR	PBP	IRR	PBP	IRR	PBP
Revenue	−3.1	NA	1.2	13.8	4.3	10.3	6.8	8.7	9.1	7.6
Costs	7.4	8.5	6.0	9.3	4.3	10.3	2.3	12.1	0.0	15.6
Operation and Maintenance	4.5	10.1	4.4	10.2	4.3	10.3	4.2	10.5	4.0	10.6

Table 4.
Sensitivity analysis of the project IRR and payback period.

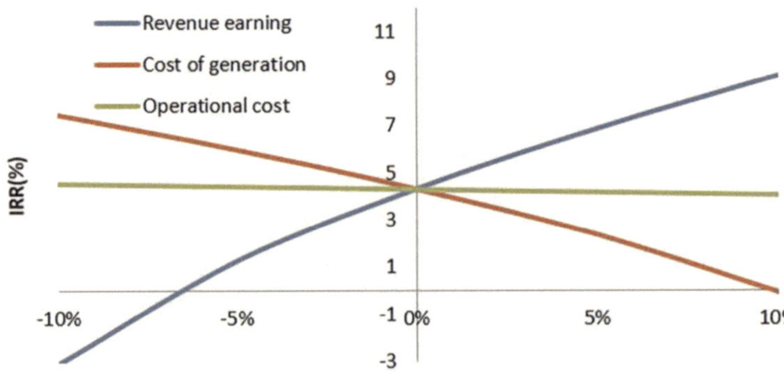

Figure 1.
Sensitivity of IRR at the variation of revenue earning, generation cost, and operational cost.

IRR becomes −3.13%. This negative IRR means the project cannot payback the investment in its lifetime and thus the payback period is not available in this condition. Similarly, the revenue earning increase by 10% causes IRR changes from 4.31% (base case) to 9.10%. Hence project turns to earn positive NPV and the corresponding payback period is 7.6 years only. Revenue earning is the sensitive factor in the case of biomass-based power generation project.

As the operational cost of a plant run on biomass cannot be expected to decrease over the years, the first cost of project installation must be curtailed. These can happen if the government ensures the tax credit and subsidy in the import items of the equipment needed.

Figure 1 shows the sensitivity of IRR with respect to revenue earning, the total cost of power generation and operational cost of generation. The internal rate of return of a biomass based power generation project is highly sensitive to revenue earning and cost of investment. The operational cost shows a less sensitivity. Perhaps, the earning is based on the selling to the utility company and the rate if low the internal rate of return is low. The implication of the IRR sensitivity curve is that the pricing of the energy generated should be increased to make the plant operation competitive with traditional power generation units.

3. Discussions

3.1 Economy of biomass combustion based power generation

Biomass based power generation is very much dependent on the source of biomass. There is a wide range of biomass feed stocks and can be procured from a variety of

Fuel type	In-sourced (ton/year)	Outsourced (ton/year)	Price (MYR/ton)	Cost (MYR)
EFB	30,500	—	16	4,88,000
EFB	—	52,000	36	1,872,000
Fruit Fiber	22,000	—	37	8,21,400
PKS	15,000		115	1,782,000
Wood		2230	50	111,500
Total	68,200	54,230		5,075,400

Table 5.
Total biomass price for combustion-based plant [12].

sources. The price of biomass is a critical factor as it is directly related to its thermal properties (calorific value, moisture content, bulk density and homogeneity etc.). The economic analysis is based on the palm oil-based fuels. **Table 5** shows the cost structure of different types of biomasses needed for a typical combustion-based plant of capacity 10 MW.

3.2 Loan financing and economic feasibility of a biomass combustion and gasification based plant

The net present value (NPV), internal rate of return (IRR), and payback period (PBP) has been re-calculated if half of the total investment is taken as loan from a

Year	Generation (kWh)	Revenue Earning (mill MYR)	Cost (MYR)	Gross Profit (MYR)	Opex (MYR)	Re-pay of loan (MYR)	Certified Emission reduction (MYR)	EAIT (MYR)	Cumulative Earn (MYR)
0						(3% p.a.)		−54,576,000	−54,576,000
1	65,700,000	13.79	7,450,366	6,346,634	586,146	3,667,279	2,436,500	4,529,709	−50,046,291
2	70,080,000	14.72	7,972,960	6,743,840	606,827	3,667,279	2,601,500	5,071,234	−44,975,057
3	79,978,000	16.80	8,889,223	7,906,325	628,282	3,667,279	2,976,215	6,586,979	−38,388,078
4	79,978,000	16.80	9,172,407	7,623,141	650,544	3,667,279	2,976,215	6,281,533	−32,106,545
5	79,978,000	16.80	9,464,912	7,330,636	673,644	3,667,279	2,976,215	5,965,928	−26,140,617
6	79,978,000	16.80	9,767,059	7,028,489	697,617	3,667,279	2,976,215	5,639,808	−20,500,809
7	79,978,000	16.80	10,079,180	6,716,368	722,497	3,667,279	2,976,215	5,302,807	−15,198,002
8	79,978,000	16.80	10,401,620	6,393,928	748,321	3,667,279	2,976,215	4,954,543	−10,243,459
9	79,978,000	16.80	10,734,737	6,060,811	775,127	3,667,279	2,976,215	4,594,620	−5,648,839
10	**79,978,000**	**16.80**	**10,734,737**	**6,060,811**	**802,955**	**3,667,279**	**2,976,215**	**4,566,792**	**−1,082,047**
							IRR	4.32%	
							PV	55,737,400	
							NPV	1,161,400	
							PBP(y)	10.34	

Table 6.
NPV, IRR, and payback period of a typical biomass combustion-based power plant with 50% loan at 3% p.a. [12].

financing company (bank, government subsidy or other stake holders of the concern). The earnings before interest and tax which is called EBIT are calculated by deducting the operating cost from the gross profit. The current earnings are discounted cash to calculate the net present value of the total plant. The NPV, IRR and PBP period is seen to have changed significantly. The detail cash flow analysis for a typical biomass combustion power plant and a typical biomass gasification power plant is presented in **Table 6**.

The loan financed project seen to have NPV, IRR, and PBP values MYR 1.16 million, 4.32%, and 10.34 years respectively for the combustion-based plant. The changes in economic performance parameters are significant and can not be accepted from economic viability point of view.

3.3 Opportunities and challenges for sustainable biomass based power generation

The advantage of biomass- based power generation relative to other available renewable enrgy forms is that it can be availed as 24/7 basis as baseload power supply. The challenges come first is the continuous and adequate supply of the feedstock in right form and at proper condition regarding the usage in the right technology whether combustion or gasification.

4. Conclusion

Energy from biomass is a need of time to face the future energy challenges that would arise by the rapid depletion of fossil fuels. Biomass extraction for energy purpose is acceptable only if it is justified economically and socially, at the same time its strategy must aim at sustainability. A drive without sustainability would create a system to be abandoned in near future. In pursuit of sustainability all the moves should be towards achieving and using technologies on the basis of economic feasibility and viability. The selection of energy production technology would be so as to sustain the ecological conditions and not to instigate the food versus fuel conflict concerning the land and water use. Also, there should have a positive environmental balance for the whole life cycle of the biomass used for energy extraction. The best alternative to the combustion-based plant a biomass integrated gasification combined cycle (BIGCC) plant can be suitable pelleted or briquetted biomass with low-cost technology and developed locally.

List of acronyms

BIGCC	Biomass integrated gasification combined cycle
CDM	Clean development mechanism
CER	Certified emission reduction
IRR	Internal rate of return
MARR	Minimum attractive rate of return
MYR	Malaysian Ringgit
NPV	Net Present Value
PBP	Payback period

Author details

A.B.M. Abdul Malek
Department of Industrial and Production Engineering, Shahjalal University of Science and Technology, Sylhet, Bangladesh

*Address all correspondence to: bashar@sust.edu

References

[1] Islam MA et al. Global renewable energy-based electricity generation and smart grid system for energy security. Scientific World Journal. 2014:1-13

[2] Hasanuzzaman M et al. Photovoltaic power generation and its economic and environmental future in Bangladesh. Journal of Renewable and Sustainable Energy. 2015;**7**(1):1-12

[3] Evans A, Strezov V, Evans TJ. Sustainability considerations for electricity generation from biomass. Renewable and Sustainable Energy Reviews. 2010;**14**(5):1419-1427

[4] Prasad R, Raturi A. Prospects of sustainable biomass-based power generation in a Small Island country. Journal of Cleaner Production. 2021;**318**: 128519

[5] Asadullah M. Biomass gasification gas cleaning for downstream applications: A comparative critical review. Renewable and Sustainable Energy Reviews. 2014; **40**(0):118-132

[6] Kumar D. Economic assessment of photovoltaic energy production prospects in India. In: Global Challenges, Policy Framework & Sustainable Development for Mining of Mineral and Fossil Energy Resources (GCPF 2015). Karnataka: India; Elsevier Procedia; Procedia Earth and Planetary Science. 2015;**11**:425–436

[7] van de Poel I. Values in engineering design. In: Meijers A, editor. Philosophy of Technology and Engineering Sciences. Amsterdam: North-Holland; 2009. pp. 973-1006

[8] Foster R, Ghassemi M, Cota A. Solar Energy: Renewable Energy and the Environment. Florida, USA: CRC Press; 2009

[9] Abdul Malek ABM et al. Energy, economic, and environmental analysis of 10-MW biomass gasification based power generation in Malaysia. Energy & Environment. 2021;**32**(2):295-337

[10] Alam M et al. Energy and economic analysis of vacuum insulation panels (VIPs) used in non-domestic buildings. Applied Energy. 2017;**188**:1-8

[11] Orioli A, Di Gangi A. The recent change in the Italian policies for photovoltaics: Effects on the payback period and levelized cost of electricity of grid-connected photovoltaic systems installed in urban contexts. Energy. 2015;**93**:1989-2005

[12] Malek ABMA et al. Techno-economic analysis and environmental impact assessment of a 10 MW biomass-based power plant in Malaysia. Journal of Cleaner Production. 2017;**141** (Supplement C):502-513

[13] IRENA, RENA. Renewable Capacity Statistics, IRENA, Abu Dhabi, 2017. Abu Dhabi, UAE: IRENA; 2017

Chapter 3

Assessment of the Impacts of an Inheritance Taxation Relief on the Profitability of Forest Investments

Jean-Philippe Terreaux

Abstract

The place and importance of forest biomass production is widely recognized in natural resources and energy policy in many countries. However, for a part of them, including France, the forest belongs mainly to private owners. Consequently, fiscal policy, including inheritance taxes, is an essential tool to orient biomass production. France is one of the countries where an inheritance tax is levied. In the case of forests, given the slow production cycle, this means that each tree is taxed several times before it reaches maturity. This situation could discourage the practice of forestry. For this reason, a tax abatement has been introduced, which consists of taxing forests at only one-quarter of their value in the calculation of the inheritance tax. This abatement is subject to a commitment to good management for 30 years. Thus not all forests benefit from it. In this work, we intend to quantify this advantage when it is attributed, so that the interested parties can compare it to the costs and inconveniences of the commitment, and above all, to estimate the additional profitability that it provides to the forest compared to other investment alternatives, all other things being equal. To this end, we set up a demographic model to represent the inheritance sequence and an economic model with the current tax rates. In the end, we find that this tax rebate is a good incentive to invest in the forest, and therefore to produce more biomass on the long term and a good incentive to produce the significant positive externalities associated with the presence of forests.

Keywords: economy, forest, inheritance, succession, taxation, valuation

1. Introduction

Biomass production through the forestry sector are particularly characterized by three phenomena, which are not specific to them but are at the origin of regulations, taxation or management rules that are different from those used in other fields of economic activity. Firstly, the standing trees are both the productive capital and the products; secondly is the length of the production cycle (40 years for a maritime pine, two centuries for some oaks); and thirdly, the importance of the externalities of forestry on the economic, social and environmental levels ("Forests precede peoples, deserts follow them", falsely attributed to Chateaubriand).

However, the government is subject to budgetary constraints, requiring different sectors of the economy to contribute to the expenditures, including forestry

IntechOpen

(e.g. see [1, 2]). In this context, many governments have adapted tax regulations where they have to be applied to forests. Broadly speaking, forest-related taxes can be classified (see [3]) into the following categories: (1) taxes based on the assumed productivity of woodlands (such as the land tax or forest income tax in France), (2) taxes on production (such as the value-added tax, where applicable), (3) taxes on wealth (such as the IFI—tax on real estate wealth in France) and (4) taxes on inheritance.

The effects of the first three taxes have been studied by forest economists: what are their impacts on the profitability of forests, the silviculture practiced, the interest of forestry vis-à-vis other activities or investments (see [4–6]). Some particular aspects have been the subject of detailed work. For example, Aschan (in [7]) shows how a progressive income tax directly impacts harvests and thus silviculture; the impact of various financial market conditions has been studied [8–10]. Some authors (see [11, 12]) have shown how these taxes decrease the value of forests, but also how, by inducing owners to change their forest management, these taxes create distortions leading to a further economic loss (e.g., by inducing to reduce or increase the rotations, i.e., the age at which the trees are cut before the forest is regenerated, compared to a situation without taxes).

The inheritance tax, applied when the owner dies, or when he gives his forest to a child or grandchild, is another possible instrument providing revenue to the government. It has a significant impact on the decisions taken by nonindustrial private forest owners and on the allocation of their capital between forest and other investments, as shown in Barua et al. [13] with a two-period theoretical model (see also [14]). As a result, it can be used to implement forest policy [15, 16]. Such a tool is used, for example, in France, but also in 23 other OECD countries [17], with very different modalities (e.g., exemption of the equivalent of the first inherited 17,000 dollars in Belgium versus the first 11,000,000 dollars in the USA) for a parent-child transmission; moreover, many assets are sometimes exempted, such as the principal residence, farms, life insurance, etc. The separation of usufruct and bare ownership is then in some countries a way of reducing the burden of this tax.

Here we are interested in the situation in France, where forests can benefit from exemption from inheritance tax for three-quarters of their value (only one-quarter is taxed), subject to a commitment to good forest management for 30 years (a commitment to be respected by the heir and possibly by his successors). The legislator's idea was to avoid taxing the same tree several times before it was harvested, and above all to avoid premature cutting of trees simply to pay this tax. On the basis of the approximation that the value of trees is on average (according to species, age, region, economic conditions, etc.) equal to three times the value of the forest land, this amounted in a way to taxing the land but not the trees. This is a very general average, as the value of the trees can be anywhere from zero to more than 20 times the value of the land (see [18]). This commitment to good future management gives the owner an incentive to abstain from harvesting trees prematurely, and this incentive is materialized in a lower amount of tax to be paid to fiscal authorities.

Our objective here is to calculate the burden that this tax represents under the present conditions, depending on whether or not this abatement (known as the "Monichon" abatement, named after the French senator Max Monichon, 1900–1977) is obtained, so as to better quantify the incentive it provides to subscribe to this commitment to good forest management. And above all, to better quantify the competitive advantage it gives to the forest among other possible investments that would not benefit from this partial exoneration.

The transmission of a legacy to future generations is also an important motive for forestry (see [19]), especially since, beyond a capital asset, a whole set of values is transmitted [20, 21]. And for private forests, the lifetime of investments often exceeds the remaining life expectancy of the owners (cf. for example [22], and the models of overlapping generations; see also [7], which illustrates how an initial investment can allow for a sequence of revenues, but only after a long duration).

In the remainder of this chapter, we build a demographic model to represent the sequence of transmissions. We then obtain the evolution of the age of the owner of a woodlot, or any other asset transmitted from generation to generation. For this, we use data for the French population. In a second step, we describe the economic model, present its results, and in a third step, we make some comments.

2. The demographic model

The demographic model is constructed to represent the transmission of the relevant part of the estate from its owner to one of his/her heirs. Various details of its construction are mentioned in Appendix 1.

We use directly the most recent data available from Insee, the French National Institute of Statistics and Economic Studies, corresponding to the year 2019 [23]. Note in this regard that the data for the years 2020 and 2021 may have been affected by the COVID-19 pandemic.

These data represent average values for the French population, and it is clear that for a particular investor, his/her own values concerning the age of children or life expectancy may differ significantly. Our results will therefore be average values, and may therefore differ from the result of a valuation that would be made for a particular case.

2.1 Generation gap

Data from Insee [23] allow us to calculate the probability distribution of the age gap between two generations. We represent below (**Figure 1**) the number of children born alive according to the age of the mother, which has the same shape as this distribution. The average age of the mother is 31 years, with a standard deviation of 5.27 years.

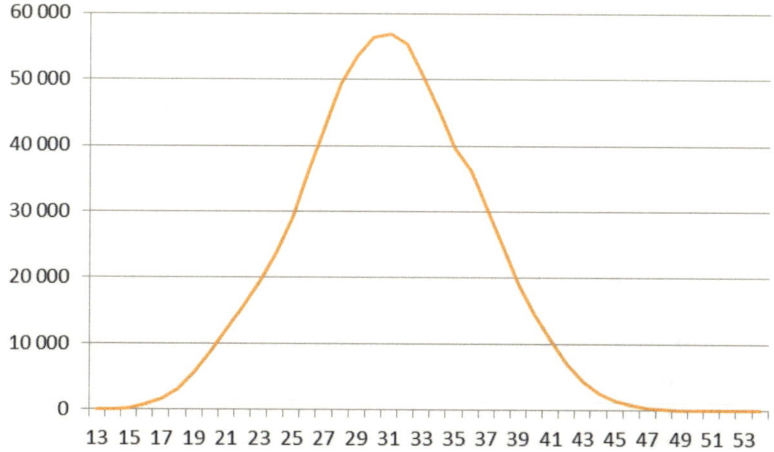

Figure 1.
Number of children born alive by age of mother. x-axis: age of mother in years; y-axis: number of children. Data for France (excluding Mayotte), 2019 (source: [23]).

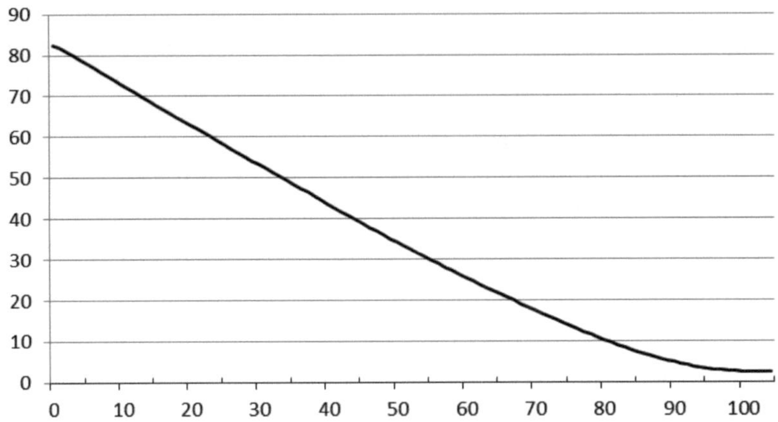

Figure 2.
Life expectancy by age (men and women). x-axis: age; y-axis: life expectancy, in years. Data for France, 2017–2019 (source: [23]).

2.2 Life expectancy as a function of age

According to the same source, we know the life expectancy as a function of age, for men and women taken together. In **Figure 2**, we represent this expectation, which has a convex shape, especially after the age of 80, meaning that at each birthday, the estimated date of death is pushed forward.

For instance, if at the age of 70, life expectancy for a woman (resp. man) is 19.20 years (resp. 15.91 years), ten years later, for a woman who has reached the age of 80, it is not 9.20 years (resp. 5.91 years), but 11.28 years (resp. 9.20 years). Note that the COVID-19 pandemic has recently reduced life expectancy in most countries by a few months.

2.3 Mortality quotient

We represent below (**Figure 3**) the mortality quotient per 100,000 survivors at age x, i.e., assuming a representative population of 100,000 persons of the same age x, the number of persons dying in year n.

2.4 Evolution of the age of the owner of a plot of forested land

Let us now suppose that we examine the evolution of the age of the owner of a well-identified plot of forested land, or a forest as a whole but which will not be divided in the future by inheritance. For example, let us assume that the owner has at the beginning (t = 1) an age a(1) = 38 years. The following year, at t = 2, the probability of death being very low at this age, the owner will have, with a high probability, the age a(2) = 39. And so on, finally leading him/her to pass on the plot, following his/her death, whose probabilities have been evaluated according to his/her increasing age (see **Figure 3**).

This transmission benefits a direct descendant (a child, whose age probability distribution is calculated from the data presented in **Figure 1**), or an indirect descendant (grandchild), if the direct descendant is already deceased (the probability is known); and so on if the indirect descendant is himself/herself deceased (see more details in Appendix 1).

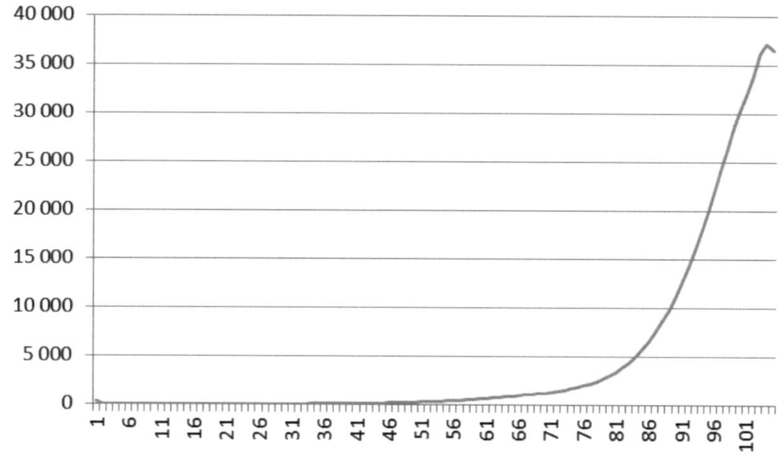

Figure 3.
Number of deaths in a year based on a population of 100,000 people of the relevant age (men and women). x-axis: age; y-axis: number of deaths. Data for France, 2017–2019 (source: [23]).

Figure 4 allows us to visualize that the probability distribution of this age converges to a stable distribution, which is, in fact, independent of the starting age a(1) of the woodlot owner.

2.5 Comparison of model results and forest owner ages

We present in **Figure 5** the year-by-year probability distribution of the age of the owner of the woodlot or forest under consideration, after a sufficiently long time for this distribution to stabilize.

We can now compare these probabilities with data from the general population in France and from the Agreste survey of forest owners [24] in Aquitaine. As there are

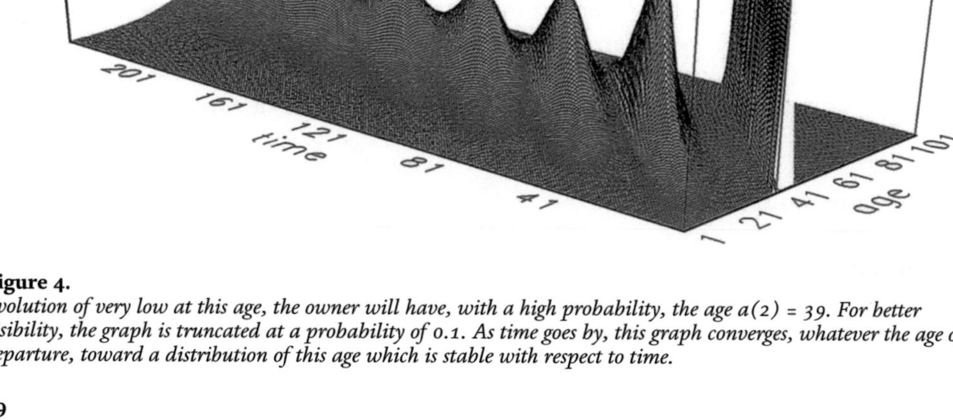

Figure 4.
Evolution of very low at this age, the owner will have, with a high probability, the age a(2) = 39. For better visibility, the graph is truncated at a probability of 0.1. As time goes by, this graph converges, whatever the age of departure, toward a distribution of this age which is stable with respect to time.

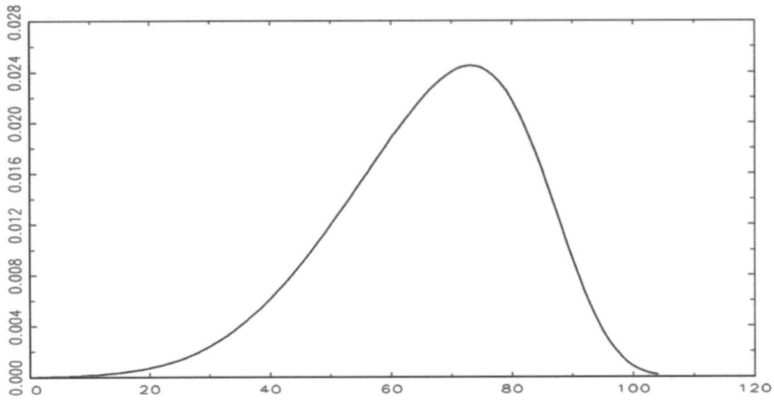

Figure 5.
Age limit distribution of the owner of the forest or woodlot under consideration. x-axis: age of owner; y-axis: probability year by year. Result of the model presented above and in Annex 1.

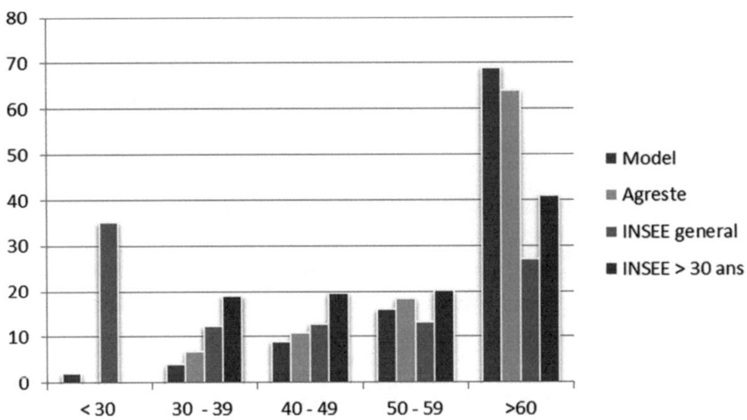

Figure 6.
Comparison of model results (left bars), then Agreste survey data [24] on forest owners, then [23] on the general population, and finally the same Insee data [23] for the population over 30 years old. x-axis: age group; y-axis: percentage (see text).

very few forest owners under 30 years old, we also show the distribution of the French population (see [23]) for only those over 30 years old (**Figure 6**).

Overall, we see that the results of the model are very close to the results of the Agreste survey and quite different from those of the general population. This can be explained by and corroborates the fact that "family transmission appears to be the essential factor in the acquisition process. Nearly three out of four owners received their first "forestry property" by inheritance or donation. The purchase, with a view to building up a forest estate, concerns 27% of owners (30% of surfaces) and the creation by planting of wooded territories less than 1%" [24].

3. The economic model

3.1 The objective

We assume that an investor has a capital that can be invested in a forest and that the required conditions (commitment to good management over 30 years) are then satisfied to benefit from the 75% deduction for inheritance tax. This capital can also be used for an alternative investment (forest without the commitment of good management, finance, real estate, etc.). To facilitate the understanding of the analysis, we assume that the investments provide the same return without this inheritance tax. Our objective is to quantify this benefit of the partial exemption from this tax in terms of additional profitability, depending on the general inheritance tax rate, the time horizon, and the current age of the investor.

3.2 Assumptions on tax rates and wealth growth

We use here the current (2021) inheritance tax rates in France. The practical details have been simplified over the last 30 years (see [15]) since the marginal tax rates are now the same for the transmissions between (a) parents and children, (b) parents and grandchildren, and (c) parents and great-grandchildren. On the other hand, an exemption from inheritance tax applies for the first euros according to the degree of parenthood (respectively (a) €100,000, (b) €31,865, and (c) €5,310). Depending on the total value of the inherited wealth, this exemption is likely to change the marginal tax rate of the forest, but for simplicity, we assume that this is not the case (otherwise, the numerical results are only slightly changed, since the difference between these marginal rates is relatively small, 5% or 10%).

The tax rates, after the aforementioned partial exemption, are presented in **Table 1** (source: e.g., Le Particulier, 1183, July–August 2021). We will use these different marginal tax rates in the following sections.

To simplify the presentation of the results, we assume that these rates will remain the same in the future. We also assume that the overall value of the estate held by the heir(s) concerned by the forest may change in the future, but without involving a change in these marginal tax rates, so that successive heirs face the same marginal tax rates.

We will assume that the annual return on capital invested in and out of the forest, regardless of inheritance tax, is constant and equal to r. The annual returns are capitalized (added to the capital) and the value of the capital, therefore, grows regularly at the rate of r, except in the case of payment of inheritance tax, in which case the tax is deducted from the capital transmitted. Furthermore, the nature of the investment (forest or non-forest) is assumed not to change in the future.

Amount	Marginal tax rate
Less than €8,072	5%
Between €8,073 and €12,109	10%
Between €12,110 and €15,932	15%
Between €15,933 and €552,324	20%
Between €552,325 and €902,838	30%
Between €902,839 and €1,805,677	40%
Greater than €1,805,677	45%

Table 1.
Marginal tax rate according to the amount of wealth transferred to the heir under consideration, after exemption of the first euros (see text).

Future values are discounted at a constant rate of a. To simplify the interpretation of the results, and thus assuming that forest owners are perfect altruists, we do not change the discount rate when an inheritance occurs. Numerically, if we take $a = r$, this leads to a present value of capital that is constant excluding inheritance taxes. Numerically, we use r = 4% (for the forest this corresponds to the results of [18] and a = 4% (see e.g., [25–27]).

3.3 The importance of the inheritance tax

The model of the evolution of the wealth subject to inheritance tax is presented in more detail in Appendix 2. The results make it possible to construct **Figure 7**, in which we present the percentage of the wealth that will be used to pay this inheritance tax over the next 20 years, depending on the marginal tax rate and whether or not the partial allowance is obtained.

We can then deduce the additional profitability induced by this partial inheritance tax relief, which we express in terms of additional annual growth of the capital invested (**Figures 8** and **9**). Obviously, this interest in the allowance is closely linked to the marginal tax rate, i.e., indirectly, to the capital transmitted to each heir. It is also closely linked to the age of the current owner (**Figure 8**) and to the considered time horizon (**Figure 9**).

The rate is higher when the current owner is older (the transmission is closer, so the benefit obtained from this abatement is relatively greater, due to discounting). In the case of a relatively old investor, it is more important when the horizon of the calculation is not very distant, as we see in the **Figure 9**.

Whatever the tax rate, **Figure 9** shows that this exemption first increases, then decreases according to the time horizon considered, taking a maximum between 25 and 30 years, for an owner who is 70 years old: for a short time horizon, he/she has little probability of dying before this time horizon, and the advantage provided by this abatement is not very significant. For a long time horizon, the successive transmissions are smoothed out over a longer period of time, and likewise the advantage provided by this abatement.

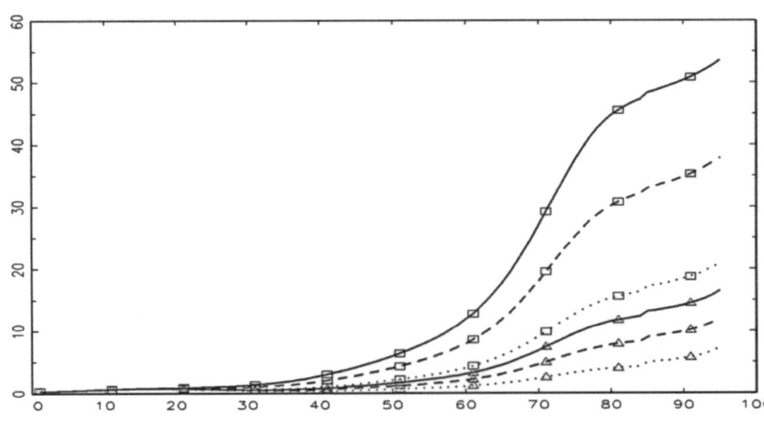

Figure 7.
On the x-axis, the age of the owner (of the forest or of the investment); on the y-axis, the share of this wealth represented by the inheritance tax to be paid over the next 20 years. Curves with squares: without tax abatement. Curves with triangles: with partial tax abatement (Monichon). Solid curve: marginal tax rate: 45%; dashed: 30%; dotted: 15%.

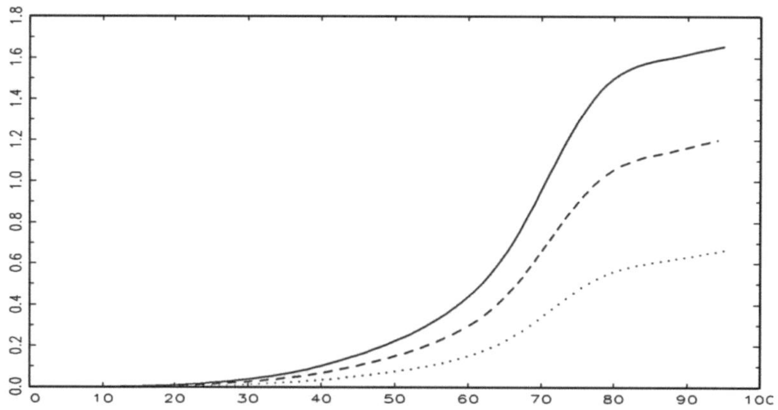

Figure 8.
For a time horizon of 20 years: on the x-axis, the age of the owner; on the y-axis, the equivalent investment performance increase (in yield points; 1 = 1% more return) due to the partial abatement (Monichon), depending on the tax rate: solid curve: marginal tax rate: 45%; dashed: 30%; dotted: 15%.

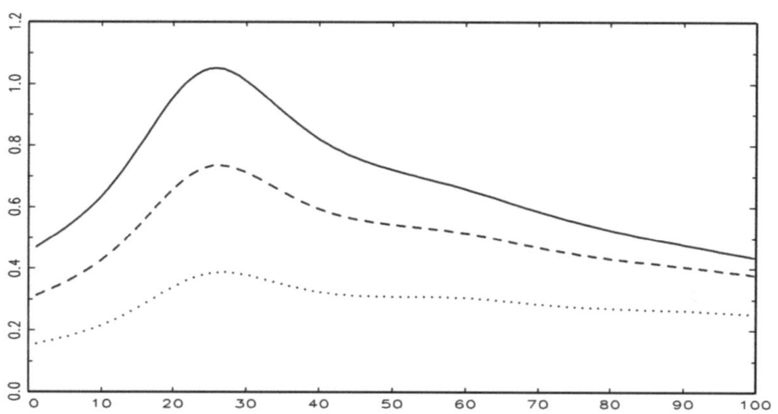

Figure 9.
For a 70-year-old owner, on the x-axis, the time horizon of the computation; on the y-axis, the equivalent performance increase of the investment (in yield points; 1 = 1% more return) due to the partial abatement (Monichon), depending on the tax rate, for the tax payable in the coming years up to the horizon of the calculations. Solid curve: marginal tax rate: 45%; dashed: 30%; dotted: 15%.

4. Conclusion

Our results concerning the age structure of French forest owners confirm that forests are most often inherited, conserved and managed, and then are passed on to heirs. Furthermore, we have a better understanding of why older forest owners generally cut fewer trees than younger ones, as noted, for example, in [22]. This is not without consequence on the production of biomass.

Some of the reasons could be that at the age of inheritance, in a country where longevity is relatively high, and different means (pension system, different forms of financial savings ...) may be sufficient to meet the current needs of retirees, forests are kept in the portfolio firstly for philosophical reasons and motives other than financial (feeling of stability provided by trees, various amenities). Secondly, forests are also seen more as precautionary savings (in case of major temporary difficulties) than as a source of income. Finally, they are a means of transmitting a heritage marked for the following generations by the personal investments and forest management decisions of the owner. All this encourages the retention of standing trees and the delaying of harvesting.

And from an economic point of view, as we have seen, inheritance tax relief is not an incentive for the owner to sell his/her forest or cut down his/her trees, but rather to pass on his/her heritage in the form of woodland.

We have also seen that the older the owner, the more he/she has an interest in doing so, and in particular in postponing the age at which trees are cut, but also in investing in silviculture (pruning, maintenance, etc.) to give more value to his/her forests. In doing so, forest owners create externalities that benefit society as a whole, most of which are positive: more biodiversity (cf. [28]), more carbon storage, more attractive forests for walkers, etc. Tax relief on forests, of the type studied here, can thus be a very useful tool for public authorities to obtain such externalities at a low cost. It can also be used to guide the short- or long-term commercialization of the biomass produced.

However, in France, these effects may be partly counterbalanced, for certain estates, by the tax on forest assets (named IFI: Impôt sur la Fortune Immobilière). If one compares forest investments that are subject to this tax (also with an abatement of three-quarters of the value of the forest, under the same conditions of commitment as the tax on inheritance studied here) with financial investments that are not subject to this burden, this IFI encourages cutting down trees and passing on financial assets. The calculation of this incentive remains to be done, and for the forests that are subject to it, the synthesis of the two effects to be calculated, both on the biomass production and on the externalities; it is a new research to be undertaken.

Finally, it should be remembered that the quantitative results presented here are based on average parameter values for the demographic and economic models, and are not a substitute for an expert appraisal, which is the only way to advise a particular forest owner or individual investor.

Acknowledgements

This study has been carried out with financial support from the French National Research Agency (ANR) in the frame of the Investments for the Future Program, within the Cluster of Excellence COTE (ANR-10-LABX45), thanks to the LUCAS Project.

A. Appendix 1: additional information on the demographic model

We consider that the evolution of the population of owners of the assets considered (forest, financial portfolio ...) can be entirely deduced from its current state. Consequently, a Markov model can be used [29]. We still have to implement it.

For simplicity, and in the absence of any other realistic hypothesis, we assume in the following that the demographic parameters (life expectancy, etc.) do not change. We use Insee data (see [23], data for the year 2019, before the COVID-19 pandemic).

In the model, time, denoted by t, is discrete, the unit being a year; $t = 1$ is the present. Suppose that in year n, the owner of the forest (or of any other property or portfolio considered) has the age of a. Insee [23] tells us directly the probability that he/she will not die in year n. Otherwise, there is inheritance.

The publication [23] also provides us with the age of the mother for every birth in France (for fathers, there is no data; perhaps a problem of uncertainties ...); we deduce the probability distribution of the age gap between a generation (between mothers and children).

If the owner (generation G) dies in year n, we thus have the probability distribution of the age of the heir child (generation G + 1). But he/she himself may have died (we know the probability, since [23] directly mentions the survival rate at a given age). In this case, the forest is passed on to the descendant of this heir, who is already deceased. This descendant (generation G + 2) himself may be already deceased, and in the calculation, we take this possibility into account by integrating the fact that the forest can be transmitted directly from generation G to G + 3. This consideration is important because the age of the heir, second or even third rank, does not follow the same probability distribution as in the case of a parent-child transmission.

In the (unlikely) case that the heir at G + 3 is also deceased, we assume that the forest is transmitted to another "branch" of the family, and we return to G + 1, to repeat the same calculations. We also suppose that the considered part of the inheritance is never divided, until the time horizon of the calculations. This is a weak assumption because if it were not the case, one can imagine that the calculation relates in fact only to one of the parts, after the partition.

For practical purposes, we consider a maximum age of 104 years: we assume that at this age, the owner voluntarily passes on his/her property to his/her heirs, under the same tax conditions.

We then define the real vector $X_t(104,1)$ with coordinates $X_t(i)$, each equal to the probability that the owner of the asset under consideration is i years old in year t.

We then define the Markov matrix M(104,104): M(i,j) is the probability that the assets owned by an owner aged j years in year t are owned by an owner aged i years in year t + 1. M(i,j) is calculated using the data presented in the text.

The evolution of Xt is given by:

$$X_{t+1} = M \cdot X_t \tag{1}$$

B. Appendix 2: additional information on the economic model

We start with an asset belonging to an owner of any age (less than 104 years). After a sufficiently long period of time, the after-tax value of this asset will depend on the past sequences of transfers, which also depends the present value of the taxes that will have to be paid.

We introduce $V_t(i) \in \mathfrak{R}^{*104}$, where i is the age of the owner at time t: If $t > 1$, $V_t(i)$ is the undiscounted after-tax value at time t of the investment if the owner is i years old, multiplied by the probability that the owner is that age. $V_1(i)$ is the initial value of the capital under consideration, with i the current age of the investor.

Since we assume that the tax rates do not change in the future, we are dealing with a Markov process.

In the case where there is no partial tax relief, we can define N, a 104×104 matrix of real coefficients, as follows:

$$V_{t+1} = N \cdot V_t, \forall t \geq 1; \tag{2}$$

N is calculated in a similar way to M, but the coefficients corresponding to a transmission are multiplied by a coefficient (1 − F) representing the loss in value of the part of the estate in question due to taxation. The model takes into account the fact that the transmission may take place via one or more generation gaps: for example, the transmission of capital to an heir 40 years younger may involve either a direct transmission (parent-child) or a transmission with a generation skip (with a child 20 years younger but previously deceased, and a grandchild heir 40 years younger than the grandparent).

In the case where a partial tax relief ('Monichon') is obtained for a capital invested in forest, we define a new matrix N′ in the same way. The only difference with N is due to the use of the tax parameters F′ taking into account this abatement instead of the parameters F:

$$V_{t+1} = N' \cdot V_t \tag{3}$$

B.1 Expected present value of inheritance tax

We are now able to calculate E(t) (resp. E′(t)), the present value of the capital at time t, in the case of an investment not benefiting from the abatement (resp. a forestry investment benefiting from it), *a* being the discount rate:

$$E(t) = \frac{\sum_{k=1}^{104} V_t(k)}{(1+a)^t} \tag{4}$$

We then define the discounted portion of the value of the estate that will be used in the future to pay inheritance taxes as follows

$$V_1(i) - E(t)\ (\text{resp.}\ V_1(i) - E'(t)) \tag{5}$$

with i the current age of the owner of the capital.

The numerical values of r (the annual return on the invested capital) and *a* (the discount rate) have both been taken to be equal to 4% per year, in real terms (zero inflation is assumed in the future, which does not affect the results presented in the text but simplifies their presentation).

B.2 Additional rate of return induced by the tax abatement

Finally, we define the additional rate of return s due to the partial estate tax abatement as the additional rate at which the non-forestry investment would have to grow to yield an expected value equal to the expected value of a forestry investment benefiting from the allowance, at the given time horizon t.

This additional rate s is defined by:

$$V_1(i) \cdot (1 + r + s)^t = V_1(i) \cdot (1 + r)^t + (E'(t) - E(t)) \cdot (1 + r)^t \tag{6}$$

Author details

Jean-Philippe Terreaux
INRAE, ETTIS Research Unit, France

*Address all correspondence to: jean-philippe.terreaux@inrae.fr

References

[1] Amacher GS. The design of forest taxation: A synthesis with new directions. Silva Fennica. 1997;**31**(1): 101-119

[2] Amacher GS, Brazee RJ. Designing forest taxes with varying government preferences and budget targets. Journal of Environmental Economics and Management. 1997;**32**:323-340

[3] Ovaskainen V. Forest taxation, timber supply and economic efficiency. Acta Forestalia Fennica. 1992;(23):88 p.

[4] Johansson PO, Löfgren KG. The economics of forestry and natural resources. Oxford: Basil Blackwell Ltd; 1985. 292 p.

[5] Terreaux JP. Impacts of different taxes and subsidies on optimal forest management in a non-random universe. Annales des Sciences Forestières. 1989; **46**:397-410

[6] Amacher GS, Brazee RJ, Thomson TA. The effect of forest productivity taxes on timber stand investment and rotation length. Forest Science. 1991;**37**(4):1099-1118

[7] Aschan W. Does a new tax system have an economic impact on a forest investment? [Master's thesis 989]. Uppsala: Swedish University of Agricultural Sciences; 2015. 58 p.

[8] Koskela E. Forest taxation and timber supply under price uncertainty: Perfect capital markets. Forest Science. 1989; **35**(1):137-159

[9] Koskela E. Forest taxation and timber supply under price uncertainty: Credit rationing in capital markets. Forest Science. 1989;**35**(1): 160-172

[10] Koskela E, Ollikainen M. Optimal design of forest taxation with multiple-use characteristics of forest stands. Environmental and Resource Economics. 1997;**10**:41-62

[11] Gamponia V, Mendelsohn R. The economic efficiency of forest taxes. Forest Science. 1987;**33**(2):367-378

[12] Klemperer WD. The economic efficiency of forest taxes: A comment. Forest Science. 1987;**33**(2):379-380

[13] Barua SK, Kuuluvainen J, Uusivuori J. Taxation, life-time uncertainty and non-industrial private forest-owner's decision-making. Journal of Forest Economics. 2011;**17**:267-284

[14] Terreaux JP. Did you say 10%? What share for the forest in a well-balanced heritage? La Forêt Privée. 2007;**297**:32-34

[15] Terreaux JP. Fiscalité sur les successions et rentabilité forestière. Cahiers d'économie et sociologie Rurales. 1995;**34/35**:59-76

[16] Amacher GS, Brazee RJ, Koskela E, Ollikainen M. Taxation, Bequests, and Short and Long Run Timber Supplies: An Overlapping Generations Problem. Department of Economics, University of Helsinki (Finland); 1997. 38p. Discussion Papers 415. ISBN: 951-45-7789-2

[17] OECD. Inheritance taxation in OECD countries. In: OECD Tax Policy Studies. Vol. 28. Paris: OECD Publishing; 2021. 149 p.

[18] Terreaux JP. In: EGD, editor. Eléments d'économie forestière, application au pin maritime dans les Landes de Gascogne. 2022 (to appear). 200 p.

[19] Amacher GS, Koskela E, Ollikainen M, Conway MC. Bequest intentions of forest landowners: Theory and empirical evidence. American Journal of Agricultural Economics. 2002; **84**(4):1103-1114

[20] Karppinen H, Korhonen M. Do forest owners share the public's values? An application of Schwartz's value theory. Silva Fennica. 2013;**47**(1): 1-16

[21] Terreaux JP, Chavet M. La propriété forestière privée, les valeurs et la fiscalité forestière. In: Actes des 1ères journées de la Fiscalité Forestière. Bordeaux: Maison de la Forêt; 2013. pp. 49-55

[22] Hultkrantz L. Forestry and the bequest motive. Journal of Environmental Economics and Management. 1992;**22**:164-177

[23] Insee. La situation démographique en 2019, Etat civil et estimation de population. Insee Résultats. 2021. Available from: https://www.insee.fr/fr/information/2410043 [Accessed: June 02, 2021]

[24] Draaf Aquitaine. La forêt privée en Aquitaine, entre patrimoine familial et outil de production. Agreste Aquitaine. 2014;**80**:4

[25] CGP—Commissariat Général au Plan. Révision du taux d'actualisation des investissements publics. Baumstark L (rapporteur), Hirtzman P (coordinator). Commissariat Général au Plan; 2005. 112 p.

[26] Terreaux JP. Taux d'actualisation décroissants et cohérence temporelle des décisions de sylviculture. Revue Forestière Française. 2008;**60**(4): 467-476

[27] Terreaux JP. Let us not forget the future—Values, justice and discount rates. Ethique et économique/Ethics and Economics. 2018;**15**(1):66-80

[28] Brahic E, Terreaux JP. Évaluation économique de la biodiversité, Méthodes et exemples pour les forêts tempérées. Paris: Quae; 2009. 200 p.

[29] Ventsel H. Theory of Probability. Moscow: MIR Publishing; 1973. 584 p.

Section 2

Biomass Production and Treatment

Chapter 4

Effects of Veld Degradation on Biomass Production in the Arable Lands of South Africa

Nkosikhona Madolo and Francis B. Lewu

Abstract

This paper reviews the impacts of veld degradation on species diversity, veld ecological condition. The major focus of this review is to assess the major critical factors that contributeto veld degradation. It is imperative to revitalize information on the effects of veld degradation in the South African pastoral farming systems. Current studies have indicated the limited research gaps that identify the adverse effects of veld degradation on species composition and biomass production. Grazing behavior in different grazing patterns has not been clear. Finally, this review will assist farmers, policymakers, and pastoralists to broaden their knowledge on policy development, and appropriate the veld management practices, coping measures of veld degradation, particularly those from resource-poor communities. Whereby, livestock production is the focus for food security and poverty alleviation. However, the use of legumes intercropped with temperate grass species can improve animal performance and herbage production during critical periods. The review further evaluates the veld management practices and their ability in providing adequate foliar cover with the use of the edible perennial grass plant that ensures long-term sustainable production with maximum economic returns during critical grazing seasons.

Keywords: arable, land, degradation, biomass, species composition

1. Introduction

Land degradation is one of the most serious global environmental issues of our time [1]. Land degradation is referred to as a major pillar that threatens most environmental issues that trigger poor land productivity, vegetation decline in most global arable lands. According to Wessels et al. [1], land degradation is defined as the persistent reduction of land's biophysical and economic production potential or can be regarded as the long-term loss of land ecosystem functions and services. Generally, land degradation is reported as the most critical factor that triggers most global environmental issues, such as climate change [2]. Land degradation has also been reported in South Africa as one of the very common environmental problems that affect biomass production across pastures and rangelands, which often lead to soil erosion and nutrient depletion [3]. In some instances, veld degradation has been reported to have a tremendous impact on nitrogen and phosphorus inputs that can potentially have adverse effects on water resources in many parts of the world. Rangeland degradation has also been regarded as a major threat to sustainable livestock production in South Africa [4]. Approximately, 69% of agricultural land in South Africa has been reported to use extensive grazing systems, of which it is unsuitable to produce quality livestock commodities for commercial purposes [5]. However, based on the current studies, the land degradation issue has become a topical subject in many parts of the world, due to the lack of relevant information on processes that lead to veld degradation as well as ineffective programs for sustainable biomass production of livestock [3]. Concurrently, communal grazing in the areas that are commonly used in South Africa has declined in the 1990s, due to expanding human settlements, land reform dynamics, climatic changes, agricultural activities (such as crops, forestry, conservation, and mining). It is also vital in assessing the threat that veld degradation poses to people on the urban-wildland interface. Recently, it has been reported that South Africa is a drought-prone country, which is attributed to rainfall distribution that is erratic and unpredictable. According to Oluwole et al. [3], argues that very clear and detailed information on factors causing veld degradation is still limited. On the other hand, Mapiye et al. [4] reported that the low quality and quantity of feed produced during the dry season can have a negative impact on the off-takes rates; therefore, nutritional improvements are crucial in order to understand the nutritional status of the rangeland. For example, protein, energy, and minerals are the most critical nutrients for animal productivity in the semi-arid-communal production systems [4]. Generally, "veld condition" is defined as the ecological status of the veld, in terms of its botanical composition and cover, as well as its fodder value, productivity, and palatability.

2. Types of veld degradation

There are six major forms of soil and veld degradation, which were identified in South Africa. These include the loss of cover, species composition, bush encroachment, alien plant invasions and deforestation, and general category of the other [5]. However, the loss of vegetative cover and species composition are the most prominent forms of degradation, although it remains difficult to separate changes in veld condition due to environmental factors (such as in mean annual precipitation) from those due to mismanagement *per se*. It is argued that the change does not always equate with veld degradation, hence, the changes in species composition can occur as a consequence of natural variably, for example, the precipitation inputs [5].

However, the environmental factors and land management are clearly subjected to significantly elevated levels of soil erosion expressed, such as sheet, rill, and gully erosion.

3. Causes of veld degradation

According to Oluwole et al. [3], it is reported that the major factor that triggers land degradation in rangelands is excessive utilization often termed overgrazing. However, Mandal et al. [6] argues soil and water erosion are the most important natural resources which are major causes of land degradation. The poor farming practices as well the trend toward agricultural intensification have been considered to be a major cause of soil erosion. The prolonged soil erosion causes irreversible soil loss over time (temporal), thus, reducing the following rangeland parameter can be negatively affected (biomass production) and hydrological functions (e.g., filtering, infiltration, and water holding capacity) of soil [7]. Veld condition is determined by the following factors e.g., species composition; the vigor of palatable grass species; basal cover; soil surface condition [8]. In South Africa, bush encroachment is a common phenomenon which is problematic because it reduces the forage quality in arable lands.

The problem of *Acarcia.karroo*, bush encroachment is most prevalent in the arable areas. Therefore, the understanding of constraints by a communal farmer is critical because the high stocking rates are often practiced by communal farmers can adversely affect growth performance and reproductive efficiency, and ultimately affect cattle market value. Thus, Communal ownership of rangeland resources also complicates the introduction and of improved rangeland management. *A.karro* is commonly dominant in most arable in the false thorn veld region of the Eastern Cape in South Africa. Where in most cases is regarded as the invader. The high stocking rates observed in most communal areas have the consequence of degrading the rangelands and reducing the feed resource base for cattle [4].

This, in turn, adversely affects growth and reproductive performance, and ultimately cattle market value. Communal ownership of rangeland resources also complicates the introduction and adoption of improved rangeland management practices in the communal areas. Information on farmers' challenges and perceptions on rangeland management, which is useful in developing sustainable communal rangeland and cattle health management practices, is still poorly understood [9].

4. Spatial heterogeneity

Spatial heterogeneity of resources, and particularly the seasonal separation of resource use, leads to distinction between equilibrium (static events) and non-equilibrium(stochastic events) [10]. Similar results obtained by Sainge et al. [11] reported that the changes in species composition, vegetation structure, and diversity across environmental and geographic gradients vegetation structure are influenced strongly by elevation [12]. Factors controlling the spatial distribution of grazing pressure may be less familiar to some ecologists [13]. Changes in spatial heterogeneity caused by grazing imply changes in habitat diversity and influence the diversity of consumers ranging from insects to birds and mammals.

Selective grazing under continuous pattern is a common grazing pattern in most arable lands that have been affected by degradation in South African pastoral farming system. The literature has reported various experiments and interesting results. Some of the findings indicate that strategies and techniques to enhance biomass production must be geared around water conservation, soil management practices, protective irrigation, and maximizing the use of fertilizers, indigenous crop varieties [14].

Equilibrium areas are referred to as those areas in which animals are in some sort of balance with their resources because of their dependence on them during the dry season. Climatic variation will cause a balance to fluctuate annually. None equilibrium areas support animals in the season of plant regrowth but the size of the animal population is not determined by these resources [15]. It is on these non-equilibrium areas that variable and periodically high defoliation intensity may be imposed because of climatic variation, causing fluctuations in the ratio of animal population size to resource abundance.

Vegetation use during the dry season range is unlikely to suffer such impacts because there is a likelihood of such vegetation being insensitive to defoliation during dry season. Vegetation cover plays important role in preventing soil cover from land degradation [3].

Together with spatial localization of herbivore impacts, due to seasonal grazing behavior and plant species, and patch-level selection, this is likely to make these environments more, and not less, prone to ecological changes [5]. Ecologists and policy-makers should seek to identify the characteristics of grazing systems that predispose such systems to veld degradation, while others appear to be resistant [16].

5. Effects of animal grazing patterns on arable lands

FAO [17], indicated that the utilization-animal relationship may be described by developing the model of animal responses and production per hectare, where it can be noticed that the production per hectare rapidly declines at optimum stocking rate. However, under-grazed areas with few animals can produce a greater total production than overgrazing with more animals. Consequently, the retrogression which is referred to as the replacement of community plants of high ecological order with a community of low ecological order can result [18]. In turn, the cattle grazing pattern often changes during the dry season, which results in high mortality rates and high cull rates in smallholder farmers. In South Africa, rangelands are divided into two veld types, which are Sweetveld type and Sourveld types. Sweetveld types are generally characterized by palatable grass species and low rainfall distribution, whereas Sourveld type is characterized by unpalatable grass species with low rainfall distribution.

Invaders are also commonly found in degraded areas. Invaders are defined as the species that were absent or present in a small amount in the original vegetation, which invade the following disturbance of continued grazing overgrazing.

Invader is less productive than increasers and is of little value as regards soil and water conservation. In some instances, animals often refrain from drinking water, giving nothing in return, and livestock refuses to graze some species. Eventually, the animals are forced to graze even unpalatable species or die due to starvation, which more productive animals and leaves those unproductive and demanding animals which manage to survive, resulting in reduced economic returns.

Hoffman et al. [19], reported that keeping animals too long in a paddock results in reduced grass vigor. Not allowing a grassland sufficient time to restore the carbohydrates reserves. Increased grazing capacity results in decreased grassland productivity, decreased biodiversity, and ultimately lead to soil erosion and loss of nutrients [2].

6. Forage legumes effects on veld degraded areas

Most of the forage is available over much of the year to dairy cattle in the tropics is its low quality compared to temperate areas. It can be overemphasized that higher production can be obtained for certain grass species, for example, *Paspalumdilatatum* incorporated with white clover (*Trifoliumrepens*) [20].

However, once pastures are established, without doubt, the most critical aspect of dairy production is maintaining pastures at a level to provide sufficient quality to enable genetically high producing dairy animals to reach their genetic potential.

7. In-situ (in site) economic impact on soil loss

Different cropping, tillage, management systems often change the structurally related soil's physical and biological properties. Compaction caused by farm implements and grazing animals increases soil bulk density and reduces infiltration rates. Furthermore, the foliar cover [18] of live plants or crop residues can reduce water runoff by reducing the impact of rainfall on bare patches, reducing the detrimental impact of rainfall, crusting, and ultimately reducing soil water evaporation [21].

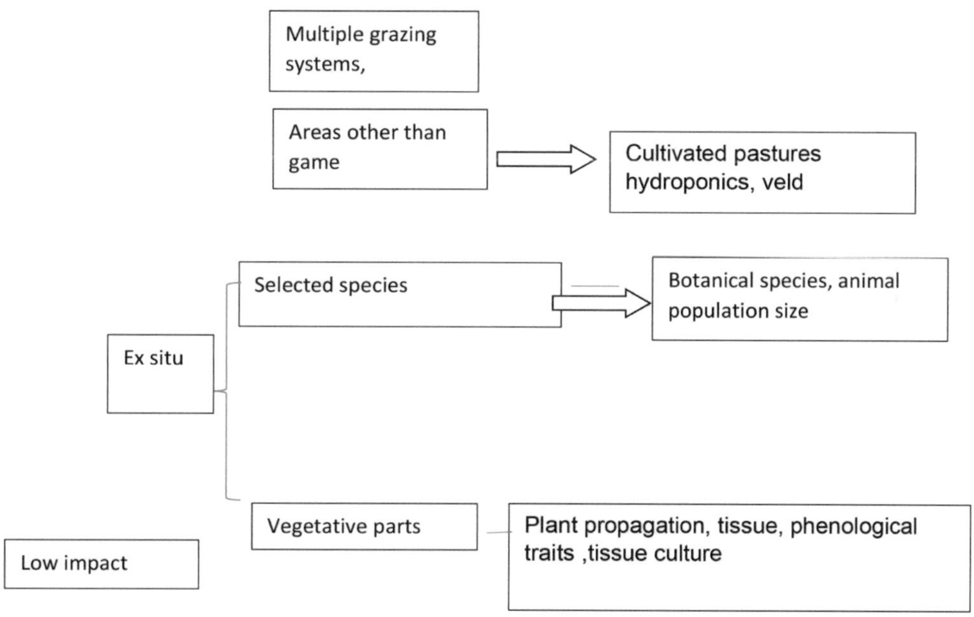

8. Ex-situ (offsite) economic impact on soil

The approaches of soil conversation must be practiced with a clear understanding of the impacts of grazing forage production. The significance of the socio-economic impact of ex-situ practices on the environment should consider higher than that of in situ conservation. It is imperative that the complexities associated with biodiversity, rapid loss of biodiversity, and their realizationis increased to implement cost-effective programs, in turn, developing realistic and viable strategies and setting priorities for effective conservation and management of genetic resources will always be necessary, particularly a profound indigenous knowledge of potential benefits of indigenous forage legumes still warrant further investigation.

9. Conclusion and recommendations

It is imperative that assessment of veld condition scoring is aligned in the context of biodiversity with different approaches. Relevance of information on extension, advisory services of biomass production of veld degraded area for determining grazing capacity, stocking rates & monitoring changes in herbaceous species composition must be maintained in the optimization of livestock production. The knowledge and research still need further investigation on introduction of local adaptable, drought-tolerant, resistant forage crops that could assist farmers to diversity on feed availability and cheaply supplementation of protein in cases of nutritional deficiency in mitigating effects of veld degradation. It is recommended that veld management for decision making should be aimed at the development vegetation, adaption, and mitigation measure should then a priority in veld rehabilitation programs in areas that are prone to veld degradation. It is necessary to curb human population growth, which is the major driving force for environmental and socioeconomic problems. There is a need to take urgent actions and interventions to protect biodiversity from threats including climate change; To ensure the maintenance of biodiversity in arable lands of South Africa.

Author details

Nkosikhona Madolo* and Francis B. Lewu
Faculty of Applied Sciences, Department of Agriculture, Cape Peninsula University, Cape Town, South Africa

*Address all correspondence to: madolon@cput.ac.za

References

[1] Wessels KJ, Prince SD, Malherbe J, Small J, Frost PE, Van Zyl D. Can human-induced land degradation be distinguished from the effects of rainfall variability? A case study in South Africa. Journal of Arid Environments. 2007;**68**(2):271-297. DOI: 10.1016/j.jaridenv.2006.05.015

[2] Nkonya E, Von Braun J, Mirzabaev A. Concepts and Methods of Global Assessment of the Economics of Land Degradation and Improvement. 2016. pp. 15-32. DOI: 10.1007/978-3-319-19168-3

[3] Oluwole FA, Sikhalazo D. Land degradation evaluation in a game reserve in Eastern Cape of South Africa: Soil properties and vegetation cover. Scientific Research and Essays. 2008;**3**(3):111-119

[4] Mapiye C, Chimonyo M, Dzama K, Marufu MC. Asian-Australasian Journal of Animal Sciences. 2010;**23**(2):213-225

[5] Meadows ME, Hoffman MT. The nature, extent and causes of land degradation in South Africa: Legacy of the past, lessons for the future? Area. 2002;**34**(4):428-437. DOI: 10.1111/1475-4762.00100

[6] Mandal D, Srivastava P, Giri N, Kaushal R, Cerda A, Alam NM. Reversing land degradation through grasses: A systematic meta-analysis in the Indian tropics. 2017:217-233. DOI: 10.5194/se-8-217-2017

[7] Le Roux J. Soil erosion in South Africa—its nature and distribution [Online]. Graan SA; 2014. pp. 1-7. Available from: https://www.grainsa.co.za/soil-erosion-in-south-africa---its-nature-and-distribution

[8] du Toit PCV et al. Estimating grazing-index values for Karoo plants [Online]. 1995. no. 2. p. 15. Available from: http://gadi.agric.za/articles/Agric/tegnies.php

[9] Malherbe J. Water erosion prediction at a national scale for South Africa. 2008;**34**(3):305-314

[10] Moreira EF, Boscolo D, Viana BF. Spatial heterogeneity regulates plant-pollinator networks across multiple landscape scales. 2015:1-19. DOI: 10.1371/journal.pone.0123628

[11] Sainge MN, Lyonga NM, Mbatchou GPT, Kenfack D, Nchu F, Peterson AT. Vegetation, floristic composition and structure of a tropical montane forest in Cameroon. Bothalia. 2019;**49**(1):1-12. DOI: 10.4102/abc.v49i1.2270

[12] Zhou Z, Sun OJ, Luo Z, Jin H, Chen Q, Han X. Variation in small-scale spatial heterogeneity of soil properties and vegetation with different land use in semiarid grassland ecosystem. Plant and Soil. 2008;**310**(1-2):103-112. DOI: 10.1007/s11104-008-9633-1

[13] Adler P, Raff D, Lauenroth W. The effect of grazing on the spatial heterogeneity of vegetation. Oecologia. 2001;**128**(4):465-479. DOI: 10.1007/s004420100737

[14] Rockstrom J. Biomass production in dry tropical zones: How to increase water productivity. In: L. Water Integr. River Basin Manag. Land & Water Bulletin No. 1. 1995. pp. 31-49

[15] Mucina L, Rutherford MC. The Vegetation of South Africa, Lesotho and Swaziland. 2006

[16] Lal R. Climate Change and Agriculture. 2016

[17] FAO. Drought impact mitigation and prevention in the Limpopo River Basin: A situation analysis. In: L. Water Discuss. Pap. 4. Vol. 4. 2004

[18] Maponya P, Mpandeli S. © Kamla-Raj 2013 perception of farmers on climate change and adaptation in Limpopo Province of South Africa. 2013

[19] Hoffman T, Todd S. Chapter 7: Vegetation degradation. In: L. Degrad. South Africa. 1997. pp. 108-160

[20] Baloyi JJ, Ngongoni NT, Hamudikuwanda H. The effect feeding forage legumes as nitrogen supplement on growth performance of sheep. Tropical Animal Health and Production. 2008;**40**(6):457-462. DOI: 10.1007/s11250-007-9120-3

[21] Truter WF et al. Southern African pasture and forage science entering the 21st century: Past to present. African Journal of Range & Forage Science. 2015;**32**(2):73-89. DOI: 10.2989/10220119.2015.1054429

Chapter 5

Steam Explosion Pretreatment: Biomass Waste Utilization for Methane Production

Sholahuddin Sholahuddin, Yoshitoshi Nakamura and Chikako Asada

Abstract

Lignocellulosic biomass as a second-generation biofuel resource such as waste from agricultural, forester industry, and unutilized wood and non-wood biomass was widely reported to use it as feedstock for methane production. As the carbon-neutral resources, biomass waste conversion for biofuel is in line with the SDGs 7 and 15 goal that can meet the needs and qualify to the standard of sustainable consumption and production pattern, and increasing the renewable energy. The wood and non-wood unutilized biomass and biomass waste are commonly faced with the recalcitrant character of the lignocellulose complex (LCC) which impacted the digestion process of the methane fermentation. Steam explosion pretreatment was enhanced the methane production by breaking the LCC into cellulose, hemicellulose, and lignin-derived product generated from the pretreatment process. Those steam-exploded products were reported effective in the conversion process into methane. The combination of steam explosion pretreatment which is an environmentally friendly pretreatment, and the use of carbon-neutral resources will provide the green biofuel which helps decrease the greenhouse gasses from the biomass waste dumping process and convert it into sustainable biofuel i.e. methane. This chapter will describe the steam explosion system development on the utilization of biomass for methane production, and the action of methane production enhancement.

Keywords: biomass conversion, biomass waste, biomass utilization, biofuel, biogas, methane, steam explosion, environmentally friendly, second-generation biofuel

1. Introduction

The carbon neutrality or the net-zero carbon dioxide emission could be fulfilled by the way to used energy and fuel from biomass resources. The plant from the agricultural and forestry sector could help the achievement of balancing the carbon dioxide from the utilization of biomass waste produced from its process. Other than that, the utilization of biomass waste could counter the production of greenhouses gas (GHG) produced from the biomass waste dumping process. The conversion from the biomass waste into methane through anaerobic digestion could maintain the GHG release from biomass waste. The use of biomass waste as carbon neutral resources can be through biomass conversion by steam explosion pretreatment, anaerobic digestion where the biogas could use for LNG substitution for household use, for power generation fuel which produces the electricity that could fulfill the self-sufficient off-grid and for the on-grid electricity system. The biogas also could convert into hydrogen for transportation fuel and other utilization. The compressed biogas with methane-rich (CH_4) and hydrogen (H_2) was potentially utilized as secondary energy, which is widely introduced in several sectors such as public transportation, household application, and other application (**Figure 1**).

The steam explosion pretreatment was commonly used for biomass treatment to break the recalcitrant of lignin carbohydrate complex (LCC) or lignin-carbohydrate polymer which is the main structure of biomass in addition to other content such as resin that makes biomass known as a substrate that is difficult to convert into biofuel through the digestion process or as a source of lignin and cellulose base of biomaterials. The steam explosion also generated the cellulose and low molecular lignin that could be utilized as a biomaterial, where the low molecular lignin could be separated by an extraction process using various types of solvents such as water, ethanol, and acetone and used as polymer-based substitute products such as epoxy resin and thermosetting resin by converting low molecular lignin into lignin-epoxy resin or using it directly as a curing agent [1–6]. The steam-exploded lignocellulosic biomass also could be utilized as an antioxidant resource which is rich in polyphenol content [7–11], and its cellulose content also could utilize as cellulose-nanofiber (CNF) resource that is widely used for sustainable biomaterials [12–14].

As the psychochemical pretreatment, the steam explosion could break the LCC and also change the chemical content as a derivative product of the content of cellulose, hemicellulose, lignin, and other specific contents that differ from one biomass to another. The steam explosion pretreatment which is based on the hydrothermal pretreatment method with high pressure and short retention time then suddenly depressurized to make the explosion effect from the pressure differences between the pressure of the steaming chamber and the normal pressure of the explosion chamber [15]. The explosion effect disrupts the structure of LCC fibrils which break

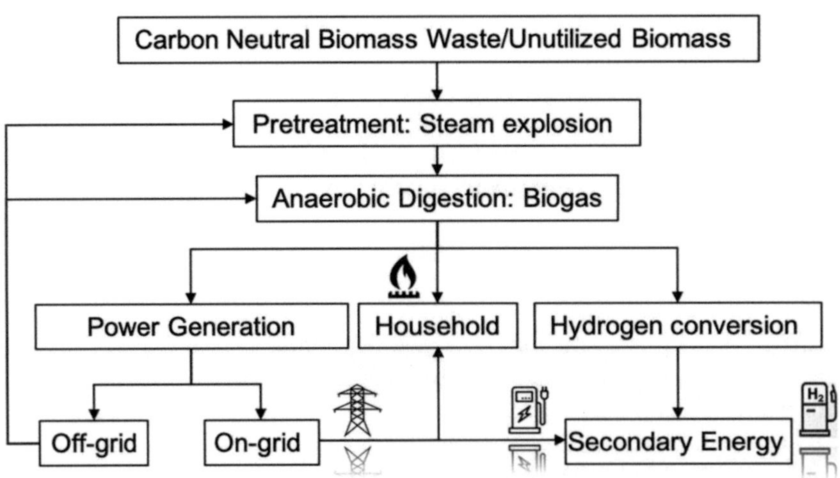

Figure 1.
Carbon neutral biomass waste and unutilized biomass anaerobic digestion scheme via steam explosion pretreatment.

its polymer chain and become small particle size that could facilitate the digestion process easily [16]. Other than that, the chemical content from the LCC could change become derived product such as cellulose that could continuedly to be degraded into cellobiose-glucose-HMF(5-(hydroxymethyl)furfural)-levulinic acid; hemicellulose that could degrade into the pentoses (xylose, arabinose) and could continuedly be degraded into furfural and formic acid, the hexoses (mannose, glucose, galactose) that could continue to degrade into HMF and continue into formic acid or levulinic acid, and hemicellulose also could produce acetyl and continue to degrade into acetic acid; the lignin content could degrade into the lignin precursors such as sinapyl alcohol, p-coumaryl alcohol, and coniferyl alcohol, those compound could continuedly degrade into phenolic compounds such as catechol, guaiacol, vanillin, syringaldehyde, 4-hydroxybenzaldehyde, 4-hydroxybenzoic acid, and vanillic acid. The compounds degradation from steam explosion pretreatment was influenced by the temperature, pressure, and steaming time. That condition was influenced by the degree of severity factor (R_0 or S_0 SF) which caused from the temperature condition and residence time [17]. The other factor i.e., pH condition was also affected the physiochemical products such as the acid addition as a catalysator, which knownly as combined severity factor (CSF) [18]. Since the severity factor could not faithfully describe the steam explosion disregard the effect of the explosion condition, Yu et al., [19] added a comprehensive factor which quantified the explosion severity that could better describing the steam explosion severity condition by explosion power density (EPD). The severity factor, combined severity factor, and explosion power density could be calculated with the equations:

$$R_0 = t \; x \; e^{[(T_r - 100)/14.75]} \tag{1}$$

Where T_r represent the temperature reaction (°C), and t represent the resident time (minutes) [20].

$$S_0 = \log \int_0^t \exp\left(\frac{T[°C] - 100°C}{14.75}\right) dt \tag{2}$$

The time integral of S_0 was described the process of non-isothermal heating character [20, 21].

$$CSF = \log(R_0) - pH \tag{3}$$

Where the *Log* (R_0) as a severity factor value and pH represent the pH level after the acid was added [18].

$$P_e = \frac{\Delta H_s + \Delta H_1 + \Delta H_m}{(t \; x \; V)} \tag{4}$$

Where the ΔH represent as the enthalpy drop from the steam (s), liquid water (1), and biomass (m), t represent the duration of the explosion, and V represent the volume of reactor [19].

The derived product from cellulose, hemicellulose, and lignin could affect the fermentation process on the anaerobic digestion as the fermentation inhibitors, nevertheless, it can be controlled by adjusting the inhibitor threshold. On the other hand, the inhibitor from physicochemical pretreatment product could be handled by detoxification process through biological, physical, or chemical. The biological detoxification via hired the microorganism that could produce enzymes that change the chemical structures of the fermentation inhibitor compounds which present in the biomass hydroxylate [22–24]. The physical detoxification could remove the inhibitor compounds without changing the chemical structure such as using activated charcoal or activated carbon for neutralizing the hydrolysate, and also by an extraction process using trialkyl amine as an alkali detoxication, n-octanol, and kerosene [25–27]. The chemical detoxification was treated by adding the modified pH such as water extraction, sodium hydroxide, and reductive substance [16, 23, 28, 29]. The potential compounds that could be converted into methane from steam-exploded biomass fraction, is not only cellulose, hemicellulose, and monosaccharides compound, the steam-exploded aromatic lignin fraction and its derived product such as syringaldehyde and vanillin also could be converted into methane by the anaerobic digestion process [15, 30–36].

The use of methane as secondary energy has been widely used, such as a substitute for liquified natural gas (LNG) for household networks and as a fuel for transportation. In addition, methane can also be converted into other secondary energy such as hydrogen by separating its carbon and is included in a cheap hydrogen source similar to LNG [37], compared to other hydrogen sources. Other than that, the methane produced from biomass waste and unutilized biomass has several advantages such as renewable, sustainable, and carbon-neutral compared with LNG which included depleted natural resources that cannot be renewable. The common hydrogen conversion system from the methane can be done in several ways such as steam reforming methane (SRM), dry-reforming methane (DRM), catalytic decomposition methane (CDM), and partial-oxidation methane (POM), those systems were widely introduced in laboratory-scale or existing technology industrial used.

In this chapter, we will try to delineate state the art of methane conversion and its derived products from biomass waste and fast-growing unutilized biomass by steam explosion pretreatment. The combination of carbon-neutral resources and environmentally friendly pretreatment could give the alternative perception from only combustion utilization to the system that vaporization the biomass waste and unutilized biomass into more potentially produces more product from one system.

2. Potential biomass waste and unutilized wood and non-wood biomass

The agriculture and forestry industries were producing sustainable and renewable biomass waste which included carbon-neutral resources that could be converted into methane by an anaerobic digestion process. The utilization of biomass waste from this sector also could help to reduce land-use change from the biomass that is mainly used only for the biofuel feedstock. The conversion of the biomass waste into methane is free from quality problems of biomass as combustion fuel that need specific calorimetry and density that could not be fulfilled by all the biomass waste. **Table 1** showed the agricultural commodity that produces biomass waste with minimum utilization such as palm oil, barley, corn, rice, sorghum, wheat, and sugarcane. Other than that, the forestry industry such as pulp and paper mills, and unutilized fast-growing biomass such as reed and grassland are potentially utilized for methane conversion.

Commodity	World production (1000 MT)	Production share top 10 country	Potential biomass waste
Palm oil	76.538	Indonesia 58%, Malaysia 26%, Thailand 4%, Colombia 2%, Nigeria 2%, Guatemala 1%, Honduras 1%, Papua New Guinea 1%, Equator 1%, Brazil 1%	Empty Fruit Bunches, Kernel Fibbers, Kernel Shell, Midrib, Trunk
Barley	145–511	EU 36%, Russia 12%, Australia 9%, Ukraine 7%, UK, Canada 5%, Argentina 3%, Turkey 3%, Morocco 2%, Iran 2%	Barley straw, Brewer Spent Grain
Corn	1.208.734	US 32%, China 23%, Brazil 10%, EU 6%, Argentina 5%, Ukraine 3%, India 3%, Mexico 2%, South Africa 1%, Russia 1%	Stem, Leave, Cobs
Rice	510.776	China 29%, India 24%, Bangladesh 7%, Indonesia 7%, Vietnam 5%, Thailand 4%, Burma 2%, Philippines 2%, Pakistan 2%, Brazil 2%	Rice Husk, Rice Straw
Sorghum	66.301	US 18%, Nigeria 10%, Ethiopia 8%, Sudan 8%, Mexico 7%, India 7%, Argentina 6%, China 5%, Brazil 4% Burkina Faso 3%	Stem, Leave, Sorghum Grain Waste
Wheat	777.890	EU 18%, China 18%, India 14%, Russia 10%, US 4%, Ukraine 4%, Pakistan 3%, Canada 3%, Argentina 3%	Straw
Sugarcane	181.082	Brazil 19%, India 18%, EU 9%, China 6%, Thailand 5%, US 5%, Pakistan 4%, Russia 4%, Mexico 4%, Australia 2%,	Sugarcane Bagasse

Table 1.
World production agricultural potential commodity with minimum biomass waste utilization [38].

3. Steam explosion pretreatment

The steam explosion pretreatment for lignocellulosic biomass that was used for methane conversion was widely reported in several studies with various experiment conditions and biomass feedstock. The steam explosion pretreatment was reported as stand-alone pretreatment for lignocellulosic biomass for methane production feedstock. Kobayashi et al., [39] used the abundant and fast-growing such as bamboo as a feedstock for methane production by an anaerobic fermentation process which operated in mesophilic condition (37°C), where the steam explosion was set in 3.53 MPa (243°C) for 0,1, 3, 5, 10, and 20 minutes of steaming time. The 5 minutes steaming time was produced the higher methane with 215 ml/g, that amount was 80% from the methane amount prediction that calculated from cellulose and hemicellulose amount from 1 gram of steam-exploded bamboo. Wu et al. [40] was used palm oil mill waste such as empty fruit bunches and palm oil fronds to convert it by steam explosion treatment at 1.5 MPa for 1 minute of steaming time. They concluded that steam explosion pretreatment enhanced the biogas production, and improved the energy values (gross energy, digestible energy, metabolic energy, net energy for maintenance, and net energy for lactation) from palm oil frond and empty fruit bunches. Lizasoain et al. [41] were used reed biomass for methane conversion using various steam explosion conditions from 160 to 220°C with 5, 10, 15, and 20 minutes of steaming time resulted in the severity factor from 2.47 to 4.83. That study has resulted in the 89% enhancement compared to untreated feedstock from steam explosion condition at 200°C for 15 minutes. Theuretzbacher et al. [42] reported utilizing wheat straw as a methane production feedstock by steam explosion pretreatment at 140, 160, and 178°C with 30, 60, and 120 minutes of steaming time which resulted in various severity factors from 2.7 to 4.4 SF Log (R_0). The highest methane production was from 140°C for 60 minutes steaming time at 3.0 SF Log (R_0) which produced 286 l_n kgVS-1. Steinbach et al. [43] were used steam explosion for rice straw to produce biogas by various severity factor 3.05 to 5.29 (S_0) from 162 to 240°C for 12 to 30 minutes steaming time. They concluded the moderate severity increases the methane production whereas severe condition dramatically drops the methane production caused by an inhibitor that formed in high severity condition. Those were similar conditions to the report from Lizasoain et al. [41]. Vivekanand et al. [44] was used the rape straw steam-exploded with emphasizing in chemical composition changes under various severity (3.5 to 5) that could impact the methane production under mesophilic conditions for 81 days. The steam-exploded rape straw was treated under 190 to 230°C with 5, 10, and 15 minutes. They concluded that the formation of the inhibitor compounds does not impact methane production. The other report explained the compounds that could be formed from biomass steam-exploded were known as an inhibitor such as HMF and furfural, also the other lignin-derived products in form of phenol and polyphenol as lignin polymers and/or lignin oligomers such as vanillin and syringaldehyde could also convert into methane. They resulted that the HMF could produce methane 450 ml CH_4/gMV, furfural 430 ml CH_4/gMV, syringaldehyde 453 ml CH_4/gMV, vanillin 105 ml CH_4/gMV. This study also reported examining the various lignin polymers such as, organosolv, lignosulfonates, and kraft lignins that could produce 14 to 46 ml CH_4/gMV. They concluded that a higher syringyl/guaiacyl ratio that generated the syringaldehyde and vanillin by partial depolymerization of lignin polymer, and lower molecular weight of lignin polymer could conduct high methane production [36]. The steam explosion pretreatment was reported to generate the low molecular lignin in line with the increased degree of the SF values [1, 5, 45–47].

The comparation between steam-explosion pretreatment and other pretreatment was reported in several studies. Take et al. [48] reported examined the Japanese cedar chip *Cryptomeria japonica* as methane production feedstock by comparation psychochemical pretreatment using steam explosion at various pressure conditions at 3.53 MPa (243°C) and 4.51 MPa (258°C) for 5 minutes steaming, steaming pretreatment at 170°C for 30 minutes, and biological pretreatment using *Ischnoderma resinosum, Fomitella fraxinea, Mycoleptodonoides aitchisonii, Trichaptum abietinum, Cyathus stercoreus*, and *Trametes hirsute*. The result from the steam explosion pretreatment could produce the highest methane with 180 ml/g with less energy use, compare with steam treatment and biological pretreatment from *Cyathus stercoreus* which only produces methane in 45 and 43 ml/g, respectively. The combination pretreatment between the steam explosion and other treatments for methane production feedstock was reported in several studies. Sholahuddin et al. [16] reported to utilize agricultural biomass waste i.e., rice husk which was treated using steam explosion at 2.53 MPa (224°C) for 5 and 7 minutes steaming time followed by water extraction for methane production, and without water extraction. The water extraction as a dilution treatment to lower the pH condition that increased due to acid formation of psychochemical effect and reduce the concentration of fermentation inhibitor produced from the physicochemical pretreatment into under the threshold. The anaerobic digestion was operated in mesophilic condition (37°C) by using activated cow dung for the inoculum which is naturally rich in cellulolytic microflora resulted produced 199 ml/g methane from 41% cellulose content, that amount was reached 96.1% of methane conversion from the prediction, compared to without water extraction which only 28 ml/g of methane from the same steam explosion condition i.e., 7 minutes of steaming time. Theuretzbacher et al. [49] reported to use a wheat straw for methane production by combination pretreatment using biological using *Scheffersomyces stipitis* and thermo-mechanical using steam explosion at 180, 200, and 220°C, those combinations was examined to reduce the thermal energy input where the biological condition could facilitate the steam explosion to break the LCC in low-temperature condition. The highest methane production from the combination of biological pretreatment and steam explosion 250 and 252 $l_n$kg VS-1 with no significance from 180 and 200°C, respectively. Bauer et al. [50] used late-harvested hay that pretreated using steam explosion at 160 to 220°C for 5, 10, and 15 minutes steaming time followed by enzymatic hydrolysis using b ß-glucosidases and hemicellulases that resulted in high yield glucose from 220°C for 15 minutes, xylose 175°C for 10 minutes. Those combinations resulted in 15.9% methane enhancement compared to the untreated. The anaerobic digestion. The anaerobic digestion. Matsakas et al. [51] reported to used hybrid pretreatment which combines the steam explosion and organosolv where the 99,8% ethanol with 1:2 ratio between biomass chips: ethanol, and heated in 200°C (1.519 MPa) with 15, 30, and 60 minutes of steaming time. The organosolv-steam-exploded products were filtrated using vacuum filtration, and the solid residue was washed using ethanol and dried and continued to the anaerobic digestion process. Weber et al. [52] used steam explosion with temperature setting 142, 164, and 179°C (0,38, 0,68, and 0,98 MPa), after that the solid reside of steam-exploded was separated by centrifuge. The methane production was prepared by a 2:1 ratio between inoculum and substrate. Li et al. [53] used corn stover by sequent pretreatment using potassium hydroxide (KOH) 0.5 and 1.5% and steam explosion under 1.2 MPa for 10 minutes steaming time. Those combinations were applied to improve the digestion ability of biomass which resulted in 80% improvement from untreated corn stover with 258 ml/gvs from 1.5% KOH and 1.2 MPa for 10 minutes steaming time, where the only steam exploded and KOH treatment in the same condition was only produced 143.8 and 208.6 ml/g_{VS}, respectively.

4. Methane production enhancement

The steam explosion pretreatment that disintegrated the LCC impacted the higher accessibility of the digestion process to convert the cellulose, hemicellulose, and lignin and its derived products into biogas [15]. Those pretreatments were simplified the hydrolysis process, however, to gain the economical factor is necessary to improve the production rate, solid retention time, and hydraulic retention time. The conversion of steam-exploded lignocellulosic biomass into methane was counted heavily on cellulose and hemicellulose as the main conversion source, even though the conversion of lignin-derived products from psychochemical pretreatment also contribute to the amount of methane production. **Figure 2** was described the methane production from lignocellulosic biomass was produced through the simultaneous system from saccharolytic and hydrolytic processes to convert the cellulose and hemicellulose into oligomers and monomers, hydrolytic and dissipotrophic organism as primary anaerobe process, the syntrophic process, acetogenic process, and methanogenic process [54, 55]. The saccharolytic and hydrolytic process initiates the biopolymers

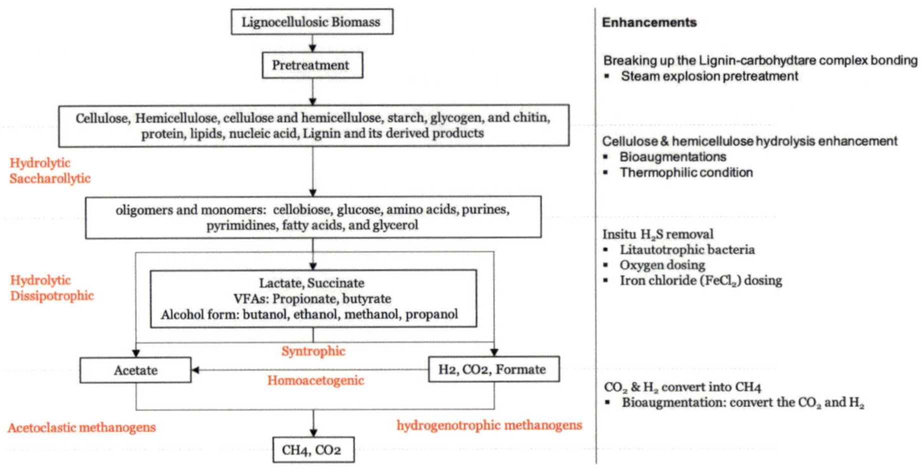

Figure 2.
Potential enhancement and low emission of lignocellulosic biomass conversion into methane.

degradation of polysaccharides such as cellulose and hemicellulose, starch, glycogen, and chitin, also the other common content such as protein, lipids, and nucleic acid. The saccharolytic and hydrolytic degraded those content into oligomers and monomers such as cellobiose, glucose, amino acids, purines, pyrimidines, fatty acids, and glycerol [56]. The cellulose and hemicellulose are commonly converted by cellulolytic microflora from the phylum of Firmicutes commonly *Ruminococcaceae* and *Clostridiaceae* families 17 such as from genus *Clostridium, Ruminococcus, Cellobacterium, Butyrivibrio, Fibrobacter,* and *Acetivibrio* [57–59]. The starch could be degraded by the genus *Thermoanaerobacterium*, *Succinimonas, Ruminobacter, Bacteroides, Prevotella, Bacteroides, Clostridium,* and *Butyrivibrio*. The protein and amino acid are commonly degraded by genus *Syntrophomanas, Bacteroides, Clostridium, Peptostreptococcus Acidaminococcus, Selenomonas, and Fusobacterium.* The xylan and pectin are commonly degraded by genus *Ruminococcus, Lachnospira Bacteroides, Butyrivibrio, Prevotella*, and *Clostridium*. The species from those genera also could degrade the other polymer such as lignin and its derived products especially the species from *Lysinibacillus* and *Paenibacillus.* The hydrolytic and dissipotrops as primary anaerobes process digest the cellobiose, glucose, amino acids, purines, pyrimidines, fatty acids, and glycerol and produce organic acid such as butyrate, succinate, lactate, pyruvate acetate, propionate, and lactate; aromatic compounds; the alcohol form such as ethanol, propanol, butanol, and methanol; carbon dioxide; hydrogen; and also produced volatile fatty acids (VFAs) [59] which dominate the degradation of cellulose. The alcohol form, VFAs, lactate, and succinate continued to degrade into single carbon compounds and hydrogen and acetate through the syntrophic process. The single carbon also could into acetate via homoacetogens process and also could directly form the methane through the hydrogenotrophic methanogens. The methane from acetate formed through the acetoclastic methanogens, however, those process was inactivated in low concentration of acetate and in high-temperature condition, other than that, acetoclastic methanogens could be blocked by the presence of high ammonia and VFAs concentration. That simultaneous system condition directly influences the SRT and HRT that affected the time consumed and energy that affected the production cost.

4.1 Enhancement: Saccharolytic and hydrolytic pathway

The methane production enhancement could be done by enhancing the simultaneous system from each process such as saccharolytic and hydrolytic, hydrolytic and dissipotrophic, syntrophic, acetogenic, and methanogenic processes. The enhancement process commonly used Biological augmentation by the addition of archaea or bacterial cultures that get high-rate of degradation time and thermophilic condition which could speed up the production rate. The bioaugmentation of the saccharolytic hydrolytic process that converts the cellulose becomes oligomers and monomers was reported in several studies. The bioaugmentation using cellulolytic bacterium from genus *Caldicellulosiruptor* that operate in thermophilic condition i.e., *Caldicellulosiruptor bescii* which focuses on the improvement of hydrolysis process that degraded the carbohydrate content from steam-exploded biomass such as cellulose, hemicellulose, and other lignocellulosic content, and fermented the C5 and C6 sugar on the simultaneous process. The *C. bescii* has a special characteristic that is quite different from other cellulolytic bacteria which has the enzymatic system in a multi-modular pathway, which secreted the individual cellulases and could bind and catalyze multiplied, wherein, this condition will support the indigenous primary anaerobes bacteria synergically [60]. Mulat et al. [61] were applied bioaugmentation for steam-exploded lignocellulosic biomass converted into methane which operated in 62°C, the *C. bescii* was added as bioaugmentation where steam-explosion pretreatment itself enhanced 118% the methane production, and the combination of steam-exploded pretreatment and bioaugmentation was enhanced 140% methane production improvement. The other species cellulolytic microflora from the genus Clostridium such as *Clostridium thermocellum* which operated in a thermophilic condition also has the capability to continuedly form ethanol directly from cellulose, and also accelerates the hydrolysis process and could produce higher H_2 that supports the hydrogenotrophic methanogens to produce more methane [62–65]. Other than that, *C. thermocellum* has the special capability to reform non-growth state into sporulation stage and L-phase in stress conditions [66]. The steam explosion and bioaugmentation using *C. thermocellum* were reported to be compared where the steam explosion was enhanced 62% methane production and bioaugmentation was enhanced 12% of methane production [64]. The other report from *C. thermocellum* enhanced the anaerobic digestion of lignocellulosic agricultural residue which resulted in an increase of 39% of methane production [67]. Tsapekos et al. [68] was used *C. thermocellum* and *Melioribacter roseus* as bioaugmentation for lignocellulosic agricultural residue conversion into methane by continuously stirred tank reactor (CSTR) which resulted in 34 and 11% methane production enhancement, respectively. The other species from *Clostridium* such *as Clostridium cellulolyticum* as a bioaugmentation agent for the wheat straw that resulted in 13% of methane production compared to non-bioaugmented [65]. Cetar et al. [69] was reported to trial bioaugmentation agents from various genus such as *Pseudobutyrivibrio* using *Pseudobutyrivibrio xylanivorans, Fibrobacter* using *Fibrobacter succinogenes, Ruminococcus* using *Ruminococcus*, and *flavefaciens* using *Clostridium cellulovorans* to enhance the hydrolysis process of brewery spent grain by comparation using two bioaugmentation agent each treatment that impacted to enhance the biogas production with resulted in 17.8% from *P. xylanivorans* alone, 6.9% from a combination of *P. xylanivorans* and *F. succinogenes,* and 4.9% from a combination of *C. cellulovorans*a and *F. succinogenes*. The other report was described to examine the bioaugmentation that combined with steam explosion using ruminal fungus such as *Pecoramyces sp.* which isolated from goat rumen to enhance the methane production from steam-exploded corn stover [70].

4.2 Enhancement: Hydrogenotrophic methanogens pathway

The other bioaugmentation pathway is to enhance hydrogenotrophic methanogens which are affected by ammonia inhibition, where the syntrophic acetate oxidation coupled with hydrogenotrophic methanogens are influenced by ammonia inhibition [71]. The bioaugmentation via syntrophic oxidation bacteria that operate in mesophilic and thermophilic conditions such as *Clostridium ultunense* [72], *Syntrophaceticus* [73], *Tepidanaerobacter acetatoxydans* [74]; and *Thermacetogenium phaeum* and *Thermotoga lettingae* [75–77], respectively. The syntrophic oxidation bacteria were syntrophic cooperation with hydrogenotrophic methanogens, which could use its ability of acetate digestion into H_2 and CO_2 and surmount the energy barriers [78]. Those systems are based on interspecies hydrogen transfer by reducing the hydrogen partial pressure which purposed H_2 and formate transfer [79]. In this case, formate plays an important role as an electron carrier at the time when the hydrogenotrophic methanogen and oxidizing bacteria have a distance gap through the Wood-Ljungdahl pathway [78, 80]. The bioaugmentation strategy was to present the syntrophic oxidation bacteria and hydrogenotrophic methanogens that could resist high ammonia levels. Tian et al. [72] was used a syntrophic acetate oxidizing bacteria i.e., *C. ultunense* that resists high ammonia levels with about 7 g NH_4^+ -NL − 1 and significantly increased with high activity in line with *Methanoculleus sp* as a hydrogenotrophic methanogen. Fotidis et al. [81] were used a combination to hire a bioaugmentation agent for syntrophic acetate oxidation association with hydrogenotrophic methanogen i.e., *C. ultunense* and *Methanoculleus bourgensis* respectively. That study was operated in mesophilic condition resulted in the increase of growth rate and incubation period of syntrophic acetate oxidation agent with 42 and 33%, respectively. Another bioaugmentation strategy to alleviate the ammonia inhibition under thermophilic conditions using *Methanoculleus thermophilu* resulted in 45 to 52% VFAs decreasing and 11 to 13% methane production improvement. This condition was described as the condition that the addition *M. thermophilu* could handle the ammonia inhibition which was proven by high activity and positive growth *of T. phaeum* is a syntrophic acetate oxidizing bacterium that stimulated by those additions [82]. The other report that examined the *M. bourgensis* as hydrogenotrophic methanogen bioaugmentation alone, added in CSTR with ammonia concentration at 5 g NH_4^+ -NL − 1 which enhanced 31.3% methane production [83].

5. Feasibility study

Steam explosion pretreatment feasibility study was reported in several studies, Shafei et al. [84] was reported the feasibility of the economic factor from biomass waste as feedstock for biogas by simulating the paper tube residual and wheat straw using steam explosion pretreatment. The result from the simulation was concluded the application of steam explosion pretreatment was increased 13% of the investment cost, however that application was decreased the production cost of methane production by 36% efficiency which brings about 80% total energy efficiency with costing 0.36 and 0.48 Euro/m3 from paper tube residual and wheat straw, respectively. In this simulation, the feedstock is unloaded from the transporter and continued to chopping process to reduce the feedstock size and collected into storage piles. The crushed feedstock continues to pretreatment process through horizontal conveyor belt which continuously processes low-pressure pre-steamer, removing non-condensable gas, high pressure with a horizontal extruder that uses steam as the driving force. The steam exploded feedstock continues to digestion process which simulated using established solid organic reactor which has 3150 m3 in total volume with 2–4 days retention time and about 20 days of residence time for fully digested by the circulated system by 5:1 ration between the residence feedstock and new feedstock. The final process is dewatering the slurry which fully digested from the digester. Kral et al. [85] was described the life cycle assessment (LCA) from a hypothetical local biogas system by adapting and integrating the steam explosion pretreatment to use unused grassland biomass as co-substrate the existing biogas reactor of Austrian alpine municipality. They used a comparation case study from the status quo of heating oil, wood chips, and grid electricity as reference scenarios for municipal energy resources; and hypothetical local biogas that is also used for municipal energy sources with 500-kWel biogas plant using unused grassland with a steam explosion as the pretreatment. The result was described that the LCA from biogas from biomass and status quo energy resources have significant differences with $\rho < 0.05$ from six categories, where the biogas electricity from steam-exploded grassland has a lower impact than the status quo energy with climate change contribution in 0.367 $CO_{2\text{-eq}}$ kWhe-1 from and 0.501 $CO_{2\text{-eq}}$ kWhe-1, respectively.

The steam explosion pretreatment was reported to enhance the full-scale biogas plant production which used a wheat straw as co-substrate for pig manure [86]. The result from the study stated that the addition of pretreated wheat straw using liquid hot water-steam explosion produced 24–34% higher methane, this condition was obtained from pretreatment at 165°C and 2.33 MPa for 10 minutes steaming time which break the LCC into low-mass polysaccharides, and at this severity factor (SF) did not generate the HMF and furfural that could inhibit the fermentation process. The steam explosion apparatus that used in this study could daily continuous process 2.300–3800 kg of wheat straw that could use 100-160 m^3 recycled water from the biogas plant with ration 20:1 and 23:1 between wheat straw and recycled water. Maroušek et al. [87] was used combination pretreatment for sunflower stalks in existing large-scale biogas reactor by maceration under 75 to 95°C for 20 to 200 seconds and continue to steam explosion pretreatment under 0.8 to 2.2 MPa for 2 to 20 minutes of steaming time, where the pretreatment was used the sole heat waste from the existing system. The optimum production was 99 m^3 methane VSt^{-1} from feedstock that macerated at 95°C for 100 seconds and continue to steam-exploded at 2 MPa for 17 minutes, where the steam explosion pretreatment higher than 2 MPa was impacted to the decreasing of methane production due to the formation of inhibitors such as furan and HMF. Pérez-Elvira et al. [88] were reported the pilot-scale feasibility study which demonstrated the hydrolysis process using steam explosion, anaerobic digestion with an energy output of cogeneration unit. This study was used an automatic continuous steam explosion of 10 L which connected to a 200 L mesophilic anaerobic digestion reactor and directly connected to the power generation where the engine exhaust gas was utilized to heat the boiler unit for steamed the hydrolysis reactor (steam explosion). The result from this study was described that the combination of steam explosion as thermal hydrolysis and anaerobic digestion which resulted considered for full-scale application. The residence time was only 40% compared to the conventional digestion and proved that this system was fully self-sufficient energy without additional energy input for all the processes. Those systems were generated 1 MW green electricity which is a 246 kW surplus compared to the conventional system, with could generate 58% less volume of bio-waste from the process.

6. Methane conversion: secondary energy

The methane conversion as secondary energy through the biogas purification to get higher methane content for household, fuel transportation, and the methane conversion into hydrogen. The biogas purification for secondary energy was mandatory to get high content methane and to reduce the carbon dioxide (CO_2) to increase the density and the calorific value, and cleaning out the hydrogen sulfide (H_2S) due to the corrosivity character for the metal part of in all the system such as gas storage tank, piping system, compressor, engine, and also the toxicity that harmful to the environment [89]. The CO_2 removal could be removed through physical absorption by water or organic scrubbing that could be physically bound with CO_2 [90, 91]. The absorption using organic solvent could also remover the H_2S, ammonia (NH_3), hydrogen cyanide (HCN) and also water vapor with low losses of CH_4, and included into regeneration system with low temperature waste, however the operation and technology investment is expensive; chemical absorption by using di-methyl ethanol amine (DMEA) or mono ethanol amine (MEA), and solution of alkali such as NaOH, $K2CO_3$, KOH, iron hydroxides ($Fe(OH)_3$), and $FeCl_2$ that could actively absorb the CO_2 [92, 93]; pressure swing absorption by sequences process of adsorption, desorption, and pressurization by hiring the synthetic resin, zeolite, activated carbon, silica gel, or activated charcoal which also could separate the N_2, H_2S and O_2 [94]; cryogenic separation which takes advantage of the different boiling points of CO2 and CH4 by condensation process on gas cooling at elevated pressures that could separate the CO_2 and also the other gas content such as O_2, N_2 and siloxanes [95]; membrane separation which base on the properties of the selective permeability of the membrane through two system i.e., gas–liquid separation where the liquid absorbs the CO_2 and also the H_2S diffusing via the membrane, gas–gas separation by the gas phase from the both side of membranes [96, 97]; hydrate formation which based on the equilibrium partition of the components between gaseous and hydrate phases, clathrate phase equilibrium for the water-phenol-carbon dioxide system [98, 99]. Other than that, CO_2 and H_2 compounds in biogas also could be utilized via biological conversion by hiring the microbial to convert the CO_2 and H_2 into methane [100, 101]. The H_2S could be removed by physical and chemical absorption by converting H_2S to elemental sulfur or metal sulfide utilizing either water or organic solvent in the physical absorption process or aqueous chemical solutions 98. The water adsorption could generate cheap operation as long as the water is available and easy to get, this system also could remove the H_2S at the same time, however, this system was included in a not-regenerative system and require high-pressure conditions and complex engineering [102]; activated carbon adsorption that catalyzed the H_2S oxidation into metal sulfide or sulfur which usually used impregnated activated carbon and catalytic-impregnated carbon which has highest oxidation rate compare with activated carbon [103, 104]; adsorption by iron oxides (Fe_2O_3), $Fe(OH)_3$ or zinc oxides (ZnS) that could easily reacted with H_2S and forming the FeS and ZnS from the reaction [105, 106]; biological biofiltration and desulfurization using litautotrophic bacteria that can convert H2S into sulfate and sulfur bases using electron donors from H_2S and carbon sources from CO_2 (**Figure 2**). Moreover, the content of H_2S in biogas could be prevented by in-situ prevented via dosing the oxygen in the digester system, where the microbiological oxidation converted the H_2S into elemental sulfur [89, 107]. The other in-situ treatment was using iron chloride ($FeCl_2$) dosing into the digester by forming the iron sulfide (FeS), where the FeS could be easily removed through the solid discharge which is a good content fertilizer nutrient [108]. Other than that, the other compounds such as nitrogen (N_2), oxygen (O_2), volatile organic compounds (VOCs), carbon monoxide (CO), and NH_3 were removed to get the methane purity [109]. Methane as secondary energy was widely applied in several countries.

The hydrogen conversion from the methane commonly through the conversion system such as SRM [37, 110–112], DRM [113, 114], CDM [115, 116], and POM [117, 118]. The SRM was widely used in industrial applications with a high theoretical H_2/CO ratio and its efficiency with low operational and production costs. The SRM system could SRM could continuedly one system with water gas shift (WGS) which could convert more hydrogen in the process where the steam and CH_4 mixed and produced syngas from hydrocarbon and water reaction [37, 112]:

$$H_2O + CH_4 \rightarrow 3H_2 + CO$$

The WGS process continue to convert the CO by water reaction [37, 112]:

$$H_2O + CO \rightarrow CO_2 + H_2$$

However, the SRM facing the complex system depends on the quality of biogas, high CO_x emission, water demand, and high investment capital [118]. The conversion through the DRM has a good point with CO_2 reduction, however, the still facing with the carbon deposition problem, influenced on CO disproportionate and reverse water gas shift reaction, and carbon deposition problem [119]. The POM was offering high selectivity and conversion rates with short residence time, and is known as a simple system with less desulphurization and not using catalyst during the process [115, 120]. Nevertheless, pure O_2 was required for the process with high CO_x emission and possibility the of producing NO_x emission with soot formation during the process [121]. The CDM was the simplest process with only one step with a single reactant, produced H_2 with high purity by mild reaction condition and no GHG emission during the process. The CDM also could produce nanocarbon material by carbon sequestration which forms a stable solid. Even though it looks promising, the CDM is still in lab level experiment which is necessary for catalyst deactivation, unreacted methane in out-stream with low purity nano-carbon, and the catalyst regeneration produced the secondary emission [114, 116, 121].

7. Conclusion

The utilization of lignocellulosic biomass waste and unitized fast-growing biomass as carbon-neutral resources by methane conversion by steam explosion pretreatment and its secondary energy (compressed biogas, nitrogen, and electric) was potentially to be the solution to fulfill the SDGs requirement which is renewable and environmentally friendly. This chapter has described the state the art, feasibility study in the full-scale application, and the life cycle assessment that could give deliberation to industry and stakeholders that consider applying the system.

Acknowledgements

The authors gratefully acknowledge the financial supports by a Grant-in-Aid for Scientific Research (A) (Grant No. 20H00664), and the Scholarship (IN: 202136) from Ministry of Education, Culture, Sport, Science, and Technology of Japan.

Conflict of interest

The authors declare no conflict of interest.

Author details

Sholahuddin Sholahuddin[1*], Yoshitoshi Nakamura[2] and Chikako Asada[2*]

1 Graduated School of Life and Material System Engineering, Tokushima University, Tokushima, Japan

2 Department of Bioscience and Bioindustry, Tokushima University, Tokushima, Japan

*Address all correspondence to: sholahudd@gmail.com
and asada.c@tokushima-u.ac.jp

References

[1] Asada C, Sholahuddin NY. Lignin as a coating and curing agent on biodegradable epoxy resins. In: Gutiérrez TJ, editor. Reactive and Functional Polymers. Vol. 1. Springer International Publishing; 2020. pp. 195-206

[2] Asada C, Nakamura Y, Kobayashi F. Waste reduction system for production of useful materials from un-utilized bamboo using steam explosion followed by various conversion methods. Biochemical Engineering Journal. 2005;**23**(2):131-137. DOI: 10.1016/j.bej.2004.11.004

[3] Sasaki C, Wanaka M, Takagi H, Tamura S, Asada C, Nakamura Y. Evaluation of epoxy resins synthesized from steam-exploded bamboo lignin. Industrial Crops and Products. 2013;**43**(1):757-761. DOI: 10.1016/j.indcrop.2012.08.018

[4] Asada C, Sasaki C, Uto Y, Sakafuji J, Nakamura Y. Effect of steam explosion pretreatment with ultra-high temperature and pressure on effective utilization of softwood biomass. Biochemical Engineering Journal. 2012;**60**:25-29. DOI: 10.1016/j.bej.2011.09.013

[5] Asada C, Basnet S, Otsuka M, Sasaki C, Nakamura Y. Epoxy resin synthesis using low molecular weight lignin separated from various lignocellulosic materials. International Journal of Biological Macromolecules. 2015;**74**:413-419. DOI: 10.1016/j.ijbiomac.2014.12.039

[6] Asada C, Honjo K, Nakamura Y. Utilization of steam-treated and milling-treated lignin from Moso Bamboo as curing agent of epoxy resin. Waste Biomass Valor. 2021;**12**:6261-6272. DOI: 10.1007/s12649-021-01444-8

[7] Basnet S, Otsuka M, Sasaki C, Asada C, Nakamura Y. Functionalization of the active ingredients of Japanese green tea (*Camellia sinensis*) for the synthesis of bio-based epoxy resin. Industrial Crops and Products. 2015;**73**:63-72. DOI: 10.1016/j.indcrop.2015.03.091

[8] Noda Y, Asada C, Sasaki C, Nakamura Y. Effects of hydrothermal methods such as steam explosion and microwave irradiation on extraction of water soluble antioxidant materials from Garlic Husk. Waste Biomass Valor. 2019;**10**:3397-3402. DOI: 10.1007/s12649-018-0353-3

[9] Noda Y, Asada C, Sasaki C, Hashimoto S, Nakamura Y. Extraction method for increasing antioxidant activity of raw garlic using steam explosion. Biochemical Engineering Journal. 2013;**73**:1-4. DOI: 10.1016/j.bej.2013.01.013

[10] Kurosumi A, Sasaki C, Kumada K, Kobayashi F, Mtui G, Nakamura Y. Novel extraction method of antioxidant compounds from Sasa palmata (Bean) Nakai using steam explosion. Process Biochemistry. 2007;**42**(10):1449-1453

[11] Kurosumi A, Kobayashi F, Nakamura Y. Development of new extraction method of natural antioxidants from Bamboo Grass. Transactions of the Material Research Society Japan. 2007;**32**(4):1139-1142

[12] Asada C, Seno M, Nakamura Y. Preparation of Biopolymer Composite Using Cedar-Derived Cellulose Nanofibers. Waste and Biomass

Valorization. 2021;**12**:6245-6254. DOI: 10.1007/s12649-021-01436-8

[13] Asada C, Sasaki C, Suzuki A, Nakamura Y. Total biorefinery process of lignocellulosic waste using steam explosion followed by water and acetone extractions. Waste and Biomass Valorization. 2018;**9**(12):2423-2432. DOI: 10.1007/s12649-017-0157-x

[14] Suzuki A, Sasaki C, Asada C, Nakamura Y. Characterization of cellulose nanofiber from steam-exploded Japanese cedar. BioResources. 2017;**12**(4):7628-7641

[15] Asada C, Sholahuddin S, Nakamura Y. Biorefinery system of lignocellulosic biomass using steam explosion. In: Sand A, Banga S, editors. Cellulose Science and Derivatives. London: IntechOpen; 2021. Available from: https://www.intechopen.com/chapters/77170. DOI: 10.5772/intechopen.98544

[16] Sholahuddin, Nakamura Y, Asada C. Effect of activated cow dung as inoculum on methane production of steam-exploded rice husks. Waste Biomass Valor. 2021;**12**:5019-5028. DOI: 10.1007/s12649-021-01365-6

[17] Duque A, Manzanares P, Ballesteros I, Ballesteros M. Steam explosion as lignocellulosic biomass pretreatment. In: Mussatto SI, editor. Biomass Fractionation Technologies for a Lignocellulosic Feedstock Based Biorefinery. Amsterdam: Elsevier Inc; 2016. pp. 349-368. DOI: 10.1016/B978-0-12-802323-5.00015-3

[18] Saddler JN, Ramos LP, Breuil C. Chapter 3: Steam pretreatment of lignocellulosic residues. In: Saddler JN, editor. Bioconversion of Forest and Agricultural Residues. 1993. pp. 73-92

[19] Yu Z, Zhang B, Yu F, Xu G, Song A. A real explosion: The requirement of steam explosion pretreatment. Bioresource Technology. 2012;**121**:335-341. DOI: 10.1016/j.biortech.2012.06.055

[20] Overend RP, Chornet E. Fractionation of lignocellulosics by steam-aqueous pretreatments. Philosophical Transactions of Royal Society London Series A, Mathematical Physical and Sciences. 1987;**321**(1561):523-536

[21] Montané D, Overend RP, Chornet E. Kinetic models for non-homogeneous complex systems with a time-dependent rate constant. Canadian Journal of Chemical Engineering. 1998;**76**(1):58-68

[22] Asada C, Sasaki C, Takamatsu T, Nakamura Y. Conversion of steam-exploded cedar into ethanol using simultaneous saccharification, fermentation and detoxification process. Bioresource Technology. 2015;**176**:203-209. DOI: 10.1016/j.biortech.2014.11.039

[23] López MJ, Moreno J, Nichols NN, Dien BS, Bothast RJ. Isolation of microorganisms for biological detoxification of lignocellulosic hydrolysates. Applied Microbiology and Biotechnology. 2004;**64**(1):125-131

[24] Chandel AK, Kapoor RK, Singh A, Kuhad RC. Detoxification of sugarcane bagasse hydrolysate improves ethanol production by Candida shehatae NCIM 3501. Bioresource Technology. 2007;**98**(10):1947-1950

[25] Villarreal MLM, Prata AMR, Felipe MGA, Almeida E Silva JB. Detoxification procedures of eucalyptus hemicellulose hydrolysate for xylitol production by Candida guilliermondii. Enzyme and Microbial Technology 2006;**40**(1):17-24. 10.1016/j.enzmictec.2005.10.032

[26] Zhu J, Yong Q, Xu Y, Yu S. Detoxification of corn stover prehydrolyzate by trialkylamine extraction to improve the ethanol production with Pichia stipitis CBS 5776. Bioresource Technology. 2011;**102**(2):1663-1668

[27] Lee JM, Venditti RA, Jameel H, Kenealy WR. Detoxification of woody hydrolyzates with activated carbon for bioconversion to ethanol by the thermophilic anaerobic bacterium Thermoanaerobacterium saccharolyticum. Biomass and Bioenergy. 2011;**35**(1):626-636

[28] Alriksson B, Cavka A, Jönsson LJ. Improving the fermentability of enzymatic hydrolysates of lignocellulose through chemical in-situ detoxification with reducing agents. Bioresource Technology. 2011;**102**(2):1254-1263

[29] Martinez A, Rodriguez ME, Wells ML, York SW, Preston JF, Ingram LO. Detoxification of dilute acid hydrolysates of lignocellulose with lime. Biotechnology Progress. 2001;**17**(2):287-293

[30] Ando S, Arai I, Kiyoto K, Hanai S. Identification of aromatic monomers in steam-exploded poplar and their influences on ethanol fermentation by Saccharomyces cerevisiae. Journal of Fermentation Technology. 1986;**64**(6):567-570

[31] Hu Z, Liu S, Yue Z, Yan L, Yang M, Yu H. Microscale analysis of in vitro anaerobic degradation of lignocellulosic wastes by Rumen microorganisms microscale analysis of in vitro anaerobic degradation of lignocellulosic wastes by Rumen microorganisms. 2008;**42**:276-281

[32] Ko JJ, Shimizu Y, Ikeda K, Kim SK, Park CH, Matsui S. Biodegradation of high molecular weight lignin under sulfate reducing conditions: Lignin degradability and degradation by-products. Bioresource Technology. 2009;**100**(4):1622-1627

[33] Chen F, Dixon RA. Lignin modification improves fermentable sugar yields for biofuel production. Nature Biotechnology. 2007;**25**(7):759-761. DOI: 10.1128/AEM.03016-13%0A

[34] Vivekanand V, Olsen EF, Eijsink VGH, Horn SJ. Effect of different steam explosion conditions on methane potential and enzymatic saccharification of birch. Bioresource Technology. 2013;**127**:343-349

[35] Healy JB, Young LY. Anaerobic biodegradation of eleven aromatic compounds to methane. Applied and Environmental Microbiology. 1979;**38**(1):84-89

[36] Barakat A, Monlau F, Steyer JP, Carrere H. Effect of lignin-derived and furan compounds found in lignocellulosic hydrolysates on biomethane production. Bioresource Technology. 2012;**104**:90-99. DOI: 10.1016/j.biortech.2011.10.060

[37] Madeira JGF, Oliveira EM, Springer MV, Cabral HL, Barbeito DF, APG S, et al. Hydrogen production from swine manure biogas via steam reforming of methane (SRM) and water gas shift (WGS): A ecological, technical, and economic analysis. International Journal of Hydrogen Energy. 2021;**46**(13): 8961-8971

[38] USDA. World Crop Production [Internet]. 2021. Available from: https://ipad.fas.usda.gov/cropexplorer/cropview/Default.aspx

[39] Kobayashi F, Take H, Asada C, Nakamura Y. Methane production from

steam-exploded bamboo. Journal of Bioscience and Bioengineering. 2004;**97**(6):426-428

[40] Wu H, Zhou Z, Yang Y, Meng Q. Effect of steam explosion of oil palm frond and empty fruit bunch on nutrient composition and ruminal fermentation characteristics. Tropical Animal Health and Production. 2020;**52**(3):1223-1228

[41] Lizasoain J, Trulea A, Gittinger J, Kral I, Piringer G, Schedl A, et al. Corn stover for biogas production: Effect of steam explosion pretreatment on the gas yields and on the biodegradation kinetics of the primary structural compounds. Bioresource Technology. 2017;**244**:949-956. DOI: 10.1016/j.biortech.2017.08.042

[42] Theuretzbacher F, Lizasoain J, Lefever C, Saylor MK, Enguidanos R, Weran N, et al. Steam explosion pretreatment of wheat straw to improve methane yields: Investigation of the degradation kinetics of structural compounds during anaerobic digestion. Bioresource Technology. 2015;**179**: 299-305

[43] Steinbach D, Wüst D, Zielonka S, Krümpel J, Munder S, Pagel M, et al. Steam explosion conditions highly influence the biogas yield of rice straw. Molecules. 2019;**24**(19):1-14

[44] Vivekanand V, Ryden P, Horn SJ, Tapp HS, Wellner N, Eijsink VGH, et al. Impact of steam explosion on biogas production from rape straw in relation to changes in chemical composition. Bioresource Technology. 2012;**123**:608-615

[45] Asada C, Megumi F, Suzuki A, Nakamura Y. Cured epoxy resin synthesized using acetone-soluble lignin and ligno-p-cresol obtained from steam-exploded wheat straw. Biomass Convers Biorefinery. 2032;**1**:3. DOI: 10.1007/s13399-021-02032-5

[46] Nakamura Y, Sawada T, Inoue E. Enhanced ethanol production from enzymatically treated steam-exploded rice straw using extractive fermentation. Journal of Chemical Technology and Biotechnology. 2001;**76**(8):879-884

[47] Fache M, Auvergne R, Boutevin B, Caillol S. New vanillin-derived diepoxy monomers for the synthesis of biobased thermosets. European Polymer Journal. 2015;**67**:527-538. DOI: 10.1016/j.eurpolymj.2014.10.011

[48] Take H, Andou Y, Nakamura Y, Kobayashi F, Kurimoto Y, Kuwahara M. Production of methane gas from Japanese cedar chips pretreated by various delignification methods. Biochemical Engineering Journal. 2006;**28**(1):30-35

[49] Theuretzbacher F, Blomqvist J, Lizasoain J, Klietz L, Potthast A, Horn SJ, et al. The effect of a combined biological and thermo-mechanical pretreatment of wheat straw on energy yields in coupled ethanol and methane generation. Bioresource Technology. 2015;**194**:7-13. DOI: 10.1016/j.biortech.2015.06.093

[50] Bauer A, Lizasoain J, Theuretzbacher F, Agger JW, Rincón M, Menardo S, et al. Steam explosion pretreatment for enhancing biogas production of late harvested hay. Bioresource Technology. 2014;**166**:403-410

[51] Matsakas L, Sarkar O, Jansson S, Rova U, Christakopoulos P. A novel hybrid organosolv-steam explosion pretreatment and fractionation method delivers solids with superior thermophilic digestibility to methane. Bioresource Technology. 2020;**316**

[52] Weber B, Estrada-Maya A, Sandoval-Moctezuma AC,

Martínez-Cienfuegos IG. Anaerobic digestion of extracts from steam exploded Agave tequilana bagasse. Journal of Environmental Management. 2019;**245**:489-495

[53] Li J, Zhang R, Siddhu MAH, He Y, Wang W, Li Y, et al. Enhancing methane production of corn stover through a novel way: Sequent pretreatment of potassium hydroxide and steam explosion. Bioresource Technology. 2015;**181**:345-350

[54] Ferry JG. Fundamentals of methanogenic pathways that are key to the biomethanation of complex biomass. Current Opinion in Biotechnology. 2011;**22**(3):351-357

[55] Vasta V, Daghio M, Cappucci A, Buccioni A, Serra A, Viti C, et al. Invited review: Plant polyphenols and Rumen microbiota responsible for fatty acid biohydrogenation, fiber digestion, and methane emission: Experimental evidence and methodological approaches. Journal of Dairy Science. 2019;**102**(5):3781-3804

[56] Ruff SE, Wietz M, Wegener A, Wagner-Doebler I, Cordero OX, Sichert A. Polysaccharide-bacteria interactions from the lens of evolutionary ecology. Frontiers in Microbiology. 2021;**12**:705082

[57] Ziemer CJ. Newly cultured bacteria with broad diversity isolated from eight-week continuous culture enrichments of cow feces on complex polysaccharides. Applied in Environmental Microbiology. 2014;**80**(2):574-585

[58] Rabee AE, Forster R, Sabra EA. Lignocelluloytic activities and composition of bacterial community in the camel rumen. AIMS Microbiology. 2021;7(3):354-367

[59] Achinas S, Achinas V, Euverink GJW. Microbiology and biochemistry of anaerobic digesters: An overview. Bioreactors. 2020:17-26

[60] Bruneckey R, Alahuta M, Qi X, Donohoe BS, Crowley MF, Kataeva IA, et al. Revealing nature's cellulase diversity: The digestion mechanism of *Caldicellulosiruptor bescii* CelA. Science (80-). 2013;**342**(6155):1513-1516

[61] Mulat DG, Huerta SG, Kalyani D, Horn SJ. Enhancing methane production from lignocellulosic biomass by combined steam-explosion pretreatment and bioaugmentation with cellulolytic bacterium *Caldicellulosiruptor bescii*. Biotechnology for Biofuels. 2018;**11**

[62] Lü F, Ji J, Shao L, He P. Bacterial bioaugmentation for improving methane and hydrogen production from microalgae. Biotechnology for Biofuels. 2013;**6**(1):1-11

[63] Cheng XY, Li Q, Liu CZ. Coproduction of hydrogen and methane via anaerobic fermentation of cornstalk waste in continuous stirred tank reactor integrated with up-flow anaerobic sludge bed. Bioresource Technology. 2012;**114**:327-333. DOI: 10.1016/j.biortech.2012.03.038

[64] Lavrič L, Cerar A, Fanedl L, Lazar B, Žitnik M, Logar RM. Thermal pretreatment and bioaugmentation improve methane yield of microalgal mix produced in thermophilic anaerobic digestate. Anaerobe. 2017;**46**:162-169. DOI: 10.1016/j.anaerobe.2017.02.001

[65] Peng X, Börner RA, Nges IA, Liu J. Impact of bioaugmentation on biochemical methane potential for wheat straw with addition of *Clostridium* cellulolyticum. Bioresource Technology. 2014;**152**:567-571

[66] Mearls EB, Lynd LR. The identification of four histidine kinases that influence sporulation in *Clostridium thermocellum*. Anaerobe. 2014;**28**:109-119

[67] Ecem Öner B, Akyol Ç, Bozan M, Ince O, Aydin S, Ince B. Bioaugmentation with *Clostridium thermocellum* to enhance the anaerobic biodegradation of lignocellulosic agricultural residues. Bioresource Technology. 2018;**249**: 620-625

[68] Tsapekos P, Kougias PG, Vasileiou SA, Treu L, Campanaro S, Lyberatos G, et al. Bioaugmentation with hydrolytic microbes to improve the anaerobic biodegradability of lignocellulosic agricultural residues. Bioresource Technology. 2017;**234**:350-359

[69] Čater M, Fanedl L, Malovrh Š, Marinšek LR. Biogas production from brewery spent grain enhanced by bioaugmentation with hydrolytic anaerobic bacteria. Bioresource Technology. 2015;**186**:261-269

[70] Shi Q, Li Y, Li Y, Cheng Y, Zhu W. Effects of steam explosion on lignocellulosic degradation of, and methane production from, corn stover by a co-cultured anaerobic fungus and methanogen. Bioresource Technology. 2019;**290**

[71] Fotidis IA, Karakashev D, Kotsopoulos TA, Martzopoulos GG, Angelidaki I. Effect of ammonium and acetate on methanogenic pathway and methanogenic community composition. FEMS Microbiology Ecology. 2013;**83**(1):38-48

[72] Tian H, Fotidis IA, Mancini E, Treu L, Mahdy A, Ballesteros M, et al. Acclimation to extremely high ammonia levels in continuous biomethanation process and the associated microbial community dynamics. Bioresource Technology. Jan 1 2018;**247**:616-623

[73] Manzoor S, Bongcam-Rudloff E, Schnürer A, Müller B. Genome-guided analysis and whole transcriptome profiling of the mesophilic syntrophic acetate oxidising bacterium *Syntrophaceticus schinkii*. PLoS ONE. 2016;**11**(11). DOI: 10.1371/journal.pone.0166520

[74] Shikata A, Sermsathanaswadi J, Thianheng P, Baramee S, Tachaapaikoon C, Waeonukul R, et al. Characterization of an anaerobic, thermophilic, alkaliphilic, high lignocellulosic biomass-degrading bacterial community, ISHI-3, isolated from biocompost. Enzyme and Microbial Technology. 2018;**118**:66-75

[75] Westerholm M, Roos S, Schnürer A. Tepidanaerobacter acetatoxydans sp. nov., an anaerobic, syntrophic acetate-oxidizing bacterium isolated from two ammonium-enriched mesophilic methanogenic processes. Systematic and Applied Microbiology. 2011;**34**(4):260-266

[76] Ahlert S, Zimmermann R, Ebling J, König H. Analysis of propionate-degrading consortia from agricultural biogas plants. Microbiology. 2016;**5**(6):1027-1037

[77] Sun L, Müller B, Westerholm M, Schnürer A. Syntrophic acetate oxidation in industrial CSTR biogas digesters. Journal of Biotechnology. 2014;**171**(1):39-44

[78] Manzoor S, Schnürer A, Bongcam-Rudloff E, Müller B. Genome-guided analysis of clostridium ultunense and comparative genomics reveal different strategies for acetate oxidation and energy conservation in syntrophic acetate-oxidising bacteria. Genes (Basel). 2018;**9**(4):1-24

[79] De Bok FAM, Plugge CM, Stams AJM. Interspecies electron transfer in methanogenic propionate degrading consortia. Water Research. 2004;**38**(6):1368-1375

[80] Stams AJM, De Bok FAM, Plugge CM, Van Eekert MHA, Dolfing J, Schraa G. Minireview exocellular electron transfer in anaerobic microbial communities. Environmental Microbiology. 2006;**8**(3):371-382

[81] Fotidis IA, Karakashev D, Angelidaki I. Bioaugmentation with an acetate-oxidising consortium as a tool to tackle ammonia inhibition of anaerobic digestion. Bioresource Technology. 2013;**146**:57-62

[82] Tian H, Yan M, Treu L, Angelidaki I, Fotidis IA. Hydrogenotrophic methanogens are the key for a successful bioaugmentation to alleviate ammonia inhibition in thermophilic anaerobic digesters. Bioresource Technology. 2019;**293**:122070

[83] Fotidis I, Wang H, Fiedel N, Luo G, Karakashev D, Angelidaki I. Bioaugmentation as a solution to increase methane production from an ammonia-rich substrate. Environmental Science and Technology. 2014;**48**(13):7669-7676

[84] Shafiei M, Kabir MM, Zilouei H, Sárvári Horváth I, Karimi K. Techno-economical study of biogas production improved by steam explosion pretreatment. Bioresource Technology. 2013;**148**:53-60

[85] Kral I, Piringer G, Saylor MK, Lizasoain J, Gronauer A, Bauer A. Life cycle assessment of biogas production from unused grassland biomass pretreated by steam explosion using a system expansion method. Sustainability (Switzerland). 2020;**12**:1-17

[86] Gaworski M, Jabłoński S, Pawlaczyk-Graja I, Ziewiecki R, Rutkowski P, Wieczyńska A, et al. Enhancing biogas plant production using pig manure and corn silage by adding wheat straw processed with liquid hot water and steam explosion. Biotechnology for Biofuels. 2017;**10**(1):1-13

[87] Maroušek J. Pretreatment of sunflower stalks for biogas production. Clean Technologies and Environmental Policy. 2013;**15**(4):735-740

[88] Pérez-Elvira SI, Fernández-Polanco F, Fernández-Polanco M, Rodríguez P, Rouge P. Hydrothermal multivariable approach. Full-scale feasibility study. Electronic Journal of Biotechnology. 2008;**11**(4)

[89] Huertas JI, Giraldo N, Izquierdo S. Removal of H2S and CO2 from biogas by amine absorption. In: Markoš J, editor. Mass Transfer in Chemical Engineering Processes. IntechOpen; 2011

[90] Awe OW, Zhao Y, Nzihou A, Minh DP, Lyczko N. A review of biogas utilisation, purification and upgrading technologies. Waste and Biomass Valorization. 2017;**8**(2):267-283

[91] Walozi R, Nabuuma B, Sebiti A. Application of low pressure water scrubbing technique for increasing methane content in biogas. Universal Journal of Agricultural Research. 2016;**4**(2):60-65

[92] Lasocki J, Kołodziejczyk K, Matuszewska A. Laboratory-scale investigation of biogas treatment by removal of hydrogen sulfide and Carbon Dioxide. Polish Journal of Environmental Studies. 2015;**24**(3):1427-1434

[93] Leonzio G. Upgrading of biogas to bio-methane with chemical absorption process: Simulation and environmental

impact. Journal of Cleaner Production. 2016;**131**:364-375

[94] Abd AA, Othman MR, Naji SZ, Hashim AS. Methane enrichment in biogas mixture using pressure swing adsorption: Process fundamental and design parameters. Materials Today Sustainability. 2021;**11-12**:100063

[95] Baena-Moreno FM, Rodríguez-Galán M, Vega F, Vilches LF, Navarrete B, Zhang Z. Biogas upgrading by cryogenic techniques. Environmental Chemistry Letters. 2019;**17**(3):1251-1261. DOI: 10.1007/s10311-019-00872-2

[96] Saedi S, Madaeni SS, Arabi Shamsabadi A, Mottaghi F. The effect of surfactants on the structure and performance of PES membrane for separation of carbon dioxide from methane. Separation and Purification Technology. 2012;**99**:104-119. DOI: 10.1016/j.seppur.2012.08.028

[97] Uchytil P, Schauer J, Petrychkovych R, Setnickova K, Suen SY. Ionic liquid membranes for carbon dioxide–methane separation. Journal of Membrane Science. 2011;**383**(1-2):262-271

[98] Gambelli AM. Analyses on CH4 and CO2 hydrate formation to define the optimal pressure for CO2 injection to maximize the replacement efficiency into natural gas hydrate in presence of a silica-based natural porous medium, via depressurization techniques. Chemical Engineering and Processing Process Intensification. 2021;**167**:108512

[99] Pahlavanzadeh H, Khanlarkhani M, Mohammadi AH. Clathrate hydrate formation in (methane, carbon dioxide or nitrogen + tetrahydropyran or furan + water) system: Thermodynamic and kinetic study. The Journal of Chemical Thermodynamics. 2016;**92**:168-174

[100] Luo G, Johansson S, Boe K, Xie L, Zhou Q, Angelidaki I. Simultaneous hydrogen utilization and in situ biogas upgrading in an anaerobic reactor. Biotechnology and Bioengineering. 2012;**109**(4):1088-1094

[101] Kim S, Choi K, Chung J. Reduction in carbon dioxide and production of methane by biological reaction in the electronics industry. International Journal of Hydrogen Energy. 2013;**38**(8): 3488-3496

[102] Hosseini SE, Wahid MA. Development of biogas combustion in combined heat and power generation. Renewable and Sustainable Energy Reviews. 2014;**40**:868-875. DOI: 10.1016/j.rser.2014.07.204

[103] Nyamukamba P, Mukumba P, Chikukwa ES, Makaka G. Biogas upgrading approaches with special focus on siloxane removal—A review. Energies. 2020;**13**(22):1-17

[104] Cano PI, Brito J, Almenglo F, Ramírez M, Gómez JM, Cantero D. Influence of trickling liquid velocity, low molar ratio of nitrogen/sulfur and gas-liquid flow pattern in anoxic biotrickling filters for biogas desulfurization. Biochemical Engineering Journal. 2019;**148**:205-213

[105] Jangam K, Chen YY, Qin L, Fan LS. Perspectives on reactive separation and removal of hydrogen sulfide. Chem Eng Sci X. 2021;**11**:100105

[106] Watanabe S. Chemistry of H2S over the surface of Common solid sorbents in industrial natural gas desulfurization. Catalysis Today. 2021:204-220. DOI: 10.1016/j.cattod.2020.05.064

[107] Zytoon MA, El-Shazly AH, Noweir MH, Al-Zahrani AA. Biological treatment of hydrogen sulfide in an airlift bioreactor with direct gas injection. Environment Protection Engineering. 2015;**41**(4):131-142

[108] Ryckebosch E, Drouillon M, Vervaeren H. Techniques for transformation of biogas to biomethane. Biomass and Bioenergy. 2011;**35**(5):1633-1645

[109] Abatzoglou N, Boivin S. A review of biogas purifi cation processes. Biofuels, Bioproducts and Biorefining. 2009;(3):42-71

[110] Roh HS, Eum IH, Jeong DW. Low temperature steam reforming of methane over Ni-Ce (1-x)Zr (x)O 2 catalysts under severe conditions. Renewable Energy. 2012;**42**:212-216. DOI: 10.1016/j.renene.2011.08.013

[111] Zhu X, Wang H, Wei Y, Li K, Cheng X. Hydrogen and syngas production from two-step steam reforming of methane using CeO2 as oxygen carrier. Journal of Natural Gas Chemistry. 2011;**20**(3):281-286. DOI: 10.1016/S1003-9953(10)60185-5

[112] Zhang H, Sun Z, Hu YH. Steam reforming of methane: Current states of catalyst design and process upgrading. Renewable and Sustainable Energy Reviews;**2021**(149):111330. DOI: 10.1016/j.rser.2021.111330

[113] Minh DP, Siang TJ, Vo DVN, Phan TS, Ridart C, Nzihou A, et al. Hydrogen production from biogas reforming: An overview of steam reforming, dry reforming, dual reforming, and tri-reforming of methane. Hydrogen Supply Chain: Design, Deployment and Operation. 2018;**1**:111-166

[114] Gao Y, Jiang J, Meng Y, Yan F, Aihemaiti A. A review of recent developments in hydrogen production via biogas dry reforming. Energy Conversion and Management. 2018;**171**:133-155. DOI: 10.1016/j.enconman.2018.05.083

[115] Chaubey R, Sahu S, James OO, Maity S. A review on development of industrial processes and emerging techniques for production of hydrogen from renewable and sustainable sources. Renewable and Sustainable Energy Reviews. 2013;**23**:443-462. DOI: 10.1016/j.rser.2013.02.019

[116] Osman AI. Catalytic hydrogen production from methane partial oxidation: Mechanism and kinetic study. Chemical Engineering and Technology. 2020;**43**(4):641-648

[117] Figen HE, Baykara SZ. Hydrogen production by partial oxidation of methane over Co based, Ni and Ru monolithic catalysts. International Journal of Hydrogen Energy. 2015;**40**(24):7439-7451

[118] Freni S, Calogero G, Cavallaro S. Hydrogen production from methane through catalytic partial oxidation reactions. Journal of Power Sources. 2000;**87**(1-2):28-38

[119] Oyama ST, Hacarlioglu P, Gu Y, Lee D. Dry reforming of methane has no future for hydrogen production: Comparison with steam reforming at high pressure in standard and membrane reactors. International Journal of Hydrogen Energy. 2012;**37**(13): 10444-10450. DOI: 10.1016/j.ijhydene.2011.09.149

[120] Kumar S, Kumar S, Prajapati JK. Hydrogen production by partial oxidation of methane: Modeling

and simulation. International Journal of Hydrogen Energy. 2009;**34**(16):6655-6668

[121] Fan Z, Weng W, Zhou J, Gu D, Xiao W. Catalytic decomposition of methane to produce hydrogen: A review. Journal of Energy Chemistry. 2021;**58**:415-430. DOI: 10.1016/j.jechem.2020.10.049

Section 3

Biomass Utilization

Chapter 6

Utilization of Wood Biomass Ash in Concrete Industry

Nina Štirmer and Ivana Carević

Abstract

The use of energy from wood biomass plants results in the production of large quantities of wood biomass ash (WBA). Most of the WBA is disposed of and some are used as a soil supplement in agriculture. In the concrete industry, there is a high potential for substitution of certain components with suitable alternative materials. Depending on its physical and chemical properties, WBA can be used in concrete production as a partial replacement for cement or as a substitute for fine aggregates. The suitability of locally available WBA should be evaluated in terms of microtexture, chemical, and mineralogical composition. This paper presents the types of WBA produced by different combustion technology, the influence of WBA as a cement replacement on the properties of cement composites in the fresh and hardened state, an overview of the environmental impact of WBA cement composites, and the market opportunities and readiness for reuse of WBA as a new potential supplementary cementitious material.

Keywords: wood biomass ash, supplementary cementitious material, compressive strength, cement composites, concrete industry

1. Introduction

The policy of promoting and increasing the use of wood biomass as a renewable energy source affects the increase in the amount of wood biomass ash (WBA) produced [1]. Comprehensive statistics on the annual production of WBA in the European Union are not available. However, Austria, Denmark, Germany, Italy, the Netherlands, and Sweden account for about 2.9 million t/y of biomass ash [2], while a survey conducted in Croatia revealed that about 25,414 t/y of produced WBA is landfilled [3]. Existing data estimated that Europe will generate up to 15.5×10^7 tons of WBA in 2020 [4], highlighting the urgency of strategic foresight in waste management. Currently, WBA is underutilized in the EU and mostly disposed of in landfills [5–8], resulting in additional costs and risks to the environment. The cost of biomass ash disposal ranges from 100 to 500 EUR/ton [9, 10]. About, 1.7 million EUR per year are paid for the disposal of WBA in Austria [11]. In the future, an increase in the cost of landfilling in the form of waste taxes or disposal fees, as well as difficulties in acquiring new landfills and stricter EU landfill directives, may be expected. Unsystematic management of WBA can lead to environmental pollution and potential risks to human health: WBA can be easily transported through the air and consequently cause health problems related to the respiratory system of the population living in the vicinity of the landfill [12], while uncontrolled landfilling of WBA can lead to groundwater pollution through leaching of heavy metals from WBA or infiltration of rainwater [13]. European policies promote and stimulate green innovations in the reuse of waste as secondary raw materials to boost the market and new green business opportunities [14]. It is, therefore, necessary to find ways and methods for the application of WBA that are environmentally sound and economically justified. Previous studies [15–19] have shown that the resulting WBA can be reused in certain industries due to their properties and chemical composition, especially in the concrete industry. However, existing regulations and standards currently preclude the use of WBA in the concrete industry [20, 21].

The objectives of this chapter are: (1) to determine what types of combustion technologies are currently in use and what types of WBA are produced by each combustion technology, the properties of these WBAs, and the factors that most influence WBA properties, as well as the physical and chemical properties that could influence the use of WBA in cement composites; (2) to assess the influence of WBA as a cement replacement on the properties of cement composites in the fresh and hardened states; (3) to provide a brief overview of the environmental impact of the use of WBA in the mortar and concrete mixes; and finally (4) to identify the market opportunities and readiness for reuse of a new potential supplementary cementitious material (SCM).

2. Wood biomass ash characterization

There are several factors that affect the quality and quantity of WBA obtained by using wood biomass in power plants. Based on [22], these factors can be divided into three main groups as shown in **Table 1**. According to **Table 1** and a detailed review of the literature, it is necessary to highlight (1) the type of biomass used for power generation, (2) the plant technology used, (3) the combustion temperature, (4) the location of WBA collection, and (5) the conditions of WBA storage. In the following, the influence of these parameters on the characterization of WBA is discussed in detail.

One of the factors that could have an influence on the properties of WBA is the area of biomass cultivation and the condition and type of soil [24], but this influence is not very large. From the tertiary group of influences, it appears that ash from wood

Group of influence	Formation process	Influence	Time of formation	References
Primary	Natural	Biomass—type Biomass cultivation area soil condition and type combustion technology	Before and during plant growing, and cutting	[13, 15, 22–29]
Secondary	Anthropogenic (technogenic)	Temperature of combustion location of WBA collecting	During combustion	[13, 15, 22, 23, 25–30]
Tertiary	Natural	Disposal and transportation	During disposal and transportation of WBA	[22, 26]

Table 1.
Groups of influence contributing to the chemical composition of WBA (adapted from Vassilev et al. [22]).

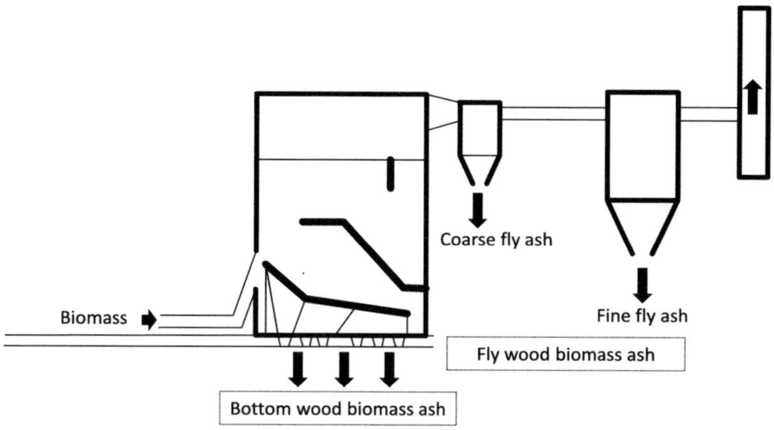

Figure 1.
WBA classification based on WBA collection in power plants (adapted from Obernberger et al. [35] and Eijk et al. [36]).

biomass undergoes certain chemical processes during its collection and disposal. The plant technology, i.e., the technology of wood biomass combustion in the power plants, as one of the factors affecting the physical and chemical properties of the produced WBA, is divided into grate combustors, fluidized bed combustors, and pulverized fuel combustors [10]. Three different types of WBA can be generated in a power plant [26, 31–34]: bottom ash (1) collected at the bottom of the chamber (bottom WBA); fly ash, which may be a relatively coarse fraction, (2) collected from cyclones or boilers; and a relatively fine fraction of fly ash, and (3) collected from electrostatic precipitators and bag filters (**Figure 1**). In some power plants bottom ash and fly ash are collected in one container as mixed WBA.

In grate combustion technology, 60–90% of the WBA from the bottom of the furnace is formed on the grate, while in fluidized bed combustion, fly WBA is the dominant ash formed [37–39]. The particles from the bottom of the furnace are larger than the fly WBA [7, 40]. This can be observed from **Figure 2**, which shows the particle size distribution of WBAs [41] and cement, and the grading curve of the bottom WBAs and aggregate (particle size 0–4 and 4–8 mm) per the combustion technology. The authors [41] proposed a cumulative grading curve for all particle sizes of the bottom WBAs as they were sieved through a 1 mm sieve to eliminate impurities and larger fractions. Grate combustion has a higher influence on the particle size distribution of the fly bottom WBAs where a generally large diversity of granulometric curve of bottom WBA compared to aggregate can be seen in **Figure 2**. Grate-fired systems are designed to cope with a degree of the sintering and partial fusion of the ash on the grate. Poor fuel distribution, relatively poor air distribution, and local high temperature on the grate can lead to the formation of relatively large ash agglomerates that reduce combustion efficiency [42]. This occurrence could lead to larger particles of the WBA sample [43]. It can also be inferred from **Figure 2** that the particles of bottom WBA from fluidized bed combustion technology and pulverized fuel combustors are smaller than those of bottom WBA from grate combustion power plants.

The WBA produced at the bottom of the combustion chamber is often mixed with mineral impurities such as sand, stones, and soil contained in the biomass, as well as sintered ash particles. In addition to the coarse and fine fraction of the fly WBA inside the plant, smoke dust of the finest fraction is also emitted together with

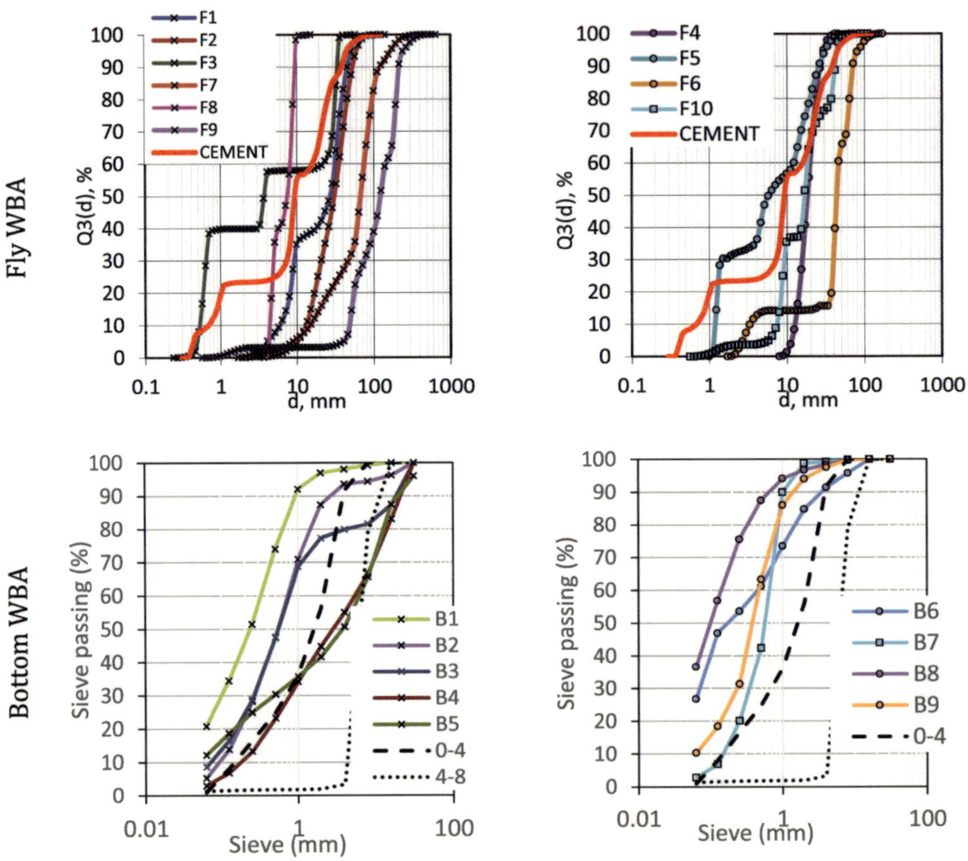

Figure 2.
Particle size distribution of fly WBA (F) (published in Carević et al. [41]) and bottom WBA (B) compared to the different combustion technologies used (x: grate combustion; o: pulverized fuel combustors; and □: fluidized bed combustors).

the flue gases [35]. In fluidized bed combustion, the lower WBA consists of sand particles, mainly quartz, added during combustion, inorganic components (soil or small stones), and unburned biomass fraction [32, 38]. Modern solutions of the combustion system on the grate may include a continuously moving and water-cooled grate, which consequently means that wet ash removal is performed from the bottom of the furnace [44]. In view of the above, it is very important to know what type of technology is used and at what location in the power plant the WBA is collected to further characterize the WBA. The choice of plant technology has a significant impact on the chemical composition of the WBA: fluidized-bed technology uses additives such as quartz sand as bed material, which can have a positive impact on the chemical composition of the WBA and contributes to a high SiO2 content compared to other combustion technologies [10, 45, 46]. The morphology of WBA (**Figure 3**) mostly showed non-uniform structure, inhomogeneous particle surface, and particles with different shapes, which could lead to higher water absorption and have a corresponding negative effect on the workability of the cement composites [28, 47, 48].

Figure 4 compares the chemical composition of 46 samples of different ash types collected from the power plants: fly, bottom ash, and mixed ash. WBA is expected to contain a higher proportion of CaO than pozzolanic oxide, the sum of SiO_2, Al_2O_3,

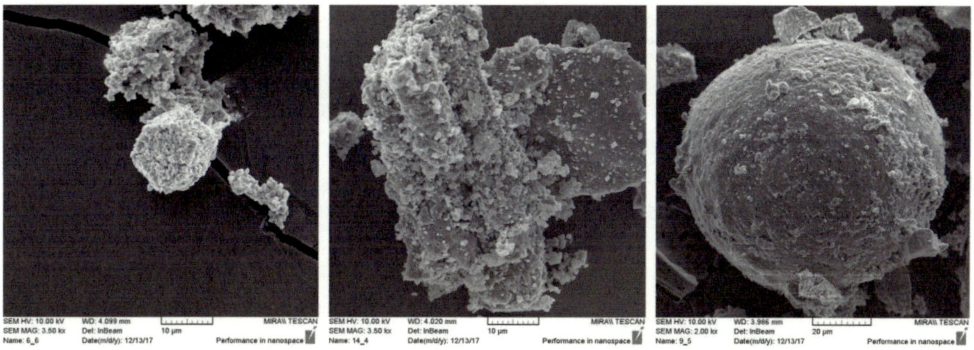

Figure 3.
Morphology of the WBA.

and Fe_2O_3 (median values for CaO were 48.61% compared to 13.49% for pozzolanic oxide for all WBA samples), indicating lower pozzolanic activity and pronounced hydraulic activity [23]. Higher alkali levels (K_2O and Na_2O) can also be observed,

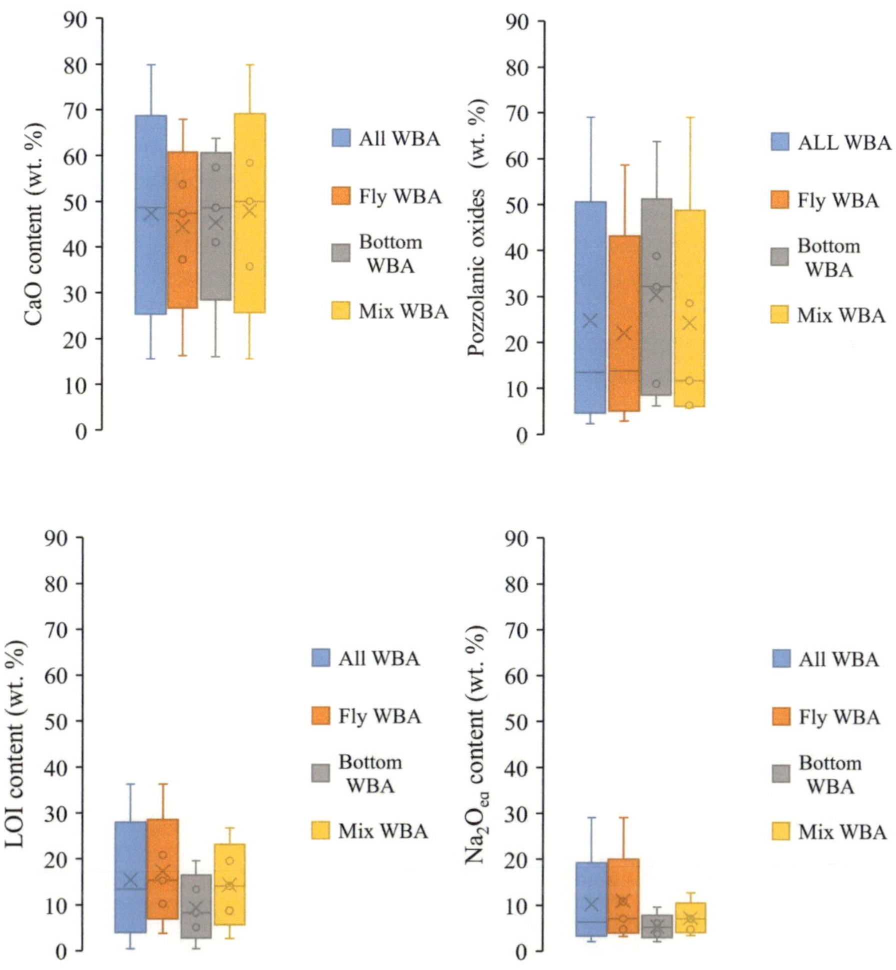

Figure 4.
Boxplots of chemical parameters from the WBA database (N = 46) by WBA type [41, 46].

which may be reflected in the mechanical and durability properties of cement composites with WBA [49]. This is particularly pronounced in the fly WBA samples. Alkali is an integral part of the characterization of untreated biomass and in woody biomass, alkalis are bound to the organic structure, so their higher content in WBA was expected. High alkali content can cause high porosity in the hardened cement matrix, resulting in lower strength and durability [15, 23, 25]. Since the CaO content is higher in all WBA specimens, free CaO is expected, a significant amount of which can cause volume instability (swelling) during the hydration process and the formation of cracks [33, 50, 51]. As shown in **Figure 4**, the fly WBA showed the highest median LOI value (15.3 wt.%) which is significantly higher than the maximum value allowed by EN 450-1 (Category C < 9 wt.%) [20]. Unburnt carbon and inorganic compounds can significantly affect the properties of concrete (workability, setting time, mechanical properties) [52].

3. Technical feasibility and valorization of WBA use as supplementary cementitious material

A review of the available literature leads to the conclusion that the application of WBA significantly depends on its properties, which depend primarily on the characteristics of the biomass used, i.e., the type of biomass, the plant technology, the combustion temperature and the location of ash collection and storage. For this reason, the chemical composition causes variation in the properties of the tested cement composites. The use of WBA in the cement composites leads to an increase in water demand, which may be related to the morphology of WBA (irregular particle shape and fineness), free CaO and alkali content, and LOI values [43, 53]. According to [23], increasing the content of WBA as a cement replacement resulted in decreased workability of cement pastes, while water treatment (washing of WBA) had a positive effect on the workability of cement mixtures due to physical modification: treatment by washing decreased the average ash particle size, porosity, and specific surface area of WBA. Increasing the proportion of WBA in mortar mixes prolonged the setting time, while cement pastes with a WBA content of 15% should be dimensionally stable despite the high content of CaO minerals in WBA (free CaO and MgO) [43]. The effect of WBA on the hydration of binders was studied by monitoring the heat release with isothermal calorimetry, where the induction period is prolonged by the addition of WBA regardless of the type and chemical properties of WBA [54]. Mixtures with WBA exhibit a slower increase in strength. However, with time the compressive strength increases so that after 28 days the compressive strength of the samples with 5 and 10% WBA is equal to or higher than that of the reference samples without ash (**Figure 5**). The effects of higher proportions of WBA on compressive strength have been shown to be unfavorable in studies. Therefore, it is not recommended to increase the proportion of WBA in structural concrete to more than 20% [16, 55, 56].

In addition to the mechanical properties of cement composites with different proportions of WBA, tests of durability properties are also important. Capillary absorption is defined as the transport of fluids due to surface tension that occurs in capillary pores. Capillary pores are the main pathway through which water and other aggressive substances penetrate cementitious composites and cause permanent problems. Therefore, capillary absorption testing is often used as one of the tests and quality assessments of cementitious composites to select a suitable concrete/mortar for the construction of structural elements exposed to liquids containing aggressive substances (usually

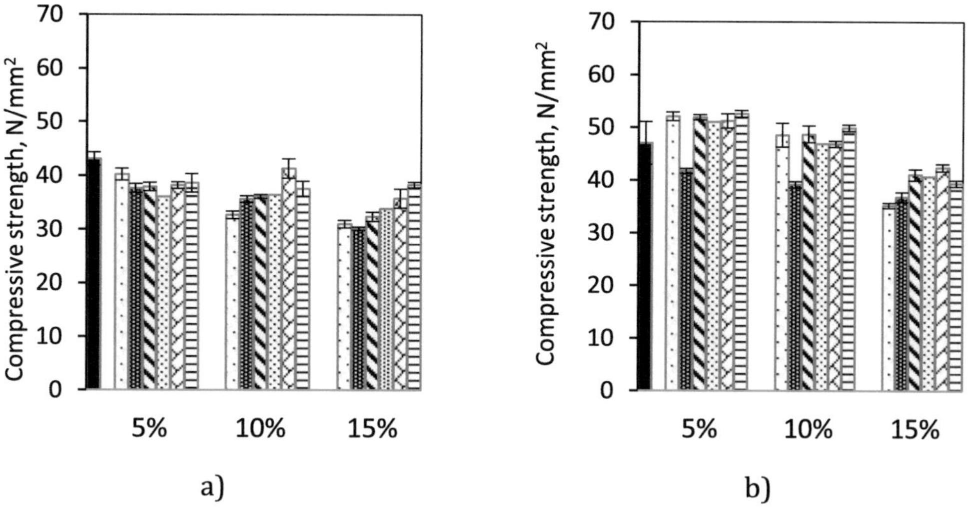

Figure 5.
Compressive strength: (a) after 7 days; and (b) after 28 days [43].

chloride or sulfate) during wetting/drying cycles. In studies [13, 43] that investigated the absorption of concrete with different proportions of WBA, an increase in absorption with WBA content was observed (an average increase in capillary absorption of up to 2.27% for mixes with 15% WBA content compared to the reference mix). The reason for the correlation between lower compressive strength and lower resistance to capillary absorption is the negative influence of the porous structure on these properties of the concrete [57]. The results of gas permeability showed the same trend as the capillary absorption coefficient: on average, the gas permeability of mortars with a WBA content of 5% decreased by 3.1%, while the cement replacement with 10 and 15% WBA increased by 12.41 and 24.31% compared to the reference mortar [58]. The researchers [59] suggested the addition of silica fume and they found that after 28 days, the gas permeability of mortar samples with 8% WBA and 7.5% silica fume decreased by

Property	**Standard**	**Influence**
Humidity	HRN EN 1097-5	Self-hardening
Visual examination	Visual examination	Durability properties: no resistance to freezing and thawing cycles (e.g., pieces of wood, etc.)
Grading	HRN EN 12620 or HRN EN 933-10	Defines the type of use (aggregate or mineral admixture)
LOI content	HRN EN 196-2	Setting time, water requirement, durability properties
SO_3 content	HRN EN 196-2	Durability properties, corrosion, volume instability
Na_2O_{eq} content	HRN EN 196-2	Alkali-aggregate reaction
MgO content	HRN EN 196-2	Volume instability (swelling, cracking)
Free CaO content	HRN EN 196-2	
Cl^- content	HRN EN 1744-1 or HRN EN 196-2	Corrosion

Table 2.
Recommended WBA properties that to be checked before use in concrete production [60].

6.6%. Chlorides are one of the main causes of corrosion and deterioration of reinforced concrete structures. Based on the results presented in [43, 58], a decrease in the chloride diffusion coefficient can be seen for all mixtures with fly WBA, except for the sample with one type of WBA, which is related to the WBA particle size.

To make WBA a valuable resource for the construction industry, technical requirements must be established. The purpose of these requirements is to enable concrete producers to ensure consistent quality and predictable behavior of the product without adverse effects on the durability and mechanical properties of the concrete [18]. Therefore, the overall effect of individual physical and chemical properties of the WBAs used on the mechanical properties and durability of cement composites was determined by evaluating the individual effects of the physical and chemical properties relative to the reference mix [58]. This study was carried out to provide concrete producers with a preliminary recommendation on the main WBA properties to be checked during reuse (**Table 2**).

4. Ecological feasibility of using WBA as supplementary cementitious material

In the construction sector, the use of industrial by-products as substitutes for natural raw materials is encouraged. When using alternative materials obtained as by-products from other industries, it is necessary to consider the environmental factor. One of the basic requirements for construction includes "hygiene, health, and environment" under the European regulation for construction products [61]. The assessment of the environmental impact of cement-based construction products is usually based on the determination of leaching, i.e. the potential release of ingredients such as trace elements (heavy metals) or organic compounds into the environment when the products come into direct contact with water or soil. The estimation of pollutant release can be done by standard short-term leaching tests and long-term tests [62, 63]. The Technical Committee of CEN TC 351 has developed laboratory tests to check the leaching of hazardous substances into nature using demineralized water as a leaching agent [63].

The authors [25, 41, 64] found that the concentration of heavy metals such as Zn, Cd, Pb, and Hg is higher in fly WBA samples than in bottom samples. Therefore, the leaching/stabilization behavior of cementitious composites prepared with fly WBA

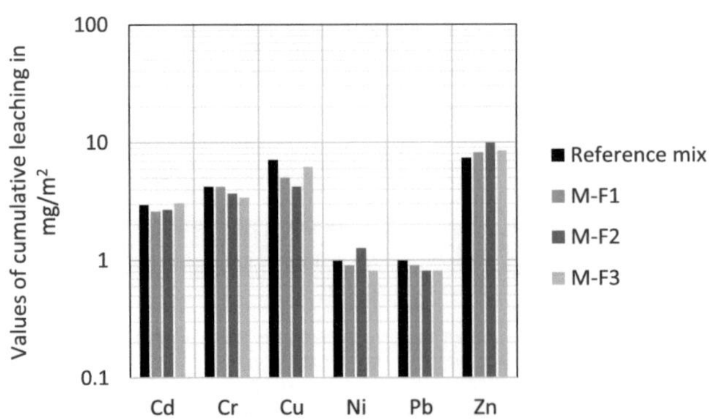

Figure 6.
Values of cumulative leaching in mg/m² for different metals (M-Fi-mortar mix with 15% of fly WBA) [65].

should be analyzed. According to the leaching results obtained by the author [65] for the observed heavy metals (Zn, Cd, CR, Cu, Ni, Pb) on monolithic specimens using 3 types of fly WBA (**Figure 6**), it was concluded that the leaching of heavy metals was acceptable, i.e., less than the limits according to the Dutch guidelines of the Soil Quality Ordinance [66] (limits for finished building materials according to the Soil Quality Ordinance for Cd: 3.8 mg/m^2; Cr: 120 mg/m^2; Cu: 98 mg/m^2; Ni: 81 mg/m^2; Pb: 400 mg/m^2; Zn: 800 mg/m^2). The same was confirmed by the authors [55, 67] when using ash from the combustion of pure wood biomass. This is explained by the ability of the cement matrix to physically and chemically bind contaminated elements (heavy metals) within the hydrate structure [68].

5. Market readiness of the WBA use as supplementary cementitious material

In order to explore the market readiness and capacity for using WBA as SCM in the concrete industry, a questionnaire was conducted among 11 concrete producers (SMEs) from Croatia with an approximate annual concrete production of at least 12,000 m3 to a maximum of 300,000 m3. The purpose of the questionnaire was to conduct a qualitative study of concrete and cement production and the views of SMEs on the reuse of WBA in their plants. According to the results of the survey, the most common strength classes in concrete production are C25/30 and C30/37 (each represented by 91%), followed by 64% of concrete use of strength classes C20/25, C35/45, and C40/50 (**Figure 7a**). The compressive strength of concrete is a common and important property in the design of concrete structures. In addition to compressive strength as a basic property of concrete,

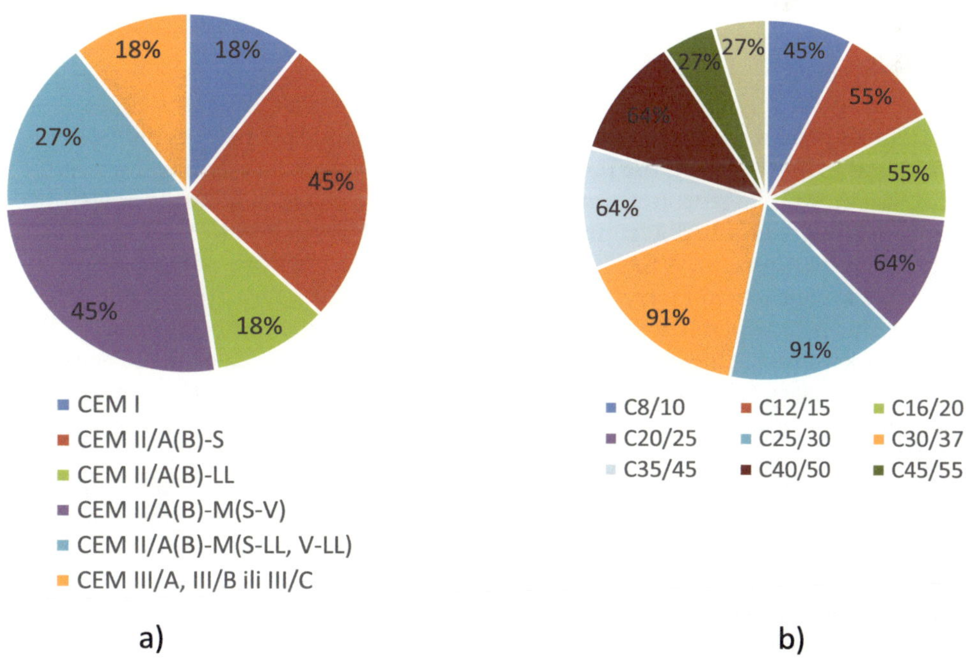

Figure 7.
(a) Concrete production share with respect to the compressive strength class; and (b) cement type share in the concrete production.

all respondents indicate water permeability. Other main properties most tested on hardened concrete are freeze-thaw resistance with or without de-icing salt (82%), wear resistance (82%), and chemical resistance (73%).

The average amount of cement used in concrete ranges from 295 to 340 kg per 1 m3 of concrete. 27% of the respondents use mineral admixtures in the production of concrete namely silica fume, coal fly ash, and metakaolin. The most common types of cement used in concrete production are shown in **Figure 7b** (multiple answers were possible): of the 15 types of cement on the market, blended cements are the most common: CEM II /A(B)-M(S-V) and CEM II /A(B)-S with 45% of use, CEM II /A(B)-M(S-LL, V-LL) with 27%, CEM II /A(B)-LL with 18% and CEM III /A(B, C), with 18%. Blended cements contain waste products as SCMs to replace clinker as the main source of CO_2 emissions in concrete production [69]. By using SCMs could result in CO^2 reduction of about 400 million tons per year [70]. These can be easily replicated as a possible circular solution for WBA management, which was recognized by concrete producers: 55% of respondents are familiar with the problem of WBA management and 91% of them are interested in using WBA in their plants. Concrete producers emphasized ensuring a consistent chemical and physical WBA quality to ensure the quality of the concrete produced.

Considering the current quantities of WBA in Croatia (25,414 tons per year [3]) and the data from the questionnaire analysis of cement and concrete production, all WBA can be used in cement and concrete production with regular quality control. For example, if 10% of cement is replaced by WBA, it is possible to reuse 1500 t of WBA per year in only one concrete plant with an average production of 50,000 m^3 concrete/year. This means that in the four concrete plants the whole amount of the finer WBA can be used, while the coarser fraction can be used as a substitute for the fine fraction of aggregates (sand).

6. Conclusions

According to all observed trends, waste ash from wood biomass combustion is expected to increase and the regulatory framework for waste management is becoming more stringent. In the design and planning phase of biomass power plants, it is important to determine the amounts of WBA generated and to find sustainable solutions for WBA management during the life cycle of the power plant. In the concrete industry, there is a high potential for substitution of certain components by adequate alternative materials, and in that context, the use of WBA has been examined. This paper presents comprehensive research of the properties of WBA necessary for its use as SCM in concrete. Based on the review of existing research and results of experimental testing shown in the paper, it can be expected that WBA reduces the workability of the cement composites, noting that cement replacement up to 10% has no significant effect on the consistency. This is probably due to the morphology of WBA, high alkali content, and LOI values. Increased setting time can also be expected, although results vary depending on the type of WBA used. For WBAs with a high CaO content, it is necessary to check the free CaO as it may affect the volume stability and durability properties of the cement composites. The comparison of the compressive strength of mortars and concretes shows a significant variability and influence of the different WBAs used on the compressive strength after 28 days with a tendency to decrease the compressive strength with a higher proportion of WBA.

The main logistical and long-term challenges that need to be considered when establishing an industrial symbiosis for sustainable WBA management are to ensure consistent WBA quality (proper storage and transportation of WBA from power suppliers to concrete producers); different types of WBA collection in power plants (e.g. mixing with water), which could affect WBA properties (self-hardening) and the need for additional pre-treatment of some WBA samples (e.g., grinding and/or screening) due to inefficient combustion of wood biomass or due to wood impurities, which could negatively affect durability properties.

Acknowledgements

The results given in this chapter were conducted under two projects: Transformation of Wood Biomass Ash into Resilient Construction Composites-TAREC[2] (IP-2016-06-7701) funded by the Croatian Science Foundation and the project Development of innovative construction products with biomass ash financed by European structural and investment funds for a 2014–2020 financial period (grant number KK.01.2.1.01.0049).

Conflict of interest

The authors declare no conflict of interest.

Author details

Nina Štirmer* and Ivana Carević
Faculty of Civil Engineering, University of Zagreb, Zagreb, Croatia

*Address all correspondence to: nina.stirmer@grad.unizg.hr

References

[1] Bioenergy Europe. Bioenergy Europe and the European Pellet Council, Brussels; 2018

[2] IEA Bioenergy. Options for increased use of ash from biomass combustion and co-firing. IEA Bioenergy. 2018. Available from: https://www.ieabioenergy.com/wp-content/uploads/2019/02/IEA-Bioenergy-Ash-management-report-revision-5-november.pdf

[3] Milovanović B, Štirmer N, Carević I, Baričević A. Wood biomass ash as a raw material in concrete industry. Građevinar. 2019;**71**:505-514. DOI: 10.14256/JCE.2546.2018

[4] Obernberger I, Supancic K. Possibilities of ash utilisation from biomass combustion plants. In: ETA-Renewable Energies, editor. Proceedings of the 17th European Biomass Conference & Exhibition. Hamburg: ETA-Renewable Energies; 2009

[5] Freire M, Lopes H, Tarelho LAC. Critical aspects of biomass ashes utilization in soils: Composition, leachability, PAH and PCDD/F. Waste Management. 2015;**46**:304-315. DOI: 10.1016/j.wasman.2015.08.036

[6] Maresca A, Hyks J, Astrup TF. Recirculation of biomass ashes onto forest soils: ash composition, mineralogy and leaching properties. Waste Management. 2017;**70**:127-138. DOI: 10.1016/j.wasman.2017.09.008

[7] Melotti R, Santagata E, Bassani M, Salvo M, Rizzo S. A preliminary investigation into the physical and chemical properties of biomass ashes used as aggregate fillers for bituminous mixtures. Waste Management. 2013;**33**(9):1906-1917. DOI: 10.1016/j.wasman.2013.05.015

[8] Pesonen J, Kuokkanen T, Rautio P, Lassi U. Bioavailability of nutrients and harmful elements in ash fertilizers: Effect of granulation. Biomass and Bioenergy. 2017;**100**:92-97. DOI: 10.1016/j.biombioe.2017.03.019

[9] Milovanović B. Types and quantities of wood biomass ash, 1st workshop "Transformation of Wood Biomass Ash into Resilient Construction Composites". Croatian Chamber of Commerce. 2017. Available from: https://www.bib.irb.hr/pretraga/?operators=and|Milovanovi%C4%87,%20Bojan%20(24088)|text|profile&year=2017

[10] van Loo S, Koppejan J. The Handbook of Biomass Combustion and Co-firing. London: Earthscan; 2012. p. 465

[11] Bohrn G, Stampfer K. Untreated wood ash as a structural stabilizing material in forest roads. Croatian Journal of Forest Engineering. 2001;**35**(1):81-90

[12] Aprianti E, Shafigh P, Bahri S, Farahani JN. Supplementary cementitious materials origin from agricultural wastes – A review. Construction and Building Materials. 2015;**74**:176-187. DOI: 10.1016/j.conbuildmat.2014.10.010

[13] Sashidhar C, Sudarsana RH. Durability studies on concrete with wood ash additive. In: 35th Conference on Our World in Concrete & Structures. Singapore: CI-PREMIER PTE LTD; 2010

[14] European Commission. The European Green Deal, Communication from the Commission, COM(2019) 640 final. Brussels, Belgium: European Commission; 2019

[15] Ottosen LM, Hansen EØ, Jensen PE, Kirkelund GM, Golterman P. Wood ash used as partly sand and/or cement replacement in mortar. International Journal of Sustainable Development and Planning. 2016;**11**(5):781-791. DOI: 10.2495/SDP-V11-N5-781-791

[16] Sklivaniti V, Tsakiridis PE, Katsiotis NS, Velissariou D, Pistofidis N, Papageorgiou D, et al. Valorisation of woody biomass bottom ash in Portland cement: A characterization and hydration study. Journal of Environmental Chemical Engineering. 2017;**5**(1):205-213. DOI: 10.1016/j.jece.2016.11.042

[17] Rissanen J, Giosué C, Ohenoja K, Kinnunen P, Marcellini M, Letizia M, et al. The effect of peat and wood fly ash on the porosity of mortar. Construction and Building Materials. 2019;**223**:421-430. DOI: 10.1016/j.conbuildmat.2019.06.228

[18] Ondrasek G, Bubalo KM, Carević I, Štirmer N, Stipičević S, Udiković-Kolić N, et al. Bioashes and their potential for reuse to sustain ecosystem services and underpin circular economy. Renewable and Sustainable Energy Reviews. 2021;**151**(July):111540. DOI: 10.1016/j.rser.2021.111540

[19] Ondrasek G, Kranjčec F, Filipović L, Filipović V, Bubalo KM, Badovinac IJ, et al. Biomass bottom ash & dolomite similarly ameliorate an acidic low-nutrient soil, improve phytonutrition and growth, but increase Cd accumulation in radish. Science of the Total Environmental. 2021;**753**:141902. DOI: 10.1016/j.scitotenv.2020.141902

[20] The European Committee for Standardization. Fly ash for concrete—Part 1: Definition, specifications and conformity criteria (EN 450-1:2012). CEN; 2012

[21] ASTM International. ASTM C 618 Standard Specification for Coal Fly Ash and Raw or Calcined Natural Pozzolan for Use. West Conshohocken, PA: ASTM International; 2010. pp. 3-6

[22] Vassilev SV, Baxter D, Andersen LK, Vassileva CG. An overview of the composition and application of biomass ash. Part 1. Phase-mineral and chemical composition and classification. Fuel. 2013;**105**:40-76. DOI: 10.1016/j.fuel.2012.09.041

[23] Berra M, Mangialardi T, Paolini AE. Reuse of woody biomass fly ash in cement-based materials. Construction and Building Materials. 2015;**76**:286-296. DOI: 10.1016/j.conbuildmat.2014.11.052

[24] Nagrockienė D, Daugėla A. Investigation into the properties of concrete modified with biomass combustion fly ash. Construction and Building Materials. 2018;**174**:369-375. DOI: 10.1016/j.conbuildmat.2018.04.125

[25] Rajamma R, Ball RJ, Tarelho LAC, Allen GC, Labrincha JA, Ferreira VM. Characterisation and use of biomass fly ash in cement-based materials. Journal of Hazardous Materials. 2009;**172**(2-3): 1049-1060. DOI: 10.1016/j.jhazmat.2009.07.109

[26] Ukrainczyk N, Vrbos N, Koenders EAB. Reuse of woody biomass ash waste in cementitious materials. Chemical and Biochemical Engineering Quarterly. 2016;**30**(2):137-148. DOI: 10.15255/CABEQ.2015.2231

[27] Cheah CB, Ramli M. The implementation of wood waste ash as a partial cement replacement material in the production of structural grade concrete and mortar: An overview. Resources, Conservation Recycling. 2011;**55**(7):669-685. DOI: 10.1016/j.resconrec.2011.02.002

[28] Naik TR, Kraus RN, McCormick S. Recycling of Wood Ash in Cement-Based

Construction Materials. Canada: Richmond; 2001

[29] Chowdhury S, Mishra M, Suganya O. The incorporation of wood waste ash as a partial cement replacement material for making structural grade concrete: An overview. Ain Shams Engineering Journal. 2015;**6**(2):429-437. DOI: 10.1016/j.asej.2014.11.005

[30] Etiégni L, Campbell AG. Physical and chemical characteristics of wood ash. Bioresource Technology. 1991;**37**(2):173-178. DOI: 10.1016/0960-8524(91)90207-Z

[31] Faaij AP. Biomass combustion. Encyclopedia of Energy. 2004;**I**:175-191. DOI: 10.1016/B0-12-176480-X/00355-7

[32] Vos J. Biomass energy for heating and hot water supply in Belarus-Best Practice Guidelines. Part A: Biomass Combustion. UNDP/GEF; 2005:125

[33] Chatterji S. Mechanism of expansion of concrete due to the presence of dead-burnt CaO and MgO. Cement and Concrete Research. 1995;**25**(1):51-56. DOI: 10.1016/0008-8846(94)00111-B

[34] Zagvozda M, Dimter S, Rukavina T, Grubeša NI. Possibilities of bioash application in road building. Građevinar. 2018;**70**(5):393-402. DOI: 10.14256/JCE.2074.2017

[35] Obernberger I, Biedermann F, Widmann W, Riedl R. Concentrations of inorganic elements in biomass fuels and recovery in the different ash fractions. Biomass and Bioenergy. 1997;**12**(3):211-224. DOI: 10.1016/S0961-9534(96)00051-7

[36] Eijk RJ, Supancic K, Obernberger I. Options for increased utilization of ash from biomass combustion and co-firing, 30102040-PGR/R&E 11-2142. IEA Bioenergy Task. 2012;**32**. Available from: https://task32.ieabioenergy.com/wp-content/uploads/sites/24/2017/03/Ash_Utilization_KEMA.pdf

[37] Obernberger I, Fluch J, Brunner T. Comparative characterization of high temperature aerosols in waste wood fired fixed-bed and fluidized-bed combustion systems. In: 17th European Biomass Conference & Exhibition. Hamburg: ETA-Renewable Energies; 2009

[38] Modolo RCE, Ferreira VM, Tarelho LA, Labrincha JA, Senff L, Silva L. Mortar formulations with bottom ash from biomass combustion. Construction and Building Materials. 2013;**45**:275-281. DOI: 10.1016/j.conbuildmat.2013.03.093

[39] Danraka MN, Aziz FNAA, Jaafar MS. Application of wood waste ash in conrete making: Revisited. In: GCEC 2017: Proceedings of the 1st Global Civil Engineering Conference. Kuala Lumpur, Malaysia: Springer; 2017. DOI: 10.1007/978-981-10-8016-6

[40] Garcia ML, Sousa-Coutinho J. Strength and durability of cement with forest waste bottom ash. Construction and Building Materials. 2013;**41**:897-910. DOI: 10.1016/j.conbuildmat.2012.11.081

[41] Carević I, Serdar M, Štirmer N, Ukrainczyk N. Preliminary screening of wood biomass ashes for partial resources replacements in cementitious materials. Journal of Cleaner Production. 2019;**229**:1045-1064. DOI: 10.1016/j.jclepro.2019.04.321

[42] Supancic K, Obernberger I, Kienzl N, Arich A. Conversion and leaching characteristics of biomass ashes during outdoor storage—Results of laboratory tests. Biomass and Bioenergy. 2014;**61**:211-226. DOI: 10.1016/j.biombioe.2013.12.014

[43] Carević I, Baričević A, Štirmer N, Bajto ŠJ. Correlation between physical and chemical properties of wood biomass ash and cement composites performances. Construction and Building Materials. 2020;**256**:119450. DOI: 10.1016/j.conbuildmat.2020.119450

[44] Lončar D, Krajačić G, Vujanović M. Podrška developerima—primjeri najbolje prakse za kogeneraciju na drvnu biomasu. Zagreb; 2009

[45] Rissanen J, Ohenoja K, Kinnunen P, Romagnoli M, Illikainen M. Milling of peat-wood fly ash: Effect on water demand of mortar and rheology of cement paste. Construction and Building Materials. 2018;**180**:143-153. DOI: 10.1016/j.conbuildmat.2018.05.014

[46] Sigvardsen NM, Kirkelund GM, Jensen PE, Geiker MR, Ottosen LM. Impact of production parameters on physiochemical characteristics of wood ash for possible utilisation in cement-based materials. Resources, Conservation Recycling. 2019;**145**(Nov):230-240. DOI: 10.1016/j.resconrec.2019.02.034

[47] Naik TR, Kraus RN, Kumar R. Wood Ash: A New Source of Pozzolanic Material, Vol. 435, Report No. CBU-2001-10. 2001. Available from: https://www4.uwm.edu/cbu/Papers/2001CBUReports/CBU2001-11.pdf [Accessed: December 12, 2019]

[48] Wang S, Miller A, Llamazos E, Fonseca F, Baxter L. Biomass fly ash in concrete: Mixture proportioning and mechanical properties. Fuel. 2008;**87**(3):365-371. DOI: 10.1016/j.fuel.2007.05.026

[49] Juenger MCG, Siddique R. Recent advances in understanding the role of supplementary cementitious materials in concrete. Cement and Concrete Research. 2015;**78**:71-80. DOI: 10.1016/j.cemconres.2015.03.018

[50] Arjunan P, Kumar A. Rapid techniques for determination of free lime and free magnesia in cement clinker and portlandite in hydrates. Cement and Concrete Research. 1994;**24**(2):343-352. DOI: 10.1016/0008-8846(94)90061-2

[51] Lamond JF, Pielert JH, editors. Significance of Tests and Properties of Concrete and Concrete-Making Materials, STP 169D. West Conshohocken, PA: ASTM International; 2006. 647

[52] Atiş CD. Strength properties of high-volume fly ash roller compacted and workable concrete, and influence of curing condition. Cement and Concrete Research. 2005;**35**(6):1112-1121. DOI: 10.1016/j.cemconres.2004.07.037

[53] Nawaz A, Julnipitawong P, Krammart P, Tangtermsirikul S. Effect and limitation of free lime content in cement-fly ash mixtures. Construction and Building Materials. 2016;**102**:515-530. DOI: 10.1016/j.conbuildmat.2015.10.174

[54] Šantek BJ, Štirmer N, Cerković S, Carević I, Kostanić JK. Pilot scale production of precast concrete elements with wood biomass ash. Materials (Basel). 2021;**14**(21):6578. DOI: 10.3390/ma14216578

[55] Tosti L, van Zomeren A, Pels JR, Comans RNJ. Technical and environmental performance of lower carbon footprint cement mortars containing biomass fly ash as a secondary cementitious material. Resources, Conservation Recycling. 2018;**134**(Jan):25-33. DOI: 10.1016/j.resconrec.2018.03.004

[56] Medina JM, Sáez del Bosque IF, Frías M, Sánchez de Rojas MI, Medina C. Durability of new blended cements addition with recycled biomass bottom ASH from electric power plants.

Construction and Building Materials. 2019;**225**:429-440. DOI: 10.1016/j.conbuildmat.2019.07.176

[57] Snellings R, Elsen J, Mertens G. Supplementary cementitious materials. Reviews in Mineralogy and Geochemistry. 2012;**74**(Dec):211-278. DOI: 10.2138/rmg.2012.74.6

[58] Carević I. Characterization of cement composites with fly ash from wood biomass. Zagreb: University of Zagreb, Faculty of Civil Engineering; 2020

[59] Cheah CB, Ramli M. The fluid transport properties of HCWA – DSF hybrid supplementary binder mortar. Composites: Part B. 2014;**56**:681-690. DOI: 10.1016/j.compositesb.2013.09.021

[60] University of Zagreb Faculty of Civil Engineering. Broshure "Transformation of Wood Biomass Ash into Resilient Construction Composites" (in Croatian), 2020

[61] EU Office. Regulation of the European Parliament and of the Council of 9 March 2011 laying down harmonised conditions for the marketing of construction products and repealing Council Directive 89/106/EEC. Official Journal of the European Union. 2011;**305**:43-88

[62] Tiwari MK, Bajpai S, Dewangan UK, Tamrakar RK. Suitability of leaching test methods for fly ash and slag: A review. Journal of Radiation Research and Applied Sciences. 2015;**8**(4):523-537. DOI: 10.1016/j.jrras.2015.06.003

[63] Kosson DS, Sloot HA, Sanchez F, Garrabrants AC. An integrated framework for evaluating leaching in waste management and utilization of secondary materials. Environmental Engineering Science. 2002;**19**(3):159-204

[64] Steenari BM, Lindqvist O. Stabilisation of biofuel ashes for recycling to forest soil. Biomass and Bioenergy. 1997;**13**(1-2):39-50. DOI: 10.1016/S0961-9534(97)00024-X

[65] Carević I, Štirmer N, Trkmić M, Jurić KK. Leaching characteristics of wood biomass fly ash cement composites. Applied Sciences. 2020;**10**(23):1-17. DOI: 10.3390/app10238704

[66] Ministry of Infrastructure and Water Management Netherland. Soil Quality Regulation. 2006. pp. 1-170

[67] Berra M, Paolini AE, Mangialardi T. Environmental quality of hardened wood fly ash-cement mixtures. Proceedings of the Institution of Civil Engineers: Waste Resource Management. 2016;**169**(1):3-13. DOI: 10.1680/warm.15.00003

[68] Grauw A, Marion A, Lane M. Study of the leaching behaviour of paving concretes : Quantification of heavy metal content in leachates issued from tank test using demineralized water. Cement and Concrete Research. 2005;**35**:951-957. DOI: 10.1016/j.cemconres.2004.06.014

[69] García-Segura T, Yepes V, Alcalá J. Life cycle greenhouse gas emissions of blended cement concrete including carbonation and durability. International Journal of Life Cycle Assessment. 2014;**19**(1):3-12. DOI: 10.1007/s11367-013-0614-0

[70] Environment UN, Scrivener KL, John VM, Gartner EM. Eco-efficient cements : Potential economically viable solutions for a low-CO2 cement-based materials industry. Cement and Concrete Research. 2018;**114**:2-26. DOI: 10.1016/j.cemconres.2018.03.015

Chapter 7

Peat as a Potential Biomass to Remove Azo Dyes in Packed Biofilters

Rosa Angélica Guillén, Cristina Lizama-Bahena, Luis Gerardo Trevino-Quintanilla, Martin Barragan-Trinidad, Victoria Bustos and Gabriela Moeller-Chavez

Abstract

Azo dyes represent a broad group of environmental pollutants that comprise between 60 and 70% of all the dyes and pigments used. The conventional processes are not efficient in treating effluents from the textile industry. Biofiltration emerges as an unconventional, easy-to-use, effective, and low-cost technology for the treatment of textile effluents. Biofiltration uses microbial consortia that form a biofilm on a filter medium. Peat is an organic matter with the ability to retain high moisture content and represents an attractive option to treat these effluents due to its high porosity, sorption capacity, availability, and low cost. The packing materials used were: peat as an organic biomass, perlite as an inorganic material, and a mixture of peat and perlite. Sorption processes in the biofilter peat-packed material and perlite are discussed dealing with its treatment capacity and as potential removers of azo dyes, their advantages and disadvantages compared with other traditional methods, and a review of operating parameters and design criteria that allow its large-scale application as a possible nonconventional treatment technology. The biofilter with the highest removal capacity was the peat-perlite mixture that achieved a 91% for the organic matter (measured as COD), and a 92% for the color removal (Direct blue 2 dye). with a retention time of 1.18 days.

Keywords: azo dyes, biofiltration, peat, perlite, sorption, biomass

1. Introduction

The textile industry is one of the most important worldwide; however, the large number of chemical compounds used in the dyeing and washing process cause its wastewater discharges to have a high content of organic and inorganic compounds that are toxic to the environment [1].

The dyes used by the textile industries contain different structures, which are in greater abundance: the acidic, basic, disperse dyes, azo, basic, anthraquinones, and metal-complex dyes [1]. Currently, the exact number of colorants produced worldwide is not known. Still, there are an estimated 10,000 colorants, with production greater than 7X10^5 tons, and an approximate 5–10% of the colorant remains in the effluents [2].

The main problem derived from the contribution of color to the waters of rivers and lakes is due to the reduction in transparency and the decrease in dissolved oxygen, due to the fact that high color loads hinder the photosynthetic function of plants [1]. Additionally, some problems associated with textile effluents are due to the presence of heavy metals or sulfur, which cause environmental problems due to their toxic nature. Some dyes of azoic nature have been found to have potential carcinogenicity, and at least 3000 commercial azo dyes have been classified as carcinogenic [3].

The production and manufacture of denim are important activities within the textile industry. However, the rise of the blue jeans maquiladora has dramatically deteriorated the environment that surrounds them. Its wastewater discharges are characterized mainly by presenting a blue color, as well as high organic loads [4].

Direct Blue 2, used mainly in denim dyeing, is an azo dye and chromophore since it involves two nitrogen molecules linked by a double bond and contains two aromatic rings in its structure (**Figure 1**). Due to its properties, it is difficult to degrade, and its discharge into the water can interfere with various biological processes that take place in bodies of water [5].

There are different physical, chemical, and biological processes that can be applied to remove colorants from wastewater; however, each process presents technical and economic limitations. Biological treatments are recognized as effective methods for the discoloration and degradation of colorants in highly polluted industrial wastewater [1, 4].

Biofiltration is a technology of easy operation, low investment, and maintenance; the influent is fed in the upper part of the biofilter and infiltrates through the filter medium; the processes that are achieved during the infiltration of the influents are slow filtration and passive, adsorption, absorption, ion exchange, and biodegradation, the latter being a destructive process through the use of microorganisms, predominantly heterotrophic bacteria, which degrade the pollutants present in industrial wastewater [6, 7]. Microorganisms are immobilized by adhering to the surface of a support medium through the formation of a film, which is in contact with wastewater continuously and intermittently [6].

There are various support materials that can be used, among the substrates that have been used for this type of technology is peat, which is partially fossilized plant material, generally dark brown, which is formed with little oxygenation and plenty of water, in places where the rate of accumulation of plant matter is greater than that of decomposition. Being a complex material, whose major constituents are lignin and cellulose, it has a surface area > 200 m^2/g and a porosity of 95% [8, 9]. These properties, together with their ability to adsorb the different compounds, make peat a material that can be used as a support for the formation of biofilms. With respect

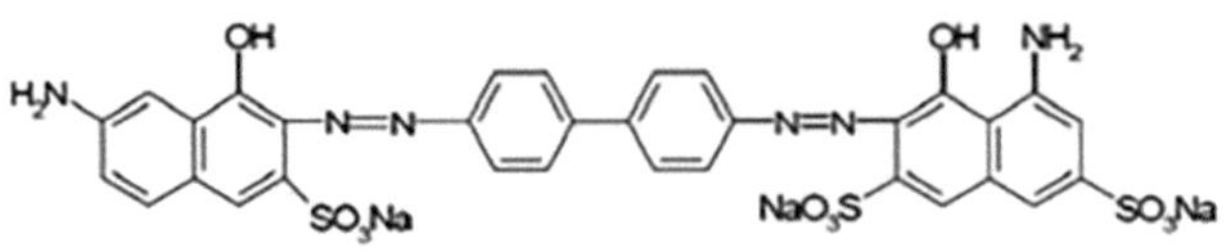

Figure 1.
Chemical structure of direct blue 2 dye.

to expanded perlite, it is a hydrated amorphous volcanic glass material with a water retention capacity of 2–5%, maintaining its original structure, it has a density of 30–150 kg/m^3, it is used to modify soils reducing its firmness and facilitating water drainage and moisture retention [10]. The composition of perlite is 70–75% silicon dioxide: SiO_2 12–15% aluminum oxide, Al_2O_3 3–4% sodium oxide, Na_2O 3–5% potassium oxide, K_2O 0.5–2% oxide iron, Fe_2O_3 0.2–0.7% magnesium oxide, MgO 0.5–1.5% calcium oxide, and CaO 3–5% [11].

The main objective of this work was to design, build, and operate a prototype of a biofiltration system to remove direct blue dye 2 present in wastewater using peat, perlite. and a mixture of peat. Perlite as packing materials.

2. Characteristics of textile wastewater

The textile industry is one of the main sources of pollutants for water worldwide due to the volume and composition of its effluents, which are characterized by being typically alkaline, hot, and colored. These effluents represent a danger to living organisms, as well as to the environment since they carry various types of toxic pollutants [1].

Textile effluents are characterized by a high level of dissimilarities in many parameters such as chemical oxygen demand (COD), pH, total solids (TS), biological oxygen demand (BOD), water use, and color [4]. The industrial manufacturing process rules out unsafe and colored dyes, mostly azo dyes. These colorants cause a great environmental problem, especially to aquatic life, due to their low biodegradability, strong color, high COD, and low BOD/COD ratio [12].

Dyes are classified into synthetic and natural. Synthetic dyes are easy to produce in a wide variety of colors and are very stable molecules; that is why they are widely used compared with natural colorants [1]. Synthetic colorants can be classified according to their mode of application and chemical structure. Based on the mode of application, they can be reactive, acidic, direct, dispersed, etc. While considering their chemical structure, they are categorized as azo, anthraquinone, triaryl methanes, among others [12].

Azo dyes are the most important family among industrial dyes, due to their ease to synthesize and their structural versatility. They are characterized by having an azo functional group (-N = N-) attached to aromatic rings. These colorants provide a practically complete range of shades and high color intensity. In addition, they are very stable to light, heat, water, and other solvents [13]. Azo dyes can be classified by the number of azo bonds they contain (monoazo, diazo, triazo, etc.) or based on the form of application in the fibers (acid, basic, direct, dispersed, mordant, reactive, and sulfurized) [14].

The typical characteristics of textile wastewater are difficult to define, because textile application methods, even the same process, are different for each industry. The concentration of colorants in textile wastewater varies in a wide range from 10 to 250 mg/L [12, 15–17] and in some cases, up to 800 mg/L [18].

Textile industries consume more than 100,000 tons/year dyes, and about 100 tons/year of dye enters the effluent water [19]. There is no exact information on the amount of dye released from various processes to the environment, but the release of the actual amounts of artificial colors into the environment has been identified as an environmental challenge.

3. Textile wastewater treatment

The textile industry uses a large amount of drinking water for the production of fibers. It is estimated that per kilogram of a textile material, 200 L of water is used, which leads to large volumes of wastewater [16]. This, together with the toxic effect of some colorants and their low biodegradability, has driven the search and implementation of technologies for the treatment and recycling of textile effluents. So, before the discharge of textile effluents to bodies of water, they must be treated either by a physical, chemical, biological process or a hybrid system.

3.1 Physical methods

Coagulation-flocculation-based methods are efficient for decolorizing wastewater containing dispersed dyes but show low efficiencies with reactive and vat dyes [20]. Filtration techniques (ultrafiltration, nanofiltration, and reverse osmosis) have been used to recover and reuse water. However, the high costs of the membranes, possible fouling of the same, and the generation of waste containing water-insoluble dyes (for example, indigo dye) limit their large-scale application [21]. On the other hand, adsorption processes (based on activated carbon) have been efficient in removing colorants present in wastewater [22]. However, its price and difficulty to regenerate it make it difficult to apply it in treatment plants.

3.2 Chemical methods

These are the degradation methods most used in the removal of colorants due to their easy application. In this category, we find the advanced oxidation processes (AOPs). These methods have the ability to degrade both the initial colorant and its by-products, either partially or totally under environmental conditions. Furthermore, they can be used in synergy with other methods [23].

Within AOP, the Fenton process (a combination of H2O2 and Fe(II) salts) is the most popular, which has been successfully applied in the degradation of soluble and insoluble dyes [24, 25]. Its main disadvantages are the generation of sludge due to the flocculation of the reagents with the dye and the cost of the reagents. However, the photo-Fenton process offers an improvement to the traditional process, so that in the presence of UV light (even sunlight can be used), it is possible to regenerate Fe(II), making the degradation process more efficient [26].

3.3 Biological methods

Biological processes, due to their cost, are the most used treatments in the removal of colorants present in industrial effluents [27, 28]. Based on oxygen requirements, biological methods are classified as aerobic, anaerobic, and anoxic or facultative, or a combination of these. Few studies have reported on the degradation in aerobic conditions, since in general long periods of acclimatization are required, and the process is sensitive to changes in the concentration of the dye [29]. On the other hand, anaerobic processes are efficient for the bleaching of textile effluents [28]. However, the aromatic amines generated are more toxic than the original compounds and are difficult to break down under anaerobic conditions. In addition, fungal cultures and enzymes have been used for the degradation of dyes [30, 31].

3.4 Hybrid methods

Coupled treatments (anaerobic-aerobic) are a good alternative for treating effluents from the textile industry [28, 32]. In the anaerobic stage, the reduction of the azo bond takes place, and the resulting aromatic amines are mineralized under aerobic conditions. An advantage of this system is the complete mineralization that is often achieved thanks to the synergistic action of different microorganisms [33]. While the main disadvantage is the long hydraulic retention times in the anaerobic stage [27, 28].

4. Nonconventional methods: biofiltration

Biofiltration, synonym for biological filtration, is a secondary treatment process for onsite wastewater. Filtration is one of the more common biological treatment processes. Filters are commonly constructed using sand, gravel, peat, or a synthetic material. These synthetic materials, such as foam, fabric, or plastic and natural materials, such as peat, are grouped together under the generic title "biofilter" [34].

Biofiltration is considered an unconventional process that involves the removal of pollutants (such as drugs, fertilizers, dyes, among others) through a physical (adsorption) and biological process simultaneously of a packed material in a filter. The packed material can be a natural one (organic or inorganic). In addition, low-cost adsorbent media can be used (which can even be an agro-industrial waste), such as bentonite, polymeric resins, or peat, which makes this process more eco-friendly and economically competitive compared with physical or chemical processes [32, 35].

5. Peat as a packing material

Biofiltration using peat as the filter medium is widely used for wastewater treatment processes in small communities and has been used to remove various pollutants and lately also used to remove emerging pollutants, due to its adsorption properties, ability to retain moisture, buffering capacity, and abundance in nature. Peat is an organic material, dark brown in color, and rich in carbon. It is formed as a result of the rotting and partial carbonization of vegetation in the acidic water of swamps, marshes, and wetlands [27]. It is formed in poorly oxygenated wetlands, where the rate of accumulation of plant matter is greater than that of decomposition. It is a very complex material, with lignin and cellulose as major constituents. The polar functional groups of lignin, which include alcohols, aldehydes, ketones, acids, phenolic hydroxides, and ethers, are involved in the formation of chemical bonds during the adsorption processes. As it has a high adsorption capacity for polar organic molecules and is a highly porous material (approx. 95% and a specific area of 200 m2/g), it is usually washed and sieved before being used in wastewater treatment [36].

Four stages in the adsorption process using porous peat are identified: (i) transport of impurities from the bulk of solution to the exterior surface of the peat; (ii) movement of pollutant across the interface and adsorption onto external surface sites; (iii) migration of pollutant molecules within the pores of the peat; and (iv) interaction of pollutant molecules with the available sites on the interior surfaces, bounding the pore and capillary spaces of the peat [36].

6. Design criteria for biofilter scale-up

The textile industry requires a large amount of water, between 100 and 200 L per kg of textile products. The wastewater obtained from the various processes is highly polluted because it contains dyes, surfactants, inorganic salts, and chemical compounds used in the production process [37]. To scale up the processes implemented in the laboratory, the hydraulic retention time (HRT) and the flow rate generated in the production systems must be considered. The following Eq. (1) establishes the volume required for the biofiltration system.

$$V = Q * t \tag{1}$$

Where: V: Usable volume of support medium (m^3), Q: Flow rate (m^3/s), and t: HRT (s).

The total effective volume of the biofilter will be affected by the porosity of the specific packing medium selected; with this information, the flow rate of the wastewater generated, the hydraulic conductivity of the packing medium, the hydraulic gradient have to be determined and applying Darcy's Law, the surface area of the treatment system calculated. This information is necessary before the scale up of these laboratory systems to a full scale.

7. Experimental procedure

7.1 Materials and methods

7.1.1 Packaging materials, inoculum, and biofilter

The reactor was built of acrylic, with the dimensions shown in **Figure 1**. These proportions between the biofilter measurements will need to be considered when scaling is required (geometric similarity). The packaging materials were selected: peat and perlite (**Table 1**). These materials are characterized by having high porosity, adsorption capacity, and availability, which implies that they are low-cost, have ideal characteristics for suitable packaging material. Peat is an organic material, dark brown in color, and rich in carbon. It is formed as a result of the rotting and partial carbonization of vegetation in the acidic water of swamps, marshes, and wetlands [9]. Perlite is a mineral of volcanic origin, whose chemical components are silica and oxides of aluminum, iron, calcium, magnesium, and sodium [11].

The packing materials were washed with plenty of water, to eliminate the color in the case of peat or powders in the case of the rest of the materials. Subsequently, they were dried by exposure to the sun. For the case of all inorganic packing materials, an

Absorbent material	Apparent density (g/cm^3)	Real density (g/cm^3)	Porosity (%)	Water retention (g/100 g)	Reference
Peat	0.1–0.5	1–1.6	94	287	[38, 39]
Perlite	0.05–0.1	0.96–1.2	95	300–400	[11, 40]

Table 1.
Physical characteristics of packing materials.

Parameter	Value
COD (mg/L)	2000
pH	6.74
Total solids (g/L)	20.26
Total suspended solids (g/L)	16.19
Total volatile solids (g/L)	11.90

Table 2.
Characterization of the inoculum.

Compound	Concentration (mg/L)
Saccharose	1000
NH_4Cl	335
KH_2PO_4	70
Yeast extract	5000
Azo dye	50

Table 3.
Synthetic wastewater composition.

average particle size of 8 mm in diameter was selected. As a filter medium, peat and perlite were used alone and, a combination of both, in a 50:50 (v/v) ratio.

The biofilters were inoculated with activated sludge (**Table 2**) from the ECCACIV Wastewater Treatment Plant, located in Jiutepec, Morelos. In total, 20% of the volume of sludge and 80% of the volume of synthetic municipal wastewater were used (**Table 3**), added with a solution containing the azo dye Direct Blue 2. The biofilters were left for up to 7 days, in order for the biofilm formation to take place (**Figure 2**).

7.2 Characterization of packaging materials

7.2.1 Adsorption and desorption isotherms

For each filter medium, adsorption kinetics was performed, based on the methodology proposed by OECD [41]. Known volumes of the test solution are added to the packing material (previously equilibrated with $CaCl_2$ 0.01 M). The mixture is stirred for an appropriate time. Subsequently, the packing material is separated by centrifugation, and the aqueous phase is analyzed by spectrophotometry. The amount of substance adsorbed on the packaging material is calculated as the difference between the amount of test substance initially present in the solution and the amount remaining at the end of the experiment.

In order to investigate whether the adsorption of the dye to the packaging material is reversible or irreversible, a desorption kinetics was carried out. From the adsorption test, once the aqueous phase is separated by centrifugation, the volume of solution removed is replaced by an equal volume of $CaCl_2$ 0.01 M (without containing dye) and stirred again, for an appropriate time. The aqueous phase is recovered (as much as possible), and it is analyzed spectrophotometrically.

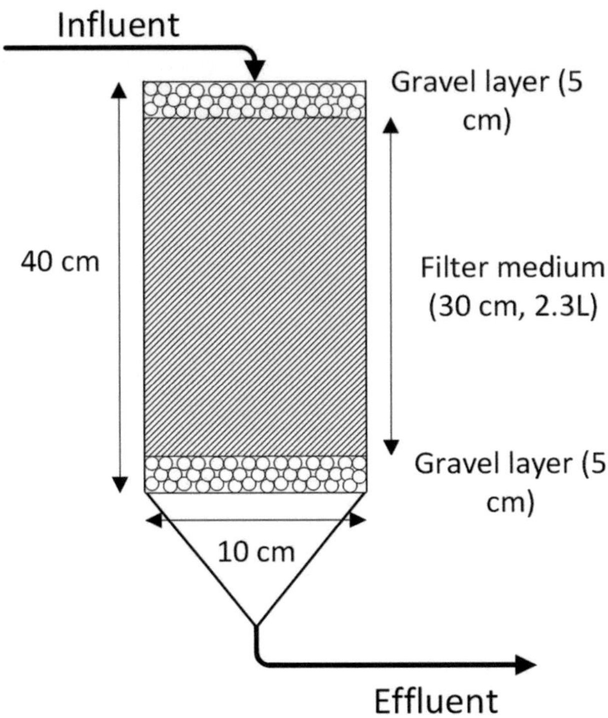

Figure 2.
Design of the biofilter used.

7.3 Determination of the porosity of the filter medium

To determine the hydraulic retention time (HRT) of the biofilters, the methodology described by Garzón-Zúñiga et al. [42] is used, which generally consists of the following steps: 1) determination of the volume of voids in the filter bed layer; 2) determination of the porosity of the filter medium and; 3) determination of HRT, based on the following Eq. (2):

$$HRT = V_t / Q \tag{2}$$

Where,
Q = flow rate (L/d).
V_t = Porosity Volume of voids in L.
Y = Volume of empty spaces (L).
The flow rate was obtained by doing emptying tests, for which it was previously necessary to fill the biofilters with water (until full coverage of the filter medium). Then, the biofilter was drained, and the volume obtained was measured at different time intervals.

7.4 Evaluation of color removal and degradation of organic matter

The removal of color was followed spectrophotometrically, in the case of the Direct Blue 2 dye, the absorbance in the effluent at 576 nm was measured. On the other hand, the removal of organic matter was determined considering the removal of COD [43].

8. Results and discussion

8.1 Biofilter flow rates and hydraulic retention times

Table 4 shows the flow rates and HRT of each biofilter, calculated using the methodology described by Garzón-Zuñiga et al., [42]. It can be seen that the biofilter with peat shows a higher HRT (1.51 d); this is because the peat can expand and has low porosity, which reduces the empty spaces. In the biofilter with the peat-perlite mixture, the HRT (1.18 d) is lower than that of the peat (HRT = 1.51 d) because the perlite increases the number of empty spaces. For the perlite biofilter, the HRT (1.0 d) is lower than the peat biofilter and the peat/perlite biofilter, because perlite is an inorganic mineral material, and it does not absorb water since it retains it on its surface.

Packing material	Flow (L)	HRT (d)	HRT (h)
Peat	1.10	1.51	36.24
Perlite	1.26	1.00	24.00
Peat/perlite	1.23	1.18	28.32

Table 4.
Hydraulic retention time (HRT) calculated from biofilters.

8.2 Organic matter removal assessment

For 110 days, the biofilters were fed with a synthetic effluent with a color concentration of 50 mg / L and consequently a constant COD. For the biofilter packed with perlite, in **Figure 3**, we observe that, at 15 days, a COD removal of 14% was achieved, and at 30 days decreased to 13%. At 50 days, the removal rate was 61%, and at 110 days, 71% removal was achieved. No studies were found in which perlite is used as packaging for biofiltration of wastewater; however, there are works carried out with inorganic packaging, Villanueva et al., [44] carried out a study with a biofilter packed with gravel, obtaining removals of 27% of the COD at 21 days.

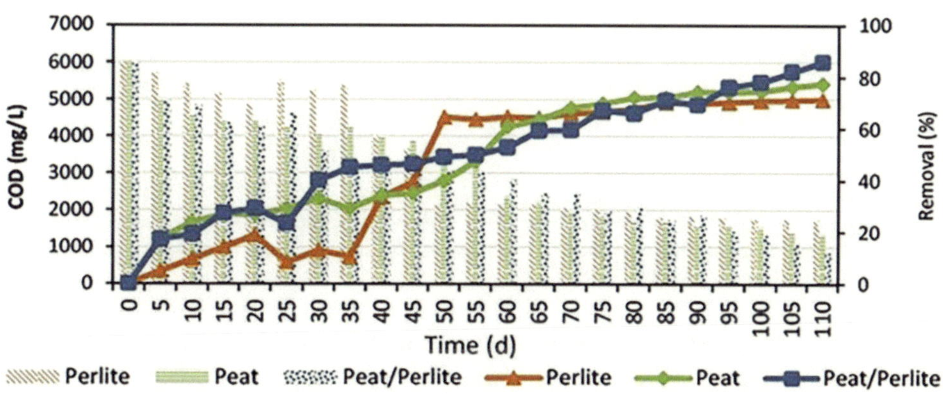

Figure 3.
Organic matter removal was measured as COD in the biofilter with the peat, perlite, and peat-perlite mixture.

For the peat-packed biofilter, **Figure 3** shows that, from day 15, COD removals of 27% were obtained, reaching at 30 days, removals of 33%. Obtaining removals up to 78% after 110 days, compared with the performance of the perlite-packed biofilter (71% COD removal), higher COD removal was achieved with the peat biofilter. In 2011, Velasco [45] reported a study of biofiltration with peat, obtaining an average organic matter removal efficiency of 75.5%, and another study by Mejia [45] reports organic matter removal efficiencies of 53.4%.

For the biofilter packed with peat-perlite, **Figure 3** shows that on day 15, organic matter removal was less than 30%. From this day on, the percentage of removal increased until reaching 70% removal on day 80, achieving a removal rate of 91% at 110 days. Comparing the results with the perlite (71%) and peat (78%) biofilters, the highest removals (86%) were obtained with this biofilter, which may be due to the use of two materials with a very different composition (organic and inorganic); however, the use of perlite helped the biofilter perform better in terms of removal. No works reported in the literature were found, with biofilters packed with peat-perlite for wastewater. In 2011, Velasco [45] carried out a study using nanoparticles of TiO_2 and MgO, in a biofilter packed with peat, reaching 97% in removal of organic matter.

8.3 Color removal assessment

For assessment of the dye concentration (mg/L), the UV–vis spectrophotometry method was used. To evaluate the dye concentration (mg/L), A UV–vis spectrophotometric method was used. First, the calibration curve for direct Blue 2 was performed with solutions of the dye from 10 to 100 mg/L concentration at a wavelength of 576 nm.

For the perlite-packed biofilter, the dye removal efficiencies are shown in **Figure 4**. On day 15, a 46% color removal was achieved, gradually increasing the removal rate. On day 25, the dye removal was 50%, reaching an 82% removal rate at 110 days. In comparison to that reported by Melgoza and De la Cruz [46], inorganic filter media such as tezontle are highly efficient (≈93%) for color removal in real textile effluent with azo dyes.

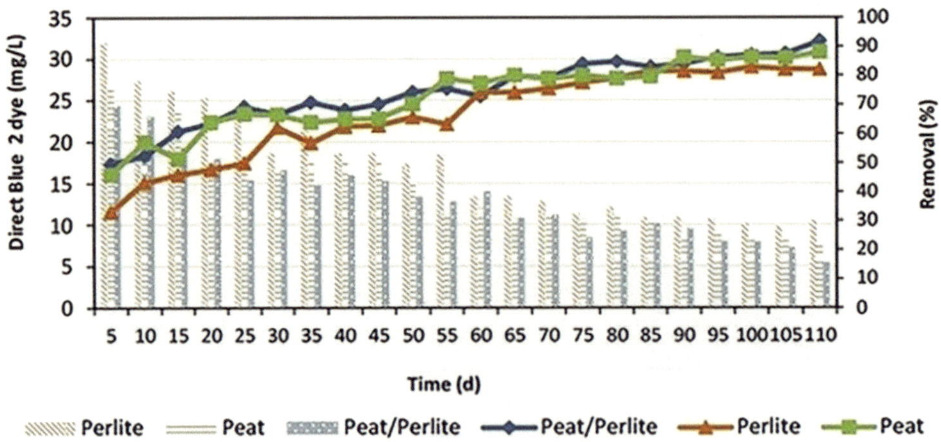

Figure 4.
Dye removal in the biofilters with peat, perlite, and peat-perlite mixture.

In the case of the peat-packed biofilter, **Figure 4** shows that on day 15, the removal of the dye achieved 51%, gradually increasing the removal rate. On day 25, the color eliminated was 67%, reaching an 88% removal rate at 110 days. In general, the performance of the color removal results shows a wide variation, which is probably due to color interferences from the peat or the biofilm formed on the peat. Mejía [47] reports a 50% removal of Terasil SRL black color in biofilters packed with peat and inoculated with Pleurotus ostreatus.

In the case of the biofilter packed with the peat-perlite mixture, **Figure 4** shows a variation in the data obtained on day 15, 61% the removal, and the day 15, the removal increases gradually (>70%), the rate removal was 79% on day 55. In 110 days, the removal reached 92%. Comparing the results with the biofilters with perlite (82%) and peat (88%), with the peat/perlite biofilter, removals of 92% were obtained. It may be due to the constituents of the two materials with different compositions (organic and inorganic) and textures. Therefore, the mixture of the two materials increases the percentage removal efficiency of the dye.

8.4 Sorption process assessment

In the adsorption kinetics, perlite has a sorption capacity of 16.2% in the first 2 hours of contact with the dye, while in the case of peat, the adsorption capacity was 87.5% during the first hour (**Figure 5**).

Adsorption and desorption were described by the linearized form of the Freundlich Eq. (3)

$$\log C_s = \log K_f + 1/n \log C_e \qquad (3)$$

where K_f is the adsorption coefficient characterizing the adsorption–desorption capacity, and n is the Freundlich equation exponent related to adsorption intensity that is used as an indicator of the adsorption isotherm nonlinearity.

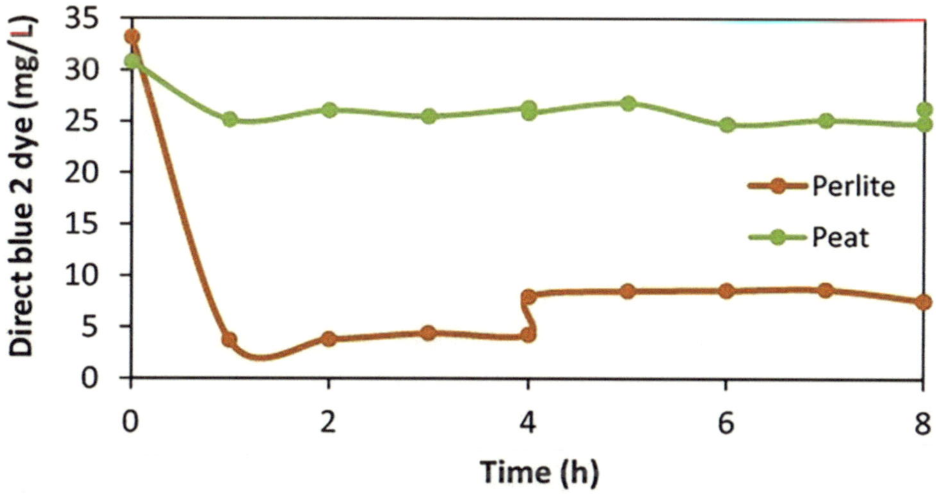

Figure 5.
Kinetics of sorption of direct blue 2 in packing materials.

$K_{f\text{-}ads}$ is the adsorption coefficient, and $K_{f\ des}$ is the desorption coefficient of the Freundlich equation.

The hysteresis coefficient, H, for the adsorption and desorption isotherms was calculated according to Eq. (4):

$$H = (1/n_{des})/(1/n_{ads}) \quad (4)$$

where, $1/n_{ads}$ and $1/n_{des}$ are the Freundlich constants obtained for the adsorption and desorption isotherms, respectively.

The organic matter (OM) normalized adsorption constant (K_{OM}) was calculated by normalizing $K_{f\text{-}ads}$ to the fraction of OM Eq. (5)

$$K_{OM} = K_{f-ads} / OM \times 100 \quad (5)$$

The sorption isotherms for the two packing materials are shown in the **Figure 6**.

Table 5 shows the parameters determined with the adsorption and desorption isotherms.

Based on the parameters determined by Freundlich, peat has a higher adsorption capacity than perlite. This is confirmed by considering the amount of organic matter contained in the materials. Since it has been shown that contaminants are adsorbed on the organic fraction of the substrates. Hysteresis in peat shows that the packing material has a dye-holding capacity since the ratio of the desorption intensity to the adsorption intensity gives a value below 1, indicating that the adsorption rate is higher than the desorption rate, which favors the retention of contaminants in the

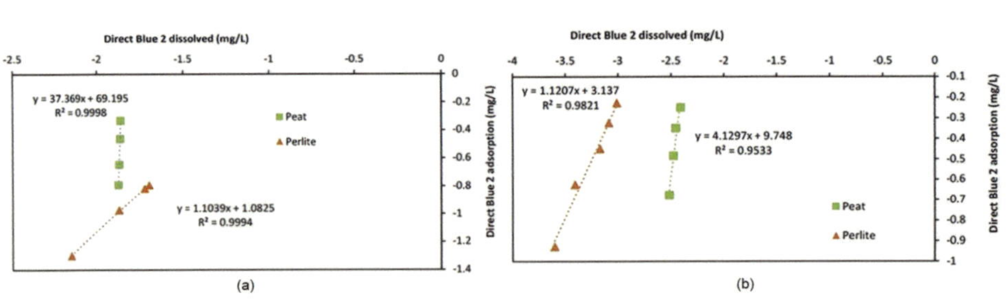

Figure 6.
Isotherms sorption for direct blue 2 dye in perlite and peat (a) Adsorption. (b) Desorption.

Packaging material	Adsorption		Desorption		H	OM* (%)	KOM(%)
	K_{ads}	1/n	K_{des}	1/n			
Peat	1.56×10^{69}	37.37	5.59×10^{69}	4.130	0. 0.11	97.51	1.59×10^{69}
Perlite	12.09	1.10	1370.88	1.121	1.09	0.62	1950

**For the organic matter determination, the methods used were the following ASTM D2974–14.*

Table 5.
Parameters of Freundlich isotherms for peat and perlite.

material. Whereas with an H value such as that of perlite close to 1, it indicates that the adsorption rate is similar to the desorption rate, so the hysteresis process does not occur [48]. Based on the characteristics of the materials used in the biofilters and adsorption data, the perlite serves as a porous and inert material, which provides the packing medium with aeration capacity and support that prevents clogging due to the peat compaction, but does not favor retention. Therefore, the pollutants present in it undergoes adsorption and desorption processes at the same rate, increasing the availability of the pollutants in the perlite-packed area. While peat provides the biofilters with the necessary nutrients for biofilm formation; moreover, adsorption support allows them to retain contaminants, favoring the contact between microorganisms and contaminants, when the pollutants present in the pore water are removed, the pollutants retained in the peat are released, favoring its availability and degradation. Therefore, the biofilter with the highest removal capacity is the peat-perlite mixture.

9. Conclusions

Perlite supplies the biofilter with support, aeration and allows to increase the availability of the pollutant due to its low adsorption capacity. While peat is a packing material that provides nutrients to the microorganisms in charge of the biodegradation process, it retains the direct blue 2 dye increasing the contact capacity between the pollutant and the microorganisms in charge of the degradation process. The perlite does not have a hysteresis process because the adsorption rate is the same as desorption. While the peat showed hysteresis, obtaining a value less than 1, which indicates that the adsorption rate is higher than the desorption rate, which favors the retention of the direct blue 2 dye. Due to the specific adsorption capacity of each material: perlite and peat, the mixture of the materials complements the properties of the packed material and improves the performance of the biofilter itself and consequently the removal capacity of the organic matter and the direct blue dye pollution of the wastewater fed into the biofilter. No reports have been found using this mixture (peat and perlite) as a packing material either in lab or pilot scale, and consequently, there are no full-scale experiences including industrial or municipal wastewater treatment reports using this nonconventional technology and packing material. This is an important opportunity to continue this research line to use this kind of nonconventional packing materials and biomasses to be used for biofilters, due to its ease of operation and economical benefits that allows us to implement them in small communities and/or for industrial wastewater treatment in small installations. Some other scale-up experiences with peat and other waste biomass indicate that it is necessary to pretreat the wastewater to be fed to eliminate solids that could clog the biofilter; therefore, the treatment train is easy to implement (septic tank or a primary settler and the biofilter packed with this mixture, and if needed a disinfection method).

Acknowledgements

The authors thanked UPEMOR for the support of chemicals and materials received to implement this research and Environmental Engineer Briseida Emilia Velázquez Vázquez for her contribution to this research.

Author details

Rosa Angélica Guillén, Cristina Lizama-Bahena, Luis Gerardo Trevino-Quintanilla, Martin Barragan-Trinidad, Victoria Bustos and Gabriela Moeller-Chavez*
Universidad Politécnica del Estado de Morelos, Jiutepec, Morelos, México

*Address all correspondence to: gabriela.moeller@gmail.com

References

[1] Saxena G, Bharagava RN. Organic and inorganic pollutants in industrial wastes: Ecotoxicological effects, health hazards, and bioremediation approaches. In: Bharagava RN, editor. Environmental Pollutants and their Bioremediation Approaches. Florida, USA: CRC Press; 2017

[2] Mohan D, Singh KP, Singh G, Kumar K. Removal of dyes from wastewater using Fly ash, a low-cost adsorbent. Industrial and Engineering Chemistry Research. 2002;**41**:3688-3695

[3] Guaratini C, Zanoni M. Textile dyes. Química Nova. 2000;**23**:71-78

[4] Shindhal T, Rakholiya P, Varjani S, Pandey A, Ngo HH, Guo W, et al. A critical review on advances in the practices and perspectives for the treatment of dye industry wastewater. Bioengineered. 2021;**12**(1):70-87. DOI: 10.1080/21655979.2020.1863034

[5] García SL. Decoloración fúngica de efluentes industriales con colorantes azo en sistemas de biofiltración con diferentes empaques orgánicos [thesis]. Mexico City: Universidad Nacional Autónoma de México; 2007

[6] Cohen Y. Biofiltration – The treatment of fluids by microorganisms immobilized into the filter bedding material: A review. Bioresource Technology. 2001;**77**(3):257-274. DOI: 10.1016/S0960-8524(00)00074-2

[7] Chaudhary DS, Vigneswaran S, Ngo H-H, Shim WG, Moon H. Biofilter in water and wastewater treatment. Korean Journal of Chemical Engineering. 2003;**20**:1054. DOI: 10.1007/BF02706936

[8] Talbot P, Bélanger G, Pelletier M, Laliberté G, Arcand Y. Development of a biofilter using an organic medium for on-site wastewater treatment. Water Science and Technology. 1996;**34**(3):435-441. DOI: 10.1016/0273-1223(96)00609-9

[9] Turetsky MR, Benscoter B, Page S, Rein G, van der Werf GR, Watts A. Global vulnerability of peatlands to fire and carbon loss. Nature Geoscience. 2015;**8**(1):11-14. DOI: 10.1038/ngeo2325

[10] Kibazohi O, Yun S-I, Anderson WA. Removal of hexane in biofilters packed with perlite and a peat–perlite mixture. World Journal of Microbiology and Biotechnology. 2004;**20**:337-343. DOI: 10.1023/B:WIBI.0000033054.15023.71

[11] Vijayaraghavan K, Raja FD. Experimental characterization and evaluation of perlite as a sorbent for heavy metal ions in single and quaternary solutions. Journal of Water Process Engineering. 2014;**4**:179-184. DOI: 10.1016/j.jwpe.2014.10.001

[12] Yaseen DA, Scholz M. Textile dye wastewater characteristics and constituents of synthetic effluents: A critical review. International journal of Environmental Science and Technology. 2019;**16**:1193-1226. DOI: 10.1007/s13762-018-2130-z

[13] Carmen Z, Daniela S. Textile Organic Dyes-Characteristics, Polluting Effects, and Separation/Elimination Procedures from an Industrial Effluents-a Critical Overview. Rijeka: IntechOpen; 2012. pp. 55-86. DOI: 10.5772/32373

[14] Nikfar S, Jaberidoost M. Dyes and colorants. In: Wexler P, editor. Encyclopedia of Toxicology. 3rd ed. Oxford: Academic Press; 2014. pp. 252-261

[15] Gähr F, Hermanutz F, Oppermann W. Ozonation – An important technique to comply with new german laws for textile wastewater treatment. Water Science and Technology. 1994;**30**:255-263. DOI: 10.2166/wst.1994.0115

[16] Ghaly A, Ananthashankar R, Alhattab M, Ramakrishnan V. Production, characterization and treatment of textile effluents: A critical review. Journal of Chemical Engineering & Process Technology. 2014;**5**:1-19. DOI: 10.4172/2157-7048.1000182

[17] Shelley T. Dye pollution clean-up by synthetic minerals. International Dyer. 1994;**79**:26-31

[18] Vandevivere PC, Bianchi R, Verstraete W. Review: Treatment and reuse of wastewater from the textile wet-processing industry: Review of emerging technologies. Journal of Chemical Technology & Biotechnology. 1998;**72**:289-302

[19] Mosbah A, Chouchane H, Abdelwahed S, Redissi A, Hamdi M, Kouidhi S, et al. Peptides fixing industrial textile dyes: A new biochemical method in wastewater treatment. Journal of Chemistry. 2019;**2019**:1-7. DOI: 10.1155/2019/5081807

[20] Liang C-Z, Sun S-P, Li F-Y, Ong Y-K, Chung T-S. Treatment of highly concentrated wastewater containing multiple synthetic dyes by a combined process of coagulation/flocculation and nanofiltration. Journal of Membrane Science. 2014;**469**:306-315. DOI: 10.1016/j.memsci.2014.06.057

[21] Koyuncu I, Güney K. Membrane-based treatment of textile industry wastewaters. In: Hoek EMV and Tarabara V, editors. Encyclopedia of Membrane Science and Technology. Hoboken, USA: John Wiley & Sons, Ltd; 2013. pp. 1-12. DOI: 10.1002/9781118522318.emst127

[22] Jadhav AJ, Srivastava VC. Adsorbed solution theory-based modeling of binary adsorption of nitrobenzene, aniline, and phenol onto granulated activated carbon. Chemical Engineering Journal. 2013;**229**:450-459. DOI: 10.1016/j.cej.2013.06.02

[23] Holkar CR, Jadhav AJ, Pinjari DV, Mahamuni NM, Pandit AB. A critical review on textile wastewater treatments: Possible approaches. Journal of Environmental Management. 2016;**182**: 351-366. DOI: 10.1016/j.jenvman.2016.07.090

[24] Fernandes NC, Brito LB, Costa GG, Taveira SF, Cunha-Filho MSS, Oliveira GAR, et al. Removal of azo dye using Fenton and Fenton-like processes: Evaluation of process factors by box–Behnken design and ecotoxicity tests. Chemico-Biological Interactions. 2018;**291**:47-54. DOI: 10.1016/j.cbi.2018.06.003

[25] Sharma A, Verma M, Haritash AK. Degradation of toxic azo dye (AO7) using Fenton's process. Advances in Environmental Research. 2016;**5**:189-200. DOI: 10.12989/aer.2016.5.3.189

[26] Ameta R, K. Chohadia A, Jain A, Punjabi PB. Chapter 3 - Fenton and photo-Fenton processes. In: Ameta SC, Ameta R, editors. Advanced Oxidation Processes for WasteWater Treatment. Cambridge, USA: Academic Press; 2018. pp. 49-87. DOI: 10.1016/B978-0-12-810499-6.00003-6

[27] dos Santos AB, Cervantes FJ, van Lier JB. Review paper on current technologies for decolorization of textile wastewaters: Perspectives for anaerobic biotechnology. Bioresource Technology. 2007;**98**:2369-2385. DOI: 10.1016/j.biortech.2006.11.013

[28] van der Zee FP, Villaverde S. Combined anaerobic-aerobic treatment of azo dyes—A short review of bioreactor studies. Water Research. 2005;**39**:1425-1440. DOI: 10.1016/j.watres.2005.03.007

[29] Buitrón G, Quezada M, Moreno G. Aerobic degradation of the azo dye acid red 151 in a sequencing batch biofilter. Bioresource Technology. 2004;**92**:143-149. DOI: 10.1016/j.biortech.2003.09.001

[30] Yesilada O, Birhanli E, Geckil H. Bioremediation and Decolorization of textile dyes by white rot fungi and laccase enzymes. In: Prasad R, editor. Mycoremediation and Environmental Sustainability. Vol. 2. Cham: Springer International Publishing; 2018. pp. 121-153. DOI: 10.1007/978-3-319-77386-5_5

[31] Chen SH, Yien Ting AS. Biodecolorization and biodegradation potential of recalcitrant triphenylmethane dyes by *Coriolopsis* sp. isolated from compost. Journal of Environmental Management. 2015;**150**:274-280. DOI: 10.1016/j.jenvman.2014.09.014

[32] Garzón-Zúñiga MA, Sandoval-Villasana AM, Moeller-Chávez GE. Decolorization of the AO24 azo dye and reduction of toxicity and genotoxicity in trickling biofilters. Water Environment Research. 2011;**83**:107-115. DOI: 10.2175/106143010X12780288627977

[33] Stolz A. Basic and applied aspects in the microbial degradation of azo dyes. Applied Microbiology and Biotechnology. 2001;**56**:69-80. DOI: 10.1007/s002530100686

[34] National Environmental Services Center. Technical Overview Biological Filtration. Morgantown, USA: West Virginia University; 2021. p. 7. Report No.: SFBLTO02

[35] Garzón-Zúñiga M, Lessard P, Aubry G, Buelna G. Nitrogen elimination mechanisms in an organic media aerated biofilter treating pig manure. Environmental Technology. 2005;**26**:361-372. DOI: 10.1080/09593332608618552

[36] Couillard D. The use of peat in wastewater treatment. Water Research. 1994;**28**:1261-1274. DOI: 10.1016/0043-1354(94)90291-7

[37] Carvalho JC, Bessegato GG, Zanoni MV. Efficiency comparison of ozonation, photolysis, photocatalysis and photoelectrocatalysis methods in real textile wastewater decolorization. Water Research. 2016;**98**:39-46. DOI: 10.1016/j.watres.2016.04.004

[38] Kolay PK, Taib SNL. Physical and Geotechnical Properties of Tropical Peat and its Stabilization. Peat: IntechOpen; 2018. pp. 93-106. DOI: 10.5772/intechopen.74173

[39] Jinming H, Xuehui M. Physical and chemical properties of peat. In: Jinsheng G, editor. Encyclopedia of Life Support Systems: Coal, Oil, Shale, Natural Bitumen, Heavy Oil and Peat. Oxford, UK: EOLSS Publications; 2002. Vol II. p. 18

[40] Patterson HBW. Chapter 6 - filtration and filters. In: List GR, editor. Bleaching and Purifying Fats and Oils. 2nd ed. Urbana, USA: AOCS Press; 2009. pp. 159-188

[41] OECD. Test No. 106: Adsorption -- Desorption Using a Batch Equilibrium Method [Internet]. Paris: Organization for Economic Co-operation and Development; 2000. Available from:

https://www.oecd-ilibrary.org/environment/test-no-106-adsorption-desorption using-a-batch-equilibrium-method_9789264069602-en [Accessed: 2022-01-08]

[42] Garzón-Zúñiga MA, Lessard P, Buelna G. Determination of the hydraulic residence time in a trickling biofilter filled with organic matter. Environmental Technology. 2003;**24**:605-614. DOI: 10.1080/09593330309385595

[43] APHA, AWWA, WFE. Standard Methods for the Examination of Water & Wastewater. 21st ed. Washington, USA: American Public Health Association; 2005. p. 1392

[44] Villanueva Hernandez JA, Vazquez Sanchez RA, Najera Aguilar HA. Evaluación de la remoción de la Demanda Química de Oxígeno (DQO) en dos biofiltros con diferentes empaques. 2012. Available from: https://repositorio.unicach.mx/handle/20.500.12753/1709 [Accessed: 2022-01-08]

[45] Velasco GY. Sistemas de biofiltración empacados con turba y nanopartículas de TiO2 y MgO para remoción de fenol [thesis]. Mexico City: Universidad Nacional Autónoma de México; 2011

[46] Melgoza Alemán RM, De la Cruz GR. Tratamiento de un efluente textil por medio de un biofiltro discontinuo secuenciado anaerobio/aerobio. En México: V Congreso Internacional y XI Nacional de Ciencias Ambientales; 2006

[47] Mejía López MP. Tratamiento de un efluente de la industria textil en biofiltros empacados con turba inoculados con Pleurotus ostreatus [thesis]. Mexico City: Universidad Nacional Autónoma de México; 2014

[48] Chunxian W, Zhang S, Nie G, Zhang Z, Wang J. Adsorption and desorption of herbicide monosulfuron-ester in Chinese soils. Journal of Environmental Sciences. 2011;**23**(9):1524-1532. DOI: 10.1016/S1001-0742(10)60583-9

Chapter 8

Reducing Clogs in Power Boiler Biomass Feeding System

Guilherme Moscato Malavazi

Abstract

With the constant increase in pulp and paper production, the demand for wood has been intensifying, and consequently, the availability of forest residues and bark for energy generation grows year after year. Seeking sustainability between forestry operations and the consumption of biomass, Klabin's paper production plant in Telêmaco Borba (Monte Alegre Unit) has been increasing the consumption of forestry residues and bark, and as a result of the particle size characteristic of these materials, occurrences of clogging of biomass transport screws became constant, reflecting in operational bottlenecks of the boiler. Seeking to solve this problem, the "Problem-Solving" methodology was used and actions were implemented in the screw that had the highest frequency of occurrences, based on the main idea of avoiding "empty spaces" and obstacles in the path of biomass. After the implementation of all items, a 75% reduction in the frequency of occurrences was obtained, reaching the objective proposed at the beginning of the work, showing that there are challenges in the pulp and paper industry that can be solved or reduced through quick solutions, cheap and effective.

Keywords: biomass, clogging, screw, boiler, residue, empty spaces

1. Introduction

The evolution of energy consumption, based on fossils, has led humanity towards an insecure and expensive energy matrix. This has led many countries to consider the need for profound changes, including an intensification of the use of other energy sources, especially renewable ones, including wood [1].

The energy use of forest biomass also promotes increased use of existing commercial forests, due to the possibility of using forest residues, which are generally left in the field after harvesting and constitute potential sources of energy; in addition, the energy use of forest residues can economically make forest management activities and silvicultural treatments feasible [2].

The main existing barriers to the greater use of renewable energies are of an economic nature. It is considered that one of the most important factors in the use of biomass as an energy input, regardless of the technique used, refers to the cost of harvesting and transporting this raw material [3].

Among the main biomasses lignocellulosic of agricultural and forestry origin, may include rice straw, rice husk, wheat straw, sorghum straw, corn husks, sugarcane bagasse, wood chips, branches and sawdust, grass, etc. In addition, this type of biomass is composed mainly of cellulose, hemicellulose, and lignin [4].

Nowadays, the integration between forest harvesting and pulp mills became closer, always seeking more yield and sustainability in the integrated production chain. Reducing the age of wood, increasing areas for planting and the proportion of total trees destined for the production of pulp keep pushing the consumption of waste generated, both in harvesting and in wood processing. For these residues, the most commonly used destination is burning in power boilers to compose the industrial energy matrix, for internal (or external) use, in addition to completing the wood cycle, completing the total use of the cultivated material.

With the frequent increase in paper production and demand for wood by the Monte Alegre Plant, the availability of this type of material for burning is constantly rising and, consequently, the consumption by power boilers (see **Figure 1**).

The valuation of forest residues for energy purposes supports some critical quality parameters that uniformity of composition is one of them. Since it is a mixed material, the ideal is to maintain the most uniform possible proportions between the various components of residual biomass (wood, bark, branches, thick roots, etc.). When it is just wood chips, it is very important to specify the contents of maximum bark and ash they may contain, in addition to the moisture content that is critical for energy performance [5].

As much as there are technological advances in the ways of harvesting and debarking, there are still several factors that hinder the consumption of forest residues and bark. The main one is based on the physical and granulometric quality of the material itself, which, residues (especially eucalyptus) and bark, have fibrous characteristics, forming the so-called "ribbons" or "strips."

At the Monte Alegre plant (Telêmaco Borba, Paraná, Brazil), there are two biomass-based power boilers to supply the steam demand for the plant. These boilers feature different operating technologies: bubbling fluidized bed (BFB) and

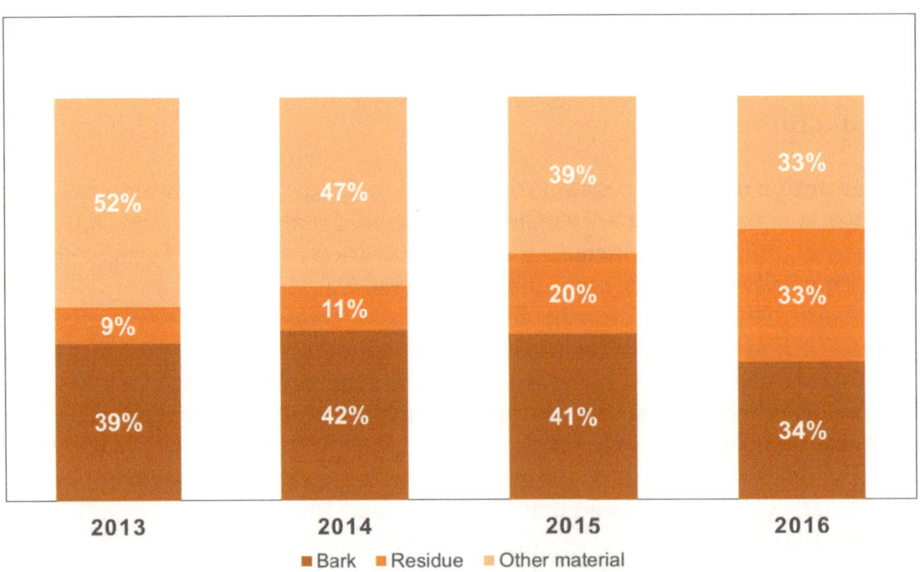

Figure 1.
Evolution in the composition of the total biomass consumed in Monte Alegre in the last four years.

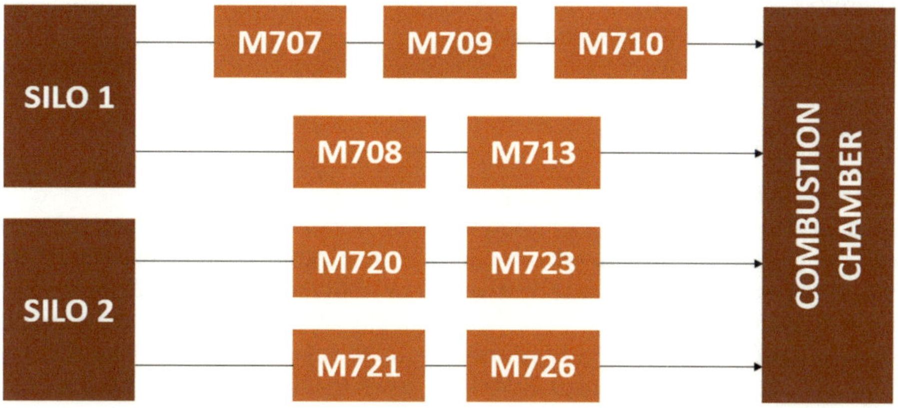

Figure 2.
Representative drawing of boiler feed system via biomass screws (adapted from Babcock Power España [6]).

circulating fluidized bed (CFB). In the CFB boiler, biomass is supplied to the power boiler and stored in two silos equipped with continuous level transmitters (weighing cells). Each biomass silo feeds two fuel lines and each silo is discharged by rotating devices with a drag arm and discharge screws. Each fuel line has a discharge screw, which transports the biomass to the metering screws and only in line 1 there is an additional transport screw [6]. **Figure 2** shows the representative design of the described system.

One of the consequences of high waste consumption is the clogging and kinking that this type of material causes. In addition, the fibrous characteristic of this biomass makes the material's specific volume larger, causing the feed screws to work at increasingly higher speeds in order to maintain constant the biomass feed mass rate and, thus, increasing the possibility of entanglements. These factors, linked to the high rate of waste consumption, contributed to one of the power boilers starting to suffer from events of this nature in 2015, increasing the unavailability of the biomass transport screws.

This deviation from an abnormal operating condition brings several problems, which are as follows:

a. Unavailability of equipment – while clogged, the screw cannot be used to feed biomass;

b. Increase in power of other screws – with the clogged screw stopped, the other power lines proportionally assume the lost load and increase the operating speed, increasing the possibility of these other positions also clogging;

c. Punctual loss of steam generation – the delay between stopping the clogged screw and compensation for fuel oil causes a punctual loss of steam generation;

d. Risk of accidents – the unclogging process is manual and depends on human interaction with the equipment, which characterizes the activity as dangerous;

e. Material wear – unwanted equipment stops always bring risks of breakage and unnecessary peripheral efforts.

Therefore, the objective of the work was to reduce the occurrence of clogging, increasing the availability of equipment.

2. Methodology

The work followed the traditional problem-solving methodology, developed in seven main steps (as shown in **Figure 3**) based on the PDCA (plan-do-control-act) cycle. This method has been highlighted in the organizational environment as a management method for process improvement and problem-solving, being the basis of continuous improvement, and can be used in any type of organization, whether it is a private company, a nonprofit organization, or in a public sector. The PDCA is a method that manages the decision-making in order to improve an organization's activities, much explored in the pursuit of improved performance. This makes the PDCA very important and contributes significantly to the achievement of better results [7].

The PDCA in organizations obtains opposite results, with extensive and voluminous plans based on the procedures followed in step "P" of the cycle PDCA that determines where you want to go by imposing effective planning, achieving a way to the desired situation, in its implementation the practice of "D" bringing the uncertainty of carrying out an important activity, because through audits it is found a large number of activities outside your procedure, following step "C" identifying something that is not going as planned. Finally, step "A" is responsible for closing the PDCA cycle, so little practiced, but through convincing actions based on failures in the previous steps ensuring problems arising giving meaning to an improvement cycle continuous process of a given process [8].

The concept of the PDCA methodology does not consist only of implementation of strategic changes, but also organizes the successive improvements in circles, consisting of four phases as described in **Table 1** [9].

Problem-solving methodology seeks to objectively define and surround the problem analyzed, identify and mitigate the root causes of each type of failure mode and implement controls, so that there are no recurrences of the problems and that earnings are routinely maintained.

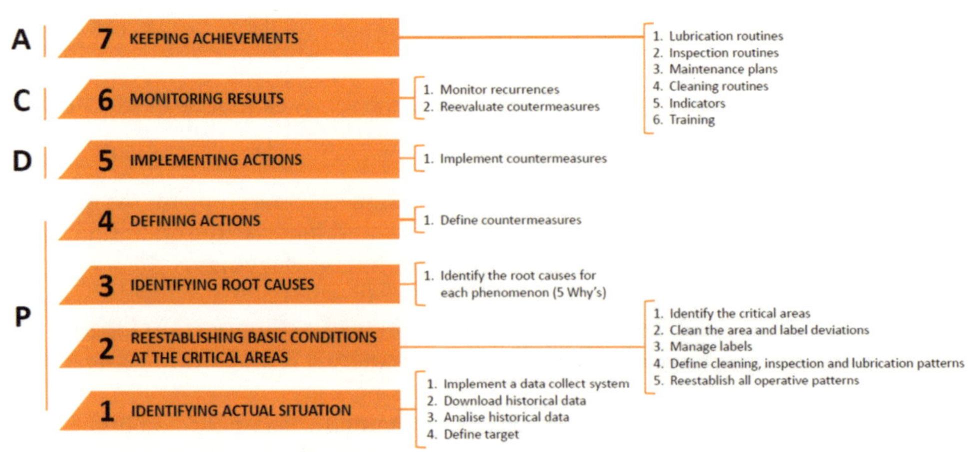

Figure 3.
Problem-solving road map (seven steps).

P	Plan – this phase starts from the preexistence of description and basic understanding of what is intended with the whole process. It consists of defining the necessary actions, sizing resources, conditions, identifying dependencies and implications, assigning responsibilities, and specifying the process for measuring performance and expected results. This phase is considered complete when a plan sufficiently detailed to support execution is proposed and approved for implementation. It is at this stage that the priority items for implementation are chosen.
D	Do – execution of the actions determined in the plan, from obtaining resources and conditions to the implementation of the measurement and control process. Its result is a set of systems, processes, equipment, or that which has been objectified in the plan, properly implemented, and in conditions to be operated and to produce the desired effects.
C	Control/Check – more than measuring, it implies ensuring that the process has been executed through careful observation of its planned performance in phase P. For this, monitoring and deviation reports are used, showing whether or not the established control parameters were met.
A	Act – in fact, more appropriately, this phase should be called "how to learn from mistakes and successes," as it is the practical use of the results of the process, good or bad, to be introjected in the culture and in the methods and systems of organization. Thus, in the previous phase (verify or control) two basic conclusions can follow—either everything went well or there were problems. In the first hypothesis, the more favorable process that was experimentally outlined in the planning and that was successful should be institutionalized and made a standard for the future. People need to be trained or educated to act in the way that worked, followed, in a new cycle, by the phases of planning, executing, verifying, and acting. This implies that the organization learns from what went right.

Table 1.
PDCA cycle steps. Adapted from Costa [9].

As a first step, the methodology provides for the definition of the focus areas of the work, since the biomass lines (four in total) contain nine screws and, through the work, the most critical position was highlighted.

Having chosen the focus area, possible problems related to the base condition of the equipment, maintenance, and lubrication routines, in addition to operating standards that, in some way, could be contributing to the problem observed were verified.

With the definition of the problem, the focus area and the guarantee of systemic maintenance and operating standards, the root causes of each failure mode that caused the stoppage of the biomass screw were investigated. Using the "5 Whys" quality tool, the reasons were broken down to the last level of knowledge, making it possible to define countermeasures to mitigate each failure mode. After the measures were implemented, the recurrence of problems was monitored and, if that happened, the analysis cycle was remade, with new countermeasures defined. Finally, the maintenance of the gains obtained was guaranteed through the systematization of controls.

3. Results

A large survey carried out over the year 2015 (see **Figure 4**) showed that position M710 was the main responsible for the blockages of the biomass system (35% of the total occurrences), being, therefore, the position chosen for the study and solution of the problem. **Figure 5** shows the simplified schematic drawing of the main components of the equipment in the M710 position.

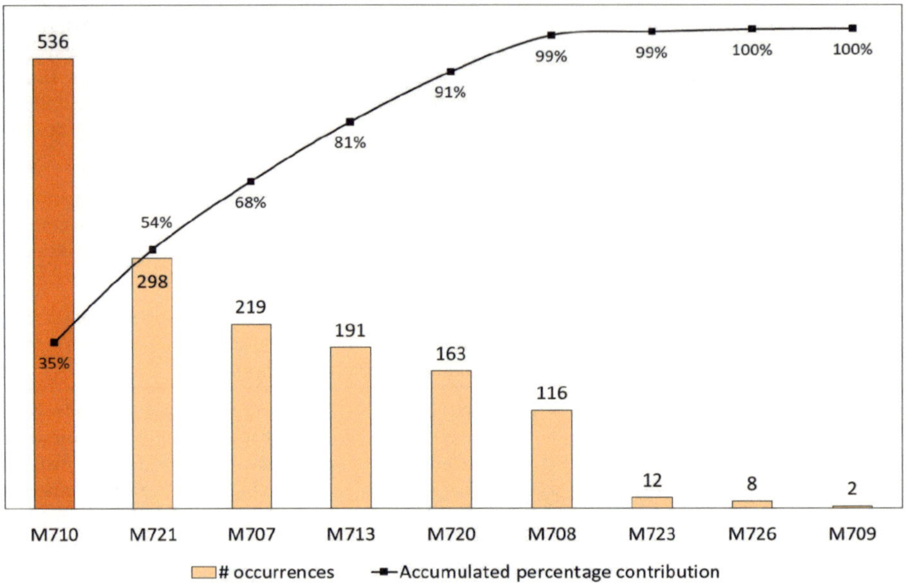

Figure 4.
Number of cloggs per position in 2015.

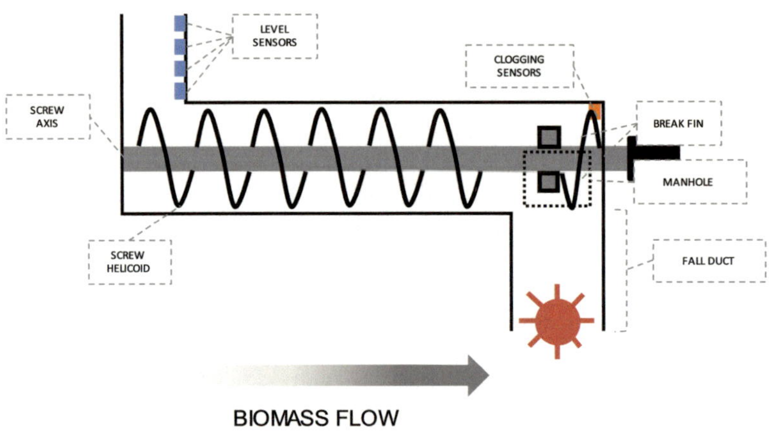

Figure 5.
Schematic drawing of the M710 thread and main items.

The initial analysis of the work on the position defined as the focus aimed to identify external factors that could contribute to the clogging being recurrent or severe. Some indicators such as average precipitation, average steam generation load, and possible operational variations between groups or work shifts did not show influence with the occurrences. As already known, the particle size quality of biomass was a point of attention, but not directly addressed, as the actions for this topic are medium and long term.

Through the "5 Whys," it was possible to observe that the biggest challenges of the M710 position were the "empty spaces" and the obstructions present in the path taken by the biomass. The actions focused on solving these root causes were:

3.1 Manhole readjustment

The manhole present in the screw fall duct was misaligned with the fall wall profile. This misalignment generated an "empty space" inside the pipeline, serving as support for the deposition of biomass, which, over time, totally obstructed the transverse profile of the pipeline, causing clogging. Thus, the simple solution was to fill the empty space with metallic material, welded to the manhole, which would eliminate the space and keep the walls of the entire duct in the same profile, as shown in **Figure 6**.

3.2 Clog sensor stem improvements

The M710 screw clogging sensor is simply a rod with tabs that when rotated by the build-up of biomass, triggers a physical sensor that stops the thread. During the observations, it was evidenced that the rod was very close to the biomass level of the screw itself, causing the material to pass over the rod, and not under, as it should be. In this way, the rod, in addition to not being activated as it should, served as a barrier for the free fall of biomass, being a major clogging point. By increasing the height of the stem by approximately 21 cm, it was possible to observe that the transported biomass returned to normal flow, eliminating an accumulation point.

3.3 Modification of the thread shaft fin

Widely known as "break-mount," the fin located at the end of the biomass screw is intended to push the material down the pipeline, avoiding agglomerations and possible clogging. During the work, it was observed that the angle between the face of the fin and the axis of the screw has a great influence on its performance, and originally, the fin had its face towards the beginning of the screw. With this configuration and direction of rotation of the thread, the fin did not push the material down, but back into the thread, in the opposite direction to the natural flow of transport.

The position of the fin was changed (according to **Figure 7**) so that it pushed the material in the same transport direction. With this new configuration, the fin, in addition to helping to transport the material, prevents the biomass from being trapped at the beginning of the drop duct.

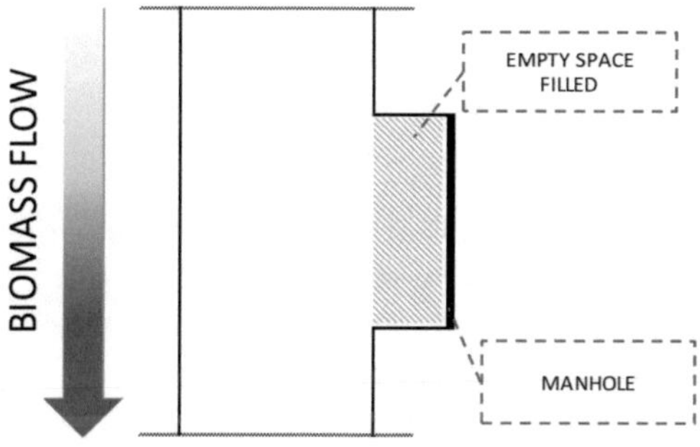

Figure 6.
Adequacy of the manhole of the biomass pipeline.

Figure 7.
Thread shaft fin position before (left) and after (right).

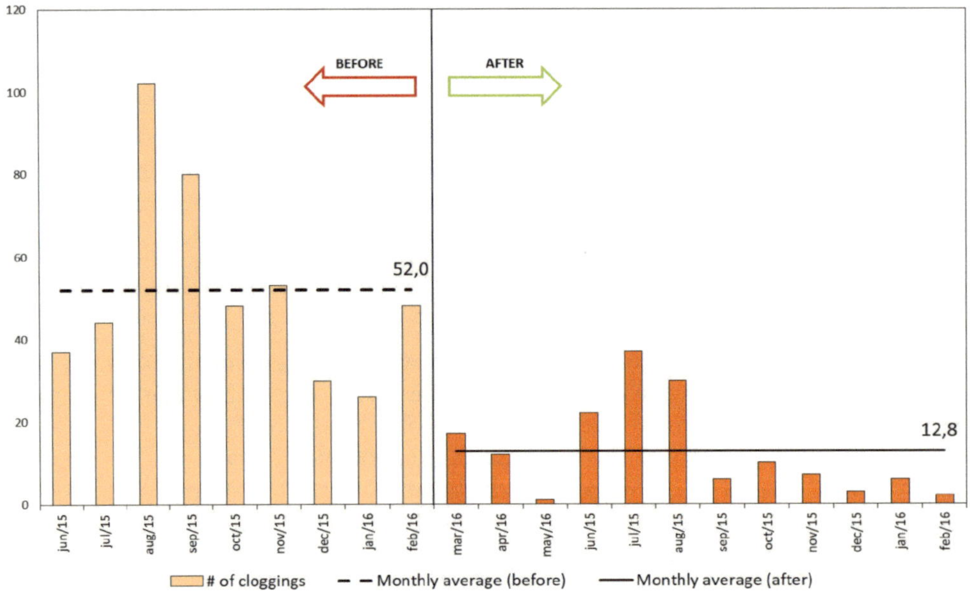

Figure 8.
Evolution of the number of cloggs of the M710 screw.

3.4 Changing the operating logic

Another important point dealt with in the work was the reactive actions taken after clogging that could prevent new occurrences or reduce the man–machine interaction in the thread unclogging process.

When the screw stops due to clogging (when the sensor is activated), an automatic operating logic was created to rotate the screw in the opposite direction to normal operation, for a few seconds and at low speed. The purpose of this sequence was to loosen any material that might be trapped above the drop duct or sensor rod. With reverse movement, the biomass detaches and falls, freeing the material duct and avoiding the need for human intervention in the machine. With the development of this logic, most of the clogging was resolved soon after the occurrence (sensor activation) and, thus, the machine availability increased significantly, while the human-machine interaction reduced.

In addition to these actions, others of lesser impact were also applied to contribute to solving other voices of the problem. The result of all the actions together can be seen in **Figure 8**, where the monthly average number of occurrences of clogs dropped 75% after the implementations. Consequently, the frequency of unclogging interventions dropped from 1.7 times a day to less than 0.5.

It is known that eliminating this type of occurrence is practically impossible for this position, since, due to the structural shape and distribution of the boiler support points, the M710 thread is the one that receives material in a different direction from the natural flow, where the entire biomass line is tortuous.

However, the actions developed were of low cost and did not require the boiler to be stopped, thus configuring a good option for solving this type of problem. In addition, any of the actions can be extended to other positions of the threads in the boiler, making it possible to drastically reduce problems related to clogging.

4. Conclusions

Using a well-known methodology, it is concluded that the actions actually attacked the root causes that promoted plugging in the biomass system, especially in position M710. The great gain of the work was the low cost and agility in carrying out the proposed actions, surpassing expectations regarding the return that was thought to be possible to achieve. Therefore, the work reached the proposed objective of reducing the occurrences in the power boiler through simple and easy-to-apply solutions, showing that, in general, there are opportunities for solving problems that involve low cost and high return.

Author details

Guilherme Moscato Malavazi
Klabin S.A, Telêmaco Borba, Brazil

*Address all correspondence to: gmalavazi@klabin.com.br

References

[1] Brito JO. O uso energético da madeira. Estudos Avançados, São Paulo. 2007;**21**(59):185

[2] Do Canto JL. Colheita mecanizada de biomassa florestal para energia. 121 f. [thesis]. Viçosa. MG: Universidade Federal de Viçosa; 2009

[3] Goldemberg J. Energia, meio ambiente & desenvolvimento. São Paulo: Editora USP; 1998. p. 125

[4] Ruan R, Zhang Y, Chen P, Liu S, Fan L, Zhou N, et al. Biofuels: Introduction. In: Padey A, Larroche C, Dussap CG, Gnansounoukhanal ESK, Ricke S, editors. Biofuels: Alternative Feedstocks and Conversion Processes for the Production of Liquid and Gaseous Biofuels. United States of America: Elsevier; 2019. pp. 3-43

[5] Foelkel, C. Utilização da Biomassa do Eucalipto para Produção de Calor, Vapor e Eletricidade - Parte 3: Resíduos Florestais Energéticos, 2016. Avaliable from: https://www.eucalyptus.com.br/eucaliptos/PT45_Residuos_Florestais_Energeticos.pdf

[6] Babcock Power España. Operation and Maintenance Manual – Sistema interno de alimentação de biomassa. Monte Alegre, Brazil: Klabin, Project MA; 2007. pp. 2-3

[7] Vieira Filho G. Gestão da Qualidade Total: Uma abordagem prática. 3rd ed. Campinas: Alínea; 2010

[8] Couto B d A, Robert MI. Gestão por processos: em sistemas de gestão da qualidade. Rio de Janeiro: Qualitymark. 1st volume. 2012

[9] Costa EA. Gestão estratégica: da empresa que temos da empresa que queremos. 2nd ed. São Paulo: Saraiva; 2007

Chapter 9

Biotisation of Vegetables

Henry Juan Javier Ninahuaman
and Grimaldo Quispe Santivañez

Abstract

The research proposes a biofertiliser from mycorrhiza and rhizobium evaluating its antagonistic capacity and biotisation in the cultivation of vegetables with a DCA, the sample considers the potato, pea, and barley in the Huasahuasi Peruvian District, with nine treatments in three formulas, considering a control group without inoculation and two repetitions. As a result, the optimal formula is obtained with 300 g of mycorrhizal and rhizobium strains + 500 g of black soil + 200 g of potato peel crust, which has an effective antagonistic capacity of 100% in pea cultivation, 90% in the barley, and 85% in the potato, besides that it achieves a biotisation in the cultivation of peas of 95%, in the barley 100% and in the potato 90%.

Keywords: biotisation, biofertiliser, mycorrhiza, rhizobium, vegetables

1. Introduction

Latin American soils have low yields, chemical fertilisers are expensive, there are phytosanitary problems, soil deterioration and nitrogen deficiency in agricultural land, and at the international level, there is a search for ways to stop soil erosion, which is of great importance for the biological diversity of vegetation and fauna (**Figure 1**) [1].

One emblematic case is camu camu, which decreased to 1.5–2.5 t/ha during 2017 due to the reduction of N, K, and Mg in the soil. For this reason, it was proposed to increase production levels with biofertilizers by using cow manure, chicken manure, island guano, and river sediment.

The use of biofertilisers promotes insect repellency, increases resistance to pest and pathogen attacks through their odour (**Figure 2**) [2].

Climate change challenges agriculture, and variations in production and costs directly affect farmers [3]. In other countries, there are no soil quality problems, but pesticide residuals in products, such as tomatoes and cape gooseberries, with up to 10 pesticides found in the fruit and on the skin in concentrations of more than 0.002 ppm, toxic compounds, such as sulfotep, phorate, heptachlor, aldrin, endosulfan sulphate and I, making export impossible due to the minimum sanitary quality requirements [4].

In response, work is being done to raise awareness, proposing other forms of energy use such as alternative energies [5] and the use of arbuscular mycorrhizal fungi (AMF) together with Twin-N as biofertilisers in potato cultivation, which would completely replace the use of chemical fertilisers with a yield per hectare of

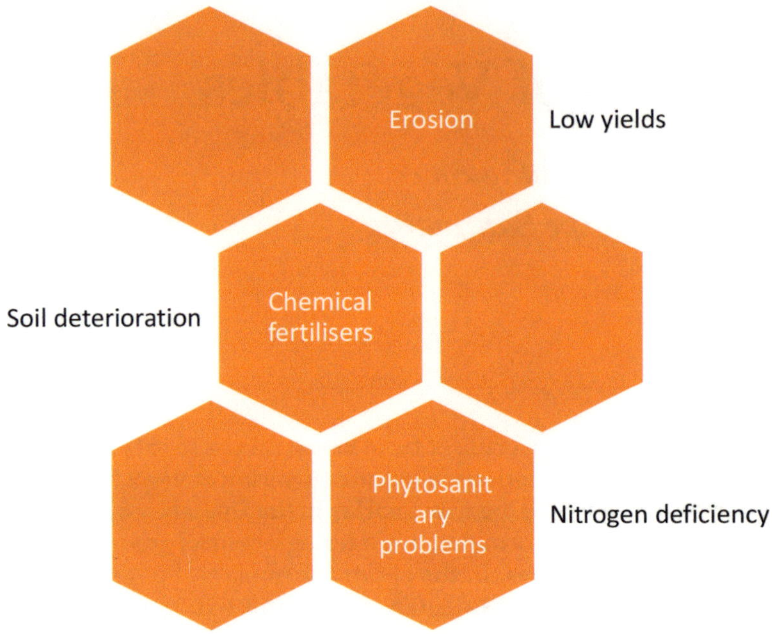

Figure 1.
Soil problems.

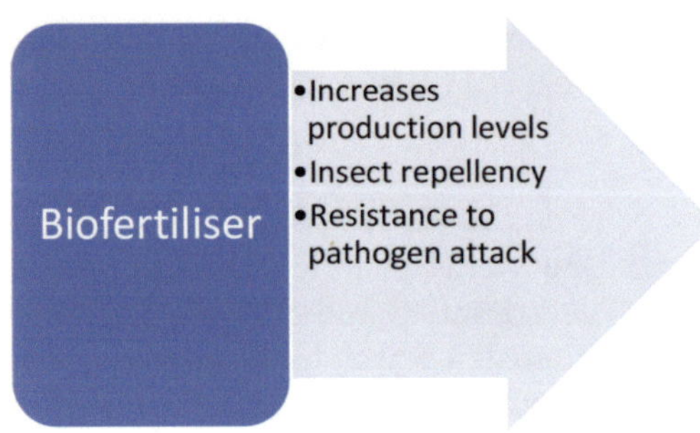

Figure 2.
Benefit of biofertiliser.

more than 116% compared to traditional fertilisation and a mostly healthy harvest of tubers with 1–10% skin lesions [6], moulds and beneficial bacteria to induce nodulation, inhibit the development of pathogenic microorganisms, fix nitrogen and other nutrients in plants, has been studied as an option for potential impact.

Mycorrhizae cover 95% of the requirements in the production of walnuts, being the production needs of 30% of nitrogen and 50% of potassium and phosphorus, the costs were 40.8% of the income from sales [7], there are studies whereby providing rhizobia a good quantity of nodules was obtained with very low weights with respect to the optimum values, but this is remedied after inoculating B. japonicum and Nod factors, offering a biotechnological alternative of acceptable yield [8].

But the antagonistic activity is another important factor, a study measures Trichoderma harzianum strains against Rhizotonia spp., Nakatea sigmoide, and Sclerotum folfsii, making T. harzianum superior in antagonism and antiparasitic activity against Garrido [9].

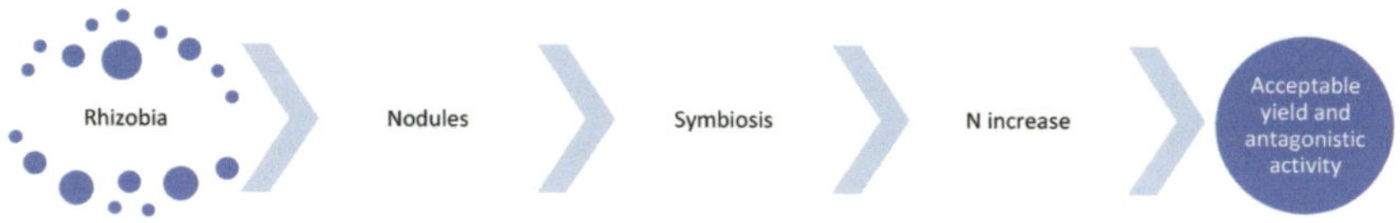

Figure 3.
Rhizobium action.

Work was carried out on wheat grains, obtaining an increase in Nitrogen (2 to 15 N/ha) and dry matter absorbed of 20–40% of that applied biofertilisers improve nutrient absorption [10].

arbuscular mycorrhizal fungi, hydrogen sulphate, and Mucoromycotina fungi are studied, which colonise 78.1% of the species, of which only 56.2% are considered to be mycorrhizal [11].

When inoculating native rhizobia on peas (Pisum sativum), 40% of the crops show the formation of nodules in symbiosis, but only 10% show their efficiency in terms of nodulation percentage and speed (**Figure 3**) [12].

Organic fertilisers in sunflower give the highest availability of nutrients, improve the weather and conditions suitable for this crop, increase the achene protein (APC), and highlight the need for water supply and sunshine on the performance of the plant development. The benefits of biofertilisation are an increase in available N which increases soil microbial activity, increases P and K content, dry matter and protein yield, the biofertiliser that obtained the highest rates of 48% oil and 14% protein is goat manure [13].

Biofertilisers were found to increase P, Ca, and Mg values but were not very effective in coffee plantations, well conventional planting systems had no differences with respect to plagiotropic branches as well as fertiliser application and type of planting [14]. Similarly, with the addition of BMV-biofertiliser, the increase in N fell and the contents of Cu and Fe decreased linearly with the increase in biofertiliser. The loss of volatile N is indicated by the alkalinity and aggregation of Ca and Mg in the oil [15].

A biofertiliser obtained by anaerobic digestion of cassava effluent was applied to the development of Crambe plants, the results indicated that the higher the percentage of biofertiliser, the oil values obtained were lower than those of the control, even that the minimum value was achieved with the highest inoculation, in addition to potassium deficiency results in decreased productivity in Crambe grains [16]. Another case is the application of cattle manure biofertiliser to strawberry plants, where it was found that production was greater than 1,250 ml/plant/week in a protected environment and sprayed with cold water and white soil, obtaining the largest fruit size in diameter and length, but with less soluble solids content (Brix) than those grown in the environment in full sun [17].

Adding saltwater to soybean reduces photosynthesis, stomatal conductance and transpiration, with low intensity when inoculated with aerobically fermented bovine biofertiliser [18], demonstrating a plant protection mechanism. When evaluating the ectomycorrhizal fungus of pine, the accumulation of heavy metals in the roots of plants with ectomycorrhizal fungi was noted, which, contrary to expectations, had fewer shoots with this type of fungi, there was no difference with the control with respect to the rhizosphere, but there was a predominance of acidobacteria, actinobacteria, and proteobacteria [19].

This study analyses mycorrhiza strains isolated from pine fungus and rhizobium isolated from pea root, thus promoting their use as biofertiliser and taking advantage of their antagonistic capacity, considering their biotisation generated from these microorganisms in plants.

It is estimated that this process contributes between 60 and 80% of biological nitrogen fixation and this symbiosis provides a considerable part of combined nutrients and nitrogen in the soil and allows plants to grow without synthetic fertilisers and without impoverishing soils [20].

2. Methods

The present research work was carried out in the district of San Juan de Huasahuasi, located 48 km from the district of Tarma, at an altitude of 2,751 m above sea level. The raw material consists of mycorrhiza and rhizobium isolated from pea root and pine fungus, rhizobium is diazotrophic bacteria that have the ability to fix N in plant nodules and mycorrhizae are the double absorption organs that are formed when symbiont fungi live inside healthy absorption organs (roots, rhizomes, or stems) [7, 12, 21]. Black soil and potato peel bran were used as inputs, oil and potato dextrose agar were also used, the equipment used was a microorganism incubator and an analytical balance (**Figure 4**) [22–26].

Vegetable crops were sampled—potatoes, peas, and barley in the Huasahuasi district of Tarma province.

Among the methods used were the Association of Analytical Communities *in vitro* sowing method and colony counting. Once the product was obtained, a physical-chemical characterisation was carried out, evaluating fertility, antagonistic capacity, and biotisation (**Figure 5**).

The experimental process consists of obtaining strains of microorganisms and the biofertiliser mycorrhiza and rhizobium from pea root and pine fungus through two stages:

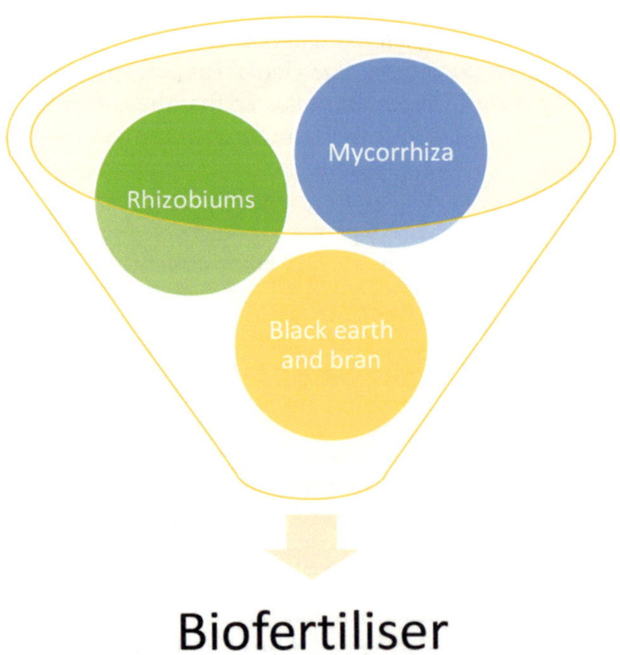

Figure 4.
Elements of biofertiliser.

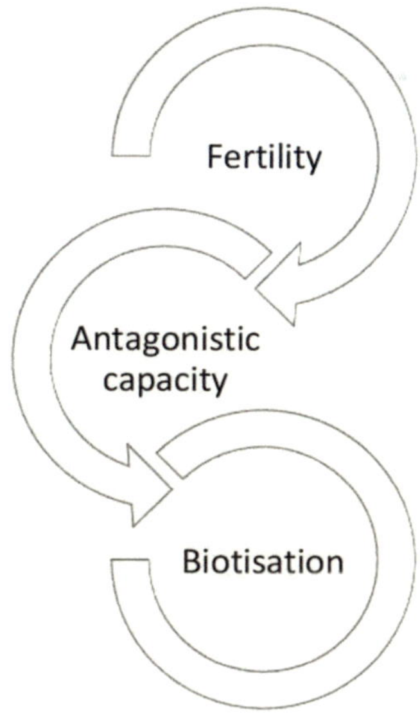

Figure 5.
Characterisation of the biofertiliser.

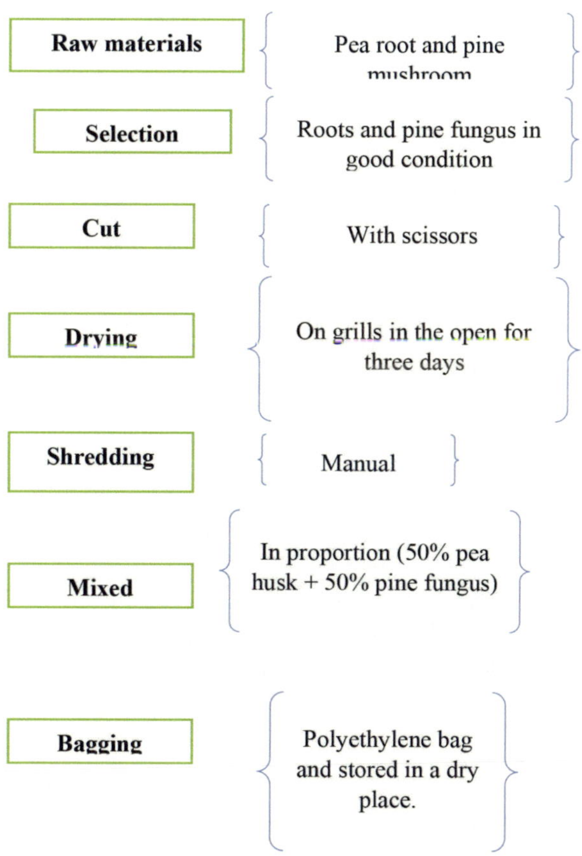

Figure 6.
First stage: breeding of strains.

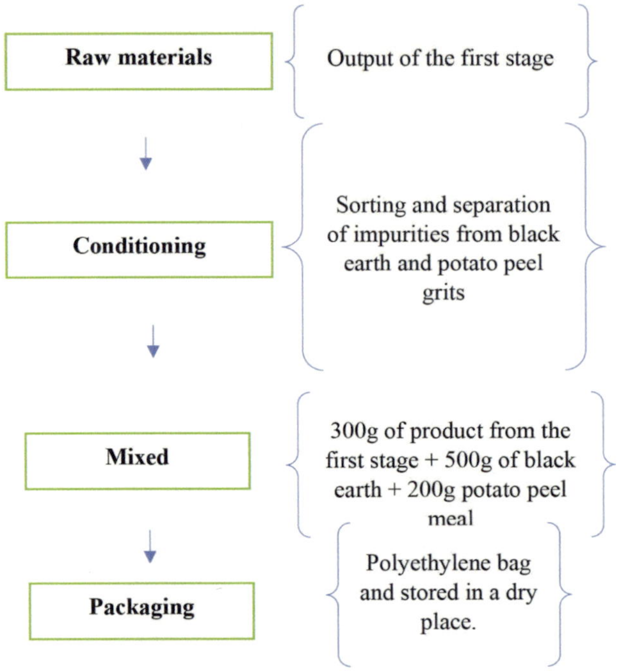

Figure 7.
Second stage: obtaining the optimal biofertiliser formula.

Figure 8.
Inoculation of biofertiliser formulation to pea seed.

The first stage consists of obtaining strains of mycorrhiza and rhizobium microorganisms, obtained from pea root and pine fungus, which is described in **Figure 6**.

The second stage consists of obtaining the optimal biofertiliser formulation of mycorrhiza and rhizobium, which is shown in **Figures 7** and **8**.

Repetitions	Treatments		Factor A		
			1	2	3
1	Factor B	1	F1C1	F2C1	F3C1
		2	F1C2	F2C2	F3C2
		3	F1C3	F2C3	F3C3
2	Factor B	1	F1C1	F2C1	F3C1
		2	F1C2	F2C2	F3C2
		3	F1C3	F2C3	F3C3

F = Biofertiliser formula; F1 = 100 g of strains of microorganisms + 500 g of black soil and 200 g of potato peel bran; F2 = 200 g of strains of microorganisms + 500 g of black soil and 200 g of potato peel grist; F3 = 300 g of strains of microorganisms + 500 g of black soil + 200 g of potato peel bran; C = Vegetable cultivation (potato, pea, and barley); C1 = Potato; C2 = Peas; and C3 = Barley.

Table 1.
Relationship of biofertiliser formulation and plant cultivation.

The statistical evaluation assessed the percentage effect of the biofertiliser in relation to its antagonistic capacity and biotisation, applying a completely randomised design (CRD) with the factorial arrangement and two replications [22], the factors were as follows:

Factor A: Inoculation of mycorrhiza and rhizobium biofertiliser formulation (F1, F2, and F3).

Factor B: Vegetable crops (potato, pea, and barley).

With a factorial arrangement of 3A × 3B = nine treatments and two replicates, the antagonistic and biotic effect of mycorrhiza and rhizobium fertiliser on vegetable crops (potato, pea and barley) is compared (**Table 1**).

3. Results and discussions

3.1 Antagonistic capacity of the biofertiliser

The analysis was applied to the treatments of the biofertiliser of mycorrhiza and rhizobium inoculating the sample with 50 g for 200 g of seed, an effective antagonistic capacity of 100% was obtained in the pea crop, 90% in barley and 85% in potato, of the biofertiliser of mycorrhiza and rhizobium with the formula F3, the biofertiliser with the formula F2 inoculated on the pea crop obtained a result of 85% effectiveness,

Results		Crops		
Formula	**C1 Pea (%)**	**C2 Barley (%)**	**C3 Potato (%)**	**Effectiveness**
F1	45	45	35	No
F2	85	80	65	Effective
F3	100	90	85	Effective

K = Ratio of strains of microorganisms 500 g mycorrhiza (pine fungus) + 500 g rhizobium (pea root).

Table 2.
Comparison of the effectiveness of antagonistic capacity.

Results		Crops		
Formula	**C1 Pea (%)**	**C2 Barley (%)**	**C3 Potato (%)**	**Effectiveness**
F1	55	60	35	No
F2	95	95	90	Effective
F3	95	100	90	Effective

Table 3.
Comparison of the effectiveness of biotisation.

80% on barley, and 65% on the potato crop, in comparison to these two formulas where the result was effective, the biofertiliser with the formula F1 the results were not very significant as the percentage of effectiveness on the pea crop was 45%, barley 45%, and potato 35%. The optimal formula of the biofertiliser of mycorrhiza and rhizobium was F3, to be used in the cultivation of vegetables, obtaining a significant result in the antagonistic capacity of the biofertiliser (**Table 2**).

3.2 Analysis of biotisation in vegetable crops

This analysis was carried out to verify the growth of the root system, the acclimatisation phase, and the increase in the functionality of the roots and, consequently, the nutritional and water status of the vegetable crops. The results obtained in relation to the inoculated formula and the vegetable crop used as a sample, which in this case was potato, pea, and barley, are shown in **Table 3**.

According to the results shown in **Table 3**, we can determine that the mycorrhiza and rhizobium biofertiliser has an effective effect on the biotisation of the plant crop by increasing the number of strains of microorganisms in the biofertiliser formula.

3.3 Balance of matter of the obtaining of the biofertiliser of Mycorrhiza and Rhizobium according to the optimal formula.

To determine the yield of the optimum formula of the mycorrhiza and Rhizobium biofertiliser, a balance of matter was carried out starting with 10 kg of pea root and 10 kg of pine fungus, the roots and fungi were selected taking into account the optimum characteristics, 16.7% was lost. The conditioning operation discards the unusable parts, stems and filaments, losing 13% during the drying operation and eliminating 55% of the water. The dry material is milled with a loss of 2%, thus obtaining a yield of 13.3 % with respect to the initial raw material (1,333 kg).

1,333 kg (50% dry pea root + 50% dry pine fungus) is mixed with 2,221 kg of black soil 0,888 kg of potato peel flour, making a total of 4,442 kg of biofertiliser for every 10 kg of fresh pea root and 10 kg of fresh pine fungus.

4. Economic viability

The economic feasibility assessment was carried out in each production phase and two stages.

The first stage is called obtaining the strains from the pea root and the pine fungus, both of the same proportion, these are selected, cut, crushed, and dried, in each process,

First phase	%	Kg
Pea root Kg		10
Pine mushroom Kg		10
Selection	Loss 16.7	3.34
Shredded	Loss 13	2.6
Crushed	Loss 2	0.4
Dried	Loss 55	11
Result	Yield 13.3	2.66

Table 4.
Result first phase.

Product	Quantity required Kg	Cost × 1 Kg	Total
Pea root Kg	10	2.00	20.00
Pine mushroom Kg	10	14.00	140.00
			160.00

Table 5.
Cost first phase.

there are diligently measured losses between them; there is a loss of 86.7%. Based on these losses, it can be deduced that the yield in this first stage amounts to 13.3% (**Table 4**).

The second phase deals with the elaboration of the biofertiliser product from the previously obtained strains. This consists of a mixture of strains from the first phase (30%), black soil (50%), and potato peel flour (20%) (**Tables 5** and **6**).

In the beginning, 10 kg of pea root at a price of 2.00 Peruvian suns (PEN) and 10 kg of pine fungus at 14.00 PEN each Kg are used, making expenses of 20.00 and 140.00, respectively.

For the second phase, black soil is required in quantities of 4,442 kg equivalent to 50% of the total mixture of 1.5 soles, amounting to 6,663 soles and potato peel flour in quantities of 1,776 kg equivalent to 20% of 1.00 PEN, amounting to 1,776 PEN.

The labour required is three daily wages of 30.00 each making 90.00 PEN.

	Quantity (Kg)	Cost × 1 Kg	Cost PEN	Cost GBP
First phase strains (30%)	2,666		160.00	29.79
Black soil (50%)	4,442	1.50	6,663	1.24
potato peel flour (20%)	1,776	1.00	1,776	0.33
Subtotal	8,884			
Labour	3 wages	30.00	90.00	16.76
	Cost 8,884 Kg		258,439	48.13
	Cost Kg		29.09	5.82

Table 6.
Cost second phase.

With these costs and wastage, a total of 8,884 kg costs 258,439 PEN, which is 29.09 soles or 5.82 GBP per kg of biofertiliser.

The yield tests in the field show a yield of 60% when using 30 g per kg of seed potato, however, it is necessary to carry out further field tests to prove the effectiveness of each product.

Regarding the analysis of the competition, there are products, such as Trichoderma, which in its presentation of 100 g has a cost of 4.00 GBP, shipped in Ecuador in South America. Another product is the blood meal whose price per 1 Kg is 140 GBP on average and the Mycoracine that in the presentation of 500 g has a value of 543.50 GBP or the Bacillus Subtilis of 500 g at a cost of 445.00 GBP

5. Discussions

Antagonism is the direct inhibitory activity exerted by one microorganism on another and controls it biologically by attenuating damage to growth systems [24].

The antagonism test against soil phytopathogens was measured with respect to the fungus Fusarium Solani, the F2 and F3 formulations were effective in the antagonistic capacity against this fungus, which represents 100% of the strains, This could be due to the fact that the number of Streptomyces strains evaluated exceeded 4,000, since the inhibition zones obtained are equivalent to the average inhibition percentages obtained in the present study [23], the mechanism of antibiosis effect is presumed to be by means of inhibitory metabolites, in the same way as [24] or by repellency, as in Abanto-Rodríguez et al. [2].

Regarding the recovery of soils, the product obtained is easily used in the prevention of soil erosion [1] and can be considered as a new form of chemical energy alternative to conventional ones [5], as both mycorrhiza- and rhizobium-based products increase the amount of N in the soil as well as K and Mg, the results are similar to those obtained by Borges et al. [13], Figueiredo et al. [14], Cardoso et al. [15], and de Sousa et al. [18] for their effectiveness in biotisation.

The methodology for obtaining the biofertiliser differs from those obtained in aerobic digestion [16], in that the method proposed in this study allows the creation of a product directly proportional to its amount of addition.

Biotisation is the use of fungi and bacteria on plants that achieve acclimatisation and creation of beneficial rhizosphere [25], the effect of biotisation showed the growth of the root system, its acclimatisation and increased root functionality, comparisons show that F3 in barley is 100% effective in direct benefit to farmers [3] and similar to the findings of Flore-Córdova with the ability to replace traditional fertilisers [7] even at a lower cost as it is not necessary to inoculate boosters like Fornasero and Toniutti [8] to achieve results, These results are supported by Grageda-Cabrera et al. [10] and Lara-pérez et al. [11], but they are better than Moreno-chirinos et al. [12] as they achieve nodule formation higher than 40 % of crops, with values of 95 % in peas and even the less effective F1 formula shows 55%.

6. Conclusions

The biofertiliser based on mycorrhiza and rhizobium is antagonistic to the fungus Fusarium Solani, increasing its antagonistic activity by increasing the dose of these strains in the formulation.

The biofertiliser based on mycorrhiza and rhizobium is able to recover soils for the cultivation of peas, potatoes and barley.

The biofertilisation effect of the biofertiliser understudy is higher in barley (100% effective) due to its higher capacity to produce substances that stimulate plant growth.

Conflict of interest

No conflict of interest.

Notes/thanks/other declarations

None.

Author details

Henry Juan Javier Ninahuaman[1*] and Grimaldo Quispe Santivañez[2]

1 Universidad Tecnológica del Perú, Cercado de Lima, Perú

2 Universidad Continental, Huancayo, Perú

*Address all correspondence to: c21259@utp.edu.pe

References

[1] FAO. Día mundial del suelo. 2019. Available from: http://www.fao.org/world-soil-day/es/ [Accessed: October 11, 2019]

[2] Abanto-Rodríguez C, Mori GMS, Panduro MHP, Castro EVV, Dávila EJP, de Oliveira EM. Uso de biofertilizantes en el desarrollo vegetativo y productivo de plantas de camu-camu en Ucayali, Perú. Revista Ceres. 2019;**66**(2):108-116

[3] Álvaro Hernán Alarcón JDS, Arias G, Díaz CJ. Sistema de control automático de variables climáticas para optimizar el rendimiento de cultivos bajo cubierta. Ingeniería Solidaria. 2017;**2017**:1-17

[4] Ávila-Orozco FD, León-Gallón LM, Pinzón-Fandiño MI, Londoño-Orozco A, Gutiérrez-Cifuentes JA. Residualidad de fitosanitarios en tomate y uchuva cultivados en Quindío (Colombia). Corpoica Ciencia y Tecnologia Agropecuaria. 2017;**18**(3):571-582

[5] Gonzáles Y. Acciones preventivas del deterioro de los suelos como alternativa para fomentar la cultura conservacionista. Revista Science. 2019;**53**(9):1689-1699

[6] Castillo C, Huenchuleo MJ, Michaud A, Solano J. Micorrización en un cultivo de papa adicionado del biofertilizante Twin-N establecido en un Andisol de la Región de La Araucanía. Idesia. 2016;**34**(1):39-45

[7] Flores-cordova MA, Parra JMS, Piña FJ, Pérez R, Sánchez E. Contribution of nutrients, organic amendments and mycorrhizae on the yield components in pecan walnut (Carya ilinoinensis). Cultivos Tropicales. 2018;**39**(1):35-42

[8] Fornasero LV, Toniutti MA. Evaluación de la nodulación y rendimiento del cultivo de soja con la aplicación de distintas formulaciones de inoculantes. Fave—Sección ciencias agrarias. 2015;**14**(1):79-90

[9] Garrido M. Capacidad antagónica de Trichoderma harzianum frente a Rhizoctonia, Nakatea sigmoidea y Sclerotium rolfsii y su efecto en cepas nativas de Trichoderma aisladas de cultivos de arroz. Scientia Agropecuaria. 2019;**10**(2):199-206

[10] Grageda-Cabrera OA, González-Figueroa SS, Vera-Nuñez JA, Aguirre-Medina JF, Peña-Cabriales JJ. Efecto de los biofertilizantes sobre la asimilación de nitrógeno por el cultivo de trigo. Revista mexicana de ciencias agrícolas. 2018;**9**(2):281-289

[11] Lara-pérez LA, Zulueta-rodríguez R, Andrade-torres A. Micorriza arbuscular, Mucoromycotina y hongos septados oscuros en helechos y licófitas con distribución en México : una revisión global. Revista de Biología Tropical. 2017;**65**(101):1062-1081

[12] Moreno-chirinos ZE, Valdez-núñez RA, Soriano BS, Ruesta-campoverde NA. Eficiencia en la nodulación por rizobios nativos, procedentes de nódulos de Pisum sativum 'arveja' colectados de diferentes departamentos del Perú. Scientia Agropecuaria. 2016;**7**(3):165-172

[13] Borges FRM, Bezerra FML, Marinho AB, Ramos EG, Adriano JDNJ. Goat manure fertilization and irrigation on production components of sunflower. Revista Caatinga. 2019;**32**(1):211-221

[14] Figueiredo LH, Miranda GRB, Vilella PMF. Biofertilizer use associated with different forms of planting in the development of the initial coffee arabic. Coffee Science. 2017;**12**(4):463-470

[15] Cardoso MO, Berni RF, Antonio IC, Kano C. Growth, production and nutrients in coriander cultivated with biofertilizer. Horticultura Brasileira. 2017;**35**(4):583-590

[16] Neves AC, Bergamini CN, de Leonardo RO, Gonçalves MP, Zenatti DC, Hermes E. Effect of biofertilizer obtained by anaerobic digestion of cassava effluent on the development of crambe plants. Revista Brasileira de Engenharia Agrícola e Ambiental. 2017;**21**(10):681-685

[17] Dos Santos EM, Viana TVDA, De Sousa GG, De Azevedo BM, Moraes JGL. Yield and quality of strawberry fruits fertilized with bovine biofertilizer. Revista Caatinga. 2019;**32**(1):16-26

[18] de Sousa GG, dos Rodrigues VS, da Soares SC, Damasceno ÍN, Fiusa JN, Saraiva SEL. Irrigation with saline water in soybean (Glycine max (L.) Merr.) in a soil with bovine biofertilizer. Revista Brasileira de Engenharia Agrícola e Ambiental. 2018;**22**(9):604-609

[19] Yu P, Sun Y, Huang Z, Zhu F, Sun Y, Jiang L. The effects of ectomycorrhizal fungi on heavy metals' transport in Pinus massoniana and bacteria community in rhizosphere soil in mine tailing area. Journal of Hazardous Materials. 2020;**381**(July):121203

[20] Ventura S, Bernilla BS. Efecto de Trichoderma viride y Bradyrhizobium yuanmingense en el crecimiento de Capsicum Annuum en condiciones de laboratorio. Rebiolest. 2014;**2**(2)

[21] Ramírez M, Rolon M, Moncada A, Serralde DP. Biofertilización con hongos formadores de micorrizas arbusculares (HFMA) en especies forestales en vivero. Biotecnología En El Sector Agropecuario Y Agroindustrial;**16**(2):15-25

[22] Sampieri RH, Collado CF, Lucio PB. Metodología de la investigación. 5ta ed. México D.F.: McGraw-Hill / Interamericana Editores, S A de C V; 2010

[23] Ikeda K, Saito H, Sato SI, Kodama T. Growth-inhibition effect of Streptomyces sp. 39L40C to mulberry twig blight pathogen, Fusarium lateritium f. sp. mori. Journal of Sericultural Science of Japan. 2000;**69**(3):163-168

[24] Orihuela M. Morfotipos de hongos endomicorrizógenos asociado al maíz amiláceo (Zea mays L. amiláceo), y su capacidad antagónica para el control de Fusarium oxysporum. Universidad Nacional de San Cristobal de Huamanga. 2016;**1**(1):7-120

[25] Infante D, Martinez B, Gonzáles N, Reyes Y. Mecanismos de acción de Trichoderma frente a hongos fitopatogenos. Protección. 2009;**24**(2):14-21

[26] Carrazana D, Santos A, Alderete Y, Galvez D, Cupull R, Navarro M. Bacteria endófita latente no vitropatógena en el cultivo in vitro de Xanthosoma sagittifolium (L. Schot). Centro Agrícola. 2011;**38**(4):21-29

Section 4

Biomass Biorefineries

Chapter 10

Challenging Biomass Feedstocks for Energy and Chemicals

Meheretu Jaleta Dirbeba and Johan Werkelin

Abstract

The Nordic countries have a long tradition of utilizing agro-industrial sidestreams for heat and power production and recovery of chemicals. A typical example is black liquor from pulp mills. Here, the woody biomass undergoes a digestion process where the fibers are separated to produce pulp for paper production. The liquid by-product from the digester, black liquor, contains wood lignin and the spent cooking chemicals. Through the chemical recovery cycle, the black liquor is utilized for heat and power production and recovery of cooking chemicals. Worldwide, there are several challenging biomass sidestreams that can be utilized in a similar fashion as with black liquor. Some examples of these are vinasse from the integrated sugar-ethanol production process; straw and manure from agriculture sources; forest residues; by-products from the food industry; etc. This book chapter will review the availability of these types of feedstocks and discuss their applicability and challenges to be used for energy and chemicals. Pyrolysis, gasification, and combustion are the potential thermal conversion options considered for the utilization of these types of challenging biomass feedstocks.

Keywords: biomass feedstock, ash, impurities, thermal conversion, renewable energy, circular economy

1. Introduction

This chapter deals with the worldwide and local resources of challenging (or low-grade) biomass feedstocks available for the production of energy and chemicals. It aims to highlight the potential of different sources of low-grade biomass and make aware of their content of impurities, mainly ash-forming elements (e.g., Na, K, Ca, Si, P, S, and Cl) and nitrogen (N). It also suggests what kind of utilization techniques, such as combustion, pyrolysis, and gasification render the best yields and the least problems in industrial conversion systems.

1.1 Challenging biomass feedstocks as a renewable source for energy and chemicals

Biomass is a renewable resource and a short-term carbon sink [1]. The carbon cycle explains how carbon atoms continuously travel from the atmosphere to the ground and then back again as carbon dioxide or methane into the atmosphere.

The biomass on earth both binds and emits greenhouse gases in the atmosphere. When dead biomass degrades, it becomes humus (soil), water, and carbon dioxide. In anaerobic conditions, every second of carbon dioxide will form methane, a 28 times more potent greenhouse gas than carbon dioxide [1].

Carbon dioxide and methane are the two most dominant greenhouse gases from anthropogenic emissions [1]. Emissions lead to increasing concentrations in the atmosphere and cause the Earth's temperature to rise. Therefore, the focus must be on all unutilized and low-quality biomass feedstocks available worldwide. These low-grade biomass feedstocks are present in different forms and have the potential to replace fossil-based feedstocks for energy and chemicals production. If they are not utilized for energy or chemicals production, they will inevitably contribute to greenhouse gas emissions. This chapter aims to shed light on different low-grade biomass feedstocks for energy and chemicals and discusses the concentrations and roles of impurities in the thermal conversion of the feedstocks.

1.2 Low-grade biomass of different sources

Agriculture and forestry give rise to a large amount of non-used biomass [2]. Only a small fraction of the field crop ends up as food or some other product, maybe as little as 10–20% [2] of the total above-ground mass of biomass. Some of it finds use in farming or as a soil fertilizer. In forestry, only the trunk of a tree is of industrial value. The rest 30% of the above-ground biomass of a tree neither becomes timber nor fiber [2]. Non-utilized sidestreams from agriculture and forestry are important biomass feedstocks for energy and chemicals. Some of these are challenging due to their content of impurities.

Industrial processes also render large amounts of biomass feedstocks as sidestreams. The largest sidestreams come from industries producing food and beverage, textile and fibers, liquid biomass fuels and wood, pulp, and paper. Sometimes, an industrial biomass feedstock contains large concentrations of impurities, but just as often, it is only slightly processed and quite low in biomass impurities.

The last sector to produce large amounts of low-grade biomass feedstocks is the household consumers and the service sector businesses. These produce biomass feedstocks in several aspects such as gardening and park managing waste, construction demolition of wood and furniture waste, packaging and food waste, and municipal solid waste. Finally, via the sewage system, it produces biomass sludge from the wastewater treatment plants.

1.3 The waste hierarchy

In a circular economy [3], the waste hierarchy model states that the first goal is to prevent or minimize the formation of waste. The most significant potential to do so for biomass waste is within the households and in the service industry. In the forestry and agricultural sectors and the manufacturing industry, the prevention or minimization of biomass waste is not possible without compromising the volume of food and materials production from biomass.

The next step in the waste hierarchy is to reuse or recycle the waste material. Reusing means, for instance, renovating an old sofa or using milk cartons as plant pots, whereas recycling constitutes the conversion of waste streams into new products and chemicals. Returning the biomass back to the soil as a fertilizer is also a way of recycling the biomass; the only problem is that half of the biomass will form carbon dioxide, and some of this also forms methane if it is done in an uncontrolled way.

The last option in the waste hierarchy is the recovery of the organic fraction of waste streams as energy, and the very last option is landfilling the waste material. The European Union has banned the landfilling of any organic material in all its member states since 2018 [4]. The best option for waste biomass feedstocks is to utilize them for energy and chemical production and return the final residues as fertilizer to the soil.

The final residues, mainly the impurities, from utilizing the low-grade biomass feedstocks for energy and chemicals should be returned to the soil to complete the nutrient cycle and in part for carbon storage. One interesting way of long-time storage of the carbon bound in biomass feedstocks is to produce biochar for use as a soil fertilizer for growing crops. The biochar also serves as a way of carbon sequestering and storage.

2. Challenging biomass feedstocks

The biomass feedstocks considered challenging for thermal conversion can be categorized as agricultural residues, e.g., wheat and rice straws and husks; industrial by-products such as rapeseed oil cake, molasses, vinasse, and black liquor; herbaceous energy crops, e.g., miscanthus, switchgrass, and reed; forestry by-products including forest residues and wood barks; and municipal solid wastes. Compared to wood, these feedstocks are of low quality and several challenges are associated with them for utilizing in thermal conversion processes. The challenges are primarily due to the high levels of impurities in the feedstocks. The impurities are mainly ash-forming elements (e.g., Na, K, Ca, Si, P, S, and Cl) and nitrogen (N). **Figure 1** shows the concentrations of the impurities in these feedstocks and woody biomasses from refs. [5–8]. As seen from the figure, most of the industrial side streams and agricultural residues contain the highest total concentration of impurities, followed by herbaceous energy crops, forest residues, and wood barks. However, the woody biomasses contain the least,

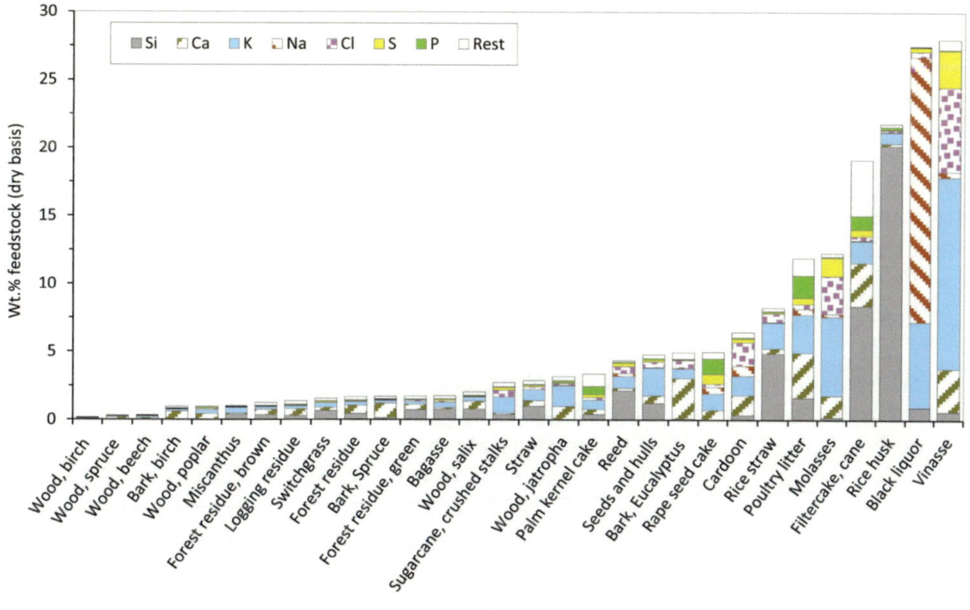

Figure 1.
Concentration of impurities in the woody and low-grade biomass feedstocks.

indicating that they are less problematic for thermal conversion systems. The main thermal conversion problems caused by the impurities are ash-related problems (e.g., corrosion and ash-deposit formation) and air emissions (NO_x and SO_x). These problems are discussed in Section 5 of this Chapter.

The causes for the high levels of impurities in the low-grade feedstocks are very variable and versatile. The main ones are (1) type of feedstock, (2) application of chemical fertilizer(s) to the soil, (3) contamination during collection and handling of the feedstock, (4) environmental factors including soil type, water quality, and climatic conditions, and (5) type of the industrial process generating the feedstock and chemical additives used during the industrial process. The influences of these factors on the concentration of impurities in the feedstocks are briefly described below, one after the other.

2.1 Feedstock type

The majority of the low-grade feedstocks described above originated, one way or another, from plants (woody or herbaceous). These plants require impurities as nutrients for their growth, and the degree of nutrient uptake from the soil depends, among others, on the type of the plant. For example, high concentrations of Si in rice plants, and thus in the rice straw and husk given in **Figure 1**, are ascribed to the presence of a gene, *Ls1* [9], specific to rice-plant roots. This gene is reported to be the primary transporter of Si from the soil to rice plant roots. Similarly, reports, e.g. [10], indicate that the concentration of impurities in a plant is directly related to the water uptake capacity of the plant. This is due to the increased amounts of the water-soluble fractions of impurities with increased water uptake by the plant. For instance, the cause for the higher concentration of the impurities, such as Si, K, and Cl shown in **Figure 1**, in the reed than in the switchgrass and miscanthus may be attributed to the higher water uptake ability of reed than the latter plants. Bakker and Elbersen [10] mentioned that the reed has a higher water uptake capacity than switchgrass and miscanthus.

Apart from feedstock type, it is well established that the different parts of a plant have different levels of impurities. For example, in the woody biomass samples used in the work by Werkelin et al. [11], the concentrations of the impurities are mostly higher in the leaves, shoots, needles, and twigs of the biomasses than in their stems (woods). This is likely one of the reasons why forest residues, which are mainly composed of tree branches, leaves, and tops, have higher levels of impurities than the woods shown in **Figure 1**.

2.2 Chemical fertilizers

Another factor for the high levels of impurities in the low-grade feedstocks is the type and amount of chemical fertilizers applied to the soil. This is especially true for agricultural residues and industrial byproducts, e.g., wheat and rice straws and husks, rapeseed cake, and molasses originating from the production of food crops where chemical fertilizers are used to enhance soil fertility (or productivity). The chemical fertilizers are mostly applied to the soil in the form of nitrates (for N), phosphates (for P), and potassium salts, mainly potassium sulfate and chloride (for K and S). The extent to which these minerals are taken up by the crops partly depends on the amount of chemical fertilizers applied to the soil.

2.3 Feedstock contamination

Contamination is a typical cause for the high level of impurities in a low-grade feedstock. It occurs primarily when the feedstock comes in contact with soil during harvesting and transporting. Feedstock contamination with soil is often the case with agricultural and forest residues and herbaceous energy crops, where mechanical harvesting techniques by swathing or raking [12] are used. However, according to Bakker and Elbersen [10], feedstock contamination during storage is less common.

2.4 Environmental factors

The environmental conditions in which plants grow play a dominant role in determining the mineral (impurity) contents of the feedstocks. These environmental factors include soil type, warm or cold weather conditions, rain or irrigation water supply, and location (latitude, longitude, or altitude). For example, switchgrass grown on clay soil has shown higher Si contents than that grown on sandy soils.

2.5 Type of industrial process

The high level of impurities in the vinasse, given in **Figure 1**, is mainly due to the influence of the industrial process used. **Figure 2** shows a simplified schematic diagram of the integrated sugar-ethanol production process. The concentrations of impurities in the crushed sugarcane and byproducts, i.e., bagasse, filter cake, molasses, and vinasse, from the integrated process are as shown in **Figure 1**. Detailed descriptions of the integrated process and the fate of impurities in the process are available from Dirbeba et al. [8]. Here, the influence of the process steps on the concentrations of the major impurities in the various byproducts is described.

As seen from **Figure 1**, vinasse > filter cake > molasses > crushed cane > bagasse in terms of the total concentration of impurities. These variations in the concentration of impurities in the cane and byproducts from the integrated process arise mainly from the sugar and ethanol production process steps shown in **Figure 2**. The influences of the process units are summarized as follows: (1) The low total concentration of impurities in the bagasse is due to the leaching of most of the impurities from the crushed cane by the imbibition water added during the milling and extraction process step. (2) The raw juice treatment involves first heating the juice, then liming and sulfiting it with quick lime (CaO) and SO_2 gas, respectively, and finally sedimenting and filtering the treated juice to remove soils, sediments, and other suspended solids in it as a filter cake. This and the removal of most of the CaO and SO_2 added for the juice treatment with the filter cake as sulfites and phosphates of calcium make the

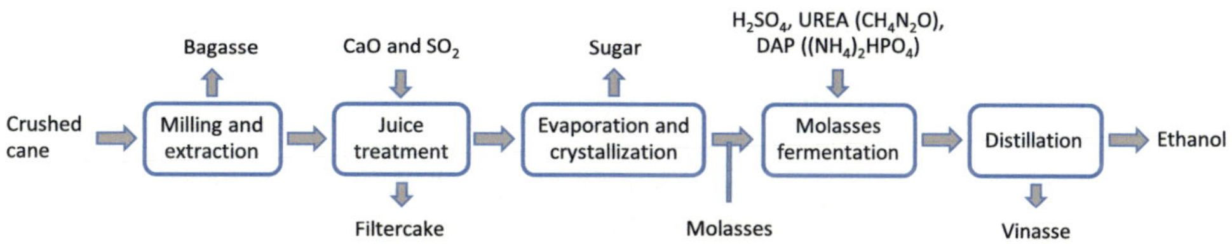

Figure 2.
Simplified schematic diagram of the integrated sugar-ethanol process.

concentration of impurities in the filter cake considerably high. (3) Vinasse, the final byproduct from the integrated process, has the highest concentration of impurities. There are two main process-related causes for the high level of impurities in the vinasse: First, most of the impurities (ash-forming elements) left in the treated juice end up in the vinasse while the organic fractions in the juice are removed as products, sugar, and ethanol, leaving the vinasse concentrated with the impurities. Second, other chemicals such as H_2SO_4, UREA, and DAP are added during the molasses fermentation stage. These chemicals contain some impurities, S, N, and P, that are partly removed with the vinasse.

Another example of an industrial process where the process steps influence the concentration of impurities in the by-product is a pulp mill. In a pulp mill, the pulp is the main product and black liquor is the sidestream. As seen in **Figure 1**, the total concentration of impurities in the black liquor is very high, whereas the levels of the impurities in the input feedstocks, woody biomasses, for pulp mills are low. The high concentration of impurities in the black liquor is due to the addition of wood pulping chemicals, NaOH and Na_2S, during the wood digestion process.

3. Availability of different types of challenging biomass feedstock

Low-grade biomass feedstocks from primary production like agricultural residues, clearing and thinning residues, and energy crops are largely available in many parts of the world [2]. The utilization of these feedstocks for energy and chemicals involves large-scale industrial processes. Despite their availability in large quantities and at low prices, their low energy densities and high moisture contents decrease their availability in practice. This is because of the high transportation costs and long distances involved with the centralized processing of these feedstocks.

The biomass feedstocks from industrial sidestreams are food or material industry by-products. The forest industry produces sawdust and bark or more processed feedstocks like black liquor or tall oil. These types of feedstocks are already inside the fence of a production site, and they pose severe waste-related problems if not utilized. However, there are still some challenges. Heat, steam, or electricity production is not always in the interest of the industry where the feedstocks are generated, or there might be a lack of competence or experience to utilize them for energy and chemicals production.

Table 1 shows the 2019 world production of the top 10 crops and estimates of the crop residues they generated in the field during harvesting and after they were processed on industrial sites. The estimates for the crop residues were made based on the data obtained from The Food and Agriculture Organization of the United Nations (FAO) [2]. As seen from the table, close to 15,000 million metric tons of agricultural residues were generated, indicating the high availability of these feedstocks for energy and chemicals production.

3.1 Availability and energy density

In the Nordic countries, residues from primary production like wheat straw and logging residues find their way to the local heat and power plants for conversion by combustion to district heating and electricity. Only a certain distance from the heat and power plant is suitable for collecting these biomasses; too long distances make the transportation costs too high [14].

	Crop type	World annual production		Harvest residues from each crop (by residue to crop ratio, RPR)			Process residues from each crop (by residue to crop ratio, RPR)		
		Million tons	% of total	Residue	RPR kg/kg	Million tons	Residue	RPR kg/kg	Million tons
Top 10 crops in the world	Sugarcane	1955	20	Tops	0.3	587	Bagasse	0.33	645
	Maize	1141	12	Stalks	2	2283	Cob/Husks	0.473	540
	Wheat	765	8	Straw/husk	1.75	1339			
	Rice, paddy	749	8	Straw	1.757	1316	Husk	0.267	200
	Oil palm fruit	416	4				Fibre/Shell	0.435	181
	Potatoes	355	4						
	Soybeans	336	3	Straw	2.5	841	Pods	1	336
	Cassava	299	3	Stalks	0.062	19	Peelings	0.015	4
	Sugar beet	281	3				Pulp	0.075	21
	Cotton	250	3	Stalks	2.755	689			
	Sum	6548	66			7072			1927
Total production		9862	100	Estimate:		*10651*	Estimate:		*2902*

Table 1.
World production of the top 10 crops and their residues generated in the field and on industrial processing sites [2, 13].

It is mainly the demand for heat in the winter that makes this feasible. The Nordic countries have systems for district heating in all cities and even in smaller municipalities. In most countries globally, there is no market or infrastructure for district heating. Instead, converting the biomass into high-grade chemicals for materials and fuels for transportation is a sustainable alternative to replace fossil-based raw materials for these commodities.

Low energy density is the result of low bulk densities (100 kg/m^3), high moisture contents (typically 40%), and low heating values (about 20 MJ/kg dry solids) of the feedstocks. This results in low energy densities, around 1000 MJ/m^3. Compared to crude oil, 35,000 MJ/m^3, and bituminous coal, 25,000 MJ/m^3, biomass feedstocks should not be transported long distances without first upgrading.

The oxygen content of the biomass feedstocks is high; a typical empirical formula for biomass is CH_2O. The maximum available thermal energy per kilogram from these feedstocks is 20 MJ, which is obtained when they are fully oxidized to CO_2 and H_2O [15]. This is relatively low compared to other primary energy sources, like natural gas, crude oil, and bituminous coal, which are 55, 45, and 30 MJ/kg, respectively.

High porosity is due to the vascular structure of biomass. It leads to the overall low density: maximum 900 kg/m^3 for dry solid hardwood, but typically much lower bulk densities: 30–170 kg dry solids per cubic meter, $kg_{D.S.}/m^3$ [13]. Higher bulk densities usually include moisture, which is of no value for its utilization for energy and chemicals.

Biomass feedstocks are naturally hygroscopic and contain some 20% moisture in equilibrium with air humidity. It dries further by applying heat and may obtain close to zero moisture content before utilization. Fresh biomass from newly harvested feedstock contains over 50% of moisture. Each percent of moisture content lowers the effective heating value by 1.125%; i.e., moisture content of 40% reduces the effective heating value of the biomass by 45%, expressed as energy released per kilogram biomass combusted.

3.2 Availability of typical industrial by-products

Biomass feedstocks from industrial by-products such as rapeseed oil cake, molasses, vinasse, and black liquor are much easier to access since these biomass feedstocks are already inside the industry gate. The challenge is if the industries where these feedstocks are generated do not find use(s) for them and if there are no proven techniques to have them processed.

The pulp and paper industry have a long tradition of utilizing all the sidestreams it generates. The largest sidestream is the spent liquor from wood pulping: black liquor. Its utilization has a long history in Scandinavian countries, but the primary purpose of processing it further within the pulp mill is to recover the inorganic cooking chemicals, which are contained in the black liquor. For every ton of pulp, seven tons of black liquor are produced. After concentrating the black liquor to a dry solid content of about 75%, it is burned in a chemical recovery boiler to produce heat and electricity for the pulp mill, which is often self-sufficient in energy. Roughly 195 million metric tons of black liquor are produced annually as a by-product from all the Kraft pulping processes in the world [16].

The integrated sugar-ethanol industry produces molasses and vinasse as by-products. The amount of molasses produced annually is about 70 million metric tons with a thermal energy value of approximately 225 TWh [17]. For every liter of ethanol produced, 10–15 liters of vinasse form as a by-product. In Brazil alone, 370 million cubic meters of vinasse is generated annually [18]. There is not yet a sustainable use for these by-product streams. They are both potential biomass feedstock for the production of energy and chemicals.

4. Thermal conversion processes as options for utilizing challenging biomass feedstocks

There are two main energy production routes from biomass: biochemical and thermochemical (herein referred to as thermal) conversion routes. Biochemical conversion of biomass involves the production of liquid (ethanol) or gaseous (methane) fuel using microorganisms, which break down the organic fraction of biomass into ethanol or methane depending on whether fermentation or anaerobic biodigestion process is used. According to Christofoletti et al. [19], biochemical conversion processes are mentioned to be slow and expensive and produce other harmful gases, such as hydrogen sulfide. Moreover, these processes generate effluents, such as vinasse, that are difficult to treat and have potential environmental pollution. However, a review of the applicability of low-grade biomass feedstocks to biochemical conversion is beyond the scope of this chapter.

On the other hand, the second option, the thermal conversion route, uses heat to disintegrate biomass into often solid, liquid, and/or gaseous fractions depending on the type of thermal conversion used. The main biomass thermal conversion processes are combustion, gasification, pyrolysis, and hydrothermal liquefaction. These processes are described briefly and discussed more in detail below in connection with the utilization of the challenging biomass feedstocks.

4.1 Combustion

Combustion is a well-established and most commonly used thermal conversion technology for the production of heat and power from biomass. It is also a proven means for waste disposal. In the latter case, combustion is often referred to as incineration. In addition to eliminating wastes that otherwise would cause environmental damage(s), incineration also produces heat utilized, for example, for district heating. Among the available technologies for biomass combustion, the fluidized bed (FB) combustion is the most advanced and efficient technology for heat and electricity production from biomass feedstocks containing low levels of impurities. There are two types of FB combustion technologies: bubbling fluidized bed (BFB) and circulating fluidized bed (CFB).

BFB and CFB technologies that utilize some low-grade biomass feedstocks have been developed and operating in some European countries. **Table 2** lists some examples of these technologies, designed and supplied by Valmet [20], along with their capacities and locations as well as the type of challenging feedstocks used.

As seen from the table, solid recovered fuel (SRF), refuse-derived fuel (RDF), and recycled fuel (REF) are the main problematic feedstocks used in the FB boilers. These feedstocks are obtained after crushing and pretreating their sources—recycled wood, MSW, and industrial and commercial wastes. The pretreatments, e.g., removing mechanical or coarse impurities such as plastic wastes, minimize the ash-related problems (discussed in the next section) that would have been caused by utilizing these feedstocks in FB boilers. In addition to the pretreatments, special design features are incorporated in these boilers to partly offset the adverse impacts of the impurities contained in the feedstocks. For example, the use of highly alloyed steels for the construction of superheater tubes of the boilers and placement of the superheater tubes in the flue gas path where the flue gas temperature is lower are some technological options for alleviating the adverse impacts of the impurities.

Company name	Type	Capacity	Location	Challenging feedstock used
Termomeccanica Ecologia	BFB	2x30 MW_{th}	Calabria, Italy	RDF
Borås Energi och Miljö	BFB	2x20 MW	Borås, Sweden	RDF, SRF
Stora Enso Langerbrugge nv	CFB	125 MW_{th}	Gent, Belgium	RDF
Mälarenergi AB	CFB	155 MW_{th}	Västerås, Sweden	RDF, SRF
Lahti Energia Oy	CFB	2x80 MW	Lahti, Finland	RDF, REF, SRF

Table 2.
Some examples of BFB and CFB boilers using low-grade feedstocks for heat and power production [20].

Another well-developed combustion technology to burn a specific challenging biomass feedstock is the Kraft recovery boiler. As discussed in the previous section, this boiler is solely designed for burning black liquor from pulp mills. It generates not only heat and electricity from the black liquor for the pulp mills but also recovers the wood pulping chemicals. However, efforts to combust a similar challenging fuel-vinasse in a recovery boiler have not been successful so far. This is in part due to the higher levels of K and Cl in the vinasse than in the black liquor as shown in **Figure 1**. Nevertheless, a recent Ph.D. thesis work by Dirbeba [21] suggests a recovery boiler-type system with a simpler lower furnace than that of the black liquor for vinasse combustion. Such a system could decrease the ash-related problems (see next section) while at the same time allowing most of the ash in the vinasse to be recovered for use as fertilizer. However, this system will inevitably produce steam with low temperatures and pressures, ultimately leading to low electrical power efficiency.

4.2 Gasification

Gasification is one of the promising routes for biomass thermal conversion due to its potential for providing high energy efficiency cycles [22]. The primary product from biomass gasification is syngas, which is composed of mainly CO and H_2. The syngas can be combusted to produce heat and power, or it serves as a feedstock for the production of liquid fuels and other value-added chemicals via, for instance, the Fischer-Tropsch process.

A novel gasification technology that has been demonstrated for low-grade biomass feedstocks is a CFB gasifier coupled with a syngas cleaning system and subsequently combustion of the clean syngas in a boiler as shown in **Figure 3**. Here, the syngas cleaning system removes impurities released during the gasification of the biomass feedstock in the CFB gasifier. As a result, combusting the clean syngas in the boiler enables to obtain higher steam parameters (and thus higher energy efficiencies) than the steam parameters that would be obtained from direct combustion of the feedstock [23]. A commercial-scale plant of such a process has been installed in Lahti, Finland, by Valmet [20]. The plant uses SRF as a feedstock, and it has a capacity to gasify 250,000 tons of SRF per year, which is equivalent to 150 MW of combined heat and power supply.

Another promising gasification technology for low-grade biomass feedstocks is the high temperatures (up to 1500°C) and high pressures (up to 3 MPa) entrained flow gasifier. One of the advantages of this technology is its feedstock flexibility-dried

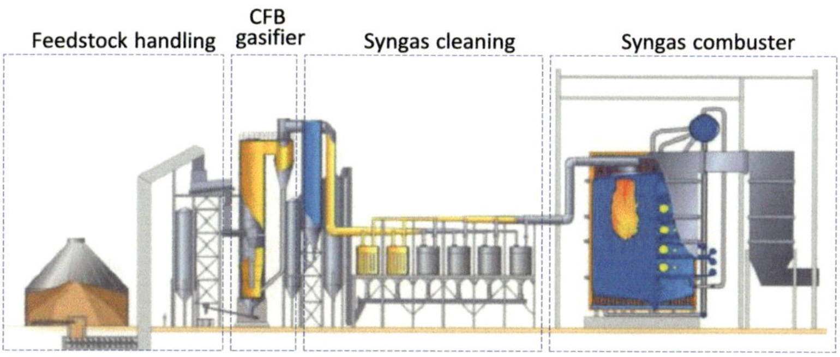

Figure 3.
Schematic of low-grade biomass feedstock gasifier coupled with syngas cleaning and combustion systems. Adapted with permission from [23].

and ground biomass feedstocks or biomass feedstocks with high moisture contents, such as black liquor and vinasse, can be injected into the gasifier with the gasifying agent. Moreover, the smelt (composed of mostly molten ash) from this process can be recovered as an aqueous phase bottom product. A pilot-scale plant of this technology has been demonstrated for black liquor to be economically feasible.

Another form of the gasification process, supercritical water gasification (SCWG), converts wet biomass feedstocks into gaseous fuels, composed of mainly methane (CH_4), hydrogen (H_2), and carbon monoxide (CO), at temperatures and pressures above the critical point of water. Several studies, e.g., [24, 25], have reported that SCWG is more suitable for biomass feedstocks with very high ($\geq$80 wt.%) moisture contents. This makes challenging biomass feedstocks such as black liquor and vinasse potential feedstocks for SCWG processes. However, SCWG technologies have not yet found their way into commercialization due to the challenges discussed later in Section 5.

4.3 Pyrolysis

Pyrolysis is a thermal conversion process where a feedstock is heated under inert gas conditions, i.e., in the absence of oxygen, to produce solid, liquid, and gaseous products often referred to as biochar, bio-oil, and non-condensable pyrolysis gases, respectively. Based on how fast the feedstock is heated to the pyrolysis reaction temperature and on the type of the final product sought to be maximized, there are mainly two types of pyrolysis processes: slow and fast pyrolysis. Slow pyrolysis, also known as conventional pyrolysis, is characterized by slow heating rates, long residence times of the pyrolysis products in the pyrolysis reactor, and biochar is the target product. In the fast pyrolysis processes, however, the feedstock is rapidly heated to the reaction temperature, at heating rates of as high as 10^{4}°C/s, and the pyrolysis vapors are rapidly withdrawn from the pyrolyzer and cooled to maximize the bio-oil yield.

In recent years, more emphasis is given to research in fast pyrolysis compared to that of the slow, as shown in **Figure 4**. This is because the fast pyrolysis bio-oil has attracted interest for use as a renewable fuel and as a feedstock for the production of chemicals. In addition, reduced storage and transportation costs and higher energy density make the bio-oil more advantageous than the original biomass feedstock from which the bio-oil is produced. Besides the bio-oil, there are growing market interests in the biochars from the fast pyrolysis: biochars can be used as a soil conditioner/ fertilizer, and they have the potential to substitute fossil-based industrial carbons

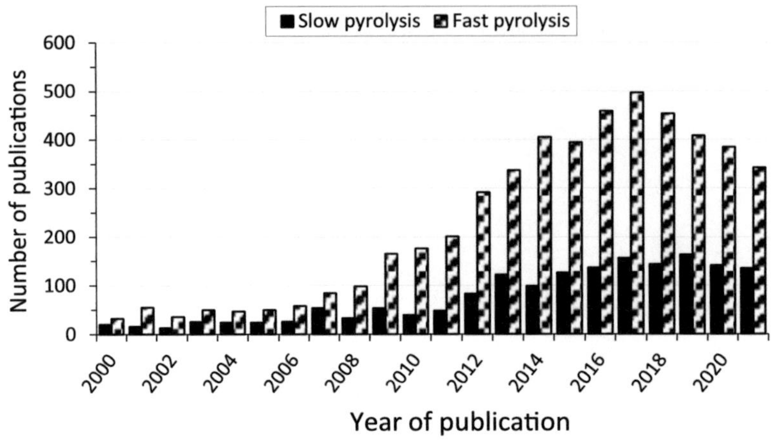

Figure 4.
The number of yearly publications on slow and fast pyrolysis. The data was retrieved from SciFinder^n with the key search words "slow" and "pyrolysis" and "fast" and "pyrolysis". The types of publications considered for the data were journal articles, review papers, conference papers, books, and dissertations.

(e.g., activated carbon). Moreover, returning biochars to the soil as fertilizers serves as CO_2 sequestration, thereby contributing to greenhouse gas emission reduction [26].

Technologies for fast pyrolysis that utilize woody biomass as a feedstock have been introduced as the first demonstration plants. For instance, a 30 MW_{th} Savon Voima's (formerly Fortum's) fast pyrolysis process has been built integrated with a CHP plant in Joensuu, Finland [23], and other industrial-scale plants are under construction [27]. However, commercial-scale fast pyrolysis technologies for low-grade biomass feedstocks have not been developed so far.

4.4 Hydrothermal liquefaction

Hydrothermal liquefaction (HTL), also known as direct liquefaction, is similar to SCWG: water is used as a solvent (or reaction medium) in both processes, and wet biomass feedstocks do not require drying for liquefaction. However, liquefaction is distinct from SCWG in the following aspects. (1) Unlike SCWG processes whose products are gaseous fuels, bio-oil is the main product from liquefaction systems. (2) HTL processes are carried out under subcritical water conditions and at moderate temperatures, 250–350°C. Although there are some pilot-scale HTL processes, as listed in [28], for low-grade biomass feedstocks, none of them have been developed into a commercial-scale technology so far.

5. Challenges and opportunities in thermal conversion of the feedstocks

As discussed in the previous section, the utilization of low-grade biomass feedstocks in thermal conversion processes has started to show a green light in some cases. However, there are still versatile challenges for marketizing these feedstocks-based thermal conversion technologies. **Table 3** lists these challenges. The challenges can be categorized into process- and product quality-related challenges. Both types of challenges are primarily due to the type and level of impurities (ash-forming elements) present in the feedstocks.

Thermal conversion process	Challenges	Opportunities/remedies
1. Fluidized bed (BFB and CFB) combustion	• Corrosion • Bed agglomeration	• Well-developed technology • Development of additives, such as kaolin, to minimize bed agglomeration • Use of corrosion-resistant metal alloys
2. Fluidized bed (BFB and CFB) gasification	• Same as in (1) • Syngas cleaning	• Same as in (1) • High energy efficiency cycles • Development of syngas cleaning technologies • Syngas conversion to other high value-added chemicals through processes such as Fischer Tropsch
3. Supercritical water gasification (SCWG)	• Corrosion • Extreme process conditions, i.e., high pressures • Handling the aqueous phase product • Less-developed and no large-scale technology • Expensive	• Potential technology for feedstocks with very high moisture content • Syngas production and conversion to other high value-added chemicals through processes such as Fischer Tropsch • Development of SCWG reactors with corrosion-resistant materials
4. Hydrothermal liquefaction (HTL)	• Same as in (3)	• Potential technology for feedstocks with very high moisture content • Bio-oil production and upgrading bio-oils to transportation fuels and high value-added chemicals • Development of HTL reactors with corrosion-resistant materials
5. High-temperature entrained flow gasification	• Corrosion • Extreme process conditions, i.e., high pressures and temperatures • Syngas cleaning • Risk of explosion • Handling the aqueous phase bottom product • Less-developed technology • No commercial-scale process • Expensive	• High flexibility in biomass feedstocks as a feed • Potential technology for biomass feedstocks with very high moisture content • Syngas production and conversion to other high value-added chemicals through processes such as Fischer-Tropsch • Recovery of inorganic chemicals with the aqueous bottom product

Thermal conversion process	Challenges	Opportunities/remedies
6. Low-temperature fast pyrolysis	• Low bio-oil yield • Unfavorable bio-oil physicochemical properties • Low heating value of the non-condensable pyrolysis gases (NCG) • Market problems	• Upgradation of pyrolysis oils to transportation fuel through catalytic fast pyrolysis and hydrodeoxygenation • Production of high value-added chemicals from the bio-oils • Production of bio-chars for fertilizer and carbon sequestration • Combustion of pyrolysis oils and gases for heat and power production • Less risk of ash-related problems from the combustion of the bio-oils and NCG • Demonstration-scale commercial plants are available

Table 3.
Challenges and opportunities/remedies for thermal conversion of low-grade biomass feedstocks.

The process-related thermal conversion problems associated with the type and concentration of impurities in the feedstocks include ash-deposit formation, corrosion, bed agglomeration (hence bed defluidization), fouling, and slagging [29, 30]. These problems often limit heat transfer in thermal converters, lower electrical power efficiency, decrease plant availability due to unplanned shutdowns for maintenance, and even cause irreversible damage(s) to the installations, leading to permanent loss of capital investment.

Moreover, several reports, e.g., [31–33], show that the impurities in the biomass feedstocks considerably influence the quantity and quality of products from thermal conversion systems. For example, alkali and alkaline earth metals in the feedstocks decrease the yield and quality of bio-oils from fast pyrolysis and HTL processes. These metals are known to render the bio-oils unfavorable physicochemical characteristics such as acidity, corrosivity, inhomogeneity, phase separation, instability, low heating value, and high solids, water, and oxygen contents. These unfavorable physicochemical properties make the direct utilization of the bio-oils as a transport fuel and a feedstock for the production of high-quality value-added chemicals unsuitable.

Nevertheless, **Table 3** also lists some opportunities or remedies for the challenges arising from the thermal conversion of low-grade biomass feedstocks. The solutions involve both technological innovations and political (regulatory) commitments. Some examples of the former case include extensive efforts in designing and developing technologies for syngas cleaning, bio-oil upgrading, and minimizing corrosion and bed-agglomeration-related problems via the use of high-quality metal alloys and bed additives, such as kaolin. The latter (or policy) option requires commitments from governments and incentives for businesses to utilize low-grade biomass feedstocks. A typical example is the adoption of circular economy, at least by most European countries, where companies implementing the policy are incentivized, climate change challenges are tackled, and dependence of economies on depleting natural resources is minimized. In this regard, the fast pyrolysis of low-grade biomass feedstocks seems promising. According to a recent review paper by Oasmaa et al. [27], using low-grade biomass and waste feedstocks including waste plastics as input for fast pyrolysis processes is environmentally and economically sustainable. Moreover, the EU renewable energy directive (EU RED II) [34] lists and promotes low-grade biomass and waste feedstocks for bio-oil production. Upgrading of the fast pyrolysis oils to transportation fuels through, for example, catalytic fast pyrolysis and hydrodeoxygenation are increasingly gaining attention and attracting interest from the industry. Moreover, the biochars from the fast pyrolysis processes have not only the potential to replace the non-renewable chemical fertilizers but also minimize greenhouse gas emissions via carbon sequestration. Thus, the future of utilizing challenging biomass feedstocks in thermal conversion systems appears encouraging.

6. Conclusions

This book chapter sheds some light on the use of low-grade biomass feedstocks as a sustainable and renewable source for the production of energy and chemicals through thermal conversion processes. The chapter assesses the availability of the feedstocks for thermal conversion and provides the sources of impurities (ash-forming elements) contained in them. Also, it emphasizes that the main challenges associated with the utilization of the feedstocks in thermal conversion systems are related to the type and concentration of the impurities in the feedstocks. Furthermore, it details the challenges of low-grade biomass combustion, gasification, pyrolysis, and liquefaction and the potential alternative options to address them. Evaluation of the existing information on the thermal conversion of these feedstocks reveals that the fast pyrolysis process is a promising thermal conversion route for these feedstocks. The pyrolysis oils from this process can be upgraded to transportation fuels or can be used for the production of high value-added chemicals. Moreover, the fast pyrolysis biochars can be returned to the soil for use as fertilizer and at the same time minimize CO_2 emission through carbon sequestration. Overall, this work provides useful information for the design and development of state-of-the-art thermal conversion technologies for challenging biomass feedstocks.

Acknowledgements

This work has been carried out at the Laboratory of Molecular Science and Engineering, Åbo Akademi University, as part of the activities at the Johan Gadolin Process Chemistry Centre (PCC). The authors are grateful to Svenska Kulturfonden and PoDoCo (Post Docs in Companies) for the grant for Dr. Meheretu Jaleta Dirbeba under the project “Role of feedstock impurities in novel pyrolysis based technologies for low-grade biomass and waste feedstocks” (PoDoCo application no. 173788). Support from Valmet Technologies Oy is also gratefully acknowledged.

Conflict of interest

The authors declare no conflict of interest.

Author details

Meheretu Jaleta Dirbeba and Johan Werkelin*
Johan Gadolin Process Chemistry Centre, Laboratory of Molecular Science and Engineering, Åbo Akademi University, Turku/Åbo, Finland

*Address all correspondence to: johan.werkelin@abo.fi

References

[1] Masson-Delmotte V, Zhai P, Pirani A, Connors SL, Péan C, Berger S, et al. Climate Change 2021: The Physical Science Basis. Contribution of Working Group I to the Sixth Assessment Report of the Intergovernmental Panel on Climate Change. Cambridge: Cambridge University Press; 2021

[2] Available from: https://www.fao.org/faostat/en/#home [Accessed: February 12, 2022]

[3] Stahel WR. Circular economy. Nature. 2016;**531**:425-438

[4] Directive (EU) 2018/850. 2018. Available from: https://eur-lex.europa.eu/legal-content/EN/TXT/?uri=CELEX%3A32018L0850 [Accessed: February 12, 2022]

[5] Hupa M, Karlström O, Vainio E. Biomass combustion technology development—It is all about chemical details. Proceedings of the Combustion Institute. 2017;**36**:113-134. DOI: 10.1016/j.proci.2016.06.152

[6] Martin M, Brice D, Martin S, André N, Labbé N. Inorganic characterization of switchgrass biomass using laser-induced breakdown spectroscopy. Spectrochimica Acta—Part B Atomic Spectroscopy. 2021;**186**:106323. DOI: 10.1016/j.sab.2021.106323

[7] Dirbeba MJ, Aho A, Demartini N, Brink A, Hupa M. Pyrolysis of sugarcane vinasse and black liquor at 400 and 500 °C. In: The Proceedings of the 13th International Conference on Energy for a Clean Environment. Ponta Delgada, São Miguel, Azores: University of Lisbon; 2017

[8] Dirbeba MJ, Brink A, DeMartini N, Zevenhoven M, Hupa M. Potential for thermochemical conversion of biomass residues from the integrated sugar-ethanol process—Fate of ash and ash-forming elements. Bioresource Technology. 2017;**234**:188-197. DOI: 10.1016/j.biortech.2017.03.021

[9] Ma JF, Yamaji N. Silicon uptake and accumulation in higher plants. Trends in Plant Science. 2006;**11**:392-397. DOI: 10.1016/j.tplants.2006.06.007

[10] Bakker RR, Elbersen HW. Managing ash content and quality in herbaceous biomass: An analysis from plant to product. In: The Proceedings of 14th European Biomass Conference. Paris: European Biomass Conference and Exhibition; 2005

[11] Werkelin J, Skrifvars BJ, Zevenhoven M, Holmbom B, Hupa M. Chemical forms of ash-forming elements in woody biomass fuels. Fuel. 2010;**89**:481-493. DOI: 10.1016/j.fuel.2009.09.005

[12] Bakker RR, Jenkins BM. Feasibility of collecting naturally leached rice straw for thermal conversion. Biomass and Bioenergy. 2003;**25**:597-614. DOI: 10.1016/S0961-9534(03)00053-9

[13] Koopmans A, Koppejan J. Agricultural and forest residues-generation, utilization and availability. Regional Consultation on Modern Applications of Biomass Energy. Rome, Italy: Food and Agriculture Organization of the United Nations; 1997. pp. 1-23

[14] Börjesson P, Gustavsson L. Regional production and utilization of biomass in Sweden. Energy. 1996;**21**:747-164. DOI: 10.1016/0360-5442(96)00029-1

[15] Friedl A, Padouvas E, Rotter H, Varmuza K. Prediction of heating values of

biomass fuel from elemental composition. Analytica Chimica Acta. 2005;**544**:191-198. DOI: 10.1016/j.aca.2005.01.041

[16] Kim CH, Lee JY, Park SH, Moon SO. Global trends and prospects of black liquor as bioenergy. Palpu Chongi Gisul/Journal of Korea Technical Association of the Pulp and Paper Industry. 2019;**51**:3-15. DOI: 10.7584/JKTAPPI.2019.10.51.5.3

[17] Dirbeba MJ, Brink A, Lindberg D, Hupa M, Hupa L. Thermal conversion characteristics of molasses. ACS Omega. 2021;**6**:21631-21645. DOI: 10.1021/acsomega.1c03024

[18] Dirbeba MJ, Aho A, Demartini N, Brink A, Mattsson I, Hupa L, et al. Fast pyrolysis of dried sugar cane vinasse at 400 and 500 °C: Product distribution and yield. Energy and Fuels. 2019;**33**: 1236-1247. DOI: 10.1021/acs.energyfuels.8b03757

[19] Christofoletti CA, Escher JP, Correia JE, Marinho JFU, Fontanetti CS. Sugarcane vinasse: Environmental implications of its use. Waste Management. 2013;**33**:2752-2761. DOI: 10.1016/j.wasman.2013.09.005

[20] Available from: https://www.valmet.com/ [Accessed: February 06, 2022]

[21] Dirbeba MJ. Thermochemical conversion characteristics of vinasse (PhD thesis). Turku, Finland: Åbo Akademi University; 2020

[22] Knoef HAM. Handbook on Biomass Gasification. 1st ed. BTG Biomass Technology Group: Enschede, Netherlands; 2005

[23] Enestam S, Björklund P, Engblom N, Hamaguchi M, Rautanen M, Wallmo H. Energy trends-recent and future fuel related challenges. In: The Proceedings of Impacts of Fuel Quality on Power Production and the Environment. Snowbird, Utah: University of Utah; 2014

[24] Reddy SN, Nanda S, Dalai AK, Kozinski JA. Supercritical water gasification of biomass for hydrogen production. International Journal of Hydrogen Energy. 2014;**39**:6912-6926. DOI: 10.1016/j.ijhydene.2014.02.125

[25] Kruse A. Supercritical water gasification. Biofuels, Bioproducts and Biorefining. 2008;**2**:415-437. DOI: 10.1002/bbb.93

[26] Matovic D. Biochar as a viable carbon sequestration option: Global and Canadian perspective. Energy. 2011;**36**:2011-2016. DOI: 10.1016/j.energy.2010.09.031

[27] Oasmaa A, Lehto J, Solantausta Y, Kallio S. Historical Review on VTT fast pyrolysis bio-oil production and upgrading. Energy and Fuels. 2021;**35**(7): 5683-5695. DOI: 10.1021/acs.energyfuels.1c00177

[28] Toor SS, Rosendahl L, Rudolf A. Hydrothermal liquefaction of biomass: A review of subcritical water technologies. Energy. 2011;**36**:2328-2342. DOI: 10.1016/j.energy.2011.03.013

[29] Baxter LL, Miles TR, Jenkins BM, Milne T, Dayton D, Bryers RW, et al. The behavior of inorganic material in biomass-fired power boilers: Field and laboratory experiences. Fuel Processing Technology. 1998;**54**:47-78. DOI: 10.1016/S0378-3820(97)00060-X

[30] Wang L, Weller CL, Jones DD, Hanna MA. Contemporary issues in thermal gasification of biomass and its application to electricity and fuel production. Biomass and Bioenergy. 2008;**32**:573-581. DOI: 10.1016/j.biombioe.2007.12.007

[31] Perander M, DeMartini N, Brink A, Kramb J, Karlström O, Hemming J,

et al. Catalytic effect of Ca and K on CO_2 gasification of spruce wood char. Fuel. 2015;**150**:464-472. DOI: 10.1016/j.fuel.2015.02.062

[32] Aho A, DeMartini N, Pranovich A, Krogell J, Kumar N, Eränen K, et al. Pyrolysis of pine and gasification of pine chars—Influence of organically bound metals. Bioresource Technology. 2013;**128**:22-29. DOI: 10.1016/j.biortech.2012.10.093

[33] Nazari L, Yuan Z, Souzanchi S, Ray MB, Xu C. Hydrothermal liquefaction of woody biomass in hot-compressed water: Catalyst screening and comprehensive characterization of bio-crude oils. Fuel. 2015;**162**:74-83. DOI: 10.1016/j.fuel.2015.08.055

[34] Directive (EU) 2018/2001. Available from: http://data.europa.eu/eli/dir/2018/2001/2018-12-21 [Accessed: February 12, 2022]

Chapter 11

Valorization of Biomass as a Raw Material to Obtain Products of Industrial Interest

Dulce María Diaz-Montaño

Abstract

Biomass is the biodegradable fraction of products and waste of biological origin. Biomass comes from activities such as agriculture, forestry, as well as the biodegradable fraction of industrial and municipal waste. A large amount of biomass encourages the proposal of projects aimed at the integrated use of these wastes to obtain products with high added value. In fact, the use of this waste avoids negative ecological impact on agricultural fields, rivers, and lakes, and supports new technologies that can feasibly solve the pollution problem. The presentation of studies related to the use of these wastes as raw material to produce compounds of industrial interest in areas such as agriculture, second and third-generation biofuels, biogas, pharmaceuticals, chemical industry, human and animal nutrition, through chemical, physical, thermochemical, and biological processes, is the objective of this chapter.

Keywords: biomass, agricultural waste, forestry waste, waste from the agri-food industry, waste from the livestock industry, urban wastes

1. Introduction

One of the challenges of the twenty-first century is to develop processes for the elaboration of products of industrial interest, with the following characteristics:

a. environmentally friendly processes,

b. quality products and services, and

c. products that satisfy the needs of the consumer.

The above is to meet the needs of the inhabitants of each country and avoid environmental pollution and contribute to the reduction of global warming.

Directive (EU) 2018/2001 of the European Parliament and of the Council defines biomass as the biodegradable fraction of products and waste of biological origin.

Biomass is generated in activities such as agricultural activities of plant and animal origin, forestry, and related industries such as fishing and aquaculture, as well as the biodegradable fraction of industrial and municipal waste of biological origin.

 IntechOpen

According to the above, biomass covers a wide range of organic materials that are characterized by their heterogeneity, both in terms of their origin and nature.

In 2009 alone, it has been calculated that almost 3.3 Gt of waste was generated, which makes it an inexhaustible source of carbon due to the large amount of biomass produced each year, being a resource that can be used as raw material for the large-scale production of a variety of products of industrial interest, which will be presented in this chapter.

In fact, the use of these residues avoids the negative ecological impact on agricultural fields, rivers, and lakes, and supports new technologies that can feasibly solve the problem of pollution, since biomass, being a neutral resource, reduces CO2 emissions, greenhouse gas (GHG) emissions, and finally provides economic benefits to society [1].

The abundance of biomass and the favorable techno-economic associated with the production of a wide range of products have recently changed the global perception of the use of biomass as a valuable resource and not as a waste. It should be emphasized that failure to utilize biomass can lead to serious environmental hazards, converting biomass into large volumes of waste and causing serious problems for society.

This chapter delves into the research carried out and the development of value-added products from the different types of biomasses. The chapter is divided into the origin and classification of biomass, to continue presenting the different biomass treatment methods and production processes that are currently used for the development of value-added products, and finally, several products of industrial interest and their technology are presented.

2. Origin and classification of biomass

Agricultural and forestry practices generate large amounts of residues [1]. The agricultural farming system generates residues in the harvesting of vegetables, fruits, grains, and other crops creating substantial amounts of residues called biomass. Especially agricultural cereal crops contribute significantly to biomass generation [1]. Centore et al. [2] published that globally 66% of residual plant biomass comes from cereal straw (stalk, leaves, and pods), and in second place are sugarcane stalks and leaves [2]. In the EU alone, about 23 Mton/year of dry biomass is available as residual cereal straw [3]. Tripathi et al. [1] mention that in 2009 alone almost 3.3 Gt of residues (fresh weight)/year were generated, considering the main world crops (wheat, corn, rice, soybean, barley, rapeseed, sugarcane, and sugar beet) in the selected countries/regions with high biomass potential (EU, Europe, Canada, Brazil, Argentina, China, and India). To this amount of biomass, it is necessary to include the biomass generated in the following activities: livestock, wood industry, agri-food, among others.

Due to the wide range of biomass that exists in the world, it can be classified according to its: (a) origin, (b) physical state and (c) chemical composition as shown in **Figures 1** and **2** [4, 5].

2.1 Classification of biomass according to its origin

Biomass classified according to its origin is divided into natural and residual.

a. Natural: Biomass that occurs spontaneously in nature, in ecosystems that have not suffered human intervention. Firewood or branches are an example of

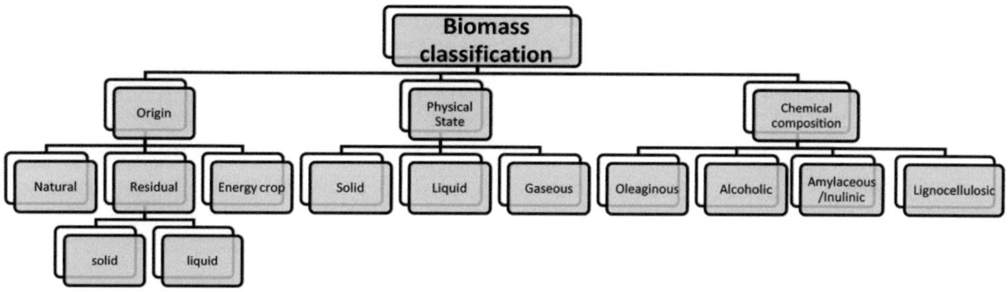

Figure 1.
Classification of biomass according to its origin, physical state, and chemical composition.

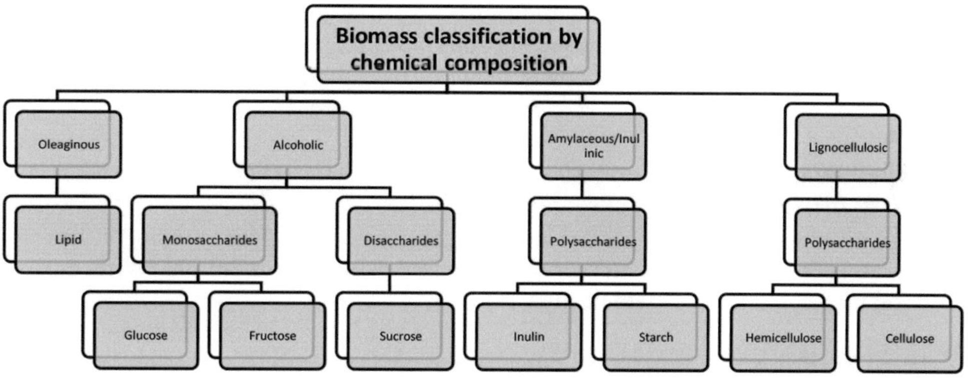

Figure 2.
Biomass classification by chemical composition.

this type of biomass and constitute the main energy source in small towns and developing countries.

b. Residual: This is the biomass that comes from waste generated by human activities, such as agriculture, livestock, the timber industry, or the agri-food industry.

In addition, biomass is classified into dry and wet, or solid and liquid, and among them can be cited:

- Residues from agricultural, forestry, and gardening activities, such as cereal straws, corn husks, agricultural surpluses, those originated in forestry treatments, etc.
- Waste from agricultural and forestry industries, such as olive oil production, olive pomace oil, wine and alcohol industry, dried fruit production, wood trimmings, sawdust, etc.
- Urban solid waste and urban wastewater.
- Livestock waste: mainly slurry.
- Agro-industrial waste: dairy industries, paper mills, distilleries, oil mills, canneries, etc.
- Used food oils.

c. Energy crops: These are agricultural crops that are not intended for food, but to produce energy; they are called agro-energy crops. Agro-energy crops are selected according to the biomass production required, so they are usually species characterized by their robustness, high cellulose concentration, to reduce cultivation costs, and the price of biomass, among the examples we have: Ethiopian rapeseed and thistle.

2.2 Classification according to physical state

Biomass can be classified according to its physical state, this can be:

a. Solid Biomass: The best-known biomass, it includes wood and forest residues, residues from wood processing and pulp and paper industries, agricultural residues (straw) and wood waste, residues obtained from pruning and cleaning of parks and gardens, energy crops, peat, agro-industrial residues (pomace, sawdust, olive pits), organic fraction of municipal solid waste, etc.

b. Liquid Biomass: This group includes biodegradable livestock and industrial waste, urban wastewater, oils, and biofuels.

c. Gaseous Biomass: This is methane or biogas obtained from animal waste, agro-food waste, landfills, waste dumps, etc.

2.3 Classification according to chemical composition

The classification of biomass according to its chemical composition can be oleaginous, alcoholic, amylaceous/inulinic, and lignocellulosic. The following is the relation of biomass according to its chemical composition.

a. Oleaginous: In this group are the lipids obtained from seeds and grains, as well as animal fat.

b. Alcoholic: Monosaccharides and disaccharides represent this group, for example, sugar pulp, sugar cane, sweet sorghum, and beet.

c. Amylaceous/Inulinic: In this group are starch and inulin, which are present in potato tuber, cereal grains, dahlia rhizomes, chicory, etc.

d. Lignocellulosic: This group is represented by cellulose and hemicellulose polysaccharides found in lignocellulosic residues such as wood in general, agricultural residues, etc.

In the same way, from an ecological point of view, it is possible to differentiate biomasses of different orders: primary, secondary, and tertiary (**Figures 3–5**).

2.4 Classification of biomass from an ecological point of view

a. Primary biomass: Primary biomass includes organic matter formed directly by photosynthetic organisms (algae, green plants, and other autotrophic organisms). This group includes natural and anthropogenic biomass (**Figure 3**). Natural

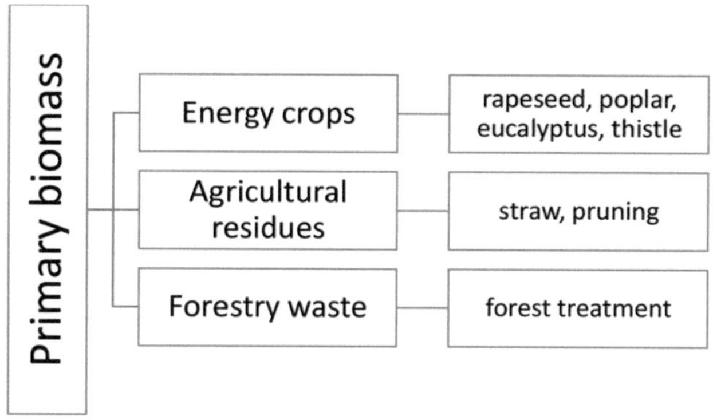

Figure 3.
Primary biomass.

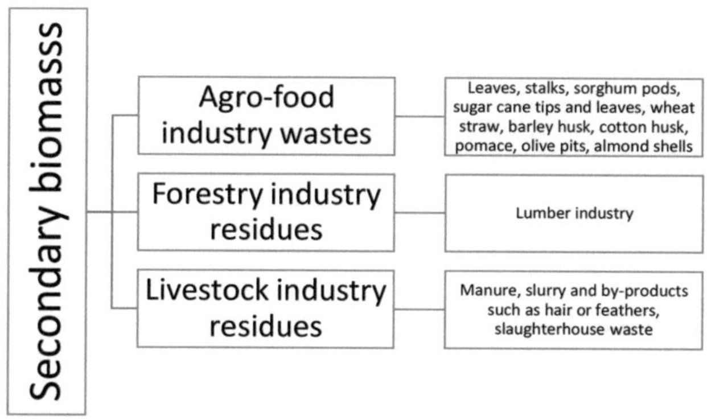

Figure 4.
Secondary biomass.

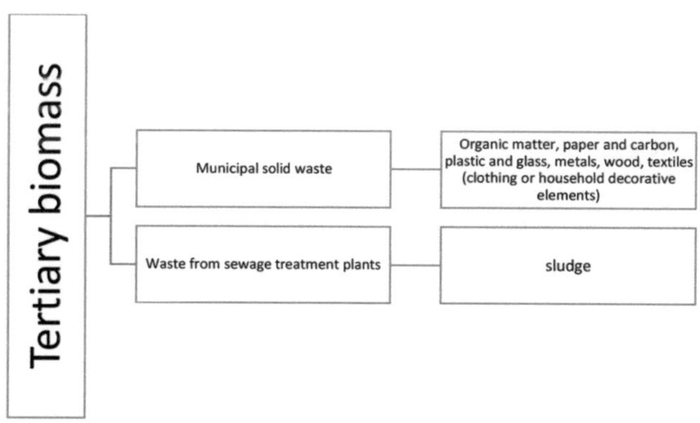

Figure 5.
Tertiary biomass.

biomass is that which is produced spontaneously in nature without any human intervention. The resources generated in the natural pruning of a forest are an example of this type of biomass. Anthropogenic biomass includes biomass obtained by human activity such as agricultural residues. Primary biomass is classified into energy crops, agricultural residues, and forestry residues. This group includes all plant biomass, including energy crops (rape, thistle, eucalyptus), algal biomass (microalgae and macroalgae), agricultural waste (straw or pruning residues), and forestry waste (forestry treatments: obtaining firewood, cleaning to prevent fires and improve access).

b. Secondary biomass: Secondary biomass falls into the category of anthropogenic biomass, which includes waste generated in the agri-food, animal, and forestry industries, such as hulls, stems, leaves, pods, bones, agro-industrial waste, animal slaughterhouse waste, and wood industry waste (**Figure 4**).

c. Tertiary biomass: Tertiary biomass includes municipal solid waste and sludge from wastewater treatment plants (**Figure 5**).

3. Biomass bioconversion technologies

Waste valorization is a process that converts waste materials into valuable products, such as chemicals, materials, and fuels. The transformation of biomass into value-added products is increasing worldwide due to the following characteristics [6–9]:

- As for chemicals and materials, biomass is an accessible and low-cost feedstock. Different forms of biomass are converted into products of industrial interest.

- As renewable energy, biomass is resource neutral, as it is generally cleaner burning than fossil fuels.

Certain types of biomass can be used directly, without any or almost no treatment, such as wood residues, such as sawmill residues, logging residues, and municipal wood residues from plants and crops, which are used as fertilizer; in other cases, pretreatment is required to condition the biomass before it is subjected to processes to obtain a product of industrial interest [8]. The most common pretreatment methods are mechanical shredding, acid or alkaline hydrolysis, extraction of the components by organic solvents or ionic liquids, and steam explosion treatment, as some examples [10, 11].

The technologies applied to modify biomass properties are grouped into 4:

- Thermochemical processes

- Chemical processes

- Biological processes

- Physical processes

Figure 6 illustrates a graphic representation of the most common technologies used in biomass valorization.

3.1 Thermochemical process

Thermochemical processes are based on the use of high temperatures to convert biomass into energy (**Figure 7**). These processes involve irreversible chemical

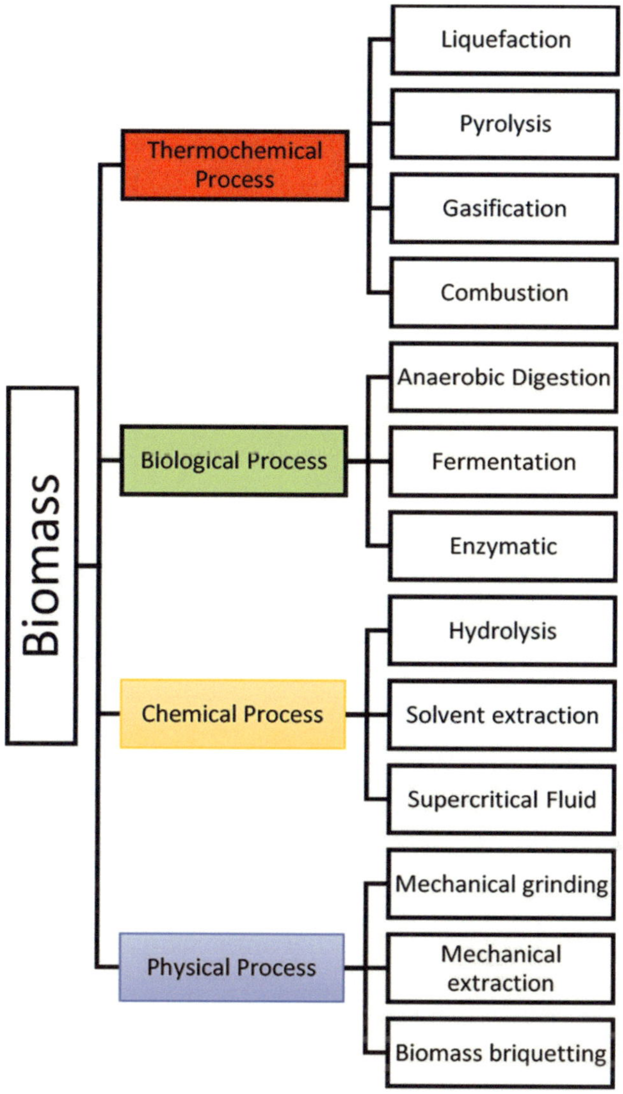

Figure 6.
Biomass transformation processes.

reactions carried out at high temperatures and a wide range of oxidation conditions [12]. These technologies have the potential to produce mainly heat, electricity, and fuels. Thermochemical transformation processes comprise liquefaction, pyrolysis, gasification, and combustion (**Figure 8**) [11–15].

3.1.1 Biomass liquefaction

Liquefaction aims to maximize the production of liquids from biomass, with the use of low temperatures (250–400°C) and high pressures (5–20 MPa) in the absence of oxygen and presence of catalysts such as carbonates and metals (zinc, copper, nickel, ruthenium) during processing. In this process the complex molecules of cellulose and lignin are fragmented by heating with steam and carbon monoxide, oxygen

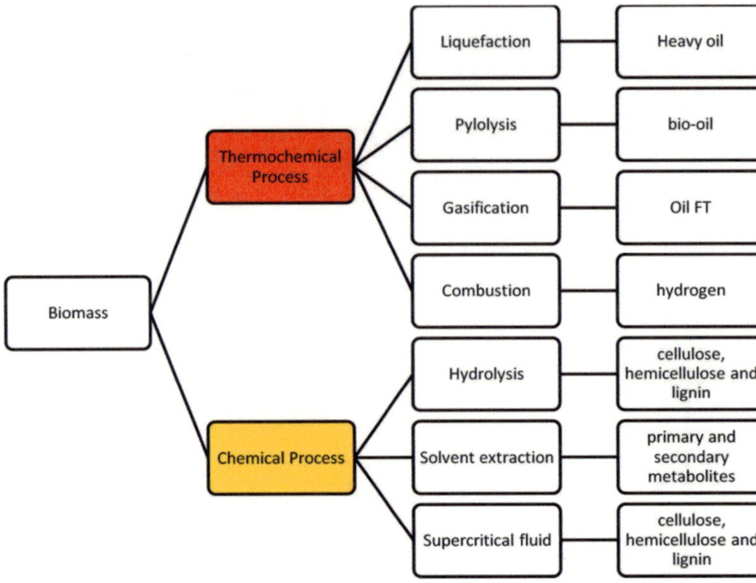

Figure 7.
Thermochemical and chemical processes of biomass and its resulting products.

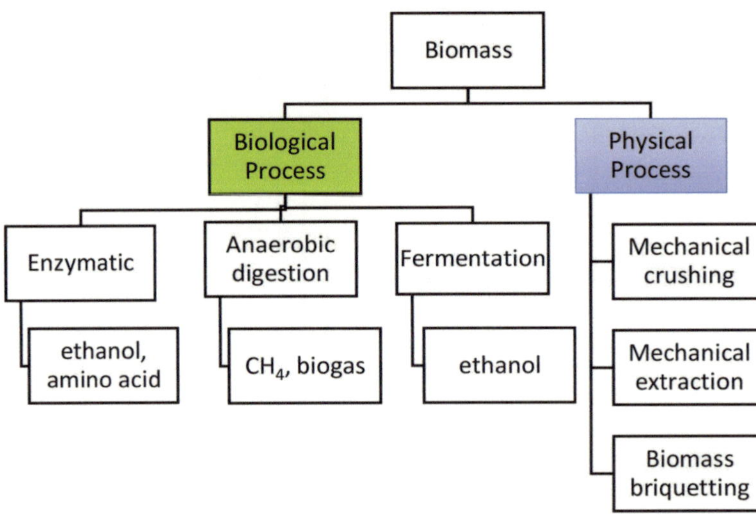

Figure 8.
Physical and biological processes of biomass transformation and resulting products.

is removed, and hydrogen atoms are added at the same time. The product of this chemical reaction is a mixture of hydrocarbons called heavy oils, which on cooling condense into a liquid fraction [13]. The heavy oil or bio-oil produced contains less oxygen since it has less water, therefore, it has a higher calorific value.

3.1.2 Pyrolysis of biomass

Pyrolysis is a process that consists of the thermal decomposition of biomass in the absence of oxygen. Pyrolysis requires temperatures up to 550°C, although it can be carried out at even higher temperatures (700–900°C), depending on the biomass treated. The product is a synthesis gas with considerable calorific value. During the pyrolysis process, solid or carbonized products, liquid products (bio-oils, tars, and water), and a gas mixture consisting mainly of CO_2, CO, H_2, and CH_4 are generated [9, 15].

3.1.3 Biomass gasification

Gasification consists of the conversion of biomass, normally of woody origin by thermal decomposition through partial oxidation reactions using a gasifying agent, such as steam, oxygen, air, or a mixture of the above and high temperatures (700–900°C), to obtain a synthesis gas also called as syngas with a considerable calorific value. Depending on the final feedstock conversion requirements, different temperature and pressure ranges can be used, as well as different types of gasifying agents, such as air, oxygen, steam, hydrogen, or carbon dioxide. The gas produced contains CO, H_2, CH_4, N_2, and steam, which is used in internal combustion engines and gas turbines. Fuel gas is mainly used to produce electricity or thermal energy [15].

3.1.4 Biomass combustion

Combustion is a thermochemical process used for heat production, consisting of a chemical reaction in the presence of oxygen at temperatures between 800 and 1000°C, in which fuel is oxidized, and a large amount of energy is released in the form of heat (exothermic reaction). Depending on the amount of oxygen present in the process, combustion can be complete when the amount of air is sufficient to oxidize all the organic elements that make up the fuel to produce mainly CO_2 and H_2O, or incomplete when the concentration of air is insufficient to oxidize the fuel and generate CO. This process converts the stored chemical energy of the biomass into heat, mechanical energy or electricity depending on the process equipment used such as furnaces, boilers, steam turbines, turbo generators, etc. [12, 15].

3.2 Chemical processes

Chemical processes include structural modifications or breaking of chemical bonds to either alter or form new molecules, as well as to hydrolyze macromolecules. Several of the chemical processes presented in this section are used as pretreatments to improve the efficiencies of biological processes, enzymatic reactions, such as fermentation and anaerobic digestion of biomass.

3.2.1 Hydrolysis

Chemical hydrolysis treatments are classified into acid hydrolysis and alkaline hydrolysis.

In alkaline hydrolysis, effective lignin removal and low inhibitor formation have been observed, although the reaction times are relatively long and the cost of the alkaline catalyst is high; however, it does not degrade sugars. The most commonly used reagents in alkaline hydrolysis are NaOH, NH_3, CaO, and $Ca(OH)_2$, and unlike acid hydrolysis, the temperatures are lower, in the range of 50–90°C. The use of an alkali causes the degradation of the ester and side chains, altering the structure of the lignin. This causes a loss of cellulose crystallinity and partial solvation of hemicellulose [16].

It has been reported that acid hydrolysis of biomass removes hemicellulose and partially lignin at high reaction rates; the limitation of acid hydrolysis is the corrosion of the reactor material, as well as a high formation of sugar degradation inhibitors. In acid hydrolysis, dilute or concentrated acid is used, the most used being H_2SO_4; the biomass is subjected to temperatures in the range of 100–160°C [17].

3.2.2 Solvent extraction

In recent years, research has been conducted on the generation of third-generation biofuels, also called advanced biofuels due to the raw materials and technological processes used for their production. The raw material for third-generation fuels are microalgae, which promise a high production of biodiesel per unit area due to their high lipid content, which surpasses all biodiesel sources currently used. Microalgae are cultivated in photobioreactors, which only need a liquid culture medium, some nutrients, and sunlight to stimulate the growth of the microalgae biomass. This makes it feasible to use land that is not suitable for the cultivation of human and animal food products for the assembly of photobioreactors. Studies for the extraction of oil from algae for subsequent transformation into biodiesel, either chemically or enzymatically, have been the subject of numerous investigations in numerous countries [18].

The study of the extraction process of lipids from microalgae begins with the knowledge of the composition of the cell wall of the algal biomass to be extracted, to select the solvents that allow high extraction efficiency and the lowest cost of the process. A wide variety of organic solvents have been used in the extraction of algal oil, the most popular being hexane and ethanol, with the extraction of more than 98% of the fatty acids present in the algal biomass [19]. Since ethanol is a polar solvent, its selectivity towards lipids is relatively low compared to other solvents, so that other components of the microalgae such as sugars, pigments, or amino acids (primary and secondary metabolites) may appear in extractions with ethanol.

3.2.3 Supercritical fluids

Supercritical fluids (SCFs) are good solvents due to their ability to dissolve substances in a similar way to organic solvents, and because their viscosity and diffusion coefficient are close to those of gases, thus facilitating the transport properties of these fluids. Moreover, since the surface tension of FSCs is equal to zero, these fluids are particularly suitable for the extraction of substances contained in solid matrices such as lignocellulosic biomass to obtain cellulose, hemicellulose, and lignin [18, 20]. A fluid is called supercritical when it is forced to remain at conditions of pressure and temperature higher than its critical pressures and temperatures, under these conditions, the fluid has characteristics of both a gas and a liquid, which gives it some special properties such as low viscosity and high relative diffusivity, which allows them to easily penetrate the solids and provide a faster extraction.

All supercritical solid extraction processes consist of two stages: extraction and separation of the solvent from the extract produced. In extraction, supercritical CO2 flows through the solid and dissolves the extractable components. The solvent loaded with the extract is evacuated from the extractor and fed to the separator, where the pressure is reduced so that the solute is not soluble and precipitates. Another advantage is the use of FSCs is the possibility of changing their solvating power by variations of the pressure and/or temperature of the fluid, thus allowing fractional extraction of the solutes, and complete recovery of the solvent by simple pressure adjustments [20, 21].

Of all the supercritical fluids that have been studied, carbon dioxide (CO2) is the most widely used due to its low critical temperature (TC = 31°C) and pressure (PC = 74 bar), non-toxicity, availability, and low cost. CO2 is a "green" solvent that is found in the atmosphere, in food and beverages, and of which no minimum content needs to be fixed in extracts, so it can be safely used [21]. In fact, it is considered a GRAS solvent. The supercritical fluid method emerged as an alternative to the traditional use of large quantities of toxic solvents for extractions, being this type of processes the most promising, besides these techniques are characterized by having short extraction times and high selectivities [20].

3.3 Physical processes

The physical processes most used in the transformation of biomass into value-added products are presented.

3.3.1 Mechanical crushing

The reduction of wood to a size compatible with the subsequent process is the first step in the pretreatment of biomass. The reduction of lignocellulosic materials through a combination of chipping and/or grinding can be applied to reduce cellulose crystallinity, increase mass transfer due to a larger contact area and increase the efficiency of the subsequent process, whether chemical, thermochemical, or biological. The size of the materials is usually 10–30 mm after chipping and 0.2–2 mm after milling [22].

3.3.2 Mechanical extraction

Mechanical extraction is usually performed through an expeller press also called screw or extruder press. This press is a continuous mechanical extractor, where the oil is extracted from the raw material in a single step, with high pressure. Mechanical extraction has been used as a tool for the extraction of microalgae components and includes several kinds of mechanical devices such as cell homogenizers, ball mills, pressing systems [10], concluding that the highest percentage of oil extraction was obtained when using a ball mill with 1 mm crystal spheres for one minute. Mechanical extraction methods have the disadvantage of difficulty in recovering the extracted oil, so these kinds of methods are used in combination with chemical solvent methods.

3.3.3 Biomass briquetting

Biomass briquettes are a biofuel, made mostly from dried and compressed green waste and other organic materials (rice and groundnut hulls, bagasse, municipal solid waste, and agricultural residues), which can be used in boilers to generate steam or electricity from it, also used in ovens for cooking and heating. Briquettes are burned together with coal to generate heat through combustion, generating low total net greenhouse gas emissions compared to fossil fuels. The dimensions of briquettes are diameter > 5 cm and length between 50 and 80 cm [23].

3.4 Biological processes

Biological processes use biological agents (microorganisms, algae, or enzymes) to convert biomass into value-added products such as electricity, heat, bioproducts, and fuels. Biological processes can be divided into biocatalysis (enzymes are used as biocatalysts), fermentation, and anaerobic digestion.

3.4.1 Enzymatic process

Enzymatic processes are present in several areas of biotechnology, such as pharmaceuticals, food, energy, detergents, textiles, as well as in the environment, mainly in water and waste treatment processes and in the formation of biofuel, specifically biodiesel. Biodiesel can be generated from the triglycerides of tallow, vegetable oil, or microalgae oil by transesterification [24].

It is important to highlight that in the processes of bioethanol and biogas formation and other products of interest by microbial means from biomass, there is a critical step, which is the release of fermentable sugars from the polysaccharides of the biomass to be converted with high yields into high value-added products. Therefore, the most recent research in the field of bioresources has focused on the development of certain biomass pretreatments, such as delignification and enzymatic hydrolysis of cellulose, in which a low production of inhibitory compounds and high release of fermentable sugars are achieved so that they can be efficiently transformed into value-added products via microbial means and with a low environmental impact [25].

3.4.2 Anaerobic digestion of biomass

In this process, organic matter (lignocellulosic biomass, municipal waste, livestock, and agricultural industry waste) is degraded to form biogas by the action of anaerobic bacteria at temperatures of approximately 30°C. Anaerobic digestion is the cheapest, most stable, and well-established technique that recovers a greater amount of energy from the source; the process consists of three fundamental stages: hydrolysis-acidogenesis, homoacetogenesis-acetogenesis, and methanogenesis [26]. The first stage involves acid-forming bacteria that use carbohydrates as raw material, the second stage involves acetic acid-forming bacteria that can be inhibited by H_2, and the third stage involves acetophilic and hydrogenophilic bacteria that use acetic acid, carbon monoxide, and hydrogen to generate the product of digestion, which is biogas.

Biogas is a mixture of methane (CH_4), carbon dioxide (CO_2), small amounts of hydrogen (H_2), hydrogen sulfide (SH_2), and nitrogen (N_2). Biogas can be used as an important energy source in the combustion process carried out in engines, turbines, or boilers operated in the industry. In addition, the degraded biomass that remains as a residue of the biogas production process is an excellent fertilizer for agricultural crops [27].

3.4.3 Biomass fermentation

Fermentation is an anaerobic process where the substrate is transformed into organic products through the action of microorganisms. The types of fermentation that exist, according to the microorganism present in the process are alcoholic, malic, lactic, acetic, propionic, and butyric.

Product	Organism	Use	Product	Organism	Use
Ethanol	*Saccharomyces cerevisiae, Zymomonas mobilis*	Biofuel	Lactic acid	*Lactobacillus*	Chemical and food, cosmetics, pharmaceutical, and plastics industries
Biobutanol	*Clostridium beijerinckii*	Biofuel	Propionic acid	*Propionibacteria*	Food preservative
Acetone-butanol-ethanol (ABE)	*Clostridium*	Biofuel	Succinic acid	*Anaerobiospirillum succinici*	Chemical and food industry, cosmetics, pharmaceuticals, and plastics
Poly-3-hydroxybutyrate (PHB)	*Burkholderia sacchari*	Biopolymer	Malic acid	*Aspergillus Escherichia coli*	Pharmaceutical and food industry
cellulose	*Rhodophyta, Phaeophyta Acetobacter xylinum*	Biopolymer	Acetic acid	*Acetobacter*	Food preservation
Xanthan gum	*Xanthomonas campestris*	Biopolymer	Formic acid	*Escherichia coli*	Textile and chemical industry
Isopropanol	*Clostridium*	Chemical Industry	Fumaric acid	*Rhizopus arrhizus Rhizopus oryzae*	Food preservation
Edible mushrooms	*Agaricus sp. Grifola sp*	Feed	Butyric acid	*Clostridium, Fusobacterium, Megasphera Eubacterium*	Chemical and food industry, pharmaceuticals
Unicellular protein	*Saccharomyces cerevisiae*	Livestock feed	Letinan	*Lentinula edodes*	Antiviral, anti-inflammatory, antibacterial, antitumor, immunomodulatory properties
			Pululan	*Aureobasidium pullulans*	bulking agent and binder in tablet production

Table 1.
Summary of the various products derived from biomass.

The substrate is mainly fermentable sugars, obtained from starch, cellulose, fruits, vegetables, and in general from lignocellulosic biomass. **Table 1** shows some of the products that have been obtained by fermentation using biomass [11, 16, 28, 29].

The transformation of biomass into chemical products and biofuels is increasing worldwide. **Table 1** shows some products obtained by fermentation from lignocellulosic biomass. Biomass is a neutral and economical resource, however, to transform biomass into value-added products, a pretreatment of delignification and saccharification is necessary to release fermentable sugars.

The environmental impact of using biomass is the reduction of CO2 emissions due to the substitution of fossil fuels and the valorization of certain wastes as raw materials. The use of indigenous biomass helps to convert potentially problematic waste for the future into available resources. In addition, this action would reduce forest fires and contribute to the positive management of ecosystems and to the mitigation of climate change.

The social impact of the use of biomass is to stimulate the economy of the region through the employment of groups linked to rural areas and to stop the depopulation of rural areas and the economic savings that the use of waste allows. Finally, the economic value of biomass utilization requires the mobilization of a series of human and capital resources and an intense relationship with suppliers, as biomass has to be supplied to industries. This benefits the primary sector (agriculture, forestry, and livestock), as well as the secondary sector (agri-food, forestry, chemical, pharmaceutical, food, materials, etc.).

4. Conclusions

Biomass is a valuable renewable and undervalued source of chemicals for use in the processing industry and can be used directly or indirectly to produce platform molecules or bioproducts by chemical, physical, microbial, or enzymatic treatments. Nowadays, biomass can be used for many purposes, such as chemicals, pharmaceuticals, food, biofuels (biogas/bioethanol), or energy and fodder production, which contribute significantly to the economic growth of countries.

It should be noted that as urbanization increases, more waste will be generated by society, so the integral valorization of biomass is a fundamental pillar of sustainable development. Given the origin of this biomass, as well as its composition, biomass is a vast resource for society.

Due to the diversity that biomass presents in its chemical composition, biomass is a vast resource that requires research to further develop technologies and processes with a multidisciplinary approach. It should be noted that biomass pretreatment is a critical point in the production processes to achieve high yields and productivity. This is necessary to overcome the complete transition of our production systems from a petroleum-based economy to a bio-based economy.

Acknowledgements

The author is grateful to the Autonomous University of Guadalajara for its support in the realization of this work.

Author details

Dulce María Diaz-Montaño
Autonomous University of Guadalajara, Guadalajara, Jalisco, Mexico

*Address all correspondence to: dulce.diaz@edu.uag.mx

References

[1] Tripathi N, Hills CD, Singh RS, Atkinson CJ. Mint: Biomass waste utilisation in low-carbon products: harnessing a major potential resource. NPJ Climate and Atmospheric Science. 2019;**2**:35. DOI: 10.1038/s41612-019-0093-5

[2] Centore M, Hochman G, Zilberman D. Worldwide survey of biodegradable feedstocks, waste-to-energy technologies, and adoption technologies. In: Pinto IAA, Zilberman D, editors. Handbook of Modelling, Dynamics, Optimization and Bioeconomics. 1st ed. Berlin, Germany: Springer Proceedings in Mathematics and Statistics; 2014. pp. 149-162. DOI: 10.1007/978-3-319-04849-9_11

[3] Baruya P. World Forest and Agricultural Crop Residue Resources for Co-firing. IEA, International Energy Agency; 2015. ISBN 978-92-9029-571-6

[4] Afanasjeva N, Castillo LC, Sinisterra JC. Mint: Lignocellulosic biomass. Part I: Biomass transformation. The Journal of Applied Science and Technology (JAST). 2017;**3**:27-43. DOI: 10.34294/j.jsta.17.3.22

[5] da Costa TP, Quinteiro P, Tarelho LA, Arroja L, Dias AC. Mint: Environmental assessment of valorisation alternatives for woody biomass ash in construction materials. Resources, Conservation & Recycling. 2019;**148**:67-79. DOI: 10.1016/j.resconrec.2019.04.022

[6] Kopetz H. Mint: Renewable resources: Build a biomass energy market. Nature. 2013;**494**:29-31. DOI: 10.1038/494029a

[7] Chum HL, Overend RP. Mint: Biomass and renewable fuels. Fuel Processing Technology (FPT). 2001;**1**:187-195. DOI: 10.1016/S0378-3820(01)00146-1

[8] Saldarriaga-Hernández S, Velasco-Ayala C, Leal-Isla Flores P, Rostro-Alanis M, Parra-Saldivar R, Iqbal HM, et al. Mint: Biotransformation of lignocellulosic biomass into industrially relevant products with the aid of fungi-derived lignocellulolytic enzymes. International Journal of Biological Macromolecules. 2020;**161**:1099-1116. DOI: 10.1016/j.ijbiomac.2020.06.047

[9] Razik AHA, Khor CS, Elkamel AA. Mint: A model-based approach for biomass-to-bioproducts supply chain network planning optimization. Food and Bioproducts Processing. 2019;**118**:293-305. DOI: 10.1016/j.fbp.2019.10.001

[10] Kumar M, Sun Y, Rathour R, Pandey A, Thakur IS, Tsang DCW. Mint: Algae as potential feedstock for the production of biofuels and value-added products: Opportunities and challenges. Science of the Total Environment. 2020;**716**:137116. DOI: 10.1016/j.scitotenv.2020.137116

[11] Cho EJ, Trinh LPT, Song Y, Lee YG, Hyeun-Jong B. Mint: Bioconversion of biomass waste into high value chemicals. Bioresource Technology. 2019;**298**:122386. DOI: 10.1016/j.biortech.2019.122386

[12] Peña J, Martínez P, Cortés M, Chirivi N, Mendoza Geney L. Mint: Uso energético de la biomasa a través del proceso de gasificación. 2017. Available from: 89-Texto del artículo-156-1-10-20180118(5).pdf

[13] Moragues J, Rapallini A. Energía de la biomasa. 2017. Available from: http://www.iae.org.ar/renovables/ren_biomasa.pd

[14] Kumar M, Olajire Oyedun A, Kumar A. Mint: A review on the current

status of various hydrothermal technologies on biomass feedstock. Renewable Sustainable Energy Reviews. Elsevier. 2018;**81**(P2): 1742-1770. DOI: 10.1016/j.rser.2017.05.270

[15] Zhang L, Xu C, Champagne P. Mint: Overview of recent advances in thermo-chemical conversion of biomass. Energy Conversion and Management. 2010;**51**:969-982. DOI: 10.1016/j.enconman.2009.11.038

[16] Ning P, Yang G, Hu L, Sun J, Shi L, Zhou Y, et al. Mint: Recent advances in the valorization of plant biomass. Biotechnology for Biofuels. 2021;**14**:102. DOI: 10.1016/j.enconman.2009.11.038

[17] Taherzadeh M, Karimi K. Mint: Acid-based hydrolysis processes for ethanol from lignocellulosic materials: A bioethanol review. BioResources. 2007;**2**:707-738 Available from: www.scirp.org

[18] González AD, Viatcheslav K, Guzmán MA. Mint: Desarrollo de métodos de extracción de aceite en la cadena de producción de biodiesel a partir de microalgas. Prospect. 2009;**7**:53-60 Available from: https://www.redalyc.org/pdf/4962/496250976007.pdf

[19] Richmond A. Handbook of Microalgal Culture: Biotechnology and Applied Phycology. 1st ed. Hoboken, New Jersey, United States: Blackwell Science Ltd; 2004. p. 566. DOI: 10.1002/9780470995280

[20] Escobar ELN, da Silva TA, Pirich CL, Corazza ML, Pereira RL. Mint: Supercritical fluids: A promising technique for biomass pretreatment and fractionation. Frontiers in Bioengineering and Biotechnology. 2020;**8**:252. DOI: 10.3389/fbioe.2020.00252

[21] Gu T, Held MA, Faik A. Mint: Supercritical CO_2 and ionic liquids for the pretreatment of lignocellulosic biomass in bioethanol production. Environmental Technology. 2013;**34**:1735-1749. DOI: 10.1080/09593330.2013.809777

[22] Sun Y, Cheng J. Mint: Hydrolysis of lignocellulosic materials for ethanol production: A review. Bioresource Technology. 2002;**83**:1-11. DOI: 10.1016/S0960-8524(01)00212-7

[23] Berastegui Barranco C, Ortega Rodríguez JP, Mendoza Fandiño JM, González Doria YE, Gómez Vasquez RD. Mint: Elaboración de biocombustibles sólidos densificados a partir de tusa de maíz, bioaglomerante de yuca y carbón mineral del departamento de Córdoba. Ingeniare. Revista chilena de ingeniería. 2017;**25**:643-653. Available from: https://www.redalyc.org/pdf/772/77254022008.pdf

[24] Pasha MK, Dai L, Liu D, Guo L, Du W. Mint: An overview to process design, simulation and sustainability evaluation of biodiesel production. Biotechnology for Biofuels. 2021;**14**:129. DOI: 10.1186/s13068-021-01977-z

[25] Zhang H, Han L, Hongmin D. Mint: An insight to pretreatment, enzyme adsorption and enzymatic hydrolysis of lignocellulosic biomass: Experimental and modeling studies. Renewable and Sustainable Energy Reviews. 2021;**140**:110758. DOI: 10.1016/j.rser.2021.110758

[26] Ziemiński K, Frąc M. Mint: Methane fermentation process as anaerobic digestion of biomass: Transformations, stages, and microorganisms. African Journal of Biotechnology. 2012;**11**:4127-4139. DOI: 10.5897/AJBX11.054

[27] Boontian N. Mint: Conditions of the anaerobic digestion of biomass. World Academy of Science, Engineering and Technology International Journal

of Environmental and Ecological Engineering. 2014;8:1036-1040. Available from: scholar.waset.org

[28] Kovacs B. Mint: Sustainable Agriculture, Forestry and Fisheries in the Bioeconomy: A Challenge for Europe: 4th Scar Foresight Exercise. European Commission; 2015. Available from: https://data.europa.eu/doi/10.2777/51435

[29] Cheng H, Wang L. Lignocelluloses feedstock biorefinery as petrorefinery substitutes. In: Matovic MD, editor. Handbook of Biomass Now. Sustainable Growth and Use. 1st ed. London: IntechOpen; 2013. p. 462. DOI: 10.5772/2583

Chapter 12

Conventional and Unconventional Transformation of Cocoa Pod Husks into Value-Added Products

Martina Francisca Baidoo, Nana Yaw Asiedu, Lawrence Darkwah, David Arhin-Dodoo, Jun Zhao, Francois Jerome and Prince Nana Amaniampong

Abstract

The drive for a sustainable society and a circular economy has motivated researchers around the globe to turn to the transformation of renewable raw materials like biomass into value-added products that are akin or superior to their fossil counterparts. Among these biomass raw materials, cocoa pod husks (CPH) which is the non-edible portion of cocoa (ca. 70–75% weight of the while cocoa fruit) remains a promising bio-resource raw material for the production high-value added chemicals but yet largely underexploited. Currently, the most popular applications of CPH involves its use as low-value application products such as animal feed, raw material for soap making, and activated carbon. However, the rich source of lignocellulosic content, pectin, and phenolic compounds of CPH means it could be used as raw materials for the production industrially relevant platform chemicals with high potential in the agrochemicals, pharmaceutical, and food industries, if efficient transformations routes are developed by scientists. In this chapter, we will shed light on some of the works related to the transformation of CPH into various value-added products. An economic evaluation of the transformation of cocoa pod husk into relevant chemicals and products is also discussed.

Keywords: cocoa pod husks, biomass, value-added products, valorization, pretreatment

1. Introduction

Cocoa (*Theobroma cacao* L.) is one of the most cultivated and valuable crops in many developing tropical countries including Ivory Coast, Ghana, Nigeria, and Cameroon whose collective efforts alone accounts for about 74.5% of annual global cocoa beans. Three species of *T. cacao* L. (*Sterculiaceae*) namely *Criollo*, *Forastero*, and *Trinitario* are the dominant market produce and commercial cocoa species of all 22 species present in that genus [1].

Cocoa pod husks (CPH) are the non-edible part of the cocoa pod with a percentage composition of 67–76% of the total cocoa pod wet weight. This translates to every kilogram of dry cocoa bean produced generating 10 kg of wet cocoa pod husks [2]. For instance, it has been estimated that the annual world crop of 1 million tons of cocoa produces about 10 million tons of pod husks as by-product, and constitutes about 67% of the fresh pod weight. After removal of the cocoa beans, treated and exported abroad, CPH is usually discarded on the farm, which often is left to decompose as an organic fertilizer. However, CPH left on the soil surface also act as a source of inoculum for plant diseases such as black pod rot (BPR) due to the development of *Phytophthora* spp. bacteria. BPR causes an annual cocoa yield loss from 20 to 30% worldwide, while individual farms may suffer an annual cocoa yield loss from 30% up to 90%. A graph of the production of cocoa bean and cocoa pod husks generated from around the world by countries known to be among the leading producers of cocoa is shown in **Figure 1**.

The development of cutting-edge technologies that can efficiently transform these hitherto waste materials generated from cocoa into useful chemicals that could potentially improve the global value chain of cacao production, is crucial and highly sort after and concomitantly reduce the negative environmental impact. Many researchers have developed interests in this area of study because of the vast availability of CPH which poses a major waste management challenge confronting cocoa-producing nations. In light of this, there have been multiple reports on the valorization of CPH into value-added products in an attempt to contribute to our drive for a sustainable society and a circular economy. Nonetheless, CPH have been hugely underexploited even though there have been numerous published literatures on this subject matter. In fact, research interest in CPH valorization dates back 1905 with a single publication. The publications increased significantly from 2003 and has continued to grow ever since. Averagely, for the past decade there has been about 18 publications per year on CPH (**Figure 2**).

Majority of these publications related to CPH were journal articles, hugely representing over 50% of the global works related to CPH transformations to various value-added products. However, a number of patents have also been filed (representing about 15% of the global publications related to CPH transformations),

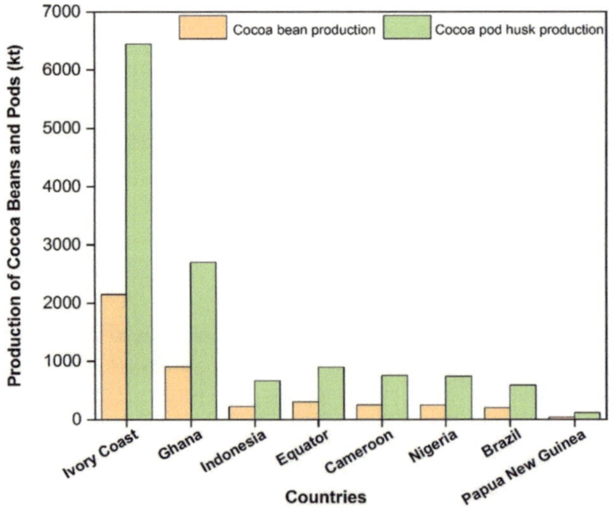

Figure 1.
Generation of cocoa bean and cocoa pod husks by various countries.

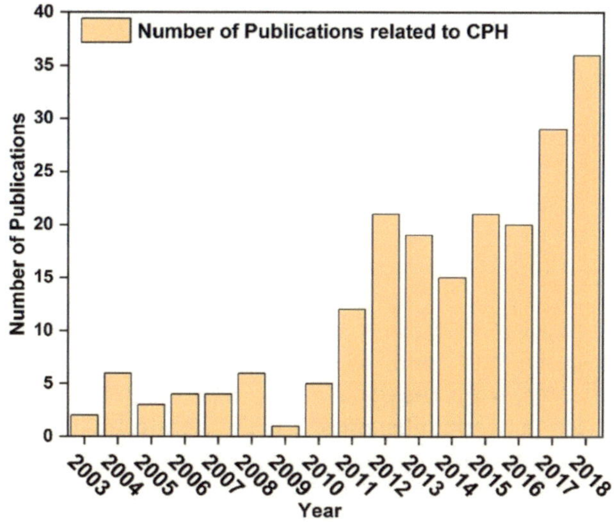

Figure 2.
Publications produced annually related to CPH transformations.

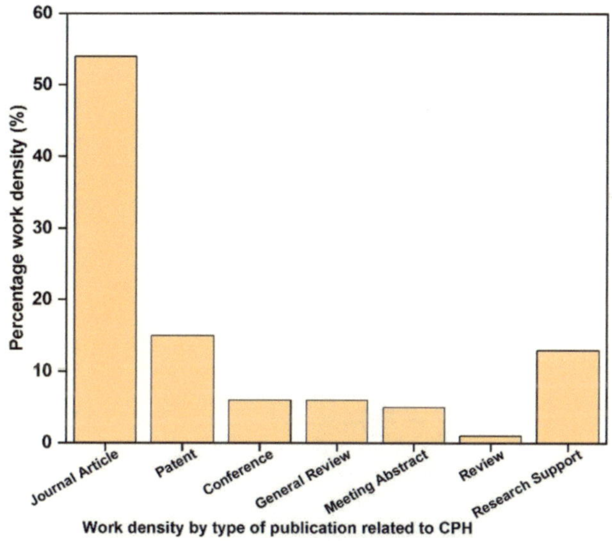

Figure 3.
Publication work density on cocoa pod husks (reproduced and modified with permission from: Ref. [3]).

signifying the importance of the works and results discovered in relation to CPH as a bio-resource raw material. **Figure 3** below shows the work density by type of publication CPH.

The renewed and increased interest in CPH can be attributed to the enormous quantities generated on the farm, the environmental challenge that rotten CPH poses as well as the concomitant spread of black pod diseases that has accounted for the huge losses recorded by cocoa farmers [1–3]. Besides CPH has been found to be a valuable bio-resource due to the myriad of value-added products such as activated carbon, soap, animal feed, soil manure and fertilizer, biofuels, paper, biofuels, and nutraceuticals that it can be transformed into. It has also been found to be a repository of base chemicals of high value such as aldehydes, ketones, theobromine, phenols, potash, and pectin [4–9]. CPH applications in several areas including radial electrochemical agrochemical bio-regulators, thermal energy technology, soil fertilization, manure and fertilizer production, food and animal chemistry, plastic treatment and waste treatment, and disposal are still being explored. Whilst soil fertilization, plant nutrition, and food and feed chemistry aspects of CPH application have been extensively exploited, plastic manufacturing, and processing is still underexplored and deserve special attention [3]. Compositionally, CPH comprises of mesocarp, sclerotic part, and epicarp (**Figure 4**).

Primarily, CPH consists of fibrous materials that includes ~19–26% cellulose, 9–13% hemicellulose, 14–28% lignin, and 6–13% pectin. The mesocarp contains mainly (~50%) cellulose, while the epicarp is enriched with lignin and the endocarp on the other hand rich in pectic substances [9]. The hemicellulose fraction of CPH has been reported to consist of arabinan, arabinoxylan, and xylan, which have been deduced from the high amount of isolable arabinose and xylose [10], along with other hemicelluloses fractions such as xyloglucans, galactomannans, and

Figure 4.
Fresh cocoa pod fruit (a) and dried cocoa pod husk (b and c).

glucomannans [11]. CPH is also a good source of phenolic acids, with quantities ranging from 4.6 to 6.9 g GAE/100 g.

Numerous technologies and transformation routes have been explored for the valorization of CPH into valuable products. Among these transformation routes are biochemical, physical, physicochemical, and thermochemical processes. Unconventional valorization routes such as supercritical carbon dioxide extraction, microwave, and ultrasound technologies have also been investigated and are still under exploration.

The main objective of this chapter is to shed light on some of the scientific efforts tailored at valorizing CPH either by conventional or unconventional approaches into valuable platform chemicals and products, as well as the challenges and future perspectives on the efficient use of CPH as a potential agro-waste resource and its economic viabilities.

2. CPH valorization routes and technological approaches into chemical platforms, fuels, and low value products

To date, conventional valorization routes for transforming CPH to specialty chemicals occur either *via* biochemical, thermochemical, or physicochemical techniques. A combination of these techniques is also possible, given that lignocellulosic biomass usually requires pretreatment especially before biochemical conversion.

2.1 Biochemical transformation of CPH into fuels

Biochemical transformation of renewable raw materials involves the use microorganisms as catalyst to transform biomass into valuable products. It is often regarded as a cheaper approach for converting biomass to chemical, energy, and fuels. However, due to the recalcitrant nature of lignin component in biomass, the use of microbes to transform crude biomass into valuable products is often challenging and difficult. In this context, it is imperative to pretreat the biomass raw material in order to render cellulose and hemicellulose susceptible to microbial action. The pretreatment processes may be physical, thermochemical, biological, or physicochemical. The nature of pretreatment approach dictates the types of the intermediate chemical that would be obtained for further conversion to final product. The main biochemical routes that have been investigated using CPH as raw material are fermentation and anaerobic digestion.

2.1.1 Anaerobic digestion of CPH

Anaerobic digestion (AD) is a sequence of processes by which microorganisms break down biodegradable material in the absence of oxygen. AD basically occurs in three steps: decomposition or hydrolysis of biomass, followed by conversion of treated biomass to organic acids, and finally conversion of acids into methane gas. The main product of AD is biogas which contains methane, carbon dioxide, and some traces of hydrogen sulfide which is one of the main sources of renewable energy. The process also produces an aqueous mixture consisting of microorganisms involved in the degradation. Large volumes of CPH generated and its composition makes it a viable candidate for AD biogas production.

In 2018, Acosta and co-workers [12] investigated the production of methane and biogas yields from CPH and compared it to other agricultural residues, to evaluate the quality of the biomass raw material as a new feedstock for biogas production. The authors concluded that 50% of organic matter from CPH was transformed to biogas with 60% yield of methane. Dry AD was the preferred process choice for the authors because it gave the highest yields of methane and also, the operating conditions were stable [12].

In another interesting work, Antwi et al. [13] investigated the potential of valorizing CPH *via* anaerobic digestion and the impact of hydrothermal pretreatment on biogas yield. They compared the biogas yield and methane content of untreated anaerobically digested CPH to those obtained from the hydrothermally pretreated CPH at different severity levels. Based on their results they concluded that AD is an effective process of converting CPH to fuels. Furthermore, the impact of the pretreatment is diverse in that biogas yield increased for CPH treated at low severity levels up to 3.0. Hydrothermal pretreatment at severity levels above 3.0 lead to inhibitions in the AD process that lowered the biogas yield.

Several reports on the valorization of CPH or cocoa related residue to biogas *via* AD has proven that to be an effective approach, however, a form of pretreatment (physical, thermochemical, biological, or physicochemical) of the biomass is required to separate lignin from cellulose and hemicellulose [5, 14–17].

2.1.2 Fermentation of CPH

Fermentation is the conversion of sugars contained in biomass hydrosylate to specialty chemicals using microbes. The type of microbe used dictates the fermentation pathway as well as the end products. The conversion of CPH to bioethanol, bio-butatnol, and propanoic acid by fermentation reported in literature has been highlighted below.

Shet et al. [17] hydrolyzed CPH with HCl to release reducing sugars under optimized conditions (8.36% W/V of CPH, 3.6 N HCl, and 7.36 hours) using response surface methodology (RSM). The hydrosylate was neutralized using 5 N NaOH followed by fermentation to produce bioethanol. The inoculum was *Pichia stipites* at 2% V/V. After 72 hours of fermentation, bioethanol was distilled from the broth at a concentration of 2 g/L. They demonstrated that CPH to ethanol conversion is feasible and that CPH offers a cheaper and renewable feedstock for ethanol production. A similar work was done by Samah and co-workers [18], where CPH was hydrolyzed with HCl, H_2SO_4, and HNO_3 at different concentrations (0.25, 0.50, 0.75, 1.00, and 1.25 M). They were further heated to 75 and 90°C for 2 and 4 hours. The highest glucose content of 30.7% W/V was obtained for CPH samples treated with 1.00 M of HCL at 75°C and 4 hours. The hydrosylate was then fermented using *Saccharomyces cerevisiae* for 48 hours at room temperature to obtain a maximum ethanol concentration of 17.3% V/V after 26 hours of fermentation.

Hernández-Mendoza et al., 2021 on the other hand performed alkaline hydrolysis on CPH and examined the effect of NaOH concentration, residence time, and temperature using a central composite design (CDD). The solid fraction was examined with X-ray diffraction (XRD) and scanning electron microscopy (SEM) in order to investigate morphological changes. It was further subjected to enzymatic hydrolysis which optimized the enzyme and solid loadings to convert cellulose to reducing sugars. The yeast *S. cerevisiae* was applied to ferment the hydrosylate. The optimum condition for the alkaline hydrolysis process occurred at 5% W/V NaOH for 30 minutes at 120°C which led to an increased in the cellulose content of CPH to 57 ± 0.25% relative to that of the untreated sample of 27.68 ± 0.15%. SEM revealed changes in porosity and structure of CPH, whilst XRD showed increase in crystallinity. Enzymatic hydrolysis yielded 66.80 g/L of reducing sugars of which 80.74% were consumed during fermentation producing 18.06 g/L of ethanol in 24 hours. They concluded that CPH is a promising feedstock for bioethanol production [19].

Propionic acid production from CPH was reported for the first time by Sarmiento-Vásquez et al. [20]. In their work, alkaline and enzymatic treatment is conducted with 2.3% W/V NaOH and 2.4% V/V Cellic® CTec2, respectively to convert CPH to fermentable sugars such as glucose to a maximum yield of 275 mg glucose/g CPH. Subsequently 7.5 g/L CPH hydrosylate is fermented with *Propionibacterium jensenii* (DSM 20274) in the presence of 7.5 g/L of glycerol. A maximum propionic concentration of 10.28 ± 1.05 g/L after 75 hours of fermentation.

Sandesh et al. [21] successfully produced acetone, bio-butanol, and ethanol from inductive assisted H_2SO_4 hydrolyzed CPH using *Clostridium acetobutylicum*. A product distribution of 5.04 ± 0.32 g/L of acetone, 11.73 ± 0.84 g/L butanol, and 1.43 ± 0.04 ethanol is reported to have been obtained after 312 hours of fermentation.

These results are a demonstration of the potential of CPH as a cheap feedstock for the production of biochemicals *via* fermentation techniques after different pretreatment approaches have been applied to the CPH biomass to convert it to fermentable sugars.

2.2 Thermochemical approaches

Thermochemical biomass conversion approach involves all processes in which heat is used to transform biomass in the solid form to other states in the presence or absence of oxygen. Processes that fall under this category are direct combustion, gasification, pyrolysis, hydrothermal liquefaction, and torrefaction. This section examines how thermochemical conversion processes have been applied in CPH valorization.

2.2.1 Direct combustion

In direct combustion, biomass is burnt in ovens, kilns, fluidized bed combustors, furnaces with excess oxygen or air to obtain gases and ash. The combustion chambers are usually operated at temperature above 900°C. Gases and ash are the key products. The ash has been found to contain 40% potash which consists of 43% potassium carbonate and 27% potassium hydroxide. This is the process soap-makers in most West African countries harness potash from CPH to produce soft soap known locally as *alata samina* [22]. These CPH potash soap have been found to contain superior properties such as higher solubility, lathering capacity, cleansing power, and consistency compared with those produced with chemical KOH [23]. Furthermore, CPH ash has also been applied as fertilizer. Studies shows that replacing about 50% of conventional NPK fertilizer with CPH ash has had positive impact on nutrients uptake by maize plants and grain yield [24]. It has had similar effect on soil fertility, fruit growth, and yield in tomato production [25]. CPH ash obtained in a furnace at 650°C for 4 hours was evaluated by [26] as a heterogeneous catalyst for the transesterification of soya bean oil to biodiesel. Their results demonstrated that CPH ash is a superior catalyst for generating high yield of biodiesel with quality and engine performance close to that of diesel from petroleum.

2.2.2 Pyrolysis

In pyrolysis biomass is thermally decomposed in an inert atmosphere at elevated temperatures. The biomass is usually converted to volatile products with solid residue called char where the proportion of each fraction depends on the conditions of pyrolysis that the biomass was subjected to. The volatile fractions are usually condensed to obtain the liquid (bio-oil) and non-condensable gaseous fractions. Operating parameters such as reaction temperature, pressure, catalysts, hot vapor residence time, solid's residence time, etc., affect the overall process performance. The conditions of pyrolysis fall into three categories namely slow pyrolysis, fast pyrolysis, and flash pyrolysis. In slow pyrolysis, the temperature of the biomass is raised to about 500°C at low heating rates with long residence times. The solid char is the main product and it is the main route of producing charcoal which can used as fuel, activated carbon, soil conditioners, and feedstock for producing chemicals. On the other hand, in fast and flash pyrolysis, the liquid fraction or bio-oil is the preferred product. In fast pyrolysis, temperatures of about 500°C and short vapor residence time of about 2 seconds are typical to generate bio-oil from biomass. Flash pyrolysis is similar to fast pyrolysis except that the residence time is shorter in the former [27].

Pyrolysis is the most widely exploited biomass to liquid (BTL) conversion route in that the crude bio-oil can be directly used in boilers and turbines to generate electricity and heat as well as feedstock for synthesizing fuels, base, and fine chemicals [28]. By this technology, bio-oils that of high value and substitute for fuels from non-renewable sources can be produced [29]. Tsai and co-worker [30] demonstrated that slow pyrolysis of CPH produces bio-chars of more than 60% carbon content and a calorific value greater than 25 MJ/kg, dry basis at temperatures between 190 and 370°C for 30–120 minutes. They concluded that though this type of biochar exhibited lignite-like feature, it is not suitable for use as fuel in boilers due to the high potassium content. Several researchers have applied this process to CPH and have generated similar products [31–33].

CPH was pyrolyzed under fast pyrolysis conditions at temperatures 550–600°C by [29] for 2–4 minutes to yield 58 wt.% bio-oil, 30 wt.% biochar, and 12 wt.% non-condensable gases. Analysis of the bio-oil shows it contained a complex mixture of carboxylic acids and ketones with 9,12-octadecadienoic acid being the most abundant.

In another work by Mansur et al., the authors [2] reported the possibility of upgrading pyrolysis oil obtained from CPH *via* the use of heterogeneous catalysis. Firstly, they pyrolyzed CPH at 500°C for 50 minutes to yield pyrolysis oil which contained several chemical compounds including benzenediols, ketones, carboxylic acids, aldehydes, furans, heterocyclic aromatics, alkyl benzenes, and phenols. This oil was subjected to catalytic upgrade using ZrO_2-FeO_x where ketonization, selective oxidation, and demethoxylation reactions occurred and selectively yielded acetone, 2-butanone, phenol, cresol, xylenol, and ethyl phenol.

Prior to pyrolysis, it is imperative to pretreat the biomass by sun drying, oven drying to avoid moisture saturation, and mechanical comminution to increase the surface area for effective pyrolysis.

2.2.3 Gasification

Gasification is a thermochemical biomass conversion process which occurs at elevated temperatures above 700°C in a limited amount of oxygen. Usually 70–80% is transformed to synthesis gas (CO and H_2) and the remainder is biochar. It is possible to obtain some amount of bio-oil if the condition is favorable. To maximize the yields of synthesis gas and improve on the overall efficiency of the process, supercritical water, and catalyst is used [27]. The synthesis gas can be transformed to fuels and myriad of chemicals via Fischer-Tropsch synthesis [34]. CPH has been converted to gaseous products of varying composition by gasification. For instance, Gunasekaran et al. [35] investigated the numerical and experimental potential of CPH gasification in an open-core gasifier. According to their results, the composition of CO, H_2, and CH_4 in the producer gas was found to be 20–24%, 12.0–16.5%, and 2.0–3.2%, respectively for the conditions that were tested. The conversion efficiency and cold gas efficiency were determined to be 82 and 38%, respectively. Further, the predicted performance parameters and temperature distribution were found to be at par. Thus, CPH was found to be a promising raw material for an open-core gasifiers.

The application of recycle system on a CPH gasification in a fixed-bed downdraft reactor was carried out by Pranolo and co-workers [36]. The aim was to produce low tar fuel gas from CPH using recycle stream consisting of CO, H_2, CO_2, and CH_4. They successfully reduced the tar content in the product gases up to 62% at temperatures ranging from 750 to 780°C. Therefore, the gas may be used as a substitute fuel for electricity generation.

2.2.4 Physicochemical routes

The valorization of CPH by physiochemical approach has mainly been by solid phase extraction or leaching in which solutes are removed from a solid by a liquid solvent [37]. Such processes have been applied in the extraction of phytochemicals and pectin from CPH. Phytochemicals are natural functional foods that possess a rich reservoir of bioactive components and nutraceuticals. Nutraceuticals was coined by Dr. Stephen De Felice and is a derivation from words "nutrition" and "pharmaceuticals." Phytochemicals are mainly foods or parts of foods that provide medical or health benefits including the prevention and treatment of diseases. There has been rapid increase in the consumption of plant-derived bioactive. Plants produce these chemicals to protect themselves but recent studies have shown that these chemicals can protect humans, animals, and other plants against diseases compound [38].

Rachmawaty et al., 2018 studied the extraction of bioactive components from CPH and the in vitro antifungal activity assay against the pathogenic fungus *Fusarium oxysporum*. The *F. oxysporum* is a deadly fungus that can cause diseases in nearly every agriculturally important plant. In the study, CPH was dry milled using a grinder into powder. Two solvents, acetone-water (7:3) and 70% ethanol was used to extract the phytochemicals. A solvent to sample ratio of 10:1 was used such that 200 ml of solvent was used for 20 g of CPH sample. The extract was found to contain alkaloids, flavonoids, tannins, and saponins, and triterpenoids which indicates the antimicrobial potential of the CPH extract. GC-MS analysis revealed four major components in the acetone solvent namely isopropyl myristate, benzenedicarboxylic acid, 9-octadecenoic acid (Z)-, methyl ester and octadecanoic acid, methyl ester. For the ethanol solvent however, three main components were found namely octadeca methyl-9,12-dienoate; 9-octadecenoic acid (Z)-, methyl ester; hexadecanoic acid, 15-methyl-methyl ester.

The acetone extract recorded the highest phenolic content and also a higher anti-fungal activity than the ethanol extract. Agar diffusion method was employed for antifungal testing and it showed that the extract was able to inhibit the fungal growth therefore leading to the conclusion that the CPH extract has great potential as a natural fungicide.

Pectin, a family of complex, acid-rich polysaccharides found in plant cell wall have been recovered from CPH by this approach. They have been extensively applied as gelling and stabilizer in cosmetics, food, and pharmaceuticals. They have the ability to reduce serum cholesterol, glucose, cancer incidence, and improved immune response in humans [39].

Pectin recovery from CPH was studied by Valladares-Diestra et al. [40] using citric acid hydrothermal treatment of CPH with concomitant production of xylooligosaccarides via enzymatic hydrolysis of the solid fraction after extraction. An optimum condition of 120°C, 10 minutes, and 2% W/V was employed for the recovering pectin. An amount of 19.3% of the biomass was recovered as pectin. They concluded that the prospects of implementing this novel method for the extraction of valuable chemicals such as pectin is very high.

Vriesmann et al. [39] optimized the variables affecting the nitic acid extraction of pectins from CPH using RSM. The optimum extraction condition was determined as pH 1.5, a temperature of 100°C, and time of 30 minutes. By these conditions a yield and uronic acid (UA) content (representing pectin content) of about 9.5 and 80%, respectively were predicted. However, experimental results gave a yield of 9.0 ± 0.4% and UA content of 66%. The predicted and experimental yield values were in close agreement, on the contrary, experimental UA content value was 17.5% lower than the predicted. This disparity was attributed to the low quality of the model for used the prediction. They further characterized the pectin a homogalacturonan highly esterified and acetylated one with some rhamnogalacturonan insertions.

Recently, Vriesmann and de Oliveira Petkowicz [41] compared the use of nitric acid and boiling water for the extraction of pectin. The pectins obtained from both extraction process was similar and identified as low methoxyl type. Rheological analysis suggests that both formed gels at low pH in spite of their high acetyl content therefore, the pectin can be used in acidic products.

3. Unconventional CPH valorization processes

Recently, processes that are considered green have been utilized to extract bioactive chemical from biomass feedstocks. These processes are gaining popularity due to their inherent benefits such lower temperature, less activation time, and higher carbon yield. Microwave, ultrasound as well as super and subcritical fluid extraction have been applied to obtain valuable chemical from CPH and is discussed in this section.

3.1 Microwave-assisted valorization of CPH

Microwave has been utilized in recent times to extract biochemicals instead of conventional processes as uniform heating, time, and solvent savings [42–44] are the main advantages of this process. Additionally, it has been found to improve the accessibility and reactivity of cellulose when used to pretreat lignocellulosic biomass. Moreover, subsequent enzyme action is heightened [43]. This is the most widely applied unconventional process for CPH valorization.

In the work of Mashuni et al., 2020, microwave was used to assist the extraction of phenols from CPH using 85% V/V ethanol as solvent. The microwave heating power was varied from 100 to 300 W whilst the extraction time spanned 5–30 minutes. Using the Folin-Ciocalteu method with gallic acid as a standard, the total phenol content of CPH was determined. The highest amount of phenol content was found to be 853.67 mg/L after 20 minutes of extraction at 200 W of microwave power. Upon characterizing the extract with GC-MS, it was revealed that the phenols present are butylhydroxytoluene; 6,6′-methylenebis(2-(tert-butyl)-4-methyl-phenol); 3-methoxy-2-((*2E*,*6E*)-3,7,11-trimethyl-dodeca-2,6,10-trienyl) phenol; and 7-hydroxy-3-(1,1-dimethylprop-2-enyl) coumarin. They concluded that microwave assisted extraction (MAE) is a promising technique for the extracting phenols quickly and efficiently [45].

Novel research was conducted by Nguyen and co-workers [42] where they extracted saponin from CPH *via* MAE using methanol as solvent. They used RSM (CCD) to identify the optimum parameters for the process. According to their findings, the optimum MAE conditions for obtaining the maximum saponin content and extraction efficiency from dried CPH were 85% methanol concentration, 40 minutes extraction time, 600 W microwave power, 6 seconds/minute irradiation time, and 50 ml/g solvent to sample ratio. The saponin content and extraction efficiency determined under these conditions were 69.9 mg escin equivalents/g dried sample and 71.1%, respectively. Thus, the CPH has a huge potential as a source of bioactive compounds for used in the nutraceutical and functional foods industries and to harness these compounds the optimum MAE conditions should be applied for best results. MAE was applied to isolate pectin from CPH using oxalic acid by Pangestu and colleagues [46]. In their work, they used RSM to investigate how pH, liquid to solid ratio (L/S), and irradiation time interact to affect the quantity of pectin isolated. A pH of 1.16, L/S of 25, and 15 minutes of irradiation were found to give a maximum yield of 9.64%. They emphasized that this route reduced the extraction time by 2–6 times. Further the L/S ratio can be minimized without considerable impact on the results. MAE was concluded as a powerful technique for isolating pectin using a cheaper and safer acidifying agent such as oxalic acid. Villota et al. [47] carbonized H_3PO_4 and KOH activated CPH via microwave assisted pyrolysis at 450°C for 5 minutes. The effect of H_3PO_4 and KOH on the activation of char from CPH and in all cases, H_3PO_4 activated carbon was observed to have higher yield and better textural properties (BET surface area = 1237.47 m^2/g, pore volume = 1.11 cm^3/g, and mesoporous) relative to that activated with KOH which exhibited severe material loss as well as low strength. Microwave assisted pretreatment of CPH has been applied by several researchers. A summary is presented in **Table 1**.

3.2 Ultrasound-assisted valorization of CPH

This process was implemented in the work of Hennessey-Ramos and colleagues, 2021 to extract pectin from CPH. RSM was used to determine the optimum operating conditions that is 6.0% feedstock concentration, 40 μL/g enzyme, and 18.54 hours on stream. Experiments involving three processes for extracting pectin namely acid, ultrasound-assisted and enzymatic extraction were conducted and compared. The results are summarized in **Table 2**.

From the results enzymatic extraction of pectin gave the best results for pectin yield followed by ultrasound-assisted citric acid extraction. The low GA content was attributed to duration (45 minutes) and temperature (60°C) of the process. They asserted that industrial operations above 60°C for ultrasonic assisted citric acid pectin extraction with the aim of increasing GA content would not be feasible owing to the inherent advantage of low temperature operation for such technologies. In the extraction of microcrystalline cellulose from CPH, it was pretreated with alkali followed

Pretreatment method	Objective	Observation	Reference
Microwave assisted H_2SO_4 hydrolysis (15.65 g of CPH, 6% V/V acid, and 8 minutes of irradiation)	Release fermentable sugars for onward fermentation to bioethanol.	Hydrosylate (9.10 g/L max) containing glucose, galactose, cellobiose, xylulose, and arabinose.	[48]
Microwave assisted NaOH hydrolysis (3% NaOH, 100 W, 2.5 minutes, and 5 g CPH)	Delignification of CPH.	Increase in cellulose content especially when the microwave irradiation period was prolonged.	[49]
Microwave (300 W, 25 minutes)	Increase porosity in lignin covering cellulose and hemicellulose to facilitate enzymatic action.	The sugar yield CPH was low, the yield of ethanol was considered high (61 ml/kg).	[50]

Table 1.
Various microwave-assisted pretreatment of CPH.

Parameter/process	Citric acid	Ultrasound-assisted citric acid extraction	Enzymatic extraction
Yield, g pectin/100 g CPHP	8.08	8.28	10.20
GA content, g GA/100 g pectin	60.97	42.77	52.06
GA yield, g GA/100 g CPHP	—	—	5.31

CPHP, cocoa pod husk powder; GA, galacturonic acid.

Table 2.
Comparative analysis of chemical, ultrasound assisted, and enzymatic pectin processes.

by ultrasonication. Ultrasound applied after alkaline pretreatment of the feedstock brought about cavitation action that helped to effectively remove fibril aggregates from the microcrystalline cellulose. A sonication time of 60 seconds and two cycles of the ultrasonication process considerably reduced the particle size of the microcrystalline cellulose to 280 nm [51].

3.3 Super and subcritical fluid extraction of biochemicals from CPH

Long extraction periods, low yield and quality of extracts, and loss of volatile compound are among many limitations of traditional extraction processes that has warranted the development of novel and green processes that overcome these limitations. Super critical and subcritical fluid extraction are among such processes that are considered efficient and time-economic [43, 52–54]. In a recent study on the extraction of phenols from CPH using supercritical CO_2, Valadez-Carmona et al. [7] employed a Box-Behnken design to maximize the process variables that is temperature, pressure, and co-solvent. The optimum conditions obtained were 60°C, 299 bar, and 13.7% ethanol. By this approach, the extraction time was lowered even though the yield was low (0.56%), the quality of the extracts was improved whilst the loss of volatile compound was minimized. The highest total phenolic compounds (TPC) were found to be 12.97 mg GAE/g extract whereas the total antioxidant capacity was 0.213 mmol TE/g extract. These findings demonstrates that supercritical CO_2 extraction is a promising technique that can be exploited for the isolation of natural antioxidants from CPH for use in food, cosmetic, or pharmaceutical products. Another interesting work was published by Muñoz-Almagro and co-workers [55] where they compared conventional and subcritical water extraction of pectin from CPH. The latter process is a technique in which water provides H^+ and OH^- ions at high pressure and temperature for dissolving both polar and non-polar compounds. At high temperatures the hydrogen bonding in water is weakened thereby decreasing the dielectric constant value and water polarity which consequently lowers the energy required for dissociation of water molecules in solute-matrix interactions and extraction efficiency is increased [55]. In the subcritical water extraction process, a pectin yield of 10.9% as opposed to 8% obtained using conventional extraction with citric acid as solvent. Characterization of the pectin showed that high molecular weight pectin (750 kDa) was preferentially extracted during the subcritical operation. These green techniques have been shown to possess high selectivity towards targeted compounds and potential for CPH valorization.

4. Future perspective

Although several transformation techniques have been investigated for the conversion of CPH to valuable products, there is still a need to develop efficient and sustainable approaches for a holistic CPH biomass valorization process. In this context, the development of cutting-edge technologies that can efficiently transform these hitherto waste materials generated from cacao into useful chemicals that could potentially improve the global value chain of cacao production, is crucial and highly sort after. Although of interest, the uncontrolled co-production of char and gaseous products limits the overall yield of bio-chemicals so-obtained, and thus the overall efficiency of this approach. Being able to fractionate these lignocellulosic biomass waste into valuable chemicals in a selective fashion is highly desirable from economic and environmental considerations, but it remains a very important scientific challenging task due to scientific bottlenecks such as: (i) recalcitrance of lignocellulosic biomass to hydrolysis, often requiring high activation temperatures which are not compatible with the stability of sugars, the main components of lignocellulosic biomass waste, and (ii) high dilution ratio to prevent recombination reactions (for instance caramelization of monomeric sugars) leading to the unwanted formation of tar-like materials. In order to overcome such scientific hurdles, researchers should consider the coupling of mechano-catalytic technology to first release sugars contained in CPH, which can be achieved without the need of any solvent, translating into efficient and environmentally friendly synthesis approach, and a pyrolysis process to valorize lignin, the co-product of the CPH fractionation after the mechano-catalytic step.

5. Economic aspects of CPH valorization

Using pectin production as a valuable product case-study from CPH, an economic analysis using Aspen Process Economic Evaluator was modeled, and allowed the estimation of investment and return of the stimulated process with the possibility to obtain a considerable profitability with a 20 years operation plant life and a pectin production capacity of 108,127.4 Ib./year, annual interest rate of 20%, a salvage value (fraction of initial investment) of 20% and depreciation method straight line and an income tax of 40%. An Internal Rate of Return (IRR) of 33% was obtained over a capital cost of $5,509,000 (USD), operational cost of $2,135,300 (USD), 17 years durations of startup, and a 4 years payback period. These values indicated a positive suggestion that the implementation of pectin production process from cocoa pod husks as an investment project owing to its better long-term benefits compared to those generated by investing in banks [56]. An important aspect of the economic viability of CPH valorization that is often ignored is the cost of the raw material which is often considered waste and of low value. According to the findings of a study conducted in Indonesia on the need for economic and sustainability assessment of the valorization of CPH, farmers demand higher levels of compensation to collect or process the raw material than expected. Only a small section of farmers were willing to carry out collection and processing for 117GBP/t CPH. This could offer some explanation for the low patronage of CPH valorization innovations in that country [57].

6. Conclusions

CPH has been demonstrated to be an excellent source of phenolics, pectin, and lignocellulosic contents that can be used for the production of platform chemicals relevant in the agrochemical, pharmaceutical, and food industries. However, although cocoa remains a prime economic cash crop in developing countries like Ghana, Ivory Coast, Indonesia, etc., the efficient transformation of cocoa pod husks into valuable products in such countries other than leaving them on farm sites to rots are scarce. Therefore, it is paramount for such developing countries to develop end-user applications for CPH that will be beneficial for industries, consumers, researchers, and also serve as extra income for farmers. It is of no doubt that the development of processes that are easy to implement, less expensive, sustainable and environmentally friendly, to convert CPH into high high-value added products, such as biofuels could significantly prevent the excessive consumption and reliant on fuel/diesel and the production of greenhouse gas. Increased valorization techniques for CPH will concomitantly increase the overall sustainability of the cocoa agribusiness and open up new avenues for sustainable incomes for cocoa farmers.

Acknowledgements

The authors would like to thank the French National Centre for Scientific Research (CNRS) through its Support Action for Collaboration with sub-Saharan Africa Grant for supporting this work. The kind contribution and efforts of Jedidian A. Adjei (KNUST Ghana) are duly acknowledged.

Author details

Martina Francisca Baidoo[1], Nana Yaw Asiedu[1], Lawrence Darkwah[1], David Arhin-Dodoo[2], Jun Zhao[3], Francois Jerome[4] and Prince Nana Amaniampong[4]*

1 Department of Chemical Engineering, College of Engineering, Kumasi, Ghana

2 Department of Materials Science and Engineering, University of Ghana, Legon-Accra, Ghana

3 Department of Biology, Institute of Bioresource and Agriculture, Hong Kong Baptist University, Hong Kong Special Administrative Region, China

4 Institut de Chimie des Milieux et Matériaux de Poitiers (IC2MP), Université de Poitiers, CNRS, ENSIP, Poitiers, France

*Address all correspondence to: prince.nana.amaniampong@univ-poitiers.fr

References

[1] Panak Balentić J, Ačkar Đ, Jokić S, Jozinović A, Babić J, Miličević B, et al. Cocoa shell: A by-product with great potential for wide application. Molecules. 2018;**23**:1-14. DOI: 10.3390/molecules23061404

[2] Mansur D, Tago T, Masuda T, Abimanyu H. Conversion of cacao pod husks by pyrolysis and catalytic reaction to produce useful chemicals. Biomass and Bioenergy. 2014;**66**:275-285. DOI: 10.1016/j.biombioe.2014.03.065

[3] Ouattara LY, Appiah Kouassi EK, Soro D, Soro Y, Yao KB, Adouby K, et al. Cocoa pod husks as potential sources of renewable high-value-added products: A review of current valorizations and future prospects. BioResources. 2021;**16**:1988-2020. DOI: 10.15376/biores.16.1.ouattara

[4] Lu F, Rodriguez-Garcia J, Van Damme I, Westwood NJ, Shaw L, Robinson JS, et al. Valorisation strategies for cocoa pod husk and its fractions. Current Opinion in Green and Sustainable Chemistry. 2018;**14**:80-88. DOI: 10.1016/j.cogsc.2018.07.007

[5] Rachmawaty, Mu'Nisa A, Hasri, Pagarra H, Hartati, Maulana Z. Active compounds extraction of cocoa pod husk (*Thebroma cacao* L.) and potential as fungicides. Journal of Physics Conference Series. 2018;**1028**:012013. DOI: 10.1088/1742-6596/1028/1/012013

[6] Oduro-Mensah D, Ocloo A, Nortey T, Antwi S, Okine LK, Adamafio NA. Nutritional value and safety of animal feed supplemented with *Talaromyces verruculosus*-treated cocoa pod husks. Scientific Reports. 2020;**10**:1-16. DOI: 10.1038/s41598-020-69763-9

[7] Valadez-Carmona L, Ortiz-Moreno A, Ceballos-Reyes G, Mendiola JA, Ibáñez E. Valorization of cacao pod husk through supercritical fluid extraction of phenolic compounds. Journal of Supercritical Fluids. 2018;**131**:99-105. DOI: 10.1016/j.supflu.2017.09.011

[8] Syamsiro M, Saptoadi H, Tambunan BH, Pambudi NA. A preliminary study on use of cocoa pod husk as a renewable source of energy in Indonesia. Energy for Sustainable Development. 2012;**16**:74-77. DOI: 10.1016/j.esd.2011.10.005

[9] Sobamiwa O, Longe OG. The nutritive value of alkali-treated cocoa husk meal in broiler chick diets. Animal Feed Science and Technology. 1994;**46**:321-330. DOI: 10.1016/0377-8401(94)90149-X

[10] Serra Bonvehí J, Aragay Benería M. Composition of dietary fibre in cocoa husk. European Food Research and Technology. 1998;**207**:105-109. DOI: 10.1007/s002170050303

[11] Vriesmann LC, de Mello Castanho Amboni RD, de Oliveira Petkowicz CL. Cacao pod husks (*Theobroma cacao* L.): Composition and hot-water-soluble pectins. Industrial Crops and Products. 2011;**34**:1173-1181. DOI: 10.1016/j.indcrop.2011.04.004

[12] Acosta N, De Vrieze J, Sandoval V, Sinche D, Wierinck I, Rabaey K. Cocoa residues as viable biomass for renewable energy production through anaerobic digestion. Bioresource Technology. 2018;**265**:568-572. DOI: 10.1016/j.biortech.2018.05.100

[13] Antwi E, Engler N, Nelles M, Schüch A. Anaerobic digestion and the

effect of hydrothermal pretreatment on the biogas yield of cocoa pods residues. Waste Management. 2019;**88**:131-140. DOI: 10.1016/j.wasman.2019.03.034

[14] Mancini G, Papirio S, Lens PNL, Esposito G. Effect of N-methylmorpholine-N-oxide pretreatment on biogas production from rice straw, cocoa shell, and hazelnut skin. Environmental Engineering Science. 2016;**33**:843-850. DOI: 10.1089/ees.2016.0138

[15] Ward-Doria M, Arzuaga-Garrido J, Ojeda KA, Sánchez E. Production of biogas from acid and alkaline pretreated cocoa pod husk (*Theobroma cacao* L.). International Journal of ChemTech Research. 2016;**9**:252-260

[16] Dahunsi SO, Osueke CO, Olayanju TMA, Lawal AI. Co-digestion of *Theobroma cacao* (cocoa) pod husk and poultry manure for energy generation: Effects of pretreatment methods. Bioresource Technology. 2019;**283**:229-241. DOI: 10.1016/j.biortech.2019.03.093

[17] Shet VB, Sanil N, Bhat M, Naik M, Mascarenhas LN, Goveas LC, et al. Acid hydrolysis optimization of cocoa pod shell using response surface methodology approach toward ethanol production. Agriculture and Natural Resources. 2018;**52**:581-587. DOI: 10.1016/j.anres.2018.11.022

[18] Samah OA, Sias S, Hua Y, Hussin NN. Production of ethanol from cocoa pod hydrolysate. Journal of Mathematical and Fundamental Sciences. 2011;**43**:87-94

[19] Hernández-Mendoza AG, Saldaña-Trinidad S, Martínez-Hernández S, Pérez-Sariñana BY, Láinez M. Optimization of alkaline pretreatment and enzymatic hydrolysis of cocoa pod husk (*Theobroma cacao* L.) for ethanol production. Biomass and Bioenergy. 2021;**154**:106268. DOI: 10.1016/j.biombioe.2021.106268

[20] Sarmiento-Vásquez Z, Vandenberghe L, Rodrigues C, Tanobe VOA, Marín O, de Melo Pereira GV, et al. Cocoa pod husk valorization: Alkaline-enzymatic pre-treatment for propionic acid production. Cellulose. 2021;**28**:4009-4024. DOI: 10.1007/s10570-021-03770-5

[21] Sandesh K, Shishir RK, Vaman Rao C. Optimization and comparison of induction heating and LPG assisted acid pretreatment of cocoa pod for ABE fermentation. Fuel. 2020;**262**:116499. DOI: 10.1016/j.fuel.2019.116499

[22] Watson RR, Preedy VR, Zibadi S. Chocolate in Health and Nutrition. London, UK: Humana Press Inc.; 2013. DOI: 10.1007/978-1-61779-803-0

[23] Taiwo OE, Osinowo FAO. Evaluation of various agro-wastes for traditional black soap production. Bioresource Technology. 2001;**79**:95-97

[24] Ayeni LS, Adetunji MT, Ojeniyi SO, Ewulo BS, Adeyemo AJ. Comparative and cumulative effect of cocoa pod husk ash and poultry manure on soil and maize nutrient contents and yield. American-Eurasian Journal of Sustainable Agriculture. 2008;**2**:92-97

[25] Ayeni LS. Integrated application of cocoa pod ash and NPK fertilizer on soil chemical properties and yield of tomato. American-Eurasian Journal of Sustainable Agriculture. 2008;**2**:333-337

[26] Ofori-Boateng C, Lee KT. The potential of using cocoa pod husks as green solid base catalysts for the transesterification of soybean oil

into biodiesel: Effects of biodiesel on engine performance. Chemical Engineering Journal. 2013;**220**:395-401. DOI: 10.1016/j.cej.2013.01.046

[27] Daramola MO, Ayeni AO, editors. Valorization of Biomass to Value-Added Commodities: Current Trends, Challenges, and Future Prospects. Switzerland AG: Springer Nature; 2020

[28] Bridgwater AV. Principles and practice of biomass fast pyrolysis processes for liquids. Journal of Analytical and Applied Pyrolysis. 1999;**51**:3-22. DOI: 10.1016/S0165-2370(99)00005-4

[29] Adjin-Tetteh M, Asiedu N, Dodoo-Arhin D, Karam A, Amaniampong PN. Thermochemical conversion and characterization of cocoa pod husks a potential agricultural waste from Ghana. Industrial Crops and Products. 2018;**119**:304-312. DOI: 10.1016/j.indcrop.2018.02.060

[30] Tsai CH, Tsai WT, Liu SC, Lin YQ. Thermochemical characterization of biochar from cocoa pod husk prepared at low pyrolysis temperature. Biomass Conversion and Biorefinery. 2018;**8**:237-243. DOI: 10.1007/s13399-017-0259-5

[31] Ofori P, Akoto O. Production and characterisation of briquettes from carbonised cocoa pod husk and sawdust. OALib. 2020;7:1-20. DOI: 10.4236/oalib.1106029

[32] Ogunjobi JK, Lajide L. The potential of cocoa pods and plantain peels as renewable sources in Nigeria. International Journal of Green Energy. 2015;**12**:440-445. DOI: 10.1080/15435075.2013.848403

[33] Araoye AO, Agboola OS, Bello OS. Insights into chemically modified cocoa pods for enhanced removal of an anti-malaria drug. Chemical Data Collections. 2021;**36**:100775. DOI: 10.1016/j.cdc.2021.100775

[34] Moulijn JA, Makkee M, van Diepen AE. Chemical process technology, second edition. Organic Process Research and Development. 2014;**18**:1153. DOI: 10.1021/op500256y

[35] Gunasekaran AP, Chockalingam MP, Padmavathy SR, Santhappan JS. Numerical and experimental investigation on the thermochemical gasification potential of cocoa pod husk (*Theobroma cacoa*) in an open-core gasifier. Clean Technologies and Environmental Policy. 2021;**23**:1603-1615. DOI: 10.1007/s10098-021-02051-w

[36] Pranolo SH, Waluyo J, Prasetiyo J, Hanif M. Application of recycle system on a cocoa pod husks gasification in a fixed-bed downdraft gasifier to produce low tar fuel gas. Jurnal Rekayasa Kimia & Lingkungan. 2019;**14**(2):120-129. DOI: 10.23955/rkl.v14i2.14160

[37] Scovazzo P, Chen W-Y, Wang LK, Shammas NK. Solvent extraction, leaching and supercritical extraction. Advanced Physicochemical Treatment Processes. 2006;**4**:581-614. DOI: 10.1007/978-1-59745-029-4_18

[38] Thakur M, Singh K, Khedkar R. Phytochemicals: Extraction process, safety assessment, toxicological evaluations, and regulatory issues. In: Prakash B, editor. Functional and Preservative Properties of Phytochemicals. Academic Press; 2020. pp. 341-361. DOI:10.1016/b978-0-12-818593-3.00011-7

[39] Vriesmann LC, Teófilo RF, Petkowicz CLDO. Optimization of nitric acid-mediated extraction of pectin from cacao pod husks (*Theobroma cacao* L.) using response surface methodology.

Carbohydrate Polymers. 2011;**84**:1230-1236. DOI: 10.1016/j.carbpol.2011.01.009

[40] Valladares-Diestra KK, Porto de Souza Vandenberghe L, Zevallos Torres LA, Zandoná Filho A, Lorenci Woiciechowski A, Ricardo Soccol C. Citric acid assisted hydrothermal pretreatment for the extraction of pectin and xylooligosaccharides production from cocoa pod husks. Bioresource Technology. 2022;**343**:126074. DOI: 10.1016/j.biortech.2021.126074

[41] Vriesmann LC, de Oliveira Petkowicz CL. Cacao pod husks as a source of low-methoxyl, highly acetylated pectins able to gel in acidic media. International Journal of Biological Macromolecules. 2017;**101**:146-152. DOI: 10.1016/j.ijbiomac.2017.03.082

[42] Nguyen VT, Le MD, Nguyen TTT, Khong TT, Nguyen VH, Nguyen HN, et al. Microwave-assisted extraction for optimizing saponin yield and antioxidant capacity from cacao pod husk (*Theobroma cacao* L.). Journal of Food Processing & Preservation. 2021;**45**:e15134. DOI: 10.1111/jfpp.15134

[43] Chen H, Liu J, Chang X, Chen D, Xue Y, Liu P, et al. A review on the pretreatment of lignocellulose for high-value chemicals. Fuel Processing Technology. 2017;**160**:196-206. DOI: 10.1016/j.fuproc.2016.12.007

[44] Padilla-Rascón C, Romero-García JM, Ruiz E, Castro E. Optimization with response surface methodology of microwave-assisted conversion of xylose to furfural. Molecules. 2020;**25**:3574. DOI: 10.3390/molecules25163574

[45] Mashuni, Hamid FH, Muzuni, Kadidae LO, Jahiding M, Ahmad LO, et al. The determination of total phenolic content of cocoa pod husk based on microwave-assisted extraction method. AIP Conference Proceedings. 2020;**2243**:030013. DOI: 10.1063/5.0001364

[46] Pangestu R, Amanah S, Juanssilfero AB, Yopi, Perwitasari U. Response surface methodology for microwave-assisted extraction of pectin from cocoa pod husk (*Theobroma cacao*) mediated by oxalic acid. Journal of Food Measurement and Characterization. 2020;**14**:2126-2133. DOI: 10.1007/s11694-020-00459-4

[47] Villota SM, Lei H, Villota E, Qian M, Lavarias J, Taylan V, et al. Microwave-assisted activation of waste cocoa pod husk by H3PO4 and KOH—Comparative insight into textural properties and pore development. ACS Omega. 2019;**4**:7088-7095. DOI: 10.1021/acsomega.8b03514

[48] Shet VB, Shetty VC, Siddik A, Rakshith KG, Shetty NJ, Goveas LC, et al. Optimization of microwave assisted H_2SO_4 hydrolysis of cocoa pod shells: Comparison between response surface methodology and artificial neural network and production of bioethanol thereof. Journal of Microbiology, Biotechnology and Food Sciences. 2018;7:473-477. DOI: 10.15414/jmbfs.2018.7.5.473-477

[49] Muharja M, Darmayanti RF, Palupi B, Rahmawati I, Fachri BA, Setiawan FA, et al. Optimization of microwave-assisted alkali pretreatment for enhancement of delignification process of cocoa pod husk. Bulletin of Chemical Reaction Engineering and Catalysis. 2021;**16**:31-43. DOI: 10.9767/BCREC.16.1.8872.31-43

[50] Vintila T, Ionel I, Rufis Fregue TT, Wächter AR, Julean C, Gabche AS. Residual biomass from food processing industry in Cameroon as feedstock for second-generation biofuels. BioResources. 2019;**14**:3731-3745. DOI: 10.15376/biores.14.2.3731-3745

[51] Zailani ISA, Aviceena, Jimat DN, Jami MS. Extraction of microcrystalline cellulose (MCC) from cocoa pod husk via alkaline pretreatment combined with ultrasonication. International Journal of Applied Engineering Research. 2016;**11**:9876-9879

[52] Da Porto C, Porretto E, Decorti D. Comparison of ultrasound-assisted extraction with conventional extraction methods of oil and polyphenols from grape (*Vitis vinifera* L.) seeds. Ultrasonics Sonochemistry. 2013;**20**:1076-1080. DOI: 10.1016/j.ultsonch.2012.12.002

[53] Ghasemi E, Raofie F, Najafi NM. Application of response surface methodology and central composite design for the optimisation of supercritical fluid extraction of essential oils from *Myrtus communis* L. leaves. Food Chemistry. 2011;**126**:1449-1453. DOI: 10.1016/j.foodchem.2010.11.135

[54] Marques LLM, Panizzon GP, Aguiar BAA, Simionato AS, Cardozo-Filho L, Andrade G, et al. Guaraná (*Paullinia cupana*) seeds: Selective supercritical extraction of phenolic compounds. Food Chemistry. 2016;**212**:703-711. DOI: 10.1016/j.foodchem.2016.06.028

[55] Muñoz-Almagro N, Valadez-Carmona L, Mendiola JA, Ibáñez E, Villamiel M. Structural characterisation of pectin obtained from cacao pod husk. Comparison of conventional and subcritical water extraction. Carbohydrate Polymers. 2019;**217**:69-78. DOI: 10.1016/j.carbpol.2019.04.040

[56] Marsiglia-Lopez D, Ramirez-Uribe M, Gonzalez-Delgado A, Ojeda-Delgado K, Sanchez-Tuiran E. Computer-aided economic evaluation of pectin extraction from cocoa pod husk (*Theobroma cacao* L.). Contemporary Engineering Sciences. 2017;**10**:1493-1500. DOI: 10.12988/ces.2017.710140

[57] Picchioni F, Warren GP, Lambert S, Balcombe K, Robinson JS, Srinivasan C, et al. Valorisation of natural resources and the need for economic and sustainability assessment: The case of cocoa pod husk in Indonesia. Sustainability. 2020;**12**:8962. DOI: 10.3390/su12218962

Chapter 13

Systematic Generation of Reactions Pathways for Manufacturing Bulk Industrial Chemicals from Biomass

Rakesh Govind, Shiva Charan and Jack Baltzersen

Abstract

The objective of this work was to develop a systematic strategy for generating efficient, alternate reaction paths that could be used to manufacture the top 100 industrial chemicals, currently produced from crude oil, using renewable feedstocks. Manufacturing these chemicals from oil, coal, or natural gas results in increasing carbon dioxide levels in the atmosphere, responsible for global climate change. The methodology employed here uses the existing knowledge on the conversion of carbon-neutral feedstocks, such as biomass, wood, etc., to suitable precursor raw materials. Known industrial reaction paths, currently used for manufacturing the top 100 industrial organic chemicals, are then combined with the known conversion of carbon-neutral feedstocks to systematically develop and evaluate alternate carbon-efficient reaction paths. The fractional carbon economy was determined from a comprehensive listing of industrial reactions paths, which also gives the yields and efficiencies of these industrial reaction paths, currently being practiced in the chemical industry. Reaction pathways with maximum carbon economy for manufacturing the top 100 industrial chemicals from carbon-neutral feedstocks have been presented in this chapter.

Keywords: reactions, carbon, economy, carbon-neutral, industrial chemicals

1. Introduction

Sustainable production of industrial chemicals requires the use of biomass as a raw material, which can be converted into intermediate chemicals, currently being used as raw materials derived from non-renewable feedstocks, such as coal, crude oil, natural gas, etc. This allows the chemical industry to preserve its current petrochemical plants, except changing its source of feedstock from nonrenewable sources to renewable materials, such as biomass. The challenges posed by shifting to renewable feedstocks involve new chemistries which convert a variety of biomass materials into the known feedstocks, and in some cases starting with completely different raw materials. In addition, biomass conversions by fermentation involve slow reactions, conducted in the liquid phase, with low conversions, resulting in dilute aqueous solutions.

Traditionally, the chemical industry has relied on gas phase, catalytic, high temperature, and often high-pressure reactions, which require short residence times in

IntechOpen

smaller reactors and produce a high concentration of product(s). In comparison, biomass conversions using fermentation are biological, liquid-phase reactions, conducted at near ambient temperature and usually atmospheric pressure. The reaction rates in fermentation chemistry are orders of magnitude lower than in gas-phase chemical conversions.

Notwithstanding these challenges, in this chapter, known reactions for converting a variety of biomass sources into known chemical feedstocks have been detailed. Conversion and yield information from the publications of these chemical reactions was used to generate and rank these reactions based on their carbon economy. Carbon economy is the ratio of the mass of carbon atoms in the feedstock produced to the mass of carbon atoms present in the biomass source. By maximizing the carbon economy, the mass of carbon atoms present in the waste product(s) is minimized.

In addition, chemical reaction pathways, currently used to manufacture the top 100 industrial chemicals from nonrenewable feedstocks, were derived from known sources [1–4], and each reaction pathway was also evaluated by its carbon economy. A computer program was developed to link the biomass conversion reactions with the industrial chemical pathways, with the objective of maximizing the overall carbon economy starting with the biomass material and ending with the industrial chemical. This provided multiple reaction pathways, in order of decreasing the overall carbon economy, to convert a biomass feedstock to each of the top 100 industrial chemicals.

2. Biomass conversion reaction pathways

In our analysis, seventeen different biomass materials were considered and information on the conversion of these biomass materials to known feedstock chemicals was derived from publications cited in this section.

Seventeen biomass sources, considered in this paper, are as follows:

- Beech wood
- Pine sawdust
- Municipal solid waste (pilot plant)
- Sewage sludge
- Sunflower residue
- Rape residue
- Switchgrass
- Sunflower shells
- Rice husk
- Pine chip
- Tropical lauan

- Paddy straw
- Corn cob
- Yellow poplar sawdust
- Alaskan spruce
- Wheat straw
- Rice hulls

The biomass conversion processes employed to convert these biomass sources to feedstock chemicals include pyrolysis, which is heating the biomass material, either in the presence of a catalyst, such as alumina, or noncatalytically. The flash pyrolysis process is conducted in an oxygen-free, inert gas atmosphere in the temperature range of 600–1000°C and 1 atmosphere pressure. Products of pyrolysis consist of gases, such as carbon monoxide, carbon dioxide, methane, etc., and liquids, such as heavier hydrocarbon oils and ammonia.

Another biomass conversion process used is hydrothermal liquefaction, where the biomass material, once shredded into small pieces, is heated in water under

Biomass source	% Carbon	% Hydrogen	% Oxygen	% Carbon economy	Reference
Beechwood	48.4	6.2	45.0	0.48	[5]
Pine sawdust	48.3	6.5	45.2	0.48	[6]
Municipal solid waste	52.3	6.5	38.3	0.52	[7]
Sewage sludge	49.5	7.3	35.6	0.50	[8]
Sunflower residue	43.6	5.8	49.3	0.44	[9]
Rape residue	44.7	5.8	48.1	0.45	[9]
Switch grass	46.8	5.1	42.1	0.47	[10]
Sunflower shells	41.5	6.1	39.8	0.42	[11]
Rice husk	38.3	4.4	35.4	0.38	[12, 13]
Pine chips	51.7	6.1	41.8	0.52	[14]
Tropical luan	51.1	6.3	42.4	0.51	[14]
Paddy straw	35.6	5.3	43.1	0.36	[15]
corn cob	46.6	5.9	45.5	0.47	[16]
Yellow poplar sawdust	48.5	5.9	43.7	0.48	[17]
Alaskan spruce	50.1	6.2	42.9	0.50	[12]
Wheat straw	43.2	5.0	39.4	0.43	[18]
Wood	48.4	6.2	45.0	0.48	[19]
Rice hulls	66.0	7.2	25.4	0.66	[20]

Table 1.
Biomass sources, composition and carbon economy.

hydrothermal pressures and temperatures ranging from 500 to 700°C. This converts the biomass material into a liquid oil product, which is then processed as crude oil, using cracking and distillation.

Gasification of biomass under controlled oxidative conditions produces synthesis gas, which can be converted to chemicals using the well-known Fisher-Tropsch chemistry.

Hydrolysis, using acids, followed by fermentation converts biomass into chemicals, such as ethanol, acetic acid, etc. These chemicals become the feedstocks for a variety of industrial chemicals.

Table 1 lists the chemical composition of the various biomass sources and their carbon economy [5–20].

3. Reactions for manufacturing industrial chemicals

Production of industrial chemicals utilizes a variety of reactions to convert the raw materials to the desired products. The following is a list of the reactions involved in the manufacture of the top 100 industrial chemicals and their chemical classification.

- Methane → acetylene: pyrolysis
- Acetylene → ethylene: hydration
- Ethanol → ethylene: dehydration
- Propane → acetylene: pyrolysis
- Isobutane → isobutylene: dehydrogenation
- N-butane → N-butylene: dehydrogenation
- Acetylene → butadiene: reaction of acetylene and formaldehyde
- Ethanol → butadiene: dehydration/dehydrogenation
- Ethylene → ethanol: hydration
- Benzene → cyclohexane: hydrogenation
- Benzene → ethyl benzene: reaction of benzene and ethylene
- Ethylene → acetaldehyde: oxidation
- Carbon monoxide → methanol: hydrogenation
- Methanol → acetic acid: carbonylation
- Acetic acid → acetic anhydride: reaction of acetic acid and ketone
- Acetic acid → acetone: decarboxylation

- Acetaldehyde → acrolein: reaction of acetaldehyde and formaldehyde
- Acetic acid → acrylic acid: reaction of acetic acid and formaldehyde
- Butadiene → adiponitrile: chlorination of butadiene with sodium cyanide
- Propylene → allyl chloride: chlorination of propylene
- Allyl chloride → allyl alcohol: hydrolysis
- Acetylene → acetaldehyde: hydration
- Acetaldehyde → crotonaldehyde: dimerization
- Crotonaldehyde → N-butanol: hydrogenation
- Ethanol → acetaldehyde: oxidation
- Crotonaldehyde → N-butyraldehyde: hydrogenation
- N-butyraldehyde → N-butanol: hydrogenation
- N-butylene → S-butanol: sulfonation
- Benzene → chlorobenzene: oxychlorination
- Benzene → cumene: reaction of benzene and propylene
- Cyclohexane → cyclohexanol: oxidation-boron assisted
- Cyclohexanol → cyclohexanone: dehydrogenation
- Methanol → formaldehyde: oxidation
- Formaldehyde → ethylene glycol: carbonylation
- Ethylene glycol → diethylene glycol: reaction of ethylene glycol and ethylene oxide
- Toluene → dinitrotoluene: nitration
- Acrolein → epichlorohydrin: chlorination
- Ethylene → ethylene dichloride: chlorination
- Ethylene → ethylene oxide: chlorohydration
- Propylene → isopropanol: hydration
- Acetic acid → ketene: pyrolysis

- Methane → methyl chloride: chlorination
- Methanol → methyl chloride: hydrochlorination
- Benzene → nitrobenzene: nitration
- Acetaldehyde → peracetic acid: oxidation
- Benzene → phenol: sulfonation
- Carbon monoxide → phosgene: reaction of carbon monoxide and chlorine
- Naphthalene → phthalic anhydride: oxidation
- Propylene → propylene dichloride: chlorination
- Propylene → propylene oxide: chlorohydration
- Toluene → terephthalic acid: reaction of toluene and carbon monoxide
- Dinitrotoluene → toluene diamine: hydrogenation
- Acetylene → trichloroethylene: chlorination
- Ethylene dichloride → trichloroethylene: chlorination
- Acetylene → vinyl chloride: hydrochlorination
- Ethylene dichloride → vinyl chloride: dehydrochlorination
- Acetylene → acrylonitrile: cyanation
- Acetaldehyde → acrylonitrile: cyanation/dehydration
- Benzene → aniline: reaction of benzene and ammonia
- Toluene → benzoic acid: oxidation
- Phenol → bisphenol-A: reaction of phenol and acetone
- Cyclohexane → caprolactam: nitration
- Methane → chloroform: chlorination
- Methyl chloride → chloroform: chlorination
- Acetylene → chloroprene: dimerization
- Butadiene → chloroprene: chlorination

- Phenol → cresylic acid: methylation
- Methane → carbon tetrachloride: chlorination
- Carbon tetrachloride → dichlorofluoromethane: reaction with hydrogen fluoride
- Methyl chloride → carbon tetrachloride: chlorination
- Terephthalic acid → dimethyl terephthalate: esterification
- Acetic acid → ethyl acetate: esterification
- Acrylic acid → ethyl acrylate: esterification
- Ethylene → ethyl chloride: hydrochlorination
- Ethylene → ethyl dibromide: bromination
- N-butyraldehyde → 2-ethylhexanol: dimerization
- Epichlorohydrin → glycerin: hydrolysis
- Adiponitrile → hexamethylenediamine: hydrogenation
- Acetone → isoprene: reaction of acetylene and acetone
- Benzene → maleic anhydride: oxidation
- Ethylene dichloride → methyl chloroform: chlorination
- Methane → methylene dichloride: chlorination
- Methyl chloride → methyl dichloride: chlorination
- N-butylene → methyl ethyl ketone: oxidation
- Acetone → methyl isobutyl ketone: dimerization
- Acetone → methyl methacrylate: cyanation
- Carbon tetrachloride → perchloroethylene: pyrolysis
- Propylene oxide → propylene glycol: hydration
- Butadiene → styrene: cyclohydrogenation
- Toluene diamine → toluene diisocyanate: phosgenation
- Carbon tetrachloride → trichlorofluoromethane: reaction of carbon tetrachloride and hydrogen fluoride

- Ethylene oxide → ethylene glycol: hydration (in book)
- Diethylene glycol → triethylene glycol: reaction of diethylene glycol and ethylene oxide
- Carbon monoxide → urea: reaction of ammonia and carbon monoxide
- Acetic acid → vinyl acetate: reaction of acetylene and acetic acid
- Carbon monoxide → formic acid: hydrolysis
- Cyclohexanol → adipic acid: oxidation
- Methane → hydrogen cyanide: ammoxidation
- Propane → hydrogen cyanide: reaction of propane and ammonia
- Carbon monoxide → isobutanol: reaction of carbon monoxide and hydrogen

Table 2 lists the chemical reactions, yield, and the calculated atom economy, used in the analysis, based on the reported reaction yields [4]. The following equation was

Industrial reaction	Yield (product/reactant)	Atom economy
Methane → acetylene	0.4545	0.5
Acetylene → ethylene	0.9174	1.0
Ethanol → ethylene	0.5848	1.0
Propane → acetylene	0.3448	0.50
Isobutane → isobutylene	0.6667	1.0
n-Butane → N-butylene	0.6667	1.0
Acetylene → butadiene	1.4925	1.0
Ethanol → butadiene	0.3333	1.0
Ethylene → ethanol	1.5152	1.0
Benzene → cyclohexane	1.0753	1.0
Benzene → ethyl benzene	1.3158	1.0
Ethylene → acetaldehyde	1.4925	1.0
Carbon monoxide → methanol	1.0	1.0
Methanol → acetic acid	1.8519	1.0
Acetic acid → acetic anhydride	1.6129	1.0
Acetic acid → acetone	0.4587	0.75
Acetaldehyde → acrolein	0.9524	1.0
Acetic acid → acrylic acid	1.20	1.0
Butadiene → adiponitrile	1.2195	1.0
Propylene → allyl chloride	1.4286	1.0

Industrial reaction	Yield (product/reactant)	Atom economy
Allyl chloride → allyl alcohol	0.6667	1.0
Acetylene → acetaldehyde	1.6129	1.0
Acetaldehyde → crotonaldehyde	0.7407	1.0
Crotonaldehyde → n-butanol	1.0	1.0
Ethanol → acetaldehyde	0.8696	1.0
Crotonaldehyde → n-butyraldehyde	1.0	1.0
n-Butyraldehyde → n-butanol	0.9709	1.0
n-Butylene → butanol	1.1111	1.0
Benzene → chlorobenzene	1.2195	1.0
Benzene → cumene	1.2658	1.0
Cyclohexane → cyclohexanol	0.9709	1.0
Cyclohexanol → cyclohexanone	0.9524	1.0
Methanol → formaldehyde	0.8696	1.0
Formaldehyde → ethylene glycol	1.5385	1.0
Ethylene glycol → diethylene glycol	1.4286	1.0
Toluene → dinitro toluene	1.8519	1.0
Acrolein → epichlorohydrin	1.2847	1.0
Ethylene → ethylene dichloride	3.3333	1.0
Ethylene → ethylene oxide	1.25	1.0
Propylene → isopropanol	1.3889	1.0
Acetic acid → ketene	0.6289	1.0
Methane → methyl chloride	2.439	1.0
Methanol → methyl chloride	1.4286	1.0
Benzene → nitro benzene	1.5385	1.0
Acetaldehyde → peracetic acid	1.5625	0.5
Benzene → phenol	0.9009	1.0
Carbon monoxide → phosgene	0.9009	1.0
Naphthalene → phthalic anhydride	0.9524	0.8
Propylene → propylene dichloride	2.439	1.0
Propylene → propylene oxide	1.0638	1.0
Toluene → terephthalic acid	1.8043	1.0
Dinitro toluene → toluene diamine	0.6369	1.0
Acetylene → trichloroethylene	4.7619	1.0
Ethylene dichloride → trichloroethylene	1.2658	1.0
Acetylene → vinyl chloride	2.2727	1.0
Ethylene dichloride → vinyl chloride	0.5988	1.0
Acetylene → acrylonitrile	1.6667	1.0
Acetaldehyde → acrylonitrile	1.2045	1.0

Industrial reaction	Yield (product/reactant)	Atom economy
Benzene → aniline	1.1923	1.0
Toluene → benzoic acid	1.1905	1.0
Phenol → bisphenol a	1.1364	1.0
Cyclohexane → caprolactam	0.7692	1.0
Methane → chloroform	7.1429	1.0
Methyl chloride → chloroform	2.2727	1.0
Acetylene → chloroprene	1.3333	1.0
Butadiene → chloroprene	1.3333	1.0
Butadiene → chloroprene	1.25	1.0
Phenol → cresylic acid	1.1494	0.5
Methane → carbon tetrachloride	9.0909	1.0
Carbon tetrachloride → dichlorofluoromethane	9.0909	1.0
Methyl chloride → carbon tetrachloride	2.7778	1.0
Terephthalic acid → dimethyl terephthalate	1.1494	1.0
Acetic acid → ethyl acetate	1.4493	1.0
Acrylic acid → ethyl acetate	1.2987	1.0
Ethylene → ethyl chloride	2.000	1.0
Ethylene → ethyl dibromide	6.2500	1.0
N-butyraldehyde → 2-ethyl hexanol	0.8130	1.0
Epichlorohydrin → glycerine	0.9524	1.0
Adiponitrile → hexamethylenediamine	1.0753	1.0
Acetone → isoprene	1.0526	1.0
Benzene → maleic anhydride	0.7692	0.66
Ethylene dichloride → methyl chloroform	1.2195	1.0
Methane → methylene dichloride	5.0000	1.0
Methyl chloride → methyl dichloride	1.6129	1.0
n-Butylene → methyl ethyl ketone	1.1111	1.0
Acetone → methyl isobutyl ketone	0.8000	1.0
Acetone → methyl methacrylate	1.3889	1.0
Carbon tetrachloride	0.5000	1.0
Propylene oxide → propylene glycol	1.1765	1.0
Butadiene → styrene	0.9696	1.0
Toluene diamine → toluene diisocynate	1.2048	1.0
Carbon tetrachloride → trichlorofluoromethane	0.7143	1.0
Ethylene oxide → ethylene glycol	1.1364	1.0
Diethylene glycol → triethylene glycol	2.8571	.10
Carbon monoxide → urea	1.3158	1.0
Acetic acid → vinyl acetate	1.3889	1.0

Industrial reaction	Yield (product/reactant)	Atom economy
Carbon monoxide → formic acid	1.6428	1.0
Cyclohexanol → adipic acid	1.3699	1.0
Methane → hydrogen cyanide	1.2195	
Propane → hydrogen cyanide	1.5625	1.0
Carbon monoxide → isobutanol	0.1499	0.8

Table 2.
Industrial chemical reactions, commercial yield and atom economy.

used to calculate the carbon economy from the reported data and a balanced reaction pathway:

$$\begin{aligned}\%\text{Carbon economy} = {} & [(\text{Unit weight of product})/\text{Unit weight of raw material}(s)] \\ & \times[\text{Molecular Weight of raw material}(s)/\text{Molecular Weight of product}] \\ & \times[\text{Moles of carbon in product}/\text{Moles of carbon in raw materials}] \times 100.\end{aligned} \quad (1)$$

4. Reaction pathways from biomass to industrial chemicals

The reaction pathways for the top industrial chemicals, as listed in the previous section, were combined with the biomass conversion reactions to maximize the overall carbon economy. This yielded biomass conversion reaction pathways to the major industrial chemicals, and these conversion paths with the maximum carbon economy are listed in **Table 3**.

Although several biomass sources were used in the analysis, only beechwood, pine sawdust, sunflower residue, rape residue, sewage sludge, alaskan spruce, tropical luan, and rice husk were selected to maximize the overall carbon economy, with beechwood and pine sawdust being mostly used to generate the chemical intermediate. Sewage sludge was used to generate benzene as an intermediate chemical, which could then be converted to other aromatic compounds. The carbon economy for sewage sludge conversion to aromatics was less than 10%, which may render these chemical paths uneconomical.

The following examples from **Table 3** illustrate the biomass conversion reactions which had the highest atom economy for two industrial chemicals.

Butadiene can be produced from biomass using the following steps:

1. Gasification of beech wood: conducted at 700°C and atmospheric pressure produces methane with an atom economy of 83.5% [7].

2. Conversion of methane to acetylene gas: using the arc process [3], methane is converted to acetylene gas with an atom economy of 50%; byproducts produced are ethylene and hydrogen gases.

3. Reaction of acetylene with formaldehyde [3]: product is butadiene and steam.

Figure 1 shows a schematic of the reaction pathway to convert beech wood to butadiene.

Industrial chemical	Reaction path with the highest carbon economy	Overall carbon economy
Butadiene	Beech wood → methane → acetylene → butadiene	0.4173
Di ethylene glycol	Pine saw dust → carbon monoxide → methanol → formaldehyde → ethylene glycol → di ethylene glycol	0.5940
Carbon monoxide	Pine saw dust → carbon monoxide	0.5940
Carbon dioxide	Beech wood → carbon dioxide	0.2923
Methane	Beech wood → methane	0.8346
Ethylene	Beech wood → methane → acetylene → ethylene	0.4173
Ethane	Alaskan spruce → ethane	0.0713
Acetylene	Beech wood → methane → acetylene	0.4173
Propylene	Beech wood → propylene	0.0236
Propane	Tropical luan → propane	0.1700
Isobutane	Sunflower residue → isobutane	0.0100
n-Butane	Sunflower residue → n-butane	0.0400
n-Butylene	Sunflower residue → methylene dichloride → n-butylene	
n-Pentane	Cannot be produced from biomass	
Iso-Pentane	Rape residue → iso-pentane	0.0300
Ethanol	Beech wood → methanol → acetylene → ethylene → ethanol	0.4173
Cyclohexane	Sewage sludge → benzene → cyclohexane	0.0852
Benzene	Sewage sludge → benzene	0.0852
Ethyl benzene	Sewage sludge → benzene → ethyl benzene	0.0852
Naphthalene	Alaskan spruce → naphthalene	0.0203
Toluene	Rice husk → toluene	0.0388
0-Xylene, m-Xylene	Cannot be produced from biomass	
p-Xylene	Alaskan spruce → p-xylene	0.0096
Acetaldehyde	Beech wood → methane → acetylene → ethylene → acetaldehyde	0.4173
Acetic acid	Pine saw dust → carbon monoxide → methanol → acetic acid	0.5940
Acetic anhydride	Pine saw dust → carbon monoxide → methanol → acetic acid → acetic anhydride	0.5940
Acetone	Pine saw dust → carbon monoxide → methanol → acetic acid → acetone	0.4455
Acrolein	Beech wood → methane → acetylene → ethylene → acetaldehyde → acrolein	0.4173
Acrylic acid	Pine saw dust → carbon monoxide → methanol → acetic acid → acrylic acid	0.5940
Adiponitrile	Beech wood → methane → acetylene → butadiene → adiponitrile	0.4173
Allyl alcohol	Beech wood → propylene → allyl chloride → allyl alcohol	0.0236
Allyl chloride	beech wood ⇒ propylene → allyl chloride	0.0236
n-Butanol	beech wood → methane → acetylene → acetaldehyde → crotonaldehyde → n-butanol	0.3091

Industrial chemical	Reaction path with the highest carbon economy	Overall carbon economy
Iso-Butanol	sunflower residue → methylene dichloride → methyl iso butyl ketone → iso-butanol	0.0004
n-Butyraldehyde	Beech wood → methane → acetylene → acetaldehyde → crotonaldehyde → n-butyraldehyde	0.3091
Chlorobenzene	Sewage sludge → benzene → chlorobenzene	0.0852
Crotonaldehyde	Beech wood → methane → acetylene → ethylene → acetaldehyde → crotonaldehyde	0.3091
Cumene	Sewage sludge → benzene → cumene	0.0852
Cyclohexanol	Sewage sludge → benzene → cyclohexane → cyclohexanol	0.0852
Cyclohexanone	Sewage sludge → benzene → cyclohexane → cyclohexanol → cyclohexanone	0.0852
Dinitro toluene	Rice husk → toluene → dinitro toluene	0.0388
Epichlorohydrin	Beech wood → methane → acetylene → acetaldehyde → acrolein → epichlorohydrin	0.4173
Ethylene dichloride	Beech wood → methane → acetylene → ethylene → ethylene dichloride	0.4173
Ethylene oxide	Beech wood → methane → acetylene → ethylene → ethylene oxide	0.4173
Ethylene glycol	Pine saw dust → carbon monoxide → methanol → formaldehyde → ethylene glycol	0.5940
Iso-Butyraldehyde	Cannot be manufactured from biomass	
Isopropanol	Beech wood → isoprene → isopropanol	0.0236
Ketene	One saw dust → ethyl acrylate → methanol → acetic acid → ketene	0.5940
Methanol	Pine saw dust → carbon monoxide → methanol	0.5940
Methyl chloride	Beech wood → methane → methyl chloride	0.8346
Nitro benzene	Sewage sludge → benzene → nitrobenzene	0.0852
Peracetic acid	Beech wood → methane → acetylene → acetaldehyde → peracetic acid	0.2087
Phenol	Sewage sludge → benzene → phenol	0.0852
Phosgene	Pine saw dust → ethyl acrylate → phosgene	0.5940
Acrylonitrile	Beech wood → ethylene dibromide → hexamethylene diamine → acrylonitrile	0.4173
Aniline	Sewage sludge → benzene → aniline	0.0852
Benzoic acid	Rice husk → toluene → benzoic acid	0.0388
Bisphenol A	Sewage sludge → benzene → phenol → bisphenol A	0.0852
Caprolactam	Sewage sludge → benzene → cyclohexane → caprolactam	0.0852
Chloroform	Beech wood → methane → chloroform	0.8346
Chloroprene	Beech wood → methane → acetylene → chloroprene	0.4173
Cresylic acid	Sewage sludge → benzene → phenol → cresylic acid	0.0426
Dichloro difluoro methane	Beech wood → methane → carbon tetrachloride → dichloro difluoro methane	0.8346

Industrial chemical	Reaction path with the highest carbon economy	Overall carbon economy
Dimethyl terephtalate	Rice husk → toluene → terepthalic acid dimethyl terephtalate	0.0388
Ethyl acetate	Pine saw dust → carbon monoxide → methanol → acetic acid → ethyl acetate	0.5940
Ethyl acrylate	Pine saw dust → carbon monoxide → methanol → acetic acid → acrylic acid → ethyl acrylate	0.5940
Ethyl chloride	Beech wood → methane → acetylene → ethylene → ethyl chloride	0.4173
Ethylene dibromide	Beech wood → methane → acetylene → ethylene → ethylene dibromide	0.4173
2-Ethyl hexanol	Paddy straw → ethanol → acetaldehyde → crotonaldehyde → n-butyraldehyde → 2-ethyl hexanol	0.2934
Glycerine	Paddy straw → ethanol → acetaldehyde → cumene → epichlorohydrin → glycerine	0.3961
Hexamethylene diamine	Beech wood → methane → acetylene → methyl methacrylate → adiponitrile → hexamethylene diamine	0.4173
Isoprene	Pine saw dust → carbon monoxide → methanol → acetic acid → acetone → isoprene	0.4455
Maleic anhydride	Sewage sludge → benzene → maleic anhydride	0.0852
Methyl chloroform	Beech wood → methane → acetylene → ethylene → ethylene dichloride → methyl chloroform	0.4173
Methylene dichloride	Beech wood → methane → methylene dichloride	0.8346
Methyl ethyl ketone	Sunflower residue → methylene dichloride → methyl iso butyl ketone → methyl ethyl ketone	0.0400
Methyl iso butyl ketone	Pine saw dust → carbon monoxide → methanol → acetic acid → acetone → methyl iso butyl ketone	0.4455
Methyl methacrylate	Pine saw dust → carbon monoxide → methanol → acetic acid → acetone → methyl methacrylate	0.4455
Perchloroethylene	Beech wood → propylene → carbon tetrachloride → perchloroethylene	0.8346
Propylene glycol	Beech wood → propylene → propylene oxide → propylene glycol	0.0236
Styrene	Beech wood → methane → acetylene → methyl methacrylate → styrene	0.4173
Toluene di isocyanate	Rice husk → toluene → dinitro toluene → toluene diamine → toluene di iso cyanate	0.0388
Trichloro fluoro methane	Beech wood → methane → carbon tetrachloride → trichloro fluoro methane	0.8346
Triethylene glycol	Beech wood → ethylene → ethylene oxide → ethylene glycol → diethylene glycol → triethylene glycol	0.0843
Urea	Pine saw dust → carbon monoxide → urea	0.5940
Vinyl acetate	Pine saw dust → carbon monoxide → methanol → acetic acid → vinyl acetate	0.5940
Hexane	Rape residue → hexane	0.0800
Formic acid	Pine saw dust → carbon monoxide → formic acid	0.5940

Industrial chemical	Reaction path with the highest carbon economy	Overall carbon economy
Adipic acid	Sewage sludge → benzene → cyclohexane → cyclo hexanol → adipic acid	0.0852
Carbon tetrachloride	Beech wood → methane → carbon tetrachloride	0.8346
Hydrogen cyanide	Beech wood → hydrogen cyanide	0.8346
Isobutanol	Pine saw dust → carbon monoxide → iso-butanol	0.4752

Table 3.
Chemical pathways for converting biomass to industrial chemicals with the overall carbon economy.

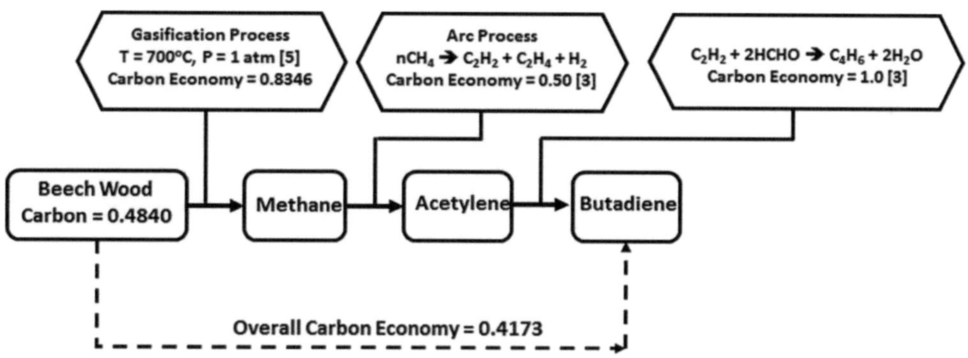

Figure 1.
Reaction path for manufacturing butadiene from beech wood.

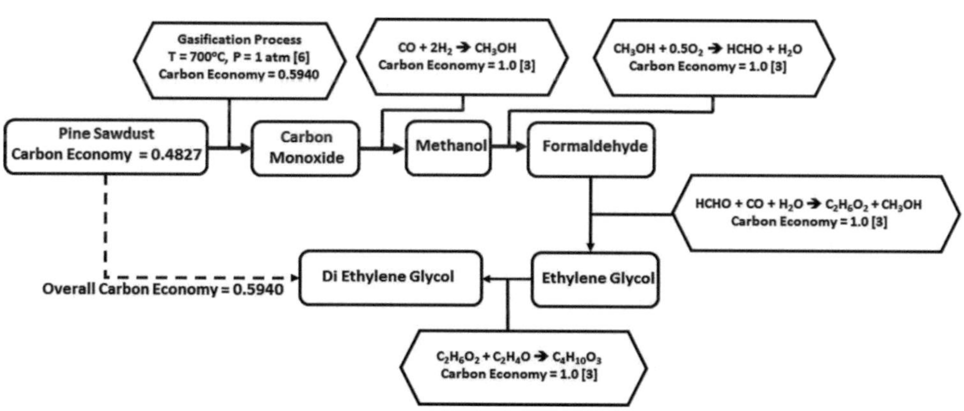

Figure 2.
Reaction path for manufacturing Di ethylene glycol from pine sawdust.

Another example of a reaction pathway is the conversion of pine sawdust to diethylene glycol, and this reaction pathway with their respective atom economies is shown in **Figure 2**. This pathway has the highest carbon economy for manufacturing diethylene glycol from a biomass source.

5. Conclusions

Sustainable industrial chemistry requires "optimum" reaction pathways, as defined by the highest carbon economy, starting with various biomass materials. Biomass is a sustainable feedstock, while currently used starting materials, such as crude oil, coal, and natural gas, are unsustainable. Furthermore, when industrial chemicals are made from unsustainable feedstocks, they eventually add additional carbon to the environment, typically in the form of carbon dioxide, an earth warming gas. Manufacturing industrial chemicals from biomass is an important step toward mitigating climate change.

The chemical industry has to recognize that continuing the use of nonsustainable feedstocks to manufacture industrial chemicals is not a viable option, especially with the growing concerns about climate change. Utilizing the existing chemical industry and simply using feedstocks derived from biomass is the most economical and expedient way to accomplish two major goals: make the chemical industry more sustainable and slow the increase in the atmospheric carbon dioxide concentration. Eventually, it will be a strategy to avoid carbon taxes on the top 100 industrial chemicals.

In this paper, a systematic method of generating the reaction pathways from various biomass sources to the top 100 industrial chemicals, which maximize the overall carbon economy, was presented. It provides a listing of multiple ways of manufacturing the industrial chemicals in the order of deceasing-carbon economy.

Author details

Rakesh Govind*, Shiva Charan and Jack Baltzersen
University of Cincinnati, Cincinnati, OH, USA

*Address all correspondence to: govindr@ucmail.uc.edu

References

[1] Wittcoff HA. Reuben BG. Plotkin JS. Industrial Organic Chemicals. 2nd ed. New York: Wiley-Interscience; 2004. p. 93. DOI: 10.1002/0471651540

[2] Industrial Organic Chemistry / Weissermel K. Arpe HJ. Transl. by Lindley CR. 4 ed. Weinheim: VCH; 1997. DOI: 10.1002/9783527619191

[3] Stadtherr MA, Rudd DF. Systems study of the petrochemical industry. Chemical Engineering Science. 1976;**31**:101-1028

[4] Blackford JL, Kashiwase D, Zalk SA. Chemical Conversion Factors and Yields: Commercial and Theoretical. Stanford Research Institute: Chemical Industries Division; 1984

[5] Corte P, Lacoste C, Traverse JP. Gasification and catalytic conversion of biomass by flash pyrolysis. Journal of Analytical and Applied Pyrolysis. 1985;**7**: 323-335

[6] Garcia L, Salvador ML, Arauzo J, Bilbao R. Catalytic pyrolysis of biomass: Influence of the catalyst pretreatment on gas yields. Journal of Analytical and Applied Pyrolysis. 2001;**58–59**:491-501

[7] Sanchez ME, Cuetos MJ, Martınez O, Moran A. Pilot scale thermolysis of municipal solid waste combustibility of the products of the process and gas cleaning treatment of the combustion gases. Journal of Analytical and Applied Pyrolysis. 2007;**78**:125-132

[8] Kaminsky W, Kummer AB. Fluidized bed pyrolysis of digested sewage sludge. Journal of Analytical and Applied Pyrolysis. 1989;**16**:27-35

[9] Sanchez ME, Lindao E, Margaleff D, Martinez O, Moran A. Pyrolysis of agricultural residues from rape and sunflowers: Production and characterization of bio-fuels and biochar soil management. Journal of Analytical and Applied Pyrolysis. 2009;**85**:142-144

[10] Boateng AA, Hicks KB, Vogel KP. Pyrolysis of switch grass (*Panicum virgatum*) harvested at several stages of maturity. Journal of Analytical and Applied Pyrolysis. 2006;**75**:55-64

[11] Guo S, Libin W, Wang C, Li J, Yang Z. Direct conversion of sunflower shells to alkanes and aromatic compound. Energy & Fuels. 2008;**22**: 3517-3522

[12] Maiti S, Banerjee P, Purakayastha S, Ghosh B. Silicon doped carbon semiconductor from rice husk char. Materials Chemistry and Physics. 2008; **109**:169-173

[13] Ji-lu Z. Bio-oil from fast pyrolysis of rice husk: Yields and related properties and improvement of the pyrolysis system. Journal of Analytical and Applied Pyrolysis. 2007;**80**:30-35

[14] Chang W, Qinglan H, Dingqiang L, Qingzhu J, Guiju L, Bo X. Production of light aromatic hydrocarbons from biomass by catalytic pyrolysis. Chinese Journal of Catalysis. 2008;**29**(9):907-912

[15] Sudha Rani K, Swamy MV, Seenayya G. Production of ethanol from various pure and natural cellulosic biomass by clostridium thermocellum strains SS21 and SS22. Process Biochemistry. 1998;**33**(4):435-440

[16] Cao NJ, Krishnan MS, Du JX, Gong CS, Ho NWY, Chen ZD, et al. Ethanol production from corn cob pretreated by the ammonia steeping process using genetically engineered

yeast. Biotechnology Letters. 1996;**18**: 1013-1018

[17] Torget R, Hatzis C, Hayward TK, Hsd T-A, Philippidis GP. Optimization of reverse-flow, two-temperature, dilute-acid pre treatment to enhance biomass conversion to ethanol. Applied Biochemistry and Biotechnology. 1996; **57/58**:85

[18] Spindler DD, Wyman CE, Grohmann K. All MohagheGHI, SIMULTANEOUS SACCHARIfication and fermentation of Pretreated wheat straw to ethanol with selected yeast strains and glycosidase supplementation. Applied Biochemistry and Biotechnology. 1989;**20/2**:I

[19] Li H, Kim N-J, Jiang M, Kang JW, Chang HN. Simultaneous saccharification and fermentation of lingo cellulosic residues pretreated with phosphoric acid–acetone for bio ethanol production. Bioresource Technology. 2009;**100**:3245-3251

[20] Saha BC, Cotta MA. Enzymatic saccharification and fermentation of alkaline peroxide pretreated rice hulls to ethanol. Enzyme and Microbial Technology. 2007;**41**:528-532

Section 5

Bioenergy Generation from Biomass

Chapter 14

Bioenergy Production: Emerging Technologies

Ifeanyi Michael Smarte Anekwe, Edward Kwaku Armah and Emmanuel Kweinor Tetteh

Abstract

Bioenergy, when compared to traditional fossil fuels, offers clear benefits due to its renewable nature and enormous supply, and so plays a critical role in ensuring energy stability while minimizing net greenhouse gas emission. However, the advancement of bioenergy can produce major environmental changes, the extent of which is unknown. This chapter highlights the overview of bioenergy, available technologies for bioenergy production, environmental implications, challenges, prospects and future work consideration for the successful transition to bioenergy economy. Consequently, a global bioenergy sector producing substantial amount of energy would be required for the transition to a low-carbon energy economy while meeting rising future energy demands.

Keywords: bioenergy, biofuel, biogas biophotolysis, combustion, fermentation, gasification, hythane, liquefaction, pyrolysis, trans-esterification

1. Introduction

The world economy has developed within a concept that is heavily dependent on fossil fuel (coal, oil, and natural gas), which supply the vast large proportion of the substrate utilized in the synthesis of fuels and chemicals. The global energy utilization is increasing tremendously, and fossil fuels currently provide around 88% of the global energy. However, due to their finite reserves and non-renewable nature, the long-term exploitation of these limited resource is unreliable [1]. According to projections, the world's energy requirement will rise by a factor of two or three throughout this century [2]. Similarly, the quantities of greenhouse gases (GHGs) in the environment are quickly increasing, with CO_2 releases from fossil fuels being the main significant contribution to this increase. It is necessary to cut greenhouse gas emissions to less than half of world emission rates of 1990 as to mitigate the consequences of global warming and climate change [3]. Another significant global concern is energy supply stability, which is complicated by the fact that the vast majority of known traditional oil and gas reserves are located in politically unstable countries.

Bioenergy is an alternative form of basic energy that offers an opportunity for greenhouse gas (GHG) reductions, provided that the feedstocks are exploited from a renewable source and that effective bioenergy technologies are utilized. It is possible that increasing the amount of electricity generated by this form of energy may help to achieve the Framework Convention on Climate Change (FCCC) goals of stabilizing atmospheric concentrations of greenhouse gases below toxic concentrations in the future. Biomass is an alternate provider of chemical feedstock and energy, and biorefining biomass is equivalent to petroleum processing [3, 4]. "A biorefinery," according to the National Renewable Energy Laboratory (NREL), is described as "a system that incorporates biomass transformation operations and technology to synthesize fuels, electricity, and chemicals from biomass" according to National Renewable Energy Laboratory. Furthermore, bioenergy obtained from biological materials has historically been considered to be a significant form of energy that will help to lessen reliance on fossil fuels [5].

The notion of biorefineries is a sustainable strategy to the biomass transformation into useful products that may easily substitute fossil oil refineries, which are used to generate a number of fuels, chemicals, and other by-products from crude oil. Using biomass as a substrate, biorefining is the method of refining a variety of bio-based products such as chemicals, fuels, and power, all of which are utilized as end products. Biofuels are liquid or gaseous fuels that are predominantly derived from biomass. They can be employed to substitute or supplement diesel, gasoline, or other fossil fuels in a variety of uses, including transportation, stationary, portable, and other purposes. Biofuels, such as biodiesel, bioethanol, biogas, and bio-oil, are the most important products of the biorefining industry. When likened to conventional fossil fuels, biofuels have outstanding characteristics in aspects of renewability, relatively clean refining, locally distributed resources, biodegradability and non-hazardous, clean combustion, a favorable economic implication, improved fuel economy, reduced reliance on petroleum oil, and improved health advantages [6, 7]. The application of green technology-based biorefinery approach results in a crude oil non-reliance future, with a prosperous industry dependent on organic and environmentally friendly raw material including agricultural residues, cheese whey, household residues, forest residues, and algae. The advancement in technology makes it possible to produce biofuel from waste raw material in an efficient manner.

1.1 Classification of biofuels

1.1.1 Generations of biofuels

Historically, there are three generations of biofuels. First generation biofuels such as bioalcohols, biodiesels, biogas, bioethers, biosyngas and vegetable oil have been produced primarily from sugar, starch, and vegetable oil sugar, or animal fats, and they are produced through conventional techniques [7]. Advances based on various biomass possibilities have resulted in the development of 2nd and 3rd generation biofuels [8]. Biofuels derived from agroforestry residues lignocellulosic materials and waste biomass (wheat stalks, maize stalks, corn, and wood) as well as dedicated non-food based bioenergy materials (e.g. miscanthus, willow, and poplar), serve as the foundation for second generation biofuel production [9]. Advanced biofuels such as biohydrogen and bioethanol are examples of the second-generation biofuels. Algae-based biofuels such as biogas (biohydrogen and biomethane) are the third generation of biofuels [10].

1.1.2 Types of biofuels

Ethanol is the most popularly used alcoholic biofuel on the industry today. There are numerous motivations for its application as a sustainable energy, including: that it is made from renewable agricultural feedstock such as corn, sugar and molasses, rather than non-sustainable sources, and that ethanol and its byproducts are less hazardous than other alcoholic fuels [11]. Biodiesel is a liquid fuel made from animal fats, vegetable oils, and waste cooking oil that can be used as a substitute for diesel fuel and is regarded as a viable replacement to fossil diesel [12]. It is sustainable, non-hazardous, biodegradable, sulfur- and benzene-free, may be applied in standard diesel engines without adjustment, and can be blended with fossil diesel at any ratio [7, 13, 14]. Bio-oil is a combination of organic components, primarily acids, alcohols, aldehydes, esters, ketones, and phenols. This liquid is usually dark brown in color and free-flowing, with a smoky fragrance [15, 16]. Bio-oil can be considered an environmentally benign fuel when compared to fossil fuels because it emits less CO2 and produces reduced NOx emissions than diesel oil [16]. Biogas is a gas combination mostly made up of CH_4 and CO_2 that is generated from agricultural residue, manure, municipal trash, plant material, sewage, green waste, or food waste while biohydrogen is produced from microalgae and bacteria metabolism. It is a form of green energy. Biogas is a diverse sustainable energy source that may be employed to substitute fossil fuels in the generation of electricity and heat, as well as a gaseous automobile fuel.

2. Biomass conversion technologies for bioenergy production

Most techniques are appropriate for direct biomass conversion or intermediate conversion [17, 18]. Because the techniques are adequately mutable, gaseous, and liquid fuels that are undistinguishable to those derived from fossil feedstocks, or that are not matching but useful as fossil fuel alternatives, can be created. It's worth noting that biomass feedstocks may be used to make practically all of the fuels and commodity chemicals that are made from fossil fuels. The techniques include a wide range of thermal [18] and thermochemical technologies [19] for the conversion of biomass via combustion, gasification, and liquefaction, as well as microbial transformation of biomass through fermentative methods to create gaseous and liquid fuels. There are numerous biomass conversion pathways for creating energy haulers from biomasses. **Figure 1** depicts significant conversion pathways for producing heat, power, and transportation fuels that are now in use or under development. The accessible technologies for development in producing transportation fuels are categorized as combustion, gasification, and digestion, followed by the technologies available.

2.1 Physicochemical conversion processes

Physicochemical biomass transformation includes the generation of products employing physical and chemical conversion techniques at relatively close ambient temperatures and pressures. It is mostly linked with the conversion of fresh or used vegetable oils, animal fats, greases, tallow, and other apt feedstocks into beneficial liquid fuels and chemicals like biodiesel.

2.1.1 Extraction or separation method

There are varieties of procedures for the extraction of biomass including liquid–solid extraction, partitioning, acid–base extractions, liquid–liquid extraction, ultrasonic extraction (UE), and microwave assisted extraction (MAE) [20]. Several

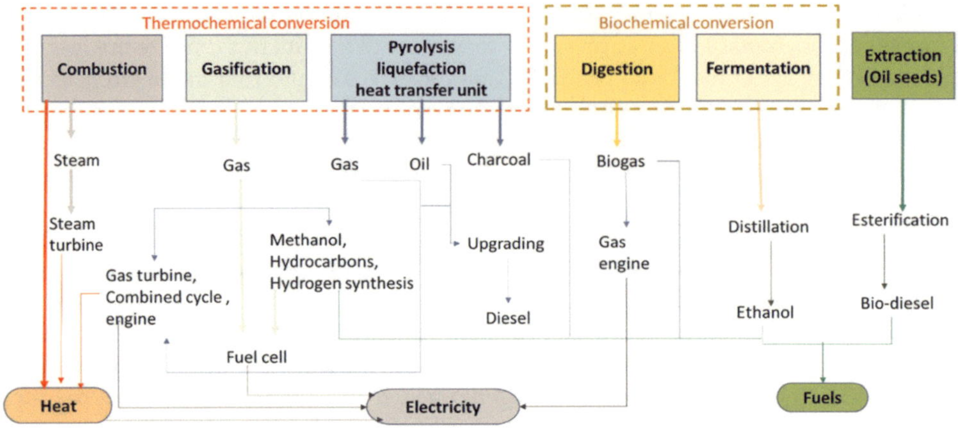

Figure 1.
Pathways for biomass conversion to finished products adapted from [19].

extraction procedures, such as enzyme assisted extraction and solvent extraction have also been examined in the past few decades [18]. However, there are certain disadvantages to these extraction processes. Liquid–liquid extraction and liquid–solid extraction are the two most used extraction methods. Two distinct solvents are typically used for liquid–liquid extraction, one of which is unvaryingly water. Cost, toxicity, and flammability are some of the downsides of this approach [21]. A solid-phase extraction (SPE) technique is also employed in separating analytes which are dissolved or suspended in a liquid mixture based on their physical and chemical properties from a wide range of matrices. Soxhlet extraction, percolation, sonication and steam distillation are examples of traditional procedures. Although these procedures are commonly used, they have numerous drawbacks: they are generally time-consuming, requiring massive quantities of polluting solvents which are susceptible to temperature, causing thermo labile metabolites to degrade (18). For extracting analytes from solid matrices, novel extraction techniques such as supercritical fluid extraction (SFE) and pressurized solvent extraction (PSE) have been developed [22]. SFE is a comparatively recent and an operative separation technology for extracting essential oils from various plant sources. Extracts could be applied as a viable substrate for pharmaceutical medications and additives in the perfume, cosmetics, and food industries. SFE has been shown to be active for essential oil separation and its derivatives for application in the food and pharmaceutical industries. This is found to yield high-quality essential oils which have more acceptable structures other than those obtained by orthodox hydro-distillation.

2.1.2 Trans-esterification

Both homogeneous and heterogeneous catalysis have been used to trans-esterify biomass such as microalgal oils for biodiesel synthesis. Because it catalyzes the reaction at low temperature and atmospheric pressure and can produce a significant conversion yield in a short period, homogeneous alkaline catalysis has been the most widely utilized method for biodiesel production. Alkaline catalysts including sodium hydroxide (NaOH) and potassium hydroxide (KOH) are extensively employed; however, because of the high free fatty acid concentration in microalgal oils, alkaline catalysts cause the free fatty acids in oils to generate soap and are not suited for microalgal biodiesel generation. As the content of free fatty acids is greater than 1%, acid catalysts are utilized to overcome the constraint of high free fatty acid content [23]. Sulfuric acid (H_2SO_4) and hydrochloric acid are the most used acid catalysts (HCl). In comparison to alkaline catalysts, they require longer response times and a higher temperature. Initially, an acid catalyst is utilized in some research to convert free fatty acids into esters by esterification. After the free fatty acid content in the oils has been decreased to less than 1%, the oils undergo a second transesterification phase employing an alkaline catalyst. Regardless of the excellent conversion yields achieved by homogeneous catalysts, catalyst loss occurs after the process. In this regard, heterogeneous catalysts are known to contribute significantly to the future for their advantages in terms of recovery and reuse [24].

2.2 Thermochemical conversion processes

This is a cost-effective technology. Dry (non-aqueous) and hydrothermal techniques are two types of dry (non-aqueous) procedures [20]. Biomass undergoes structural breakdown which degrades to condensable vapors, and eventually disintegrating to gaseous molecules in a dry thermochemical transformation method as the temperature rises. A better understanding of everything from the process of decomposition of a single component to the technoeconomic evaluation of the biofuel sector is needed to achieve commercial synthesis of biofuels via thermochemical transformation of biomass [25].

2.2.1 Conventional combustion

This is defined as the oxidative chemical reaction that produces light, heat, smoke, and gases in a flame front when combustible elements (hydrogen and carbon) are ignited in fuels. Nitrogen is relatively inert, though it burns endothermically with oxygen at high temperatures to generate the undesirable NOx pollutants [26]. Combustion techniques now provide a significant amount of biomass-based renewable energy [27]. Wood, dry leaves, hard vegetable husks, rice husks, and dried animal manure are all examples of biomass that can be burned in combustion plants. An exothermic chemical reaction occurs during the combustion process. When biomass is burn't in the presence of oxygen, chemical energy is released. At about 800 to 1000° C, combustion occurs inside the combustion chambers. It's worth noting that the biomass utilized to produce biofuels by combustion must have a moisture content of less than 50%. Traditional wood use is inefficient (sometimes as low as 10%) and causes pollution with dust and soot. The adoption of considerably improved heating systems, such as those that are automated, have catalytic gas cleaning, and use standardized fuel, has resulted from technological developments [25].

Effective biomass-to-electricity/heat conversion is achievable because of fluidized bed technologies and better gas purification. Biomass co-combustion, particularly in coal-fired power plants, is considered a single most rapidly developed biomass conversion route in numerous EU countries (including Spain, Germany, and the Netherlands). The benefits of co-firing are clear, with features such as improved total electrical efficiency (often about 40%) because of existing plant economies of scale, and little to non-existent investment costs when high-quality fuels such as pellets are utilized [26, 28]. Furthermore, direct avoided emissions are significant due to the direct substitution of coal. Since several coal-fired power plants are completely depreciated, co-firing is generally a very beneficial greenhouse gas (GHG) countermeasures alternative. Additionally, biomass combustion reduces sulfur and other emissions. Because many plants currently have some co-firing capability, there is a growing need for increased co-firing shares (up to 40%) [21].

2.2.2 Carbonization

Carbonization is the process of converting waste biomass into high-carbon, high-energy charcoal [10]. It redefines renewable energy and power producing principles. Char is made through a pyrolysis process in which biomass is burned to high temperatures in an inert atmosphere until the absorbed volatiles are released, hence increasing its heating value and energy content. Carbonization is an old process that is still employed today, but the increasing interest in it, particularly with biomass, stems from the fact that it opens new commercial and scientific opportunities. The carbon in the created char may be removed to make the valuable graphite and graphene. On a weight basis, the efficiency of these archaic systems is regarded to be quite low. For such operations, the wood to charcoal conversion rate is predicted to be between 6 and 12 tonnes of wood per tonne of charcoal [29]. Carbonization, also known as "dry wood distillation", removes most the wood's volatile components. Carbon accumulates mostly as the oxygen and hydrogen levels in the wood decline. The wood experiences a variety of physico-chemical changes as the temperature rises. The majority of water evaporates between 100 and 170°C, and gases, including condensable vapors like CO and CO2, between 170 and 270°C. Following that, condensable vapors (those with long carbon chain molecules) produce pyrolysis oil, which is used to generate chemicals or fuels. Exothermic reactions are defined as those that occur between 270 and 280°C and are characterized by the spontaneous creation of heat.

The advancement of industries such as the charcoal industry has resulted in significant improvements in production efficiency, with commercial synthesis, particularly in Brazil, currently with efficiency levels of >30%. The three main methods of generating charcoal are internally heated (by controlled burning of the raw material), externally heated (using fuelwood or fossil fuels), and hot circulating gas. Internally fired charcoal kilns are the prevalent type of kiln. It is estimated that these kilns waste 10–20% of the wood (w/w), with another 60% (w/w) lost in the transformation to, and emission of gases into the atmosphere [29]. Externally heated reactors fully eliminate oxygen, yielding higher-quality charcoal on commercial scale. They do, however, need the application of an external fuel source, which can be obtained from "producer gas" once pyrolysis has started.

2.2.3 Liquefaction

Thermochemical transformation of biomass to liquid fuels in a hot, pressurized water environ long enough to disintegrate the solid biopolymeric framework into predominantly liquid constituents is known as biomass hydrothermal liquefaction [30]. Hydrothermal processing temperatures range from 523 to 647 K, with working pressures ranging from 4 to 22 megapascal (MPa). The technique is meant to treat wet materials without the necessity for drying and provide access to ionic process parameters using a liquid water processing medium. The temperature is high enough to trigger pyrolytic process in biopolymers, and the pressure is high enough to control the liquid water processing phase. Hydrothermal method is classified into three distinct stages based on the severity of the working conditions. At temperatures <520 K, hydrothermal carbonization happens [17]. Hydrochar is the main product, and it resembles low-rank coal in qualities. The hydrochar from microalgae is largely made up of the carbohydrate and protein fractions, with the lipid fraction remaining intact, allowing the lipids to be recovered during hydrothermal carbonization.

At intermediate temperatures between 520 and 647 K, this process is called hydrothermal liquefaction (HTL), a promising thermochemical liquefaction technique and it produces a liquid fuel called bio-crude. Biocrude is like petroleum crude, and it may be used to make all the petroleum distillate fuel products. Gasification reactions take control at temperatures above 647 K, and the process is known as hydrothermal gasification, which creates synthetic fuel gas. One of the merits of hydrothermal gasification over liquefaction stems from the fact that the water phase that follows gasification contains less organic carbon, resulting in improved carbon efficiency [31]. In each case, the underlying goal is to remove oxygen to produce a final product which has a higher energy density. Unlike HTL, thermochemical liquefaction of biomass has received recognition in recent years as it provides a greater energy density and has a faster reaction time, and it can be used on a wider range of materials. HTL can efficiently treat wet and dry biomass without lipid content limitations, from lignocellulosic to organic waste. The product created in this process is known as bio-crude, which is the renewable analog to oil, because it is an energy-dense intermediate that may be refined to a fuel [22].

2.2.4 Pyrolysis

By adding heat to a feedstock in the absence of oxygen, long chain molecules are broken down into short chain molecules through pyrolysis [32]. **Figure 2** depicts different bioenergy production routes of pyrolysis. Pyrolysis occurs at temperatures between 300°C and 700°C while the mild pyrolysis know as torrefaction (of wood chip) is evident at temperatures below 300°C [9]. The process is used in the manufacturing of syngas from biomass or waste as input (a mixture of hydrogen, volatile organic compounds, and carbon monoxide). By modifying the process settings, it is necessary to synthesize fluids similar to diesel and a variety of various products. Because of a greater understanding of the physical and chemical parameters that control pyrolytic reactions, the optimisation of reactor settings required for certain forms of pyrolysis has been made possible. More research is currently ongoing

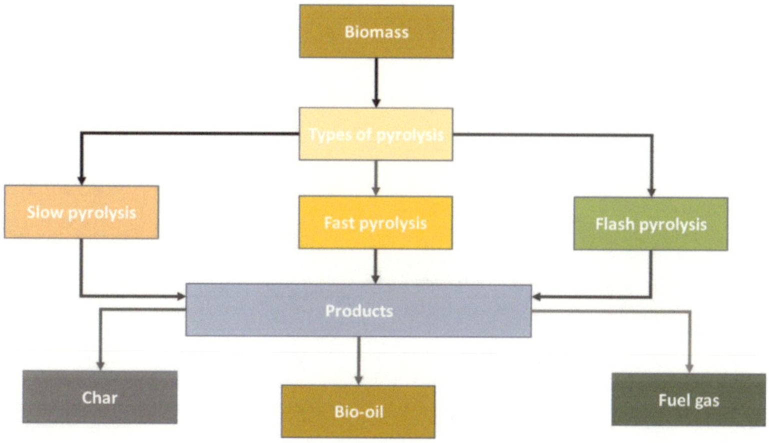

Figure 2.
Pathways of pyrolysis processes for bioenergy production adapted from [32].

to produce hydrogen using high-pressure reactors and producing alcohol from pyrolytic oil using low-pressure catalytic techniques (which require zeolites) [20]. The advantages of pyrolysis and gasification is the conversion of their solid materials into vapor which are further burnt in turbines, providing fuel flexibility and security. The heat required to drive the chemical reactions that generate syngas is a key disadvantage of both technologies. As a result, some fuel must be used in the syngas production process.

2.2.5 Gasification

Gasification is the process of partially oxidizing an organic feedstock to generate syngas (a mixture of hydrogen, volatile short chain organic compounds, and carbon monoxide) [33]. The fuel is typically biomass or waste, and the chemical proportions in the syngas can be controlled by changing the process conditions. The conversion of CO_2 from outside of a biomass into fuels such as the those in their synthetic forms are used in this technique for meet high carbon demands from renewable sources. The huge carbonate deposits on the planet and carbonates arising from the sea, containing about 360 parts per million (ppm) of CO_2 by volume, might all be used as renewable carbon resources [21]. As demonstrated in **Figure 3**, it can be produced using biomass gasification techniques and then converted into a variety of chemicals and fuels. For continuous water splitting, these can be subjected to electrochemical, biochemical, thermochemical, microbial, photolytic, and biophotolytic operations. Biomass represents about 10.5% of total energy utilization in most developed countries, according to estimates provided by the International Energy Agency (IEA) from a study of 133 countries in 2000.

2.3 Biochemical conversion processes

Biochemical conversion mechanisms disintegrate biomass using enzymes produced by bacteria and other microbes. Microbes are employed to carry out the biomass transformation operation in most cases. Biochemical conversion is one of the few methods for extracting energy from biomass that is environmentally friendly.

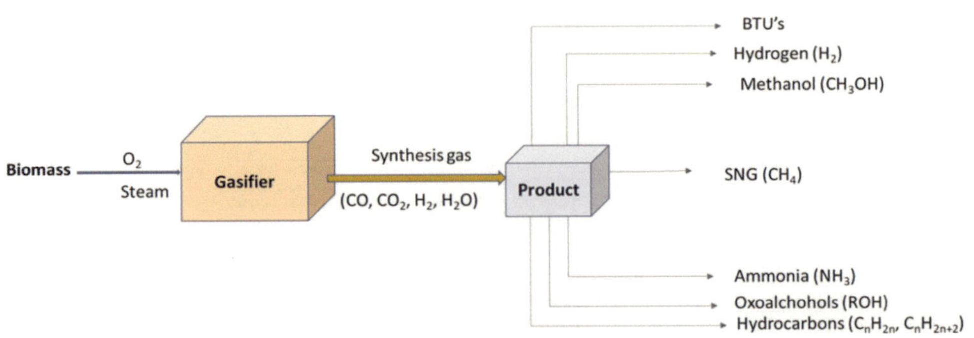

Figure 3.
Sequence for derivation of syngas from biomass adapted from [20].

2.3.1 Fermentation mechanism

Fermentation is a biochemical technique applied for bioethanol production after biomass pretreament (makes the cellulose accessible) and hydrolysis (breaks the polysaccharide in feedstock to free sugar molecules). Fermentation is a metabolic operation that uses enzymes to induce chemical reactions in organic feedstocks. There are three fermentation processes that are frequently employed in bioethanol synthesis: separate hydrolysis and fermentation (SHF), simultaneous saccharification and fermentation (SSF), and simultaneous saccharification and co-fermentation (SSCF). Separate hydrolysis and fermentation (SHF) is the most popular approach utilized in bioethanol synthesis. The hydrolysis of lignocellulosic biomass is excluded from the ethanol fermentation process in SHF. It is possible to deploy enzymes at elevated temperatures for improved efficiency while fermenting microbes can be utilized at mild temperatures for optimal sugar consumption. SSF and SSCF have a brief entire operation since the enzymatic hydrolysis and fermentation processes take place concurrently to keep the level of glucose as minimal as possible during the operation. In SSF, the fermentation of glucose is segregated from the fermentation of pentoses, but in SSCF, the fermentation of glucose and pentoses are carried out in the same facility [34]. SSF and SSCF are preferable over SHF because the procedure can be completed in the same vessel. The advantages of both procedures are cheaper costs, larger ethanol yields, and reduced operating times [35].

Fermentation of bioethanol can be done in a batch, fed-batch, repeated batch, or continuous mode, depending on the process. In a **batch method**, the feedstock is delivered at the start of the operation and the media is not added or removed throughout the operation [36]. This mode of fermentation is beneficial due to the absence of labour skills and ease of biomass management [37]. **Continuous method** is accomplished by continuously introducing feedstock, culture medium, and nutrients to a bioreactor comprising functional microbes [38]. The merits of continuous systems over batch and fed-batch systems include increased yield, smaller bioreactor volumes, and lower capital and operating expense [37]. **Fed-batch fermentation** is an integration of batch and continuous modes of fermentation that involves the input of feedstock into the fermentor without withdrawing the medium from the fermentor. It has been successfully employed to mitigate the issue of biomass inhibition in batch operations. Comparing this procedure to other modes of fermentation, it accounts for an increased efficiency, produces more dissolved oxygen in the medium, requires less fermentation duration, and has a less harmful impact on the medium constituents [39].

2.3.2 Anaerobic digestion

Anaerobic digestion (AD) is a mechanism in which microbes disintegrate organic matter in the absence of oxygen, including animal dung, wastewater biosolids, and food residues. In order to produce biogas (biomethane), anaerobic digestion must occur in an airtight vessel known as a bioreactor, which can be built in a variety of forms and dimensions to accommodate the site's and biomass requirements. These bioreactors include diverse microbial populations that decompose (or digest) the residue and generate biogas and digestate (the solid and liquid substance end-products of the AD operation), which are released from the digester once the waste has been broken down [40]. However, **anaerobic co-digestion** is the method of combining different organic substances in a single digester. Co-digested resources comprise manure, food wastes (including processing, distribution, and consumer generated materials), energy crops, crop wastes, and fats, oils, and greases (FOG) from restaurant grease traps. Co-digestion can raise the quantity of biogas produced from organic residue that is low yielding or challenging to digest.

The mechanism of anaerobic digestion is divided into four steps: hydrolysis, acidogenesis, acetogenesis, and methanogenesis. In single-stage batch bioreactors, all residues are fed at the same time, and all four approaches as shown in **Figure 4** are permitted to take place in the same reactor consecutively; the compost is then discharged after a specified retention interval or after the termination of biogas generation [39]. **Hydrolysis** is employed to break down organic macromolecules into their constituent parts, which can then be used by acidogenic bacteria [41]. During **acidogenesis**, acidogenic microbes are capable to manufacture intermediate volatile fatty acids (VFAs) and other compounds by accumulating the products of hydrolysis via their cell membranes and converting them into other products [42]. **Acetogenesis** is the mechanism by which these high VFAs and other intermediates are transformed into acetate, with H_2 and/or CO_2 being generated during the operation [42]. **Methanogenesis** is the ultimate step of anaerobic digestion, during which readily available intermediates are consumed by methanogenic microbes, resulting in the production of methane. The environmental requirements of methanogenesis are as follows: greater pH than earlier phases of anaerobic digestion, as well as lower redox potential [43].

2.4 Biological process

Using microbes (microalgae and Cyanobacteria or blue-green algae), it is possible to produce biogas by a variety of processes, including biophotolysis, photo fermentation and dark fermentation.

2.4.1 Biophotolysis

Biological photolysis occurs when light or a microbiological species is present and leads to the dissociation of H2O into molecular H2 and O2. Biophotolysis is a metabolic mechanism that is reliant on light and can be classified into two types: direct photolysis and indirect photolysis [44, 45].

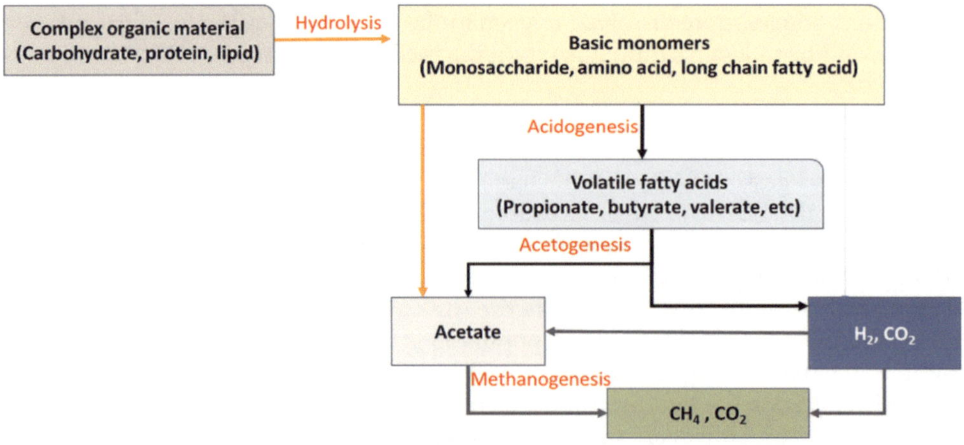

Figure 4.
Four-step anaerobic digestion process adapted from [43] with modifications.

Direct Biophotolysis is a light-dependent route for hydrogen formation which occurs in two stages: first, the breakdown of H2O molecules in photosynthesis (Eq. 1), accompanied by the synthesis of hydrogen facilitated by hydrogenases (Eq. 2), which occurs in green algae and cyanobacteria and depends on light energy [46].

$$2H_2O \rightarrow 4H^+ + 4e^- + O_2 \tag{1}$$

$$4H^+ + 4e^- \rightarrow 2H_2 \tag{2}$$

Direct bio-photolysis comprises H2O oxidation as well as a light-dependent electron exchange to the [Fe] hydrogenase, which leads to H2 generation through photosynthesis [47]. Direct bio-photolysis was based on the photosynthetic ability of microalgae and cyanobacteria to quickly breakdown H2O into oxygen and hydrogen. Microalgae can employ solar energy via proton and electron obtained from the H2O—splitting process, but cyanobacteria receive their energy from photosynthetic activity to enhance H2 generation, which takes place by direct adsorption of light and electron transfer to two enzyme cateories—hydrogenase and nitrogenase [48]—responsible for the enhancement of the transformation of hydrogen ions to hydrogen gas [49]. These techniques showed tremendous potential, but they also had major limitations, such as the discrepancies of direct bio-photolysis to simultaneously generate H_2 and O_2, as well as the fact that the O_2 produced by bacteria throughout the procedure prevents considerable H2 production from being achieved.

During indirect biophototlysis, photosynthetic H2 can be formed by green algae amid sulfur deprivation conditions, as opposed to direct bio photolysis [48]. The restriction of sulfur—nutrients in the growth media of green algae prompted a reversible impediment in the O_2 photosynthetic operation of the green algae. Sulfur deprivation triggers a decrease in the activity of the photosystem II (PSII), which is responsible for enhancing electron extraction from water through photochemical oxidation, and the photosynthetic process decreases below the respiration activity, resulting in a decrease in oxygen discharge below the amount of oxygen expended by respiration [50]. The synergistic effect between photosynthesis and respiration attributed to sulfur deprivation leads to a net utilization of oxygen by cells, which enables the growth environment to become anoxic [51]. The potential to develop ways to reuse constituents of the photobioreactor and optimize the cost of chemical nutrients that aids algae development which account for around 80% of the overall operational costs are two of the setbacks of efficient commercial application of indirect bio-photolysis for biogas synthesis [52, 53].

2.4.2 Photo fermentation

Under anoxic environments with light, photosynthetic microbes are capable of converting the majority of organic acids or volatile fatty acids (VFA) into biohydrogen and carbon dioxide [54]. Nitrogenase is the enzyme responsible for the majority of the biohydrogen produced by photosynthetic bacteria. Luminous light has a significant effect on the synthesis of nitrogenase [55]. It is essential for biohydrogen synthesis that the feedstock have an appropriate ratio of carbon and nitrogen sources (C/N ratio). Nitrogen constraints have been shown to modify the metabolic activities of photosynthetic bacteria, directing it more towards the discharge of extra energy and reducing power in the form of biohydrogen. The process of photo fermentation is influenced by some variables, such as light intensity, inoculum age, nutrient type, and temperature. Temperature has a significant impact on the metabolic routes' ability to shift to greater biohydrogen synthesis [56]. The biohydrogen metabolism of purple non-sulfur bacteria is primarily controlled by the activity of the enzymes; nitrogenase and hydrogenase [56]. As part of the process, the nitrogenase enzyme generates biohydrogen under nitrogen-deficient environments (Eq. 3), where the hydrogenase enzyme oxidizes the biohydrogen in order to reuse electrons, protons, and ATP for employ in energy metabolism [57, 58]. Because hydrogenase enzyme can operate in any direction, according to Eq. 4, some of them are physiologically dedicated to utilizing biohydrogen (in the presence of appropriate electron acceptors) while others are responsible for the synthesis of biohydrogen under stringent anaerobiosis [59].

Light

$$2H^+ + 2e^- + 4ATP \rightarrow H2v + 4ADP + 4Pi \quad (3)$$

Nitrogenase

$$H_2 \rightarrow 2H^+ + 2e^- \quad (4)$$

Nitrogenase

The overall metabolic route for the photo fermentation system is given as:

$$\text{Substrate} \rightarrow \text{TCA cycle} \rightarrow \text{NAD/NADH} \rightarrow \text{Ferredoxin} \rightarrow \text{Nitrogenase} \rightarrow H_2.$$

2.4.3 Dark fermentation

Anoxic and certain microalgae (green algae) perform heterotrophic fermentation on carbohydrate-based substrates in the absence of light energy, resulting in the synthesis of hydrogen [60]. When it comes to dark fermentation, the practicality of producing hydrogen is dependent on the fact that hydrogen can be generated by heterotopic bacteria satellites that are situated in the algae biomass slurries. The impediment of H_2-consuming microorganisms in a multi-microbial consortium that disintegrates algal biomass for the generation of H2 is a vital issue that presents a barrier to the effective use of dark fermentation technology. Dark fermentation is a mechanism in which organic feedstock are transformed by fermentative bacteria into biohydrogen, volatile fatty acids (VFA), and carbon dioxide in the absence of light. Carbohydrates (mostly glucose) are the primary energy sources for this mechanism, which results in the production of biohydrogen as well as volatile fatty acids (VFAs) such as acetic acid and butyric acid. Eqs. (5) and (6) demonstrate variation in product yield when acetic acid or butyric acid is the sole VFA product, the highest output of 4 and 2 mol H_2/mol glucose respectively can be obtained. A lesser output is frequently attained in reality, because glucose is not only utilized for biohydrogen generation, but also to nourish and sustain the development of the microbes [60]. Biohydrogen generation via this approach can be influenced by substrate, inoculum, bacteria growth conditions, and other operating parameters.

$$C_6H_{12}O_6 + 2H_2O \rightarrow 4H_2 + 2CH_3COOH + 2CO_2 \quad (5)$$

$$C_6H_{12}O_6 + 2H_2O \rightarrow 2H_2 + CH_3CH_2CH_2COOH + 2CO_2 \quad (6)$$

2.4.4 Proposed multi-stage bioreactor for biogas production

A multi-stage bioreactor can be employed for the production of biohydrogen or hythane. A four-stage bioreactor produces significant amounts of hydrogen and recovers energy. In the first step which involves direct biophotolysis, blue-green algae employ visible light whereas photosynthetic microorganisms utilize unfiltered infrared rays in the second stage photo-fermentative reactor. The second phase photosynthetic reactor discharge is passed to a third stage dark fermentation for microbial transformation of substrates into H_2 and organic acids. The fourth stage involves converting organic acid (from dark fermentation) into biohydrogen via microbial cell electrolysis in the dark (ideally at night or in low light) [47]. The growing interest in hythane has led to substantial study into dark fermentation of biomass for hythane generation in two-stage processes. Hythane is a gaseous combination of H_2 (10–30%) and CH_4 (70–90%) used as a substitute to methane in the automotive sector. Hythane is now produced mostly from fossil fuels, however using sustainable sources will significantly minimize greenhouse gas emissions. The efficient biotechnology process of two-stage anaerobic digestion (AD) can generate biohythane in two-stages, dark fermentation, and methanogenic phases, for H2 and CH_4 synthesis respectively. Because H_2 is a sustainable energy source, its existence in hythane facilitates the reduction of CO_2 and NOx emissions. This product (hythane) is a clean-burning green energy that could be used as industrial biogas [61]. However, various issues need to be addressed before the multi-stage bioreactor technology may be efficiently utilized [62].

3. Economic and environmental implications, limitations and prospects

3.1 Economic feasibility of biofuel compared to fossil fuel

The rise of international bioenergy markets is critical to maximizing the utilization of global biomass resources and market potential [63]. The global biomass and biofuel markets, on the other hand, are still expanding and are subject to tariffs and non-tariff trade restrictions, resulting in substantial and often unexpected changes in the international trade flows [64, 65]. In contrast to fossil fuel markets, bioenergy markets have limited trade flows, which exacerbates these problems. Additionally, feedstock supply (easily accessible), offtake (easily secured contracts), capacity utilization (75%) and sustainability compliance are key factors required for bioenergy plant establishment [63, 65, 66]. According to Bloomberg New Energy Finance [65] the annual value of renewable energy capacity can rise from 395 USD billion in 2020 to 460 USD billion in 2030. This can result in bioenergy market been expanded by 7 USD trillion for the next two decades. The use of biofuel can be economically and environmentally advantageous to both developed and undeveloped countries [63, 65, 66]. Consequentially, biofuels have the potential to be a sustainable, renewable, and viable energy source, especially in the transportation sector. This makes the biofuels industry to have many potentials with ecological and economic benefits [67, 68].

However, when compared to the gasoline cost of production (from fossil fuel), which is about 0.3 USD – 0.4 USD/LGE (liter per gasoline equivalent) in 2020, sugarcane and corn ethanol production cost is approximately 0.40–0.50 USD/LGE, making ethanol less competitive commercially [69]. Likewise, sugar beet, maize, or wheat ethanol cost between 0.6 USD and 0.8 USD/LGE. The comparatively higher price and energy content of ethanol are significant drawback to its utilization as a viable sustainable biofuel and as a gasoline additive. The energy content of a gallon of ethanol is approximately one-third that of a gallon of gasoline. Consequently, ethanol has not been economically viable when likened to gasoline; however, with government incentives, the cost of producing ethanol will be significantly reduced [70]. In actual fact, when compared to fossil fuels, the use of biofuels will minimize the net cost of fuel through biofuel regulations which may reduce fossil fuel use by less than 2.5% at a cost of 67 USD billion plus a 6 USD billion gas tax [63, 65, 66]. The primary concern is that, in the near future, more biofuels will make overall fuel costs more expensive than fossil fuels. Notwithstanding, the long-term savings in fuel prices may offset the initial expenditures [71].

3.2 Environmental impacts and benefit

Replacing fossil fuels with biofuels (fuels made from renewable organic material) is possible to reduce conventional and greenhouse pollutant emissions. Additionally, producing energy from biomass has substantial distinctive environmental benefits. The abatement of acid rain, soil erosion, water pollution, and landfill pressure, while also providing habitat for wildlife and improving forest reserves through proper management are among some of the advantages [72, 73]. Although there are certain uncertainties about employing biomass indirect combustion, gasification, or pyrolysis processes can provide still significant environmental benefits. For instance, the production of SO2, CO2, and ash is often much lower in biomass power systems than in coal combustion and conversion systems [68, 72, 74]. The sources and side effects of coal combustion which makes biomass combustion more advantageous include reduce emission Hazardous air pollutants (HAP) and SO2 of the following [75]. Hence, sulfur and nitrogen content of biomass combustion are so low to be neglected.

Biomass, on the surface, appears to be an appealing renewable fuel for boilers, even though its composition is liable to change. For example, the ash composition of biomass differs significantly from the ash composition of coal. Also, many undesired processes in combustion furnaces and power boilers are caused by metals in ash when combined with other fuel constituents such as silica, sulfur, and chlorine [72, 73, 75, 77]. Conversely, in biomass combustors, elements such as Si, K, Na, S, Cl, P, Ca, Mg, and Fe are engaged in processes that can contribute to ash fouling and slagging [76, 77]. The effects of biomass content on combustion are non-hazardous and provide great environmental safety. The principal benefit of using biomass energy is the reduction of greenhouse gas pollution. Furthermore, reburning of biomass fly ash as a fuel-flexible material can provide well-burnt ashes for common fuels. Additionally, eliminating ash stabilization (chemical hardness) can significantly enhance ash potential. This can reduce NOX emissions by 20% while slightly increasing CO emissions. However, the rise of CO level is usually around 100–140 ppm, which are within the permissible average limit of 150 ppm CO [67, 75, 77]. Also, the ash produced can be returned into the forest, replenishing the nutrients loss by the soil. Therefore, the nutrient compounds in the ash can be recycled or repurposed as fertilizers for good sustainable energy practices based on biomass.

3.3 Limitations of bioenergy production

Improper burning of biomass releases CO2, N2O, CH4, and other hydrocarbons, all of which are detrimental to health. Human activity contributes 60% to global climate change [67, 73]. Activities such as using chemicals like chlorofluorocarbons (15%), agricultural biomass (12%), land-use alterations (9%) and other human activities (4%) also contribute to high levels of greenhouse gases in the atmosphere [68, 75]. Currently, global greenhouse gas emissions are increasing year on year. CO2 has been increasingly linked to global warming [78, 79]. The greenhouse effect caused by gases (with three or more atoms) with higher heat capacity than O2 and N2. The primary human-caused greenhouse gas is CO2 (CO2). CO2 emissions from fossil and biomass fuel combustion significantly contribute to the greenhouse effect and global warming. The reactivity of ash in biomass combustion can be detrimental. In the diverse activities of this sustainable feedstock, trace elements found in biomass play a significant role. Trace elements (usually metals) are biochemically important, as well as nutritionally and environmentally [76–78]. The amounts of trace element levels are related to biomass species, sample growing site, plant age, and distance from the pollution source. Metals such as Cd, and Hg ions are potentially detrimental to plants. As boilers flue gas undergoes chemical processes, phase transitions, and precipitation because of a wide temperature differential, high element concentrations in both biomass and boiler fly ash are essential [9, 13, 14, 75–77].

3.4 Potentials and future work considerations for effective bioenergy production

Since fossil fuels have caused havoc on the ecosystem, it is critical to explore solutions. Biofuels can provide energy requirements while limiting environmental impact by exploiting readily available biomass as feedstocks. According to life-cycle analyses, advanced biofuels and cellulosic biofuels have the potential to achieve baseline GHG reduction targets of 50% and 60%, respectively (including indirect land-use change). Although transportation currently contributes around 23% of all CO2 emissions caused by energy use. To achieve a 50% decrease in energy-related CO2 emissions by 2050, sustainably produced biofuels could account for 27% of total transportation fuel consumption [63, 66, 80]. In essence, biofuels derived from waste biomass could be the most sustainable energy alternative to fossil fuels in the transportation industry [81–83]. Nevertheless, concerns about the biomass supply chain, energy efficiency, and product yield persist. Different processing improvement techniques, either alone or in combination with nanomaterials, may be used to tackle these problems. Advancing biomass combustion technology can result in increased conversion efficiency at a low cost. Additionally, several research have reported on the use of nanomaterials in conjunction with microwave, mechanical vibration, pulsation, and ultrasonication to enhance biofuel production [19, 20]. Compared to other nanocatalysts, ferrofluids are easy to separate and move in oscillating magnetic fields [76, 77]. Therefore, they could be used with some of the technologies to improve the biomass-based energy economy.

Continuous biofuel synthesis using microchemical and Coiled Flow Inverters (CFI) are also possible. Heat transfer fluids (HTF) and ionic liquids (IL) could also be employed in biofuel production to save energy. In the future, the use of biomass in biofuel synthesis and utilization is very promising to be explored to further improve the overall process economy. According to the EU's Renewable Energy Directive (RED), biofuels must meet certain sustainability standards before they may contribute to the binding national targets each member state [63, 65]. Several attempts to develop sustainability criteria and standards for biofuels are underway in this section. Other international initiatives include the Global Bioenergy Partnership, the Roundtable on Sustainable Biofuels (RSB), and ISO (International Organization for

Standardization) standards aimed at increasing bioenergy production's efficiency and lowering emissions [63, 64].

4. Conclusion

Bioenergy will be the most important sustainable energy source in the coming decades since it provides a cost-effective substitute to fossil fuels. The availability of low-cost biofuel and a wide range of viable forms of biofuel for the generation of heat, steam, electricity, and gas, as well as for use as a transportation fuel, will be critical to the growth of bioenergy. Many different sources, such as crops, grasses, leaves, manure, fruit and vegetable wastes, algae or other lignocellulose biomass can be used, and the procedure can be done on both small and large scale. This enables the production of biofuel everywhere in the entire globe. Significant advancements in process performance of existing technologies, as well as the establishment of novel techniques for biomass conversion, mixing, process monitoring, and process control, are required for further biofuel facility development. However, the major concern is lowering the cost of biofuel synthesis. Consequently, the biorefinery concept is required to more thoroughly exploit sustainable biomass and to produce additional value-added coproducts (e.g. bio-based products from lignin) that would lower the cost of biofuel synthesis. As a result, biofuel will be more cost efficient than fossil fuels to enhance effective transition to bioeconomy.

Author details

Ifeanyi Michael Smarte Anekwe[1]*, Edward Kwaku Armah[2] and Emmanuel Kweinor Tetteh[3]

1 School of Chemical and Metallurgical Engineering, University of the Witwatersrand, Johannesburg, South Africa

2 Department of Applied Chemistry, School of Chemical and Biochemical Sciences, C.K. Tedam University of Technology and Applied Sciences, Navrongo, Ghana

3 Department of Chemical Engineering, Durban University of Technology, Durban, South Africa

*Address all correspondence to: anekwesmarte@gmail.com

References

[1] Uihlein A, Schebek L. Environmental impacts of a lignocellulose feedstock biorefinery system: An assessment. Biomass and Bioenergy. 2009;**33**(5): 793-802

[2] IEA. Energy Technology Perspectives. Scenarios & Strategies to 2050. Paris: IEA/OECD; 2006

[3] IPCC. The IPCC Special Report on Emissions Scenarios (SRES). Geneva: IPCC; 2000

[4] Octave S, Thomas D. Biorefinery: Toward an industrial metabolism. Biochimie. 2009;**91**(6):659-664

[5] Ruane J, Sonnino A, Agostini A. Bioenergy and the potential contribution of agricultural biotechnologies in developing countries. Biomass and Bioenergy. 2010;**34**(10):1427-1439

[6] Parawira W. Biodiesel production from Jatropha curcas: A review. Scientific Research and Essays. 2010; **5**(14):1796-1808

[7] Demirbas A. Political, economic and environmental impacts of biofuels: A review. Applied Energy. 2009;**86**:S108-SS17

[8] Singh A, Olsen SI, Nigam PS. A viable technology to generate third-generation biofuel. Journal of Chemical Technology and Biotechnology. 2011;**86**(11): 1349-1353

[9] Sims RE, Mabee W, Saddler JN, Taylor M. An overview of second generation biofuel technologies. Bioresource Technology. 2010;**101**(6): 1570-1580

[10] Costa JAV, De Morais MG. The role of biochemical engineering in the production of biofuels from microalgae. Bioresource Technology. 2011;**102**(1):2-9

[11] Cheng JJ, Timilsina GR. Status and barriers of advanced biofuel technologies: A review. Renewable Energy. 2011;**36**(12):3541-3549

[12] Van Gerpen J. Biodiesel processing and production. Fuel Processing Technology. 2005;**86**(10):1097-1107

[13] Kumar A, Ergas S, Yuan X, Sahu A, Zhang Q, Dewulf J, et al. Enhanced CO2 fixation and biofuel production via microalgae: Recent developments and future directions. Trends in Biotechnology. 2010;**28**(7):371-380

[14] Khan SA, Hussain MZ, Prasad S, Banerjee U. Prospects of biodiesel production from microalgae in India. Renewable and Sustainable Energy Reviews. 2009;**13**(9):2361-2372

[15] Xiu S, Shahbazi A. Bio-oil production and upgrading research: A review. Renewable and Sustainable Energy Reviews. 2012;**16**(7):4406-4414

[16] Huber GW, Corma A. Synergies between bio-and oil refineries for the production of fuels from biomass. Angewandte Chemie, International Edition. 2007;**46**(38):7184-7201

[17] Jingura RM, Musademba D, Kamusoko R. A review of the state of biomass energy technologies in Zimbabwe. Renewable and Sustainable Energy Reviews. 2013;**26**: 652-659

[18] Demirbaş A. Biomass resource facilities and biomass conversion processing for fuels and chemicals. Energy Conversion and Management. 2001;**42**(11):1357-1378

[19] Faaij A. Modern biomass conversion technologies. Mitigation and Adaptation Strategies for Global Change. 2006; **11**(2):343-375

[20] Adams P, Bridgwater T, Lea-Langton A, Ross A, Watson I. Biomass conversion technologies. In: Greenhouse Gas Balances of Bioenergy Systems. Cambridge, Academic Press: Elsevier; 2018. pp. 107-139

[21] Suopajärvi H, Pongrácz E, Fabritius T. The potential of using biomass-based reducing agents in the blast furnace: A review of thermochemical conversion technologies and assessments related to sustainability. Renewable and Sustainable Energy Reviews. 2013;**25**:511-528

[22] Dutta J. Engineering of Polysaccharides via Nanotechnology. In Multifaceted Development and Application of Biopolymers for Biology, Biomedicine and Nanotechnology. Berlin, Heidelberg: Springer; 2013. pp. 87-134

[23] Meher LC, Sagar DV, Naik S. Technical aspects of biodiesel production by transesterification—A review. Renewable and Sustainable Energy Reviews. 2006;**10**(3):248-268

[24] Leung DY, Wu X, Leung M. A review on biodiesel production using catalyzed transesterification. Applied Energy. 2010;**87**(4): 1083-1095

[25] Rahman K, Melville L, Huq SI, Khoda S. Understanding bioenergy production and optimisation at the nanoscale–a review. Journal of Experimental Nanoscience. 2016;**11**(10): 762-775

[26] Demirbas A. Combustion systems for biomass fuel. Energy Sources, Part A: Recovery, Utilization, and Environmental Effects. 2007;**29**(4):303-312

[27] Grande L, Pedroarena I, Korili SA, Gil A. Hydrothermal liquefaction of biomass as one of the Most promising alternatives for the synthesis of advanced liquid biofuels: A review. Materials. 2021;**14**(18):5286

[28] Rizvi H, Amir A, Gupta N. Hazards and environmental effects of nanomaterials in bioenergy applications. In: Nanomaterials. Cambridge, Academic Press: Elsevier; 2021. pp. 737-744

[29] Hu B, Wang K, Wu L, Yu SH, Antonietti M, Titirici MM. Engineering carbon materials from the hydrothermal carbonization process of biomass. Advanced Materials. 2010;**22**(7):813-828

[30] Toprak S, Holzer TL. Liquefaction potential index: Field assessment. Journal of Geotechnical and Geoenvironmental Engineering. 2003; **129**(4):315-322

[31] Juang CH, Jiang T, Andrus RD. Assessing probability-based methods for liquefaction potential evaluation. Journal of Geotechnical and Geoenvironmental Engineering. 2002;**128**(7):580-589

[32] Collard F-X, Blin J. A review on pyrolysis of biomass constituents: Mechanisms and composition of the products obtained from the conversion of cellulose, hemicelluloses and lignin. Renewable and Sustainable Energy Reviews. 2014;**38**:594-608

[33] Sharma S, Meena R, Sharma A, Goyal P. Biomass conversion technologies for renewable energy and fuels: A review note. IOSR Journal of Mechanical and Civil Engineering. 2014;**11**(2):28-35

[34] Canilha L, Chandel AK, Suzane dos Santos Milessi T, Antunes FA,

Luiz da Costa Freitas W, das Graças Almeida Felipe M, da Silva SS. Bioconversion of sugarcane biomass into ethanol: An overview about composition, pretreatment methods, detoxification of hydrolysates, enzymatic saccharification, and ethanol fermentation. Journal of Biomedicine and Biotechnology. 2012;**2012**:1-15

[35] Chandel AK, Kapoor RK, Singh A, Kuhad RC. Detoxification of sugarcane bagasse hydrolysate improves ethanol production by Candida shehatae NCIM 3501. Bioresource Technology. 2007; **98**(10):1947-1950

[36] Hadiyanto H, Ariyanti D, Aini A, Pinundi D. Batch and fed-batch fermentation system on ethanol production from whey using Kluyveromyces marxianus. International Journal of Renewable Energy Development. 2013;**2**(3):127

[37] Jain A, Chaurasia SP. Bioethanol production in membrane bioreactor (MBR) system: A review. International Journal of Environmental Research and Development. 2014;**4**(4):387-394

[38] Ivanova V, Petrova P, Hristov J. Application in the ethanol fermentation of immobilized yeast cells in matrix of alginate/magnetic nanoparticles, on chitosan-magnetite microparticles and cellulose-coated magnetic nanoparticles. arXiv preprint arXiv: 11050619. 2011

[39] Cheng NG, Hasan M, Kumoro AC, Ling CF, Tham M. Production of ethanol by fed-batch fermentation. Pertanika Journal of Science & Technology. 2009; **17**(2):399-408

[40] Verma S. Anaerobic digestion of biodegradable organics in municipal solid wastes. Columbia University. 2002; 7(3):98-104

[41] Gujer W, Zehnder AJ. Conversion processes in anaerobic digestion. Water Science and Technology. 1983;**15**(8–9): 127-167

[42] Dinopoulou G, Rudd T, Lester JN. Anaerobic acidogenesis of a complex wastewater: I. the influence of operational parameters on reactor performance. Biotechnology and Bioengineering. 1988;**31**(9):958-968

[43] Meegoda JN, Li B, Patel K, Wang LB. A review of the processes, parameters, and optimization of anaerobic digestion. International Journal of Environmental Research and Public Health. 2018;**15**(10): 2224

[44] Saifuddin N, Priatharsini P. Developments in bio-hydrogen production from algae: A review. Research Journal of Applied Sciences, Engineering and Technology. 2016; **12**(9):968-982

[45] Shaishav S, Singh R, Satyendra T. Biohydrogen from algae: Fuel of the future. International Research Journal of Environmental Sciences. 2013;**2**(4): 44-47

[46] Saifuddin N, Ong M, Priatharsini P. Optimization of photosynthetic hydrogen gas production by green alga in sulfur deprived condition. Indian Journal of Science and Technology. 2016; **9**(40):93390

[47] Show K-Y, Yan Y, Ling M, Ye G, Li T, Lee D-J. Hydrogen production from algal biomass–advances, challenges and prospects. Bioresource Technology. 2018;**257**:290-300

[48] Manish S, Banerjee R. Comparison of biohydrogen production processes. International Journal of Hydrogen Energy. 2008;**33**(1):279-286

[49] Turner J, Sverdrup G, Mann MK, Maness PC, Kroposki B, Ghirardi M, et al. Renewable hydrogen production. International Journal of Energy Research. 2008;**32**(5):379-407

[50] Kosourov S, Nagy V, Shevela D, Jokel M, Messinger J, Allahverdiyeva Y. Water oxidation by photosystem II is the primary source of electrons for sustained H2 photoproduction in nutrient-replete green algae. Proceedings of the National Academy of Sciences. 2020;**117**(47): 29629-29636

[51] Benemann JR. Hydrogen production by microalgae. Journal of Applied Phycology. 2000;**12**(3–5):291-300

[52] Show K-Y, Lee D-J, Chang J-S. Bioreactor and process design for biohydrogen production. Bioresource Technology. 2011;**102**(18):8524-8533

[53] Show K-Y, Yan Y, Zong C, Guo N, Chang J-S, Lee D-J. State of the art and challenges of biohydrogen from microalgae. Bioresource Technology. 2019;**289**:121747

[54] Argun H, Kargi F. Bio-hydrogen production by different operational modes of dark and photo-fermentation: An overview. International Journal of Hydrogen Energy. 2011;**36**(13): 7443-7459

[55] Koku H, Eroğlu I, Gündüz U, Yücel M, Türker L. Aspects of the metabolism of hydrogen production by Rhodobacter sphaeroides. International Journal of Hydrogen Energy. 2002;**27** (11–12):1315-1329

[56] Basak N, Das D. The prospect of purple non-sulfur (PNS) photosynthetic bacteria for hydrogen production: The present state of the art. World Journal of Microbiology and Biotechnology. 2007; **23**(1):31-42

[57] Oh Y-K, Raj SM, Jung GY, Park S. Current status of the metabolic engineering of microorganisms for biohydrogen production. Bioresource Technology. 2011;**102**(18):8357-8367

[58] Hasyim R, Imai T, Sompong O, Sulistyowati L. Biohydrogen production from sago starch in wastewater using an enriched thermophilic mixed culture from hot spring. International Journal of Hydrogen Energy. 2011;**36**(21): 14162-14171

[59] Vignais PM, Magnin J-P, Willison JC. Increasing biohydrogen production by metabolic engineering. International Journal of Hydrogen Energy. 2006; **31**(11):1478-1483

[60] Zhang C, Kang X, Liang N, Abdullah A. Improvement of biohydrogen production from dark fermentation by cocultures and activated carbon immobilization. Energy & Fuels. 2017;**31**(11):12217-12222

[61] Cavinato C, Giuliano A, Bolzonella D, Pavan P, Cecchi F. Bio-hythane production from food waste by dark fermentation coupled with anaerobic digestion process: A long-term pilot scale experience. International Journal of Hydrogen Energy. 2012; **37**(15):11549-11555

[62] Holladay JD, Hu J, King DL, Wang Y. An overview of hydrogen production technologies. Catalysis Today. 2009;**139**(4):244-260

[63] Popp J, Lakner Z, Harangi-Rákos M, Fári M. The effect of bioenergy expansion: Food, energy, and environment. Renewable and Sustainable Energy Reviews. 2014;**32**:559-578

[64] Institute W. Biofuels for Transport: Global Potential and Implications for

Sustainable Energy and Agriculture. Sterling: Earthscan; 2012

[65] Finance BNE. Global renewable energy market outlook. Bloomberg New Energy Finance. 2011;**11**:16

[66] Searchinger T, Heimlich R, Houghton RA, Dong F, Elobeid A, Fabiosa J, et al. Use of US croplands for biofuels increases greenhouse gases through emissions from land-use change. Science. 2008;**319**(5867):1238-1240

[67] Liu Y, Cruz-Morales P, Zargar A, Belcher MS, Pang B, Englund E, et al. Biofuels for a sustainable future. Cell. 2021;**184**(6):1636-1647

[68] Azadbakht M, Ardebili SMS, Rahmani M. Potential for the production of biofuels from agricultural waste, livestock, and slaughterhouse waste in Golestan province, Iran. Biomass Conversion and Biorefinery. 2021;**2021**: 1-11

[69] EIA. Analysis & Projections. 2020

[70] Yacobucci BD. Fuel Ethanol: Background and Public Policy Issues. Washington, DC: Congressional Research Service; 2007. p. RL-30369

[71] Anekwe IMS, Khotseng L, Isa YM. The Place of Biofuel in Sustainable Living; Prospects and Challenges; Reference Module in Earth Systems and Environmental Sciences. Amsterdam, The Netherlands: Elsevier; 2021

[72] Vujanović M, Wang Q, Mohsen M, Duić N, Yan J. Recent progress in sustainable energy-efficient technologies and environmental impacts on energy systems. Applied Energy. 2021;**283**:116280

[73] Dell'Anna F. Green jobs and energy efficiency as strategies for economic growth and the reduction of environmental impacts. Energy Policy. 2021;**149**:112031

[74] Ahmed I, Zia MA, Afzal H, Ahmed S, Ahmad M, Akram Z, et al. Socio-economic and environmental impacts of biomass valorisation: A strategic drive for sustainable bioeconomy. Sustainability. 2021;**13**(8):4200

[75] Demirbas A. Potential applications of renewable energy sources, biomass combustion problems in boiler power systems and combustion related environmental issues. Progress in Energy and Combustion Science. 2005;**31**(2): 171-192

[76] Jung S, Shetti NP, Reddy KR, Nadagouda MN, Park Y-K, Aminabhavi TM, et al. Synthesis of different biofuels from livestock waste materials and their potential as sustainable feedstocks–a review. Energy Conversion and Management. 2021;**236**: 114038

[77] Kumar Y, Yogeshwar P, Bajpai S, Jaiswal P, Yadav S, Pathak DP, et al. Nanomaterials: Stimulants for biofuels and renewables, yield and energy optimization. Materials Advances. 2021; **2**(16):5318-5343

[78] Meys R, Kätelhön A, Bachmann M, Winter B, Zibunas C, Suh S, et al. Achieving net-zero greenhouse gas emission plastics by a circular carbon economy. Science. 2021;**374**(6563):71-76

[79] Liu L, Wang J, Wang F, Yang X. The impact of the planting of forest biomass energy plants under the embedded internet of things technology on the biodiversity of the local environmental ecology. Environmental Technology and Innovation. 2021;**24**:101894

[80] Melillo JM, Reilly JM, Kicklighter DW, Gurgel AC, Cronin TW,

Paltsev S, et al. Indirect emissions from biofuels: How important? Science. 2009; **326**(5958):1397-1399

[81] Tetteh EK, Asante-Sackey D, Armah EK, Rathilal S. Tapping wastewater resource: why and how? In: Handbook of Biofuels. Cambridge, Academic Press: Elsevier; 2022. pp. 125-146

[82] Mostafaeipour A, Bidokhti A, Fakhrzad M-B, Sadegheih A, Zare MY. A new model for the use of renewable electricity to reduce carbon dioxide emissions. Energy. 2022;**238**:121602

[83] Armah EK, Chetty M, Rathilal S, Asante-Sackey D, Tetteh EK. Lignin: value addition is key to profitable biomass biorefinery. In: Handbook of Biofuels. Cambridge, Academic Press: Elsevier; 2022. pp. 233-247

Chapter 15

Biomass and Energy Production: Thermochemical Methods

Alireza Shafizadeh and Payam Danesh

Abstract

In this chapter, an overview of bioenergy importance toward energy systems with low (zero or negative) greenhouse gas emissions and general conversion technologies to produce different types of bioenergy products from various biomass feedstock is presented. The bioenergy products from biomass cover all physical phases including solid (biochar), liquid (bio-oil and bio-crude oil), and gases phase (bio syngas) which make them an interesting field in terms of both academic types of research and industrial scale. A discussion on the available technologies for thermochemical, biochemical, and extraction processes is presented, which is followed by some important parameters on each separate process that cause the optimum production rate and desired products. In addition, in the final part, an overview of the technology readiness level for the processes is reported.

Keywords: biomass, bioenergy, thermochemical conversion, biochemical conversion, technology readiness level

1. Introduction

Energy is an indispensable and prominent factor to accelerate economic and social development all over the world, undoubtedly. Therefore, due to the rise of the global population and incline to growth in both developed and developing countries, the energy request has been growing [1–3]. On one side, strong concerns over the depletion of fossil fuel reserve/resource and their accessibility in the next decades for long-term planning, and on another side, serious warns related to greenhouse gas emission due to fossil fuel consumption and destructive predictions of climate change consequences at the global level necessitate a huge scale transition toward new energy arrangements with reduced or even negative greenhouse gases [4–6]. In addition, The Paris Agreement on climate change calls on members to preserve the global temperature rise below 1.5 to 2 degrees Celsius (°C) above pre-industrial levels [7]. One of the most significant measures toward energy systems with low (zero or negative) greenhouse gas emissions to mitigate global temperature rise in the long-term and is the application of renewable energies and their share into global energy consumption instead of fossil fuel [8–10]. Biomass is clean renewable energy that accumulates and transfers sun energy in the form of chemical energy during the growth of plants and trees through the photosynthesis process [11]. Therefore, biomass has been recognized as one of the renewable energy sources, with carbon capture capability

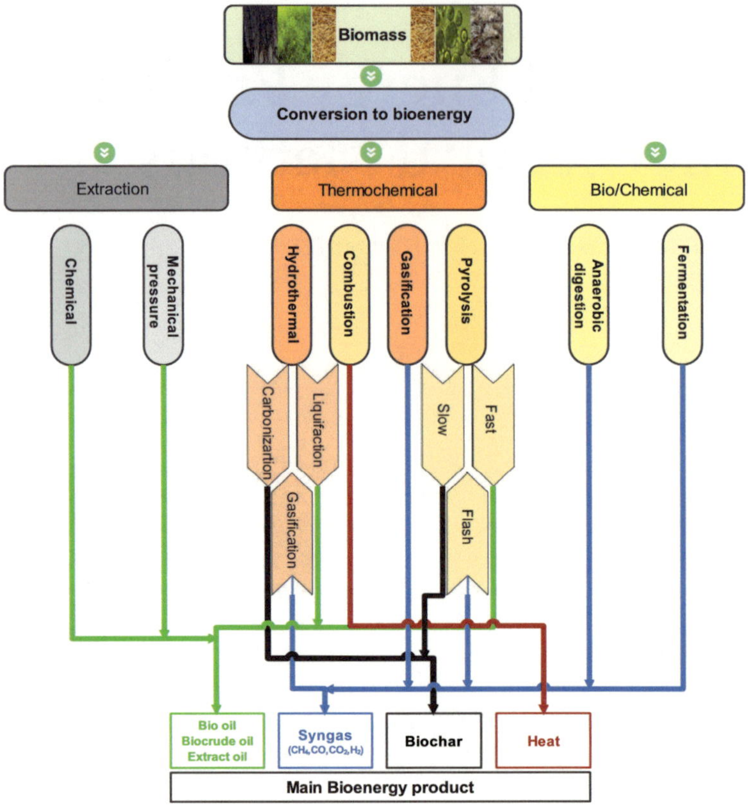

Figure 1.
General processes of bioenergy production from biomass feedstock.

and carbon neutrality [12–14]. In this context as it is shown in **Figure 1**, biomass also demonstrates the capability of transformation of the accumulated energy into multiple general forms of final energy carries such as solid, liquid, and gaseous which are compatible for various sectors comprising heat, power, and transport fuel [15]. In order to convert biomass energy to carrier energy products, some approaches such as thermochemical, biochemical, and coupled hybrid bio-refinery platforms or processes have been developed to ease access to green energetic biofuels with high value-added and clean energy chemicals [16].

2. Thermochemical conversion

Thermochemical conversion is defined as the degradation of organic matters due to heat exposition of biomass and chemical reactions. The process is mainly categorized in some processes named combustion, torrefaction, gasification, pyrolysis, and hydrothermal [17, 18]. In the thermochemical conversion of biomass, heat and catalysts are applied to transform biopolymers of biomass into biofuels and other valuable chemical components [19]. Based on the process the outputs mainly are biochar (carbon-rich solid residue,) liquid biofuel including bio-oil, bio-crude oil and tar (condensable vapors), and syngas (non-condensable gases) [20].

2.1 Combustion

Combustion is defined as high-temperature exothermic oxidation of biomass in the presence of oxygen and the presence of consecutive heterogeneous and homogeneous reactions which resulted in the production of heat as the main product. Combustion is divided into four stages: drying, pyrolysis (de-volatilization), volatiles combustion, and char combustion. As soon as biomass particles enter the burning environment, the particles moisture evaporate, on further heating, volatile gases and tars are released which follow by their combustion. The remaining char will essentially retain its original shape. The process outcomes mostly depend on the properties of the feedstock, particle size, temperature, and combustion atmosphere that can have char and ash (typically includes inorganic oxides and carbonates) as the solid byproducts of combustion [21, 22]. Carbon dioxide (CO2) and water vapor (H2O) are also produced during the complete combustion of biomass, however, it is not achieved under any conditions which cause the production of carbon monoxide (CO), methane (CH4), non-methane hydrocarbons (NMHCs), particulate matter (PM) and nitrogen and sulfur species mainly NO_x and SO_x during the incomplete combustion the biomass material [23]. The drawbacks are mainly controlled through modification of combustion processes via flue gas recirculation, boiler modification, and re-burning technology which often mitigate such emissions economically [24].

2.2 Hydrothermal conversion

The hydrothermal conversion process is a suitable technology especially for wet biomass into bio-fuel which is defined as a thermochemical transformation of biomass in high temperatures (100–700°C) and high pressures (5–40 MPa) in a liquid media or hot supercritical water [25]. In hydrothermal liquefaction (HTL) as an important hydrothermal process, raised temperatures (200–350°C) and high pressures (5–20 MPa) in the presence of solvent (sub–/super-critical water) applied to boost biomass decomposition and reformation to produce bio-crude (as the main output) bio-char, water-soluble organic polar fractions and gaseous [26–28]. During the HTL process, several complex mechanisms such as hydrolysis activate which degrade biomass macromolecules and then decompose them into smaller components to reactive fragments by bond cleavage and several reactions such as dehydration, dehydrogenation, deoxygenation, and decarboxylation while some complex chemicals such as bio-crude produce through depolymerization [29–31]. Derived bio-crude oil through HTL shows a higher heating value between 36 to 40 MJ/kg which is close to petroleum-derived oil characteristics [32–34]. HTL technology which is currently at the pilot/demonstration scale has several positive points in comparison to another thermochemical process including the ability to use high moisture content biomass inputs, lower operating temperature, higher throughput, and removal of oxygen from the bio-crude [35, 36]. In addition to biomass feedstock elemental composition, various operational parameters such as temperature, reaction time, pressure, presence of a catalyst (catalyst type and amount), solvent/biomass ratio, and reaction medium influence the process in terms of quantity and quality of produced bio-crude [37–40]. HTL in comparison with other processes reveals various advantages including application feedstock with high moisture content without drying requirement, exploitation of the properties of superheated fluids to reduce mass transfer resistances, and penetration of the solvent to biomass structure to enable the fragmentation of biomass molecules due to high pressure which result to obtain high-quality bio-crude oil [41].

Hydrothermal Carbonization (HTC) is the second hydrothermal conversion which is performed in a temperature range of 180 to 350°C during which the biomass is submerged in water and heated under pressure (2 to 6 MPa) for 5 to 240 min while the main product of HTC is hydro-char [42]. Hydrothermal gasification (Supercritical water gasification) is a thermochemical conversion process in which, wet biomass was directly converted into combustible gases under 400 to 500°C (processed till 700°C) and 24 to 36 MPa pressure with/without catalyst aid. Further, supercritical water is (<374°C, 22.1 MPa pressure) is acting as a reactant and solvent that splits organic compounds. During gasification, decomposition of biomass causes dissolution of reactive species that promote the yield of gaseous products by impeding the biochar production at supercritical [39, 43]. The hydrothermal gasification technologies) have considerable economic, environmental, and technical advantages over other high-demand energy conversion technologies. These processes are compatible with wet feedstock (not suitable candidates for another thermochemical process). Also due to the reactions taking place at lower temperatures (less energy consumption) and the use of a wide range of feedstock processing [44]. Due to the unique dissolution properties of water during hydrothermal gasification, less coke and tars are produced while pressurized produced syngas is typically free from gaseous that do not usually require further processing and can lower compression costs [45].

2.3 Pyrolysis

Pyrolysis defines as thermal decomposition in the absence of oxygen to break biomass chemical bonds in high temperatures to produce biofuels [46]. Depending on process requirement and desired product the process temperatures vary between 280 to 1000°C [47, 48]. During the process, generally three-step mechanisms including de-hydrogenation, de-polymerization and fragmentation occur to transfer biomass to biofuel [49]. The percentage of main products including bio-oil and bio-char and bio-syngas as the byproduct differ depending on heating rate, solid residence time, and temperature as the main operational parameters in the process [50]. Lower pyrolysis temperatures and longer residence times (Slow pyrolysis) tend to produce more bio-char while high temperatures and longer residence times increase the production of gas. Moderate or high temperatures and short residence times (Fast and Flash pyrolysis) resulted in more bio-oil [51]. Several technologies and reactors with the semi-continuous or continuous process have been developed on a laboratory scale and considered as suitable reactors for commercialization of pyrolysis including Bubbling Fluidized Bed (BFB), Circulating Fluidized Bed (CFB), Circulating Spouted Bed (CSB), Rotary Cone (RC), Ablative reactor and Screw/auger reactor [52]. In addition, plasma pyrolysis reactor configuration, Vacuum pyrolysis, Microwave-assisted, and solar-assisted pyrolysis have been extensively investigated as the state-of-the-art technologies related to biomass pyrolysis which demonstrates their advantages over conventional electrical-heating-assisted biomass pyrolysis [53, 54].

The higher heating value (HHV) of the bio-oils normally ranges between 15 and 20 MJ/kg which is only 40–50% of the conventional petroleum fuels with HHV between 42 to 45 MJ/kg. The HHV of the bio-oils can be approximately calculated through some empirical equations formulated by elemental analysis of the bio-oil (CHNOS analysis plus ash content) as represented in (Eq. (1)) [49].

$$\text{HHV}\left(\frac{\text{MJ}}{\text{kg}}\right) = 0.3491\times C + 1.1783\times H + 0.1005 \times S - 0.1034\times O - 0.0151\times N - 0.0211\times \text{Ash} \tag{1}$$

Since the liquid bio-fuel which contains oxygenated compounds such as acids, alcohols, phenols, ketones, and esters is commonly considered as poor quality, thus, it requires upgrading into a higher value-added product through promising methods such as catalytic steam reforming. The process of bio-oil quality upgrading and the water gas shift (WGS) reaction is presented in (Eq. (2)) and (Eq. (3)) respectively [55].

$$C_nH_mO_k + (n-k)H_2O ® nCO + \left(n + \left(\frac{m}{2}\right) - k\right)H_2 \tag{2}$$

$$CO + H_2O \rightleftharpoons CO_2 + H_2 \tag{3}$$

2.4 Gasification

In the condition in which production of biogas fuel is required, the gasification process under a reduced oxygen atmosphere applies to convert solid biomass to a gaseous fuel known as synthesis gas [56]. The biomass gasification process is conducted in four main stages including drying of the biomass particles followed by pyrolysis of the dried biomass particles(de-volatilization), in the next step partial oxidation of the pyrolysis gases and/or char occurred and finally char gasification happened (reduction). In contrast to pyrolysis, the feed is brought into contact with a gasifying agent (air) to ease the reaction between oxygen and biomass content in higher temperatures between 600°C and 1500°C. The produced gas contains various percentages of CO, H_2, CH_4, CO_2, $H2_O$, N_2, and eleven other gases depending on the quality of the biomass used and the way gasification is conducted [57, 58]. Fixed bed, fluidized bed, entrained flow, rotary kiln reactor, and plasma reactor can be utilized based on the operational conditions in gasification [59]. Briefly, biomass feedstock type and composition, particle size, moisture and ash content (higher ash content cause ash agglomeration during the process especially in high temperature), operational temperature, pressure and residence time, gasifying media, equivalence ratio (actual air-to-biomass ratio), steam-to-biomass ratio (S/B) and finally catalyst type and amount are the most prominent factors during the gasification process [60].

According to the **Figure 2** Biomass pass their steps of drying, pyrolysis, and partial oxidation before reach to the gasification point. Each stage is accrued in a specific range of temperature [61]. After the drying step, biomass is decomposed to solid char and pyrolysis which will be faced with the second decomposition stage and conversion into decomposes gases (non-condensable) and volatile hydrocarbons. Then, these products react with the oxidizing agent to produce syngas and smaller amounts of lower hydrocarbon gases (C1–C4) [62]. The global reaction inside the gasifier (except for unconverted solid carbon) can be described as (Eq. (4)) while for simplicity only the amount of hydrogen, carbon, nitrogen, oxygen, and sulfur of the biomass are considered in the model [58]:

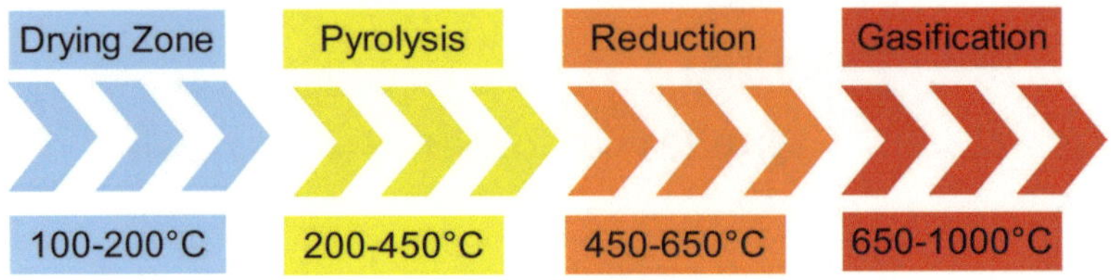

Figure 2.
Gasification steps and the temperature zones.

$$\begin{aligned} CH_aO_bN_cS_d &+ wH_2O_{(l)} + sH_2O_{(g)} + eO_2 + \rho eN_2 \leftrightarrow (1-\alpha)C_s \\ &+ n_{co}CO + n_{CO_2}CO_2 + n_{O_2}O_2 + n_{H_2}H_2 + n_{H_2O}H_2O + n_{CO_2}CO_2 \\ &+ n_{N_2}N_2 + n_{No}NO + n_{NO_2}NO_2 + n_{NH_3}NH_3 + n_{HCN}HCN \\ &+ n_{H_2s}H_2S + n_{SO_2}SO_2 + n_{SO_3}SO_3 + n_{\cos COs} \end{aligned} \tag{4}$$

One of the important issues during gasification is the removal of tar which is formed during the pyrolysis stage (as a transition step toward the gasification). Various tars components are released which can condense and form sticky deposits by quenching downstream when they contact cold points of the gasification system [63]. Tar roots severe damage to gas engines or turbines through fouling and coking in the system. Therefore, it is very important to reduce the tar content and particulate matter, in the syngas below the level of 100 mg/m3 and 50 mg/m3 respectively to apply for gas engine consumption [64]. Therefore, even though gasification is a relatively well-known technology, the share of gasification in overall energy demand is insignificant due to barriers concerning biomass harvesting and storage, biomass pre-treatment (drying, grinding, and densification), gas cleaning (physical, thermal or catalytic), process efficiency and syngas quality issues [65].

3. Biochemical conversion

3.1 Anaerobic digestion

In addition to thermochemical operation, bio-chemical processes such as anaerobic digestion (AD) and fermentation are promising technology as a renewable source of energy products [66, 67]. Regarding human health, environment, economy, and energy conservation issues, AD systems have attracted remarkable attention by the production of bio-methane gas (renewable energy source) through bio-chemical conversion of biodegradable wastes [68]. AD process has occurred in an insufficient O2 atmosphere which prepares suitable conditions for activation of the microorganism to degrade organic matter into biogas [69]. To convert the feedstock to bio-methane, a series of bi-metabolism steps including hydrolysis/acidogenesis, acetogenesis, and methanogenesis occurred in the AD systems reactors [70]. During the first stage, the high molecular weight complex insoluble organic matter is degraded into simple soluble molecules by the extracellular enzymes [69]. During the hydrolysis phase, the organic components of carbohydrate, protein, and lipid polymers are hydrolyzed into simple sugar, amino acid, and long-chain fatty acid respectively [71]. Meanwhile, monosaccharides are produced through hydrolysis of the insoluble compounds of cellulose and hemicellulose by enzymatic microorganisms (Streptococcus and Enterobacterium) [72]. However, at this step, rigid lignin structure which is resistant to the penetration of microorganisms requires delignification as a pretreatment process to undergo biodegradation [73]. In the next step acidogenic bacterizes such as Clostridium, Peptococcus Anaerobus, Lactobacillus, Psychrobacter, Anaerococcus, Bacteroides, Acetivibrio, Butyrivibrio, Halocella, and Actinomyces (highly active fermenter and the most abundant bacterizes in AD) applied to dissolve and bounded oxygen in the solution and carbon [74, 75]. At the final steps of the process, acetotrophic, hydrogenotrophic and methylotrophic pathways occurred which are the main route of methane production [76]. In the methanogenesis phase, acetic acid and hydrogen that formed in the acetogenesis phase are transformed to biomethane via methanogenic microorganisms while the pH in the system will increase to neutral values within the range of 6.8–8 [71]. The methanogenesis phase effectiveness is very reliant on the balanced relationship between bio-kinetics of microorganisms (Crenarchaeota, Euryarchaeota, etc.) with its growth environment (food supply and accessibility) [77, 78].

Working conditions in AD generally influence the formation of the produced biogas. The degradation process is affected by several factors including operation temperature, carbon to nitrogen (C: N) ratio, pH level, organic loading rate (OLR), Hydraulic retention time (HRT), and stirring [76]. Defining an optimum temperature that causes the stability of the enzymes and co-enzymes activity can have a significant influence on AD and bio-methane production while the efficient AD process is dependent on the optimum temperature [79, 80]. The optimum temperature for digestion process operation of anaerobic microorganisms could be range in psychrophilic (10–30°C), mesophilic (30–40°C), or thermophilic (50–60°C) conditions [81].

Alkalinity or acidity of the substrate is categorized by the important parameter of pH value. The stability of acidogenic activity and methanogenic bacteria is directly influenced by the changes in [82, 83]. Ideally, the optimum pH for acidogenesis and methanogenic stages place in a range from pH 5.5 to 6.5 and from 6.5 to 8.2, respectively [84]. Neutralization is essential in cases of excessively high or low pH during the anaerobic digestion feedstock especially before the plant is fed. The pH is chemically improved by adding the base, such as lime, to the reactor if negligible acidification happens during the AD process [85]. The next effective parameter in the AD process is the ratio of carbon to nitrogen in organic material [86]. A high C: N ratio indicated the low nitrogen sources that are needed to sustain the material supply for digestion. Meanwhile, the low C: N ratio signified the potential of $NH4+$ inhibition in the digestion process. Ideally, the optimum C: N ratio for the AD process is within the range of 20–35 [87]. The HRT which is defined as the retention period of the substrates inside the digester can vary based on the feedstock composition and digester temperature [88]. High HRT will result in improvement in biogas yields while the lower HTR is interested since decreasing cost of production and enhancement of process efficiency [89, 90]. The OLR also can affect The AD process negatively or positively [91]. Minor OLRs may cause malnutrition of microorganisms and adversely affects the AD while in contrast, a great ORL ratio may cause insufficient resources to support the development of microbial organisms [92, 93]. Temperature condition, characteristics of the substrates, and HRT of the AD operation impacts the OLR behavior and amount [76].

In terms of technological requirements, several types of reactors have been developed that generally can classify into wet or dry reactors based on their total solid contents [94]. In the design and operation of the anaerobic reactor, two parameters of reactor volume to daily flow and OLR have the most important value. The dry types (serve the feedstock with a solid concentration of more than 15%) itself could be categorized into three different types including horizontal plug-flow, vertical plug-flow, and non-flow (batch type) [95, 96]. In contrast, the wet digesters are defined to serve the feedstock having a total solid less than 15%value [97].

3.2 Fermentation

Fermentation is considered as another biochemical technology that can be applied to get energy from biomass. Fermentation defines as a process of central metabolism in which alcohol (for instance ethanol) or acid is produced by an organism through the conversion of carbohydrates, such as starch or sugar. Wines, beers, and ciders are traditionally carried out with fermentation process by using Saccharomyces cerevisiae strains, the most common and commercially available yeast [98, 99]. The utilization of feedstock such as wheat, corn, sugarcane, etc. for biofuel production (first generation biofuel) causes the problem of food security. The use of biomass feedstock (second generation) in bioethanol production solves this matter in many aspects [100]. Depending on fermentation conditions such as temperature, pH, aeration, and nutrient supplementation microorganisms are susceptible to lignocellulosic hydrolysate to produce bio ethanol [101]. Nevertheless, the production of biofuel through fermentation of promising sources (rice straw, wheat straw, corn straw, and sugarcane bagasse) is quite interesting but still meets some technical issues to release the fermentable sugars from lignocellulosic. The problem necessitates a pretreatment process including Physical (mechanical, extrusion, Irradiation), chemical (organosolv, ozonolysis, ionic liquid, acid, and alkali washing) physicochemical, and biological [102].

Several fermentation technologies such as batch and continues and fed-batch modes have been utilized. The complete subtract and highest conversion rate but lower volumetric production can be done through batch mode rather than continuous mode which led to high productivity (due to high dilution ratio and long duration process) and steady residual concentration [103]. Overly, batch fermentation could be applied for high viscous feedstock, while continuous fermentation methods can offer better plant capacity utilization [104]. During the batch and continuum operation, the addition of Indigenous Consortium Streptococcus sp. or enzyme glucoamylase has been reported that helps to fermentation process [105, 106].

4. Extraction

In addition to the thermochemical and biochemical process, the extraction method indeed is applied to oil from oil seeds or nuts materials such as hazelnut, almond nut, sesame seed, sunflower seed, or rapeseed. Traditionally, the oil can be extracted through cold pressing, hot pressing, or solvent extraction methods where the pressing is a mechanical method while solvent extraction is a chemical method [107, 108]. The pressing technique (solvent-free) is traditionally applied to extract edible oil from various sources such as nut or seed samples. Before the extraction sample preparation through various pretreatments on the sample is required before extraction in order to enhance the extraction efficiency [109]. The objectives of the pretreatment process are to destroy or soften the cellular structure of the sample and reduce the moisture content, which can increase the efficiency of the later extraction stage by destroying or softening the cellular structure of the sample and reduction

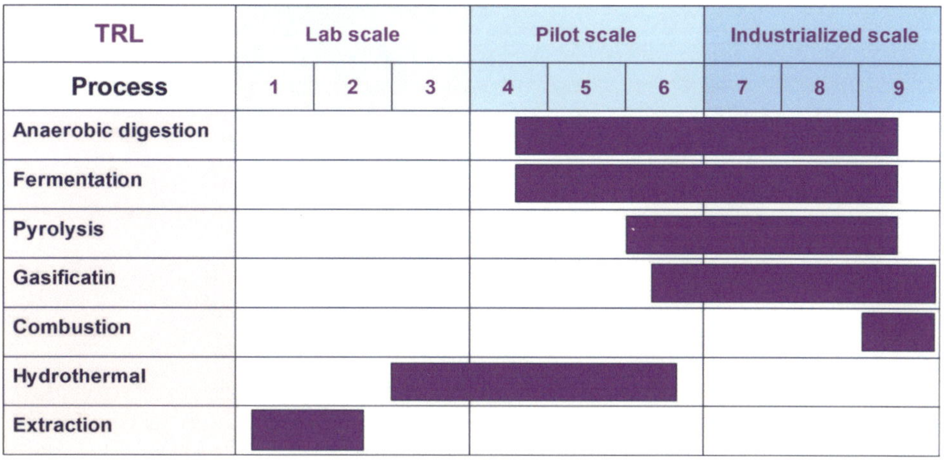

Figure 3.
General technical readiness level of each conversion process of biomass to bioenergy.

of the seed moisture content [110]. The process is normally continued with solvent extraction (use solvent polar or non-polar) process due to the significant amount of oil remaining in the press cake, which is around 20–30%100. However new techniques such as microwave-assisted extraction [111], supercritical fluid extraction [112], ultrasound-assisted extraction can be applied in order to extract separate desired oil liquid from a solid–liquid sample [113].

5. Technology readiness level

It must be noticed that each mentioned process of bioenergy production is placed in a certain level of technical maturity as briefly demonstrated in the **Figure 3** [114–116]. The maturity level of each technic is represented by a term which is called technical readiness level (TRL) and it is divided from lab scale (1–3), pilot-scale (4–6) to the highest level of maturity which is proven, tested, and qualified all parameters with a full commercial plant and industrialized scale (6–9) to produce products for public usage [114].

Acknowledgements

I would like to acknowledge and give my warmest thanks to my supporters at the University of Tehran who made this work possible.

Conflict of interest

The authors declare no conflict of interest.

Author details

Alireza Shafizadeh* and Payam Danesh
Faculty of Agricultural Engineering and Technology, Department of Mechanical Engineering of Agricultural Machinery, College of Agriculture and Natural Resources, University of Tehran, Tehran, Iran

*Address all correspondence to: a.shafizadeh@ut.ac.ir

References

[1] Baz K, Cheng J, Xu D, Abbas K, Ali I, Ali H, et al. Asymmetric impact of fossil fuel and renewable energy consumption on economic growth: A nonlinear technique. Energy [Internet]. 2021;**226**:120357. Available from: https://www.sciencedirect.com/science/article/pii/S036054422100606X

[2] Barber J. Hydrogen derived from water as a sustainable solar fuel: Learning from biology. Sustainable Energy and Fuels [Internet]. 2018;**2**(5):927-935. DOI: 10.1039/C8SE00002F

[3] Jeong J, Ko H. Bracing for Climate Impact: Renewables as a Climate Change Adaptation Strategy [Internet]. Abu Dhabi; 2021. pp. 1-104. Available from: https://www.irena.org/-/media/Files/IRENA/Agency/Publication/2021/Aug/IRENA_Bracing_for_climate_impact_2021.pdf

[4] Capellán-Pérez I, Arto I, Polanco-Martínez JM, González-Eguino M, Neumann MB. Likelihood of climate change pathways under uncertainty on fossil fuel resource availability. Energy & Environmental Science Journal [Internet]. 2016;**9**(8):2482-2496. DOI: 10.1039/C6EE01008C

[5] Shen N, Wang Y, Peng H, Hou Z. Renewable energy green innovation, fossil energy consumption, and air pollution—Spatial empirical analysis based on China. Sustainability. 2020;**12**. Article DOI: 10.3390/su12166397

[6] Schwartz SE. Uncertainty in climate sensitivity: Causes, consequences, challenges. Energy & Environmental Science Journal [Internet]. 2008;**1**(4):430-453. DOI: 10.1039/B810350J

[7] Bui M, Adjiman CS, Bardow A, Anthony EJ, Boston A, Brown S, et al. Carbon capture and storage (CCS): The way forward. Energy & Environmental Science Journal [Internet]. 2018;**11**(5):1062-1176. DOI: 10.1039/C7EE02342A

[8] Schmidt J, Gruber K, Klingler M, Klöckl C, Ramirez Camargo L, Regner P, et al. A new perspective on global renewable energy systems: Why trade in energy carriers matters. Energy & Environmental Science Journal [Internet]. 2019;**12**(7):2022-2029. DOI: 10.1039/C9EE00223E

[9] Davis M, Moronkeji A, Ahiduzzaman M, Kumar A. Assessment of renewable energy transition pathways for a fossil fuel-dependent electricity-producing jurisdiction. Energy for Sustainable Development [Internet]. 2020;**59**:243-261. Available from: https://www.sciencedirect.com/science/article/pii/S0973082620303203

[10] Atsu F, Adams S. Energy consumption, finance, and climate change: Does policy uncertainty matter? Journal of Economic Analysis & Policy [Internet]. 2021;**70**:490-501. Available from: https://www.sciencedirect.com/science/article/pii/S0313592621000485

[11] Demirbas A. Biofuels [Internet]. Angewandte Chemie International Edition. 2009;**6**(11):951-952. London: Springer London; 15-38 p. (Green Energy and Technology; vol. 13). Available from: http://link.springer.com/10.1007/978-1-84882-011-1

[12] Liu X, Li N, Liu F, Mu H, Li L, Liu X. Optimal design on fossil-to-renewable energy transition of regional integrated energy systems under CO2 emission abatement control: A case study in Dalian, China. Energies. 2021;**14**. Article DOI: 10.3390/en14102879

[13] Creutzig F, Breyer C, Hilaire J, Minx J, Peters GP, Socolow R. The mutual dependence of negative emission technologies and energy systems. Energy & Environmental Science Journal [Internet]. 2019;**12**(6):1805-1817. DOI: 10.1039/C8EE03682A

[14] Zhao B, Wang H, Hu Y, Gao J, Zhao G, Ray MB, et al. Hydrothermal Co-liquefaction of lignite and lignocellulosic biomass with the addition of formic acid: Study on product distribution, characteristics, and synergistic effects. Industrial & Engineering Chemistry Research [Internet]. 2020;**59**(50):21663-21675. DOI: 10.1021/acs.iecr.0c04619

[15] Osman AI, Mehta N, Elgarahy AM, Al-Hinai A, Al-Muhtaseb AH, Rooney DW. Conversion of biomass to biofuels and life cycle assessment: A review. Environmental Chemistry Letters [Internet]. 2021;**19**(6):4075-4118. DOI: 10.1007/s10311-021-01273-0

[16] Kumar G, Dharmaraja J, Arvindnarayan S, Shoban S, Bakonyi P, Saratale GD, et al. A comprehensive review on thermochemical, biological, biochemical and hybrid conversion methods of bio-derived lignocellulosic molecules into renewable fuels. Fuel [Internet]. 2019;**251**:352-367. Available from: https://www.sciencedirect.com/science/article/pii/S0016236119306040

[17] Nazari L, Xu C (Charles), Ray MB. Advanced Technologies (Biological and Thermochemical) for Waste-to-Energy Conversion. Singapore: Springer; 2021. pp. 55-95. Available from: http://link.springer.com/10.1007/978-981-15-9267-6_3

[18] Teh JS, Teoh YH, How HG, Sher F. Thermal analysis Technologies for Biomass Feedstocks: A state-of-the-art review. Processes [Internet]. 2021;**9**(9):1610. Available from: https://www.mdpi.com/2227-9717/9/9/1610

[19] Dhyani V, Bhaskar T. A comprehensive review on the pyrolysis of lignocellulosic biomass. Renew Energy [Internet]. 2018;**129**:695-716. Available from: https://www.sciencedirect.com/science/article/pii/S0960148117303427

[20] Daful AG, Chandraratne RM. Biochar production from biomass waste-derived material. In: Encyclopedia of Renewable and Sustainable Materials [Internet]. Amsterdam, Netherlands The Boulevard, Langford Lane, Kidlington, Oxford, USA: Elsevier Inc.; 2020. pp. 370-378. Available from: https://linkinghub.elsevier.com/retrieve/pii/B9780128035818112494

[21] Adams P, Bridgwater T, Lea-Langton A, Ross A, Watson I. Biomass conversion technologies. In: Greenhouse Gases Balances of Bioenergy Systems [Internet]. Elsevier; 2018. pp. 107-139. Available from: https://linkinghub.elsevier.com/retrieve/pii/B9780081010365000082

[22] Mandø M. Direct combustion of biomass. In: Biomass Combustion Science, Technology and Engineering [Internet]. Sawston, Cambridge, UK: Woodhead Publishing Limited, Elsevier; 2013. pp. 61-83. Available from: https://linkinghub.elsevier.com/retrieve/pii/B9780857091314500042

[23] Demirbas A. Hazardous emissions from combustion of biomass. Energy Sources, Part A: Recovery, Utilization and Environmental Effects. 2007;**30**(2):170-178. Available from: https://www.tandfonline.com/doi/full/10.1080/00908310600712406

[24] Oluwoye I, Altarawneh M, Gore J, Dlugogorski BZ. Products of incomplete combustion from biomass reburning. Fuel [Internet]. 2020;**274**:117805. Available from: https://linkinghub.elsevier.com/retrieve/pii/S0016236120308012

[25] Tran K-Q. Fast hydrothermal liquefaction for production of chemicals and biofuels from wet biomass – The need to develop a plug-flow reactor. Bioresource Technology [Internet]. 2016;**213**:327-332. Available from: https://www.sciencedirect.com/science/article/pii/S0960852416304746

[26] Leng L, Zhang W, Leng S, Chen J, Yang L, Li H, et al. Bioenergy recovery from wastewater produced by hydrothermal processing biomass: Progress, challenges, and opportunities. Science of the Total Environment [Internet]. 2020;**748**:142383. Available from: https://www.sciencedirect.com/science/article/pii/S004896972035912X

[27] Arun J, Gopinath KP, SundarRajan P, Malolan R, Adithya S, Sai Jayaraman R, et al. Hydrothermal liquefaction of Scenedesmus obliquus using a novel catalyst derived from clam shells: Solid residue as catalyst for hydrogen production. Bioresource Technology [Internet]. 2020;**310**:123443. Available from: https://www.sciencedirect.com/science/article/pii/S096085242030715X

[28] Kumar G, Shobana S, Chen W-H, Bach Q-V, Kim S-H, Atabani AE, et al. A review of thermochemical conversion of microalgal biomass for biofuels: Chemistry and processes. Green Chemistry [Internet]. 2017;**19**(1):44-67. DOI: 10.1039/C6GC01937D

[29] Gollakota ARK, Kishore N, Gu S. A review on hydrothermal liquefaction of biomass. Renewable & Sustainable Energy Reviews [Internet]. 2018;**81**:1378-1392. Available from: https://www.sciencedirect.com/science/article/pii/S1364032117308146

[30] Katakojwala R, Kopperi H, Kumar S, Venkata MS. Hydrothermal liquefaction of biogenic municipal solid waste under reduced H2 atmosphere in biorefinery format. Bioresource Technology [Internet]. 2020;**310**:123369. Available from: https://www.sciencedirect.com/science/article/pii/S0960852420306416

[31] Devi TE, Parthiban R. Hydrothermal liquefaction of Nostoc ellipsosporum biomass grown in municipal wastewater under optimized conditions for bio-oil production. Bioresource Technology [Internet]. 2020;**316**:123943. Available from: https://www.sciencedirect.com/science/article/pii/S0960852420312153

[32] Cheng F, Jarvis JM, Yu J, Jena U, Nirmalakhandan N, Schaub TM, et al. Bio-crude oil from hydrothermal liquefaction of wastewater microalgae in a pilot-scale continuous flow reactor. Bioresource Technology [Internet]. 2019;**294**:122184. Available from: https://www.sciencedirect.com/science/article/pii/S0960852419314142

[33] Khan N, Mohan S, Dinesha P. Regimes of hydrochar yield from hydrothermal degradation of various lignocellulosic biomass: A review. Journal of Cleaner Production [Internet]. 2021;**288**:125629. Available from: https://www.sciencedirect.com/science/article/pii/S0959652620356754

[34] Arun J, Gopinath KP, SundarRajan P, Malolan R, Ajay Srinivaasan P. Hydrothermal liquefaction and pyrolysis of Amphiroa fragilissima biomass: Comparative study on oxygen content and storage stability parameters of bio-oil. Bioresource Technology Reports [Internet].

2020;**11**:100465. Available from: https://www.sciencedirect.com/science/article/pii/S2589014X20300864

[35] Kim SJ, Um BH. Effect of thermochemically fractionation before hydrothermal liquefaction of herbaceous biomass on biocrude characteristics. Renew Energy [Internet]. 2020;**160**:612-622. Available from: https://www.sciencedirect.com/science/article/pii/S0960148120310788

[36] Lozano EM, Pedersen TH, Rosendahl LA. Integration of hydrothermal liquefaction and carbon capture and storage for the production of advanced liquid biofuels with negative CO2 emissions. Applied Energy [Internet]. 2020;**279**:115753. Available from: https://www.sciencedirect.com/science/article/pii/S030626192031240X

[37] Tekin K, Karagöz S, Bektaş S. A review of hydrothermal biomass processing. Renewable & Sustainable Energy Reviews [Internet]. 2014;**40**:673-687. Available from: https://www.sciencedirect.com/science/article/pii/S1364032114006807

[38] Akhtar J, Amin NAS. A review on process conditions for optimum bio-oil yield in hydrothermal liquefaction of biomass. Renewable & Sustainable Energy Reviews [Internet]. 2011;**15**(3):1615-1624. Available from: https://www.sciencedirect.com/science/article/pii/S1364032110004235

[39] Mathimani T, Mallick N. A review on the hydrothermal processing of microalgal biomass to bio-oil - knowledge gaps and recent advances. Journal of Cleaner Production [Internet]. 2019;**217**:69-84. Available from: https://www.sciencedirect.com/science/article/pii/S0959652619301465

[40] Li Y, Zhu C, Jiang J, Yang Z, Feng W, Li L, et al. Catalytic hydrothermal liquefaction of Gracilaria corticata macroalgae: Effects of process parameter on bio-oil up-gradation. Bioresource Technology [Internet]. 2021;**319**:124163. Available from: https://www.sciencedirect.com/science/article/pii/S0960852420314371

[41] Kaur R, Biswas B, Kumar J, Jha MK, Bhaskar T. Catalytic hydrothermal liquefaction of castor residue to bio-oil: Effect of alkali catalysts and optimization study. Industrial Crops and Products [Internet]. 2020;**149**:112359. Available from: https://linkinghub.elsevier.com/retrieve/pii/S0926669020302752

[42] Heidari M, Dutta A, Acharya B, Mahmud S. A review of the current knowledge and challenges of hydrothermal carbonization for biomass conversion. Journal of the Energy Institute [Internet]. 2019;**92**(6):1779-1799. Available from: https://www.sciencedirect.com/science/article/pii/S1743967118306421

[43] Rodriguez Correa C, Kruse A. Supercritical water gasification of biomass for hydrogen production – Review. The Journal of Supercritical Fluids [Internet]. 2018;**133**:573-590. Available from: https://linkinghub.elsevier.com/retrieve/pii/S0896844617303510

[44] Elias Bamaca Saquic B, Irmak S, Wilkins M, Smith T. Effect of precursors on graphene supported platinum monometalic catalysts for hydrothermal gasification of biomass compounds to hydrogen. Fuel [Internet]. 2021;**290**:120079. Available from: https://linkinghub.elsevier.com/retrieve/pii/S0016236120330763

[45] Okolie JA, Epelle EI, Nanda S, Castello D, Dalai AK, Kozinski JA. Modeling and process optimization of hydrothermal gasification for hydrogen production: A comprehensive review.

The Journal of Supercritical Fluids [Internet]. 2021;**173**:105199. Available from: https://linkinghub.elsevier.com/retrieve/pii/S0896844621000383

[46] Bridgwater AV. Review of fast pyrolysis of biomass and product upgrading. Biomass and Bioenergy [Internet]. 2012;**38**:68-94. Available from: https://www.sciencedirect.com/science/article/pii/S0961953411000638

[47] Fahmy TYA, Fahmy Y, Mobarak F, El-Sakhawy M, Abou-Zeid RE. Biomass pyrolysis: Past, present, and future. Environment, Development and Sustainability [Internet]. 2020;**22**(1):17-32. DOI: 10.1007/s10668-018-0200-5

[48] Patel A, Agrawal B, Rawal BR. Pyrolysis of biomass for efficient extraction of biofuel. Energy Sources, Part A: Recovery, Utilization and Environmental Effects. 2020;**42**(13):1649-1661. DOI: 10.1080/15567036.2019.1604875

[49] Kan T, Strezov V, Evans TJ. Lignocellulosic biomass pyrolysis: A review of product properties and effects of pyrolysis parameters. Renewable & Sustainable Energy Reviews [Internet]. 2016;**57**:1126-1140. Available from: https://linkinghub.elsevier.com/retrieve/pii/S1364032115015683

[50] Perera SMHD, Wickramasinghe C, Samarasiri BKT, Narayana M. Modeling of thermochemical conversion of waste biomass – A comprehensive review. Biofuel Research Journal [Internet]. 2021;**8**(4):1481-1528. Available from: https://www.biofueljournal.com/article_140769.html

[51] Uddin MN, Techato K, Taweekun J, Mofijur M, Rasul MG, Mahlia TMI, et al. An overview of recent developments in biomass pyrolysis technologies. Energies [Internet]. 2018;**11**(11):3115. Available from: http://www.mdpi.com/1996-1073/11/11/3115

[52] Qureshi KM, Kay Lup AN, Khan S, Abnisa F, Wan Daud WMA. A technical review on semi-continuous and continuous pyrolysis process of biomass to bio-oil. Journal of Analytical and Applied Pyrolysis [Internet]. 2018;**131**:52-75. Available from: https://linkinghub.elsevier.com/retrieve/pii/S0165237017305193

[53] Wang G, Dai Y, Yang H, Xiong Q, Wang K, Zhou J, et al. A review of recent advances in biomass pyrolysis. Energy & Fuels [Internet]. 2020;**34**(12):15557-15578. DOI: 10.1021/acs.energyfuels.0c03107

[54] Raza M, Inayat A, Ahmed A, Jamil F, Ghenai C, Naqvi SR, et al. Progress of the Pyrolyzer reactors and advanced Technologies for Biomass Pyrolysis Processing. Sustainability [Internet]. 2021;**13**(19):11061. Available from: https://www.mdpi.com/2071-1050/13/19/11061

[55] Setiabudi HD, Aziz MAA, Abdullah S, Teh LP, Jusoh R. Hydrogen production from catalytic steam reforming of biomass pyrolysis oil or bio-oil derivatives: A review. International Journal of Hydrogen Energy [Internet]. 2020;**45**(36):18376-18397. Available from: https://linkinghub.elsevier.com/retrieve/pii/S0360319919339527

[56] Cerinski D, Baleta J, Mikulčić H, Mikulandrić R, Wang J. Dynamic modelling of the biomass gasification process in a fixed bed reactor by using the artificial neural network. Cleaner Engineering and Technology [Internet]. 2020;**1**:100029. Available from: https://www.sciencedirect.com/science/article/pii/S266679082030029X

[57] Richardson Y, Drobek M, Julbe A, Blin J, Pinta F. Chapter 8 - biomass

gasification to produce syngas. In: Pandey A, Bhaskar T, Stöcker M, Sukumaran RK, editors. Recent Advances in Thermo-Chemical Conversion of Biomass [Internet]. Boston: Elsevier; 2015. pp. 213-250. Available from: https://www.sciencedirect.com/science/article/pii/B9780444632890000089

[58] Gambarotta A, Morini M, Zubani A. A non-stoichiometric equilibrium model for the simulation of the biomass gasification process. Applied Energy [Internet]. 2018;**227**:119-127. Available from: https://linkinghub.elsevier.com/retrieve/pii/S0306261917310103

[59] Ren J, Cao J-P, Zhao X-Y, Yang F-L, Wei X-Y. Recent advances in syngas production from biomass catalytic gasification: A critical review on reactors, catalysts, catalytic mechanisms and mathematical models. Renewable & Sustainable Energy Reviews [Internet]. 2019;**116**:109426. Available from: https://www.sciencedirect.com/science/article/pii/S1364032119306343

[60] Sikarwar VS, Zhao M, Fennell PS, Shah N, Anthony EJ. Progress in biofuel production from gasification. Progress in Energy and Combustion Science [Internet]. 2017;**61**:189-248. Available from: https://www.sciencedirect.com/science/article/pii/S036012851630106X

[61] Hendriyana H. Effect of equivalence ratio on the Rice husk gasification performance using updraft gasifier with air suction mode. Jurnal Bahan Alam Terbarukan [Internet]. 2020;**9**(1):30-35. Available from: https://journal.unnes.ac.id/nju/index.php/jbat/article/view/23527

[62] Saleem F, Harris J, Zhang K, Harvey A. Non-thermal plasma as a promising route for the removal of tar from the product gas of biomass gasification – A critical review. Chemical Engineering Journa [Internet]. 2020;**382**:122761. Available from: https://linkinghub.elsevier.com/retrieve/pii/S1385894719321710

[63] Valderrama Rios ML, González AM, Lora EES, Almazán del Olmo OA. Reduction of tar generated during biomass gasification: A review. Biomass and Bioenergy [Internet]. 2018;**108**:345-370. Available from: https://www.sciencedirect.com/science/article/pii/S0961953417304026

[64] Hwang JG, Choi MK, Choi DH, Choi HS. Quality improvement and tar reduction of syngas produced by bio-oil gasification. Energy [Internet]. 2021;**236**:121473. Available from: https://linkinghub.elsevier.com/retrieve/pii/S0360544221017217

[65] Mikulandrić R, Böhning D, Böhme R, Helsen L, Beckmann M, Lončar D. Dynamic modelling of biomass gasification in a co-current fixed bed gasifier. Energy Conversion and Management [Internet]. 2016;**125**:264-276. Available from: https://www.sciencedirect.com/science/article/pii/S019689041630317X

[66] Hunter SM, Blanco E, Borrion A. Expanding the anaerobic digestion map: A review of intermediates in the digestion of food waste. Science of the Total Environment [Internet]. 2021;**767**:144265. Available from: https://linkinghub.elsevier.com/retrieve/pii/S0048969720377962

[67] Batista AP, Gouveia L, Marques PASS. Fermentative hydrogen production from microalgal biomass by a single strain of bacterium Enterobacter aerogenes – Effect of operational conditions and fermentation kinetics. Renew Energy [Internet]. 2018;**119**: 203-209. Available from: https://linkinghub.elsevier.com/retrieve/pii/S0960148117312132

[68] Mao C, Feng Y, Wang X, Ren G. Review on research achievements of biogas from anaerobic digestion. Renewable & Sustainable Energy Reviews [Internet]. 2015;**45**:540-555. Available from: https://linkinghub.elsevier.com/retrieve/pii/S1364032115001203

[69] Sytar O, Prasad MNV. Production of biodiesel feedstock from the trace element contaminated lands in Ukraine. In: Bioremediation and Bioeconomy [Internet]. Amsterdam, Netherlands The Boulevard, Langford Lane, Kidlington, Oxford, USA: Elsevier Inc.; 2016. pp. 3-28. Available from: https://linkinghub.elsevier.com/retrieve/pii/B9780128028308000010

[70] Chiu SLH, Lo IMC. Reviewing the anaerobic digestion and co-digestion process of food waste from the perspectives on biogas production performance and environmental impacts. Environmental Science and Pollution Research [Internet]. 2016;**23**(24):24435-24450. Available from: http://link.springer.com/10.1007/s11356-016-7159-2

[71] Strazzera G, Battista F, Garcia NH, Frison N, Bolzonella D. Volatile fatty acids production from food wastes for biorefinery platforms: A review. Journal of Environmental Management [Internet]. 2018;**226**:278-288. Available from: https://linkinghub.elsevier.com/retrieve/pii/S0301479718309101

[72] Li W, Khalid H, Zhu Z, Zhang R, Liu G, Chen C, et al. Methane production through anaerobic digestion: Participation and digestion characteristics of cellulose, hemicellulose and lignin. Applied Energy [Internet]. 2018;**226**:1219-1228. Available from: https://linkinghub.elsevier.com/retrieve/pii/S0306261918307657

[73] Koyama M, Yamamoto S, Ishikawa K, Ban S, Toda T. Inhibition of anaerobic digestion by dissolved lignin derived from alkaline pre-treatment of an aquatic macrophyte. Chemical Engineering Journa [Internet]. 2017;**311**:55-62. Available from: https://linkinghub.elsevier.com/retrieve/pii/S1385894716316382

[74] Karthikeyan OP, Heimann K, Muthu SS, editors. Environmental footprints and eco-design of products and processes. In: Recycling of Solid Waste for Biofuels and Bio-Chemicals [Internet]. Singapore: Springer Singapore; 2016. Available from: http://link.springer.com/10.1007/978-981-10-0150-5

[75] Ahammad SZ, Sreekrishnan TR. Energy from wastewater treatment. In: Bioremediation and Bioeconomy [Internet]. Amsterdam, Netherlands The Boulevard, Langford Lane, Kidlington, Oxford, USA: Elsevier Inc.; 2016. pp. 523-536. Available from: https://linkinghub.elsevier.com/retrieve/pii/B9780128028308000204

[76] Zamri MFMA, Hasmady S, Akhiar A, Ideris F, Shamsuddin AH, Mofijur M, et al. A comprehensive review on anaerobic digestion of organic fraction of municipal solid waste. Renewable & Sustainable Energy Reviews [Internet]. 2021;**137**:110637. Available from: https://linkinghub.elsevier.com/retrieve/pii/S1364032120309217

[77] Rada EC, editor. Biological Treatment of Solid Waste [Internet]. New York: Apple Academic Press; 2015. Available from: https://www.taylorfrancis.com/books/9781771882804

[78] Kigozi R, Aboyade A, Muzenda E. Biogas production using the organic fraction of municipal solid waste as feedstock. Int'l Journal of Research in Chemical, Metallurgical and Civil Engg. (IJRCMCE) 2014;**1**(1):108-114. ISSN: 2349-1442, EISSN: 2349-1450

[79] Li D, Song L, Fang H, Shi Y, Li Y-Y, Liu R, et al. Effect of temperature on the anaerobic digestion of cardboard with waste yeast added: Dose-response kinetic assays, temperature coefficient and microbial co-metabolism. Journal of Cleaner Production [Internet]. 2020;**275**:122949. Available from: https://linkinghub.elsevier.com/retrieve/pii/S0959652620329942

[80] Tabatabaei M, Aghbashlo M, Valijanian E, Kazemi Shariat Panahi H, Nizami A-S, Ghanavati H, et al. A comprehensive review on recent biological innovations to improve biogas production, part 1: Upstream strategies. Renew Energy [Internet]. 2020;**146**:1204-1220. Available from: https://linkinghub.elsevier.com/retrieve/pii/S0960148119310572

[81] Toutian V, Barjenbruch M, Unger T, Loderer C, Remy C. Effect of temperature on biogas yield increase and formation of refractory COD during thermal hydrolysis of waste activated sludge. Water Resources [Internet]. 2020;**171**:115383. Available from: https://linkinghub.elsevier.com/retrieve/pii/S0043135419311571

[82] Rajendran K, Mahapatra D, Venkatraman AV, Muthuswamy S, Pugazhendhi A. Advancing anaerobic digestion through two-stage processes: Current developments and future trends. Renewable & Sustainable Energy Reviews [Internet]. 2020;**123**:109746. Available from: https://linkinghub.elsevier.com/retrieve/pii/S1364032120300435

[83] Zhang J, Kan X, Shen Y, Loh K-C, Wang C-H, Dai Y, et al. A hybrid biological and thermal waste-to-energy system with heat energy recovery and utilization for solid organic waste treatment. Energy [Internet]. 2018;**152**:214-222. Available from: https://linkinghub.elsevier.com/retrieve/pii/S0360544218305528

[84] Zhang F, Zhang Y, Ding J, Dai K, van Loosdrecht MCM, Zeng RJ. Stable acetate production in extreme-thermophilic (70°C) mixed culture fermentation by selective enrichment of hydrogenotrophic methanogens. Scientific Reports [Internet]. 2015;**4**(1):5268. Available from: http://www.nature.com/articles/srep05268

[85] Kouzi AI, Puranen M, Kontro MH. Evaluation of the factors limiting biogas production in full-scale processes and increasing the biogas production efficiency. Environmental Science and Pollution Research [Internet]. 2020;**27**(22):28155-28168. Available from: https://link.springer.com/10.1007/s11356-020-09035-1

[86] Messineo A, Maniscalco MP, Volpe R. Biomethane recovery from olive mill residues through anaerobic digestion: A review of the state of the art technology. Science of the Total Environment [Internet]. 2020;**703**:135508. Available from: https://linkinghub.elsevier.com/retrieve/pii/S0048969719355020

[87] Li D, Liu S, Mi L, Li Z, Yuan Y, Yan Z, et al. Effects of feedstock ratio and organic loading rate on the anaerobic mesophilic co-digestion of rice straw and cow manure. Bioresource Technology [Internet]. 2015;**189**:319-326. Available from: https://linkinghub.elsevier.com/retrieve/pii/S0960852415005167

[88] Jain S, Jain S, Wolf IT, Lee J, Tong YW. A comprehensive review on operating parameters and different pretreatment methodologies for anaerobic digestion of municipal solid waste. Renewable & Sustainable Energy Reviews [Internet]. 2015;**52**:

142-154. Available from: https://linkinghub.elsevier.com/retrieve/pii/S1364032115007388

[89] Shi X-S, Dong J-J, Yu J-H, Yin H, Hu S-M, Huang S-X, et al. Effect of hydraulic retention time on anaerobic digestion of wheat straw in the Semicontinuous continuous stirred-tank reactors. BioMed Research International [Internet]. 2017;**2017**:1-6. Available from: https://www.hindawi.com/journals/bmri/2017/2457805/

[90] Aramrueang N, Rapport J, Zhang R. Effects of hydraulic retention time and organic loading rate on performance and stability of anaerobic digestion of Spirulina platensis. Biosystems Engineering [Internet]. 2016;**147**:174-182. Available from: https://linkinghub.elsevier.com/retrieve/pii/S1537511015304670

[91] Guo J, Wang W, Liu X, Lian S, Zheng L. Effects of thermal pre-treatment on anaerobic co-digestion of municipal biowastes at high organic loading rate. Chemosphere [Internet]. 2014;**101**:66-70. Available from: https://linkinghub.elsevier.com/retrieve/pii/S0045653513016676

[92] Zhang L, Loh K-C, Zhang J. Enhanced biogas production from anaerobic digestion of solid organic wastes: Current status and prospects. Bioresource Technology Reports [Internet]. 2019;**5**:280-296. Available from: https://linkinghub.elsevier.com/retrieve/pii/S2589014X18300689

[93] Dhanya BS, Mishra A, Chandel AK, Verma ML. Development of sustainable approaches for converting the organic waste to bioenergy. Science of the Total Environment [Internet]. 2020;**723**:138109. Available from: https://linkinghub.elsevier.com/retrieve/pii/S0048969720316223

[94] Angelonidi E, Smith SR. A comparison of wet and dry anaerobic digestion processes for the treatment of municipal solid waste and food waste. Water and Environment Journal. 2015;**29**(4):549-557. Available from: https://onlinelibrary.wiley.com/doi/10.1111/wej.12130

[95] Van DP, Fujiwara T, Leu Tho B, Song Toan PP, Hoang MG. A review of anaerobic digestion systems for biodegradable waste: Configurations, operating parameters, and current trends. Environmental Engineering Research [Internet]. 2019;**25**(1):1-17. Available from: http://eeer.org/journal/view.php?doi=10.4491/eer.2018.334

[96] Hinds GR, Lens PNL, Zhang Q, Ergas SJ. Microbial biomethane production from municipal solid waste using high solids anaerobic digestion. In: Microbial Fuels [Internet]. Boca Raton: CRC Press; 2018, 2017. pp. 153-188. Available from: https://www.taylorfrancis.com/books/9781498763806/chapters/10.1201/9781351246101-5

[97] Rapport JL, Zhang R, Williams RB, Jenkins BM. Anaerobic digestion technologies for the treatment of municipal solid waste. International Journal of Environment and Waste Management [Internet]. 2012;**9**(1/2):100. Available from: http://www.inderscience.com/link.php?id=44163

[98] Maicas S. The role of yeasts in fermentation processes. Microorganisms [Internet]. 2020;**8**(8):1142. Available from: https://www.mdpi.com/2076-2607/8/8/1142

[99] Puligundla P, Smogrovicova D, Obulam VSR, Ko S. Very high gravity (VHG) ethanolic brewing and fermentation: A research update. Journal of Industrial Microbiology

and Biotechnology [Internet]. 2011;**38**(9):1133-1144. Available from: https://academic.oup.com/jimb/article/38/9/1133-1144/5994261

[100] Devi A, Singh A, Bajar S, Pant D, Din ZU. Ethanol from lignocellulosic biomass: An in-depth analysis of pre-treatment methods, fermentation approaches and detoxification processes. Journal of Environmental Chemical Engineering [Internet]. 2021;**9**(5):105798. Available from: https://linkinghub.elsevier.com/retrieve/pii/S2213343721007752

[101] Robak K, Balcerek M. Review of second-generation bioethanol production from residual biomass. Food Technology and Biotechnology [Internet]. 2018;**56**(2). Available from: http://www.ftb.com.hr/images/pdfarticles/2018/April_June/FTB-56-174.pdf

[102] Pandiyan K, Singh A, Singh S, Saxena AK, Nain L. Technological interventions for utilization of crop residues and weedy biomass for second generation bio-ethanol production. Renew Energy [Internet]. 2019;**132**:723-741. Available from: https://linkinghub.elsevier.com/retrieve/pii/S0960148118309996

[103] Ahmad A, Banat F, Taher H. A review on the lactic acid fermentation from low-cost renewable materials: Recent developments and challenges. Environmental Technology & Innovation [Internet]. 2020;**20**:101138. Available from: https://linkinghub.elsevier.com/retrieve/pii/S2352186420314383

[104] Eş I, Mousavi Khaneghah A, Barba FJ, Saraiva JA, Sant'Ana AS, SMB H. Recent advancements in lactic acid production - a review. Food Research International [Internet]. 2018;**107**:763-770. Available from: https://linkinghub.elsevier.com/retrieve/pii/S0963996918300012

[105] Peinemann JC, Demichelis F, Fiore S, Pleissner D. Techno-economic assessment of non-sterile batch and continuous production of lactic acid from food waste. Bioresource Technology [Internet]. 2019 Oct;**289**:121631 Available from: https://linkinghub.elsevier.com/retrieve/pii/S0960852419308612

[106] Xu X, Zhang W, Gu X, Guo Z, Song J, Zhu D, et al. Stabilizing lactate production through repeated batch fermentation of food waste and waste activated sludge. Bioresource Technology [Internet]. 2020;**300**:122709. Available from: https://linkinghub.elsevier.com/retrieve/pii/S0960852419319388

[107] Jahirul MI, Brown JR, Senadeera W, Ashwath N, Laing C, Leski-Taylor J, et al. Optimisation of bio-oil extraction process from beauty leaf (Calophyllum Inophyllum) oil seed as a second generation biodiesel source. Procedia Engineering [Internet]. 2013;**56**:619-624. Available from: https://linkinghub.elsevier.com/retrieve/pii/S1877705813005225

[108] Yang S, Hallett I, Oh HE, Woolf AB, Wong M. Application of electrical impedance spectroscopy and rheology to monitor changes in olive (Olea europaea L.) pulp during cold-pressed oil extraction. Journal of Food Engineering [Internet]. 2019;**245**:96-103. Available from: https://linkinghub.elsevier.com/retrieve/pii/S0260877418304400

[109] Hamm W, Hamilton RJ, Calliauw G, editors. Edible Oil Processing [Internet]. Chichester, UK: John Wiley & Sons, Ltd; 2013. Available from: http://doi.wiley.com/10.1002/9781118535202

[110] Ezeh O, Niranjan K, Gordon MH. Effect of enzyme pre-treatments on bioactive compounds in extracted Tiger nut oil and sugars in residual meals. Journal of the American Oil Chemists' Society [Internet].

2016;**93**(11):1541-1549. Available from: http://doi.wiley.com/10.1007/s11746-016-2883-9

[111] Gaber MAFM, Tujillo FJ, Mansour MP, Juliano P. Improving oil extraction from canola seeds by conventional and advanced methods. Food Engineering Reviews [Internet]. 2018;**10**(4):198-210. Available from: http://link.springer.com/10.1007/s12393-018-9182-1

[112] da Silva RPFF, Rocha-Santos TAP, Duarte AC. Supercritical fluid extraction of bioactive compounds. TrAC Trends in Analytical Chemistry [Internet]. 2016;**76**:40-51 Available from: https://linkinghub.elsevier.com/retrieve/pii/S0165993615300625

[113] Samaram S, Mirhosseini H, Tan CP, Ghazali HM. Ultrasound-assisted extraction and solvent extraction of papaya seed oil: Crystallization and thermal behavior, saturation degree, color and oxidative stability. Industrial Crops and Products [Internet]. 2014;**52**:702-708. Available from: https://linkinghub.elsevier.com/retrieve/pii/S0926669013006730

[114] Shahbaz M, Al-Ansari T, Inayat A, Inayat M. Technical readiness level of biohydrogen production process and its value chain. In: Value-Chain of Biofuels [Internet]. Elsevier; 2022. pp. 335-355. Available from: https://linkinghub.elsevier.com/retrieve/pii/B9780128243886000178

[115] Stafford W, Lotter A, Brent A, Von MG. Biofuels technology: A look forward. WIDER Work Paper Series [Internet]. 2017. Available from: https://ideas.repec.org/p/unu/wpaper/wp2017-87.html

[116] Cerruti E, Di Gruttola F, Lauro G, Valentini TD, Fiaschi P, Sorrenti R, et al. Assessment of feedstocks and Technologies for Advanced Biofuel Production. E3S Web of Conferences [Internet]. 2020;**197**:05002. Available from: https://www.e3s-conferences.org/10.1051/e3sconf/202019705002

Chapter 16

Advances in Bioenergy Production Using Fast Pyrolysis and Hydrothermal Processing

Meegalla R. Chandraratne and Asfaw Gezae Daful

Abstract

This chapter provides an overview of current efforts and advances as well as environmental and economic aspects of fast pyrolysis and hydrothermal processing, which are potential technologies for bioenergy production, mainly bio-oil and syngas. Biomass is presently the primary bioenergy resource in the world. The chapter presents a brief discussion of sources and compositions of biomass. Biomass is converted to various products using thermochemical conversions. Pyrolysis is a thermochemical process that converts biomass into carbon-rich solid residue, condensable vapors, and non-condensable gases in the absence of oxygen. It is a promising technology for converting biomass into renewable biofuels with environmental and economic advantages. Pyrolysis processes are classified based on their operating conditions and desired products. Two thermochemical processes, fast pyrolysis and hydrothermal processing are reviewed. Fast pyrolysis produces a higher quantity and quality of bio-oil and syngas than slow and intermediate pyrolysis processes. Hydrothermal processing converts wet biomass into carbonaceous biofuel. The ability to produce higher-value bioenergy by these pyrolysis technologies depends on the feedstock and operating condition of the pyrolysis processes. This chapter will present the most promising features of fast pyrolysis and hydrothermal processing along with their optimal pyrolysis conditions in maximizing the production of biofuels.

Keywords: lignocellulosic biomass, biomass, bio-oil, biofuel, syngas, pyrolysis

1. Introduction

The current global energy supply is, to a large extent, based on fossil fuels (oil, natural gas, and coal) of which the reserves are finite. As a result of industrialization, population growth, and urbanization, there has been a rapid increase in global energy demand and consumption. The necessity for long-term alternative energy sources is obvious due to the increasing energy consumption, high prices and limited reserves of fossil fuels and evidence of global warming, environmental pollution, and climate change. As a result, there is renewed interest in producing and using renewable energy resources, such as biomass, wind, solar, geothermal, and tidal. Bioenergy is a sustainable form of energy derived from biomass sources [1–4]. Recently, bioenergy is getting more attention because of its potential advantages, including renewable fuel for boilers, engines, turbines, power generation and industrial processes; inexpensive and CO_2 neutral; utilization of nonfood and waste second-generation biomass feedstocks; easy to store and transport as liquid fuels; high-energy density compared to atmospheric biomass gasification fuel gases [2, 5, 6]. Biomass is a promising eco-friendly alternative source of renewable bioenergy because of its abundant availability, relatively lower price, and zero greenhouse gas emissions in the context of current energy scenarios. However, the only renewable energy resource that can be used to produce transport fuels is biomass [2, 4].

Biomass is plant or animal-based organic matter that is living or was living in the recent past. Various biomass components, such as sugars, starches, and lignocellulosic (non-starch fibrous part of the plant) materials, can be converted to liquid transport fuels, reducing the use of fossil fuels. A promising alternative to reduce environmental issues related to waste disposal and management is converting biomass residues and wastes (such as crop residues, food wastes, animal manure, and municipal solid wastes) into useful bioenergy. Some of the advantages of converting biomass residues and wastes into bioenergy include (a) reducing the burden on waste management, (b) converting waste into valuable energy reduces the dependence on fossil fuels, (c) reducing decomposing waste and associated issues such as water contamination, greenhouse gas emissions, pests and insects breeding, and foul odor. [4, 7–10].

The biomass feedstocks can be transformed into biofuels through biochemical and thermal conversion processes. The thermal conversion approach, such as pyrolysis, gasification, and torrefaction, are applicable for a wide range of biomass types using different temperatures to breakdown the bonds of organic matter in a relatively short period of time, unlike the biochemical processes [2, 5, 6]. Lignocellulosic biomass, such as agricultural crop residues, wood and forestry residues, are readily available, inexpensive, and promising resources for biofuels. Biomass can be considered one of the best options for sustaining future energy demand. The more efficient biomass production and conversion processes are essential for the efficient utilization of biomass resources [11]. Biomass is a valuable fuel source that is considered renewable as it can be produced year after year. Compared to fossil fuels, biomass has the potential to reduce combustion emissions, such as CO_2, SO_X, and NO_X [12, 13].

2. Biomass

A commonly used biomass classification is based on the origin of biomass, such as agricultural crop residues, forestry and wood processing residues, purposely grown dedicated energy crops, aquatic biomass, animal, food, industrial and municipal waste, sewage sludge, digestate, and industrial crops. Various types of wastes, such as wastepaper, sewage sludge, cow manure, poultry litter, municipal, and many industrial wastes, are treated as biomass because these are a mixture of organic (and nonorganic) compounds. Biomass is also classified based on its chemical composition as carbohydrates, lignin, essential oils, vegetable oils, animal fats, natural resins (gums), etc. Lignocellulosic biomass is the most abundant biomass on the earth and it represents a major carbon source for bioenergy, biofuels, and chemical compounds [2, 4].

2.1 Sources of biomass

Agricultural crop biomasses are natural products of agriculture, including food-based and nonfood-based portions of crops. The food-based portion comprises simple carbohydrates and oils from crops, such as corn, sugarcane, sugar beet, rapeseed, soybean, and sunflower. The nonfood-based portion is commonly discarded, which comprises complex carbohydrates of crops that are not harvested for commercial use or byproducts from harvesting or processing, such as corn stover, sugarcane bagasse, straw residues, waste from food processing, horticulture, and food crops [4, 7, 14]. Forestry and wood processing residues include trees that are not valuable as timber and not harvested during logging, crowns and branches from fully-grown trees that are removed during logging in commercial forests, waste from forest and wood processing (such as wood pellets, woodchips, leaves, lumps, barks, and sawdust) as well as materials removed during forest management operations. Most of the biomass used today are derived from agricultural crop, forestry, and wood biomass [7, 15].

Another expanding and potentially larger source of biomass is dedicated energy crops that are grown specifically for their fuel value on marginal land unsuitable for agriculture. These are high-yield and low-maintenance crops that produce maximum energy yield. There are two types of energy crops, herbaceous and short-rotation woody crops. Herbaceous energy crops include perennial grasses, such as switchgrass, miscanthus, bluestem, elephant grass, bamboo, and wheatgrass, that are harvested annually after maturity. In 2–3 years, herbaceous energy crops reach complete production and do not require replanting for 15 years or more. The drawback of most nonwoody energy crops is that their chemical properties (high ash and salt content) make them less suitable for combustion. Woody crops are grown on short rotations, generally with more intensive management than timber plantations. These fast-growing hardwood trees include poplar, willow, maple, cottonwood, black walnut, and sweetgum. The woody crops are harvested within 5–8 years of planting [4, 14–17].

Aquatic biomass includes different types of algae, plants, and microbes found in water, such as aquatic plants, water hyacinth, seaweed, kelp, macroalgae, and microalgae [18]. Another primary biomass source is municipal, industrial, food, and animal waste. Municipal solid waste includes waste from commercial, industrial, and residential sectors containing a significant amount of biomass with energy content. The industrial waste includes waste from textile and food processing industries and waste from various industrial and manufacturing processes, such as sugar cane residues and paper sludge. Food waste includes postconsumer waste, animal fat, used cooking oil, residues from food and drink manufacturing, preparation and processing, etc. Animal and human waste includes cooked or uncooked food, fruits, paper, manure of different animals, and waste from farm and processing operations. The problem of disposing of waste is reduced to a certain extent when waste materials are treated and converted to useful energy products. Primarily, animal and human waste are free of harmful materials. In contrast, industrial waste may contain different harmful additives and toxic chemicals [4, 14, 15, 19].

Plant biomass has a carbon-to-oxygen (C/O) ratio of almost one. Because of the high level of oxygen, the energy density of biomass is relatively lower than fossil fuels, which means that issues associated with land use must be considered. The potential benefit of biomass can be reduced by environmental damage due to the expansion of land use for biomass production, leading to a high potential for deforestation, emissions, erosion, nutrient runoff, etc. When sufficient land areas are available, large-scale cultivation of energy crops for bioenergy is feasible. The agricultural lands must be used to grow food crops. Land for energy crops needs to be selected carefully to avoid food versus energy conflict. Identifying lands with minimal disturbance to food production is critical for technically and economically feasible biomass production. To achieve sustainable large-scale biomass production, infertile/marginal or abandoned agricultural land with little fertilizer or pesticides and potentially needing minimal water has been widely considered important. Energy crops are adaptive to infertile/marginal or abandoned agricultural land. Energy crops, such as switchgrass and miscanthus, generally require much less water to grow and are suitable to replace dryland crops partially. Energy crops should not be grown at the expense of biodiversity. Beyond the vast land areas needed to grow energy crops, the long-term impact of soil quality due to repeated removal of biomass and water usage are major concerns [4, 20, 21].

Plants absorb atmospheric CO_2 and produce carbohydrates in photosynthesis that form the building blocks of biomass. Water and sunlight are the other two key ingredients of photosynthesis. The burning of biomass does not add to the total CO_2 inventory of the earth as it releases CO_2 back into the atmosphere that the plants have absorbed recently in photosynthesis producing biomass. Therefore, biomass is considered the most important carbon-neutral or green carbon fuel source. But the overall biomass chain needs to be considered for true carbon neutrality of biomass. Significant cost, energy needs, and CO_2 emissions account for biomass harvesting, drying, handling, transportation, processing, and storage, which need to be considered in life-cycle analysis for sustainability. Biomass plays an integral part in the overall sustainable energy solution. Biochar facilitates the conversion of marginal lands to lands suitable for agriculture by improving soil quality. The impacts of adding biochar to soils may include reduced land area required for food production as a result of increased productivity and making marginal lands economically productive [4, 12, 20, 22].

2.2 Composition of biomass

The chemical composition of biomass is different from fossil fuels. Lignocellulosic biomass is a complex mixture of biopolymers consisting of three key elements, carbon (C), oxygen (O), and hydrogen (H). The percentages in dry matter of C, O, and H are 42–47%, 40–44%, and 6%, respectively, whose total content reaches typically above 95%. In addition, depending on the plant species and environment, plant biomass also contains various macronutrients, micronutrients, trace elements, and other heavy metals [4, 18]. The non-starch fibrous part of the plant (lignocellulosic) material is the major component of plant biomass. Three major constituents of lignocellulosic biomass comprising the cell wall of plants are cellulose, hemicellulose, and lignin. Cellulose, the main component of the plant cell wall, provides structural support. The second most abundant polymer in lignocellulosic biomass is hemicellulose. The third most abundant polymer in lignocellulosic biomass is lignin. Usually, cellulose is the major component in wooden biomasses, whereas hemicellulose is the key component in leaves and grasses and lignin in shells. Hemicellulose is thermally less stable than cellulose. Lignin is the most stable of all three. Knowledge of biomass composition in terms of cellulose, hemicellulose, and lignin can be helpful in controlling the product chemistry [2, 4, 23, 24].

The other compounds present in biomass include inorganic compounds and organic extractives. These nonstructural components include fats, waxes, proteins, terpenes, simple sugars, gums, resins, starches, and essential oils that do not constitute the cell walls or cell layers. Often these compounds are responsible for the smell, color, flavor, and natural resistance to decaying of some species. The inorganic compounds constitute less than 10% by weight of biomass, forming ash in the pyrolysis process. Depending on the type of biomass, the cellulose, hemicellulose, and lignin content fall in the range of 40–60%, 15–30%, and 10–25%, respectively. Fermentable sugars produced by hydrolyzing carbohydrates (cellulose and hemicellulose) can be converted into fuels and chemicals. The content of cellulose, hemicellulose, and lignin in wood biomass is high (~90%), while more extractives and ash are present in agricultural and herbaceous biomass [2, 4, 24].

Analysis of biomass feedstock is an essential part of understanding the behavior of biomass in energy use. The proximate analysis, ultimate analysis, and higher heating value (HHV) of biomass feedstock can provide a clear understanding of its thermochemical conversion characteristics. The proximate analysis gives information on biomass composition in terms of volatile matter (VM), fixed carbon (FC), ash content, and moisture (M) content. VM is the condensable and non-condensable vapors/gases released from biomass during heating. The amount of VM depends on the heating rate and the final biomass temperature. FC is the solid carbon (nonvolatile) that remains in the char after devolatilization. FC and VM indicate the percentage of biomass burned in solid and gaseous states, respectively. Ash is the noncombustible solid residue remaining after biomass is completely burned. These are of fundamental importance for bioenergy use. These data provide the essential information for the furnace design, including sizing and location of primary and secondary air supplies, refractory, ash removal, and exhaust handling equipment. [4, 25, 26].

The ash contains mostly inorganic residues and its composition depends on the biomass type. The inorganics in ash include silica, calcium, iron, aluminum, and small amounts of potassium, sodium, magnesium, and titanium. The content of ash in biomass is generally small. But if biomass contains alkali metals or halides, ash may play a significant role in biomass combustion or gasification. Agricultural residues, grasses, and straw generally contain potassium compounds and chlorides are particularly susceptible to this problem and can cause severe corrosion, fouling, and agglomeration in boilers or gasifiers. Burning biomass at lower temperatures mitigates the problems of corrosion and slagging. The ash produced during biomass conversion does not necessarily come from biomass itself but also from other sources like contamination as well. Biomass can pick up dirt, soil, rock, and other impurities during collection and handling, partly contributing to ash content [4, 14, 25].

The relationship between FC and char yield in biomass is positive, while VM and ash relate negatively to char yield. The greater biomass VM is expected to lead to greater gas production instead of the solid phase. Moisture content has a significant impact on the biomass conversion process. High moisture content is a major concern in biomass conversion. Thermochemical conversion processes generally require biomass with low moisture content. However, biochemical conversion processes can use biomass with high moisture content. Some moisture is required in the gasification process to produce hydrogen and with increasing moisture content, the amount of hydrogen increases. The moisture content can be very high (>90%) in some wet biomass (such as water hyacinth). As the energy used in the evaporation of moisture is not recovered, moisture drains much of the deliverable energy during conversion [4, 25–27].

The ultimate analysis provides the composition of biomass on a gravimetric basis, including major elements (C, H, O, S, and N), moisture, and ash. The ultimate analysis is usually reported on a dry and ash-free basis. These are useful for performing mass balances on biomass conversion processes. Elemental chemical composition, volatiles, moisture, and ash are essential for thermochemical conversions of biomass. Additionally, information on the polymeric composition of biomass is required for conversions, such as torrefaction, pyrolysis, and gasification. The ultimate analysis helps calculate the quantity of combustion air needed to sustain the combustion reactions. Usually, the sulfur and nitrogen content of biomass is very low and produces minimal pollutants SO_X and NO_X [25, 27].

3. Biomass conversion

Biomass can be converted to end products (such as heat, biofuels, or chemicals) through chemical, biochemical, and thermochemical conversion processes. Selection of the conversion process depends on number of factors, such as the desired form of end products, biomass feedstock available, environmental standards, policy, economic conditions, and specific factors related to the project. In most situations, the selection of the conversion process is based on two factors, the desired form of end products and biomass feedstock available. The moisture content of biomass primarily determines the biomass conversion process. Dry biomasses (such as wood or straw) are required for thermochemical conversions, such as pyrolysis, gasification, or combustion. Low-energy density due to higher moisture content makes wet biomass unsuitable for these processes. Transportation and energy costs significantly increased due to the high moisture content. Hydrothermal and biochemical processing are wet conversion processes that have gained growing attention and are more suitable for processing high moisture content biomass, including aquatic biomass, sewage sludge, food waste, and manure. Compared with thermochemical conversion, biochemical conversion consumes less energy but requires more time. Consequently, cost-effective hydrothermal processing has been given more attention than thermochemical conversion (with drying). If moisture content lies between wet and dry regions, additional parameters (such as cost and feasibility of drying) need to be considered in selecting a suitable conversion process [1, 2, 4, 10, 28–30].

Thermochemical conversion processes usually offer many advantages over biochemical conversion processes, including better conversion efficiency, handling a wide variety of feedstocks, shorter reaction times, and high-energy efficiency. As a result, thermochemical conversion processes have recently received greater attention for biofuel production. Many thermochemical conversion processes are available to convert biomass into products (solid, liquid, and gaseous). Thermochemical conversion processes use high temperatures to breakdown the bonds of biomass organic matter. These are classified according to the oxygen content used in the process, including combustion (complete oxidation), gasification (partial oxidation), and pyrolysis (thermal degradation in the absence of oxygen). Torrefaction, a mild form of pyrolysis, is also performed in the absence of oxygen. Hydrothermal processing, a thermal degradation in the absence of oxygen, is an alternative route to process wet biomass. The typical products of the thermochemical conversion of biomass are biochar (carbon-rich solid residue), bio-oil (liquid fraction, condensable vapors), and non-condensable gases. The distribution of products (biochar, bio-oil, and gases) depends primarily on the conversion process [2, 4, 9].

4. Pyrolysis

Pyrolysis is one of the thermal decomposition processes conducted in the absence of oxygen to convert biomass into three distinct product fractions—solid residue (biochar), condensable vapors resulting in liquid product fraction (bio-oil), and non-condensable gaseous products. In the absence of oxygen, combustion cannot occur; instead, pyrolysis happens. Pyrolysis processes can be classified as torrefaction, slow pyrolysis, intermediate pyrolysis, fast pyrolysis, flash pyrolysis, microwave pyrolysis, and hydrothermal processing. These pyrolysis processes differ from one another based on the operating conditions such as residence time, heating rate, and pyrolysis temperature, which in turn affect the yield of products (gas, bio-oil, and biochar) [3, 4]. Moderate temperatures and short residence times tend to produce more liquids. The operating conditions of these different thermal conversion processes, along with their product distribution and biomass feed particle size needed, are shown in **Table 1**.

Mode	Condition	Liquid (bio-oil)	Solid (biochar)	Gas (syngas)	Heating rate	Particle Size (mm)
Slow pyrolysis	Low to moderate temperatures (300–550°C), Long residence time (hours to days)	30%	35%	35%	1–0.8°C/s	5–50
Intermediate pyrolysis	Low to moderate temperatures (450–550°C), Moderate residence time (10–20 s)	50%	25%	25%	1–10°C/s	1–5
Fast pyrolysis	Moderate temperatures (425–600°C), Short vapor residence time (<2 s)	75%	12%	13%	10–1000°C/s	< 1
Flash Pyrolysis	(750–1000°C), (0.5 seconds)				>1000°C/s	<0.2
Microwave-Assisted Pyrolysis	(400–800°C)					
Torrefaction	(450–550°C), (< 2 hours)	20%	75%	5%	< 1°C/s	
Hydrothermal Carbonization	(<200°C), (minutes to hours)	35–80%			< 1°C/s	
Hydrothermal Liquefaction	(200–350°C), 5–20 MPa					
Hydrothermal Gasification	(400–600°C), 23–45 MPa, short residence time					
Gasification	High temperature (>800°C), Long vapor residence time	5% tar (55% water)	10%	85%		

Table 1.
Operating conditions of various pyrolysis processes and their product fractions (bio-oil, biochar, and gas) [2].

The three pathways char formation, depolymerization, and fragmentation describe the primary conversion of biomass during the pyrolysis process. Intra- and intermolecular rearrangement reactions generally favor char formation resulting in higher thermal stability of the residue. The formation of benzene rings and the combination of these rings into an aromatic polycyclic structure characterize char formation. The release of water or non-condensable gas (devolatilization) generally accompanies these rearrangement reactions. The breaking of polymer bonds characterizes depolymerization, a dominant reaction during the initial stages of pyrolysis. When the temperature is sufficiently greater than the activation energies for the bond dissociation, depolymerization occurs, increasing the concentration of free radicals. It is followed by stabilization reactions producing monomer, dimer, and trimer units. These volatile condensable molecules at ambient conditions are found in the liquid fraction. Fragmentation involves breaking polymer bonds and even monomer bonds, resulting in the formation of non-condensable gases and a range of organic vapors that are condensable under ambient conditions [4, 31–33].

The decomposition of three lignocellulose components (hemicellulose, cellulose, and lignin) releases condensable vapors and non-condensable gases. The condensable vapor includes methanol, acetic acid, acetone (mainly from hemicellulose), anhydrous monosaccharides, hydroxyacetaldehyde (mainly from cellulose), phenols, and heavier tars (from lignin decomposition) apart from water vapor. The water-insoluble heavier tars contain larger molecules obtained from splitting ether and C-C bonds in lignin. The condensable vapors are condensed to form bio-oil (a dark brown and free-flowing organic liquid mixture). It usually contains 15–35 wt.% water resulting from the original moisture and as a pyrolysis product. Pyrolysis temperature determines the degree of devolatilization of biomass. There are significant differences between the pyrolysis behaviors of hemicellulose, cellulose, and lignin, which are responsible for most physical and chemical property modifications during the pyrolysis process. Hemicellulose and cellulose decompose over a narrow temperature range. Lignin decomposes over a wider temperature range than hemicellulose and cellulose [4, 31, 32, 34, 35].

5. Fast pyrolysis

Fast pyrolysis typically involves high temperatures (450 and 550°C), high heating rates (10–1000°C/s), and short residence times (0.5–2 s) [36]. It is the most promising thermal process to produce a higher amount of liquid fuel (bio-oils) than other thermal conversion processes. Fast pyrolysis can produce up to 75 wt% bio-oil [37], which can be used directly or as an energy carrier after upgrading.

Fast pyrolysis suppresses secondary reactions (cracking and repolymerization) by having short vapor residence times (rapid removal and quenching of condensable primary volatile vapors) and maintaining high heating rates, thereby maximizing the yield of condensable vapors (bio-oil). This results from rapid quenching and condensing intermediate degradation products of hemicellulose, cellulose, and lignin to bio-oil without further reactions, such as breaking down larger molecular weight (MW) components into smaller MW gaseous products. The rapid quenching of intermediates results in bio-oil having many reactive species, contributing to its unusual characteristics. Rapid and simultaneous depolymerization and fragmentation of cellulose, hemicellulose, and lignin fractions with a rapid increase in temperature form condensable vapors. Rapid removal and quenching shorten the residence time at high temperatures and trap many of these fractions inhibiting further reactions (depolymerize, decompose, degrade, crack or condense with other molecules) to form more non-condensable gases [4, 38, 39].

The main product of the fast pyrolysis process is bio-oil (65–75%), with smaller amounts of biochar (10–25%) and non-condensable gases (10–20%). The distribution of bio-oil, biochar, and gases depends on the biomass composition, rate, and duration of heating. The fast pyrolysis process has the capability to produce bio-oil with high fuel-to-feed ratios. To strike a balance between thorough devolatilization and minimal secondary cracking of vapors, the optimum pyrolysis temperature range for bio-oil production is 425–600°C, with a maximum yield of around 500°C [10]. Due to the higher cellulose and hemicellulose content in wood than in energy crops and agricultural residues, woody biomass (poplar, sawdust, forest, and wood residue) produces the highest bio-oil yield of around 75%, followed by energy crops (reed) and agricultural residues (wheat straw, flax straw, etc.). Product yield in fast pyrolysis is affected by the feed particle size. Smaller particle size increases the heat transfer rate, thus, increasing bio-oil yield. Feedstock particle size and pyrolysis temperature need to be optimized for maximum bio-oil yield [4, 36, 39]. A finely ground (usually <1 mm) biomass feed is required to achieve very high heat transfer rates, thereby very high heating rates reducing heat and mass transfer limitations. Due to the absence of secondary reactions, the overall fast pyrolysis process is highly endothermic. Fast pyrolysis favors low moisture content biomass (<10 wt.%) to minimize water content in bio-oil. Low moisture content also facilitates grinding the feed to give sufficiently small particles to ensure rapid heating and hence fast pyrolysis [4, 37].

The central part of the pyrolysis process is the reactor used, where the thermal conversion reactions occur. Many reactors are used in the pyrolysis process, such as entrained flow reactor, fluidized bed reactor, fixed bed reactor, autoclave, rotating cone reactor, and plasma reactor [40]. These reactors can be classified into subcategories according to the flow of material and phenomena, such as circulating, co-current, counter-current, and crossflow. The amount of bio-oil depends on the reactors used and the operating conditions. The continuous developments in pyrolysis technologies explore many reactor designs to optimize pyrolysis performance and produce high-quality bio-oil. Because of its moisture contents, a higher heating value (HHV) of the bio-oil produced is half the HHV of crude oil. However, each reactor type has specific characteristics, bio-oil yielding capacity, advantages, and limitations. The crucial characteristic steps of the fast pyrolysis process are: the pyrolysis reaction takes place with high heat and heat transfer rates, thus, the particle sizes of biomass materials need to be small enough to enhance such heat transfer; the pyrolysis reaction temperature ranges from 450 to 550°C in the vapor phase; short residence times for the vapor up to two seconds; rapid quenching and condensing the vapors into bio-oil. Common reactor types used for fast pyrolysis are described below [41–45].

5.1 Packed bed reactor

The packed bed pyrolysis reactor system contains a reactor with a gas cooling and cleaning system. These reactors are common types of reactors with cylindrical shapes and packed with solid packing materials, such as firebricks, steel, or concrete; they can be packed with catalysts too. The feed enters from one side and the product is obtained from the other. The relatively fine biomass solids move down and contact a counter-current upward-moving product gas stream. The catalyst pellets are packed in a given section and are unmovable where the pyrolysis reactions occur in this section. Some of the advantages of these packed bed reactors are catalyst recovery and recycling, which gives good economic impacts [41, 42].

5.2 Bubbling fluidized-bed reactor

Fluidization is a phenomenon in which fine solids are transformed into a fluid-like state through contact with a gas or liquid. The particles in the fluidized bed are present in a semi-suspended state when the gas velocity maintains a critical value known as the minimum fluidization velocity. The fixed bed transforms into a fluidized bed at this stage when the fluid drag is equal to the particle weight. Bubbles are made at the openings at which the fluidizing gas enters the bed, where the packing solids above the gas entrance are pushed aside until they create a void space through which the gas can enter at the initial fluidization velocity. Uniform mixing, uniform temperature distribution, and operation in a continuous state are the main advantages of bubbling fluidized-bed reactors [43, 44].

5.3 Circulating fluidized-bed reactor

A circulating fluidized-bed reactor works on the same principle as the bubbling fluidized bed except that the bed is highly expanded and solids continuously recycle around an external loop comprising a cyclone and loop seal. In this circulating fluidized bed, the reactor does not contain any bed and does not have any separate upper surface. The most important advantages of circulating fluidized-bed reactors over other reactor configurations include internal recycling of huge bulk particles reaching the top of the vessel back to its bottom, a good void range, and no distinct upper bed surface in the column [42, 45].

5.4 Ablative pyrolysis reactor

Ablative pyrolysis reactor is basically different in concept compared to the other methods of fast pyrolysis. In ablative pyrolysis, biomass is pressed against a heated surface and rapidly moved during which the biomass melts at the heated surface and leaves an oil film behind which evaporates. In the other reactors mentioned above, the rate of reaction is limited by the rate of heat transfer through a biomass particle, that is why fine particles are required. This ablative process uses larger biomass particles and is typically limited by the heat supply rate to the reactor. The rate of reaction is strongly affected by pressure, the relative velocity of biomass on the heat exchange surface, and the reactor surface temperature [41, 42].

6. Hydrothermal processing

Biomass materials are typically wet and have a moisture content range of up to 95 wt.%. Biomass with more than 30 wt.% moisture content is not suitable for pyrolysis. It needs to be dried before being suitable for pyrolysis, which requires a large amount of energy. It becomes a net energy consumption for biomass with high moisture content because the heat available from the biomass is less than the heat of moisture evaporation. Hydrothermal processing involves applying heat and pressure in the presence of water (subcritical or supercritical). Biomass typically with 70 wt.% or more water can be converted into carbonaceous end products without atmospheric oxygen. Water plays an active role as a solvent and reactant in hydrothermal processing. It is a promising technique for converting wet biomass into carbonaceous solids at relatively high yields without energy-intensive drying before or during the process. Depending on the operating conditions (temperature, pressure, and residence time), hydrothermal processes are classified as hydrothermal carbonization (HTC), hydrothermal liquefaction (HTL), and hydrothermal gasification (HTG) [2, 4].

6.1 Hydrothermal carbonization (HTC)

When biomass feedstock in water is heated at temperatures below 200°C in a sealed vessel at autogenous pressure, mostly solids (hydrochar) are formed in a process known as HTC. The residence time of HTC varies from minutes up to several hours. Hemicellulose and cellulose decomposition temperature in subcritical water is usually around 160°C and 180 to 200°C, respectively, while lignin decomposes above 220°C. HTC converts biomass into three distinct product fractions: solid residue (hydrochar), bio-oil mixed with water in liquid fraction (aqueous solution), and a small volume of gases (consisting mainly of CO_2). HTC aims to maximize the hydrochar yield. The three factors (type of biomass, pH, and maximum temperature used) primarily influence the product distribution and characteristics. The other factors, such as solids concentration (in biomass water mixture) and reaction time, have a relatively smaller influence. The overall extent of hydrochar formation from glucose is negligible below 160°C and yield is maximum at 200°C. Hydrochar formation is reduced with the increase in temperature above 200°C as a result of gasification reactions converting part of the hydrochar formed into volatile compounds. Process conditions and the type of biomass feed are the two factors that influence energy requirements and final product composition. Hydrochar has high hydrophobic and homogeneous properties and can be easily separated from the liquid fraction. Dried hydrochar pellets can be produced from the separated solid fraction, which can be used for energy production. The liquid fraction can be used to recover mono sugars. The gas fraction has less CO and CO_2 and is less harmful. The hydrochar has carbon content similar to lignite and the yield of hydrochar varies from 35% up to 80% [2, 4, 46–48].

The HTC reduces both the oxygen and hydrogen content of the biomass through dehydration and decarboxylation. During HTC, hemicelluloses and cellulose are hydrolyzed to oligomers/monomers, whereas lignin mostly remains unchanged. The reaction mechanism of the HTC process mainly involves dehydration, decarboxylation, and polymerization. Dehydration is favored at temperatures less than 300°C. The hydroxymethylfurfural (HMF) generated from hexose (D-fructose and D-glucose) and furfural generated from pentoses (D-xylose) are well-known dehydration products of sugars. The hydrothermal process under acidic conditions allows the effective conversion of D-glucose to HMF. D-glucose first isomerizes to D-fructose and then undergoes dehydration to form HMF. The HMF, in turn, decomposes into levulinic acid, formic acid, and soluble polymeric carbonaceous material with increasing residence time [49, 50].

Hydrochar has a higher energy content than the feedstock used and lower O/C and H/C ratios than the feedstock. Hydrochar has higher H/C ratios than biochar specifications. HTC is a high-energy-consuming process. Solar energy appears to be an attractive renewable energy source to combine with HTC. HTC can combine with other processes to produce hydrochar with characteristics (morphology, porosity, conductivity, H/C ratio, O/C ratio, energy content, elemental composition, etc.) suitable for applications in many fields such as solid fuel in power generation, soil amendment, adsorbent in water purification and carbon capture. Hydrochar can be further processed to use as carbon electrodes or nanocomposites. HTC process was initially used for the degradation of organic materials, production of liquid and gaseous fuels, and production of basic chemicals. In recent years, the technology gained research interest to produce solid hydrochar and as a technique to synthesize nano- and micro-size carbon particles [46, 47, 51, 52].

The hydrochar produced by HTC directly from carbohydrates or biomass lacks porosity. Only a tiny porosity is developed even after further carbonization at a higher temperature. This is due to hydrochar being pre-carbonized material produced under autogenic pressures and temperatures between 160 and 200°C. For most industrial applications such as adsorption or catalysis, the high surface area and porosity of hydrochar are essential. This would ensure efficient transport and diffusion throughout the material. Different techniques have been developed to improve the porosity of hydrochar [47]. Some of the advantages of the HTC process include low carbonization temperatures, can be synthesized in the aqueous phase (no drying is required), and inexpensive process. Hydrochar obtained from HTC has the following properties: (a) uniform spherical micro-sized particles; (b) oxygenated functional groups at the surface (OH, C=O, COOH groups); (c) controlled porosity can be easily introduced using activation procedures, thermal treatments, etc.; (d) easily controlled surface chemistry and electronic properties via additional thermal treatment; (e) special physicochemical properties can be obtained by adding other components (such as inorganic nanoparticles) to biomass [49, 50].

6.2 Hydrothermal liquefaction (HTL)

At temperatures between 200 and 350°C and pressures of 5–20 MPa, biomass is primarily converted to a liquid fraction (aqueous soluble) in a process known as HTL. Leading reactions in HTL are considered to be free radical and ionic reactions. At ambient conditions, the dielectric constant (a measure of hydrogen bonding) of water is about 80 F/m. It decreases rapidly with increasing temperature, at 250°C and 5 MPa dielectric constant is about 27 F/m and at 350°C and 25 MPa about 14 F/m. Due to decreasing dielectric constant (number of hydrogen bonds), water displays less polar behavior. An increase in temperature increases the dissociation of water. The ionic product of water (pK_w) at 25°C is 14 and decreases to 11 at 250°C. With increasing temperature, mass transfer is enhanced because of accelerated mass-transfer-limited chemical reactions resulting from a decrease in the viscosity of water [4, 53, 54].

The primary conversion of biomass during the HTL comprises three pathways; depolymerization, decomposition, and recombination. Higher MW biomass is depolymerized and decomposed into smaller MW compounds. These compounds are highly reactive and recombined (repolymerized) to form bio-oil, gaseous and solid products. The parameters such as temperature and pressure are important for the depolymerization of long-chain polymer structures to shorter-chain hydrocarbons. The decomposition step involves three steps: dehydration (loss of water molecule), decarboxylation (loss of CO_2 molecule), and deamination (removal of amino acid content). The dehydration and decarboxylation steps remove oxygen from the biomass in the form of H_2O and CO_2, respectively. Macromolecules of biomass are hydrolyzed to form polar monomers and oligomers. Subcritical water at HTL temperatures and pressure breaks down the hydrogen bonds of the cellulose structure to form sugar monomers. It is rapidly degraded by different reactions (such as isomerization, hydrolysis, dehydration, reverse aldol defragmentation, rearrangement, and recombination) into a series of products. Most of the degradation products such as polar organic molecules, furfurals, phenols, glycolaldehyde, and organic acids are highly soluble in water. Recombination and repolymerization of light MW compounds occur due to the unavailability of the hydrogen compound or excess oxygen [53, 55, 56].

During HTL of lignin, hydrolysis and splitting of the ether and C-C bond, demethoxylation, alkylation, and condensation reactions occur. Competition occurs between these main reactions. The gaseous, liquid, and solid yield of HTL of biomass depends on several parameters, including biomass feedstock, temperature, heating rate, residence time, pressure, mass ratio of water/biomass, and catalyst. The main product of HTL is the liquid fraction (bio-oil). The temperature and pressure directly (activation energy, reaction equilibria) and indirectly (solvent properties) impact the reaction. During HTL, the major components of biomass cellulose, hemicellulose, and lignin behave differently. In general, biomass with high cellulose and hemicellulose produces higher bio-oil yields. Higher bio-oil yields have been reported from hardwood samples (cherry) than softwood (cypress). Softwood contains higher lignin than hardwood, hence, lower bio-oil yield [54, 57]. Other studies have also shown that both temperature and lignin contents of wood had a marked effect on bio-oil yield. Bio-oil production was maximum for wood with low lignin contents [58, 59]. Subcritical water in HTL acts as a heat transfer medium to overcome the heat transfer limitations. As a result, biomass particle size has negligible to minimal effects on HTL. Excessive size reduction of biomass feedstock is not required [54, 58].

Usually, the effect of temperature on the bio-oil yield is synergetic due to the increased fragmentation of biomass at higher temperatures. Depolymerization occurs when the temperature is sufficient for bond dissociation. The competition among hydrolysis, fragmentation, and repolymerization reactions describes the role of temperature during the HTL process. Depolymerization is a dominant reaction during the initial stages of HTL. Repolymerization becomes active at later stages of HTL, leading to the formation of hydrochar. Intermediate temperatures usually produce higher bio-oil yields [54, 58]. The increase in HTL temperature not only enhances the reaction rates but also changes the reaction mechanisms. Hence, lower temperatures favor ionic reactions; higher temperatures promote the formation of radicals by homolytic bond breakage. Radical reactions usually lead to a diverse product spectrum and finally to gas formation [54, 60, 61]. Various authors have observed increased bio-oil yields with increasing temperature during the HTL process. Different authors have proposed various optimum temperatures for a variety of biomasses. It can be assumed that the temperature range of 280–350°C would be suitable for the decomposition of biomass under both subcritical and supercritical conditions. Final HTL temperature varies with the type of biomass [54, 58].

The temperature gradients during the heating of biomass are important for the sequence and extent of chemical reactions. Due to the better dissolution and stabilization of fragmented compounds in subcritical water, the effect of heating rates on the product distributions in HTL is minimal compared to pyrolysis. Because of secondary reactions, slow heating rates typically tend to yield solid fraction (hydrochar). Secondary reactions are also dominant at very high heating rates and yield more gases. Furthermore, bio-oil yield is not significantly affected by large variations in high heating rates. Moderate heating rates may be suitable to overcome heat transfer limitations leading to extensive fragmentation and minimal secondary reactions. Many researchers have investigated the effect of residence times on product distribution during the HTL process. Duration of reaction time may characterize the product compositions and the overall biomass conversion. Short residence times are usually preferred during the HTL of biomass. Longer residence times can decompose preasphaltenes and asphaltene into lighter products enhancing the yield of bio-oil and gases. It is essential to inhibit the decomposition of lighter products to obtain a high liquid oil yield. Generally, bio-oil yield attains a maximum before decreasing for extended residence times, whereas gas yield and biomass conversion increase continuously until reaching saturation [54–56, 58].

Pressure helps maintain single-phase media for HTL to avoid large heat inputs required for phase change. Two-phase systems need a large heat supply to maintain the temperature of the system. Pressure increases solvent density and a high-density medium penetrates effectively into molecules of biomass components resulting in improved decomposition and extraction. Many investigations have been performed to study the influence of different solvents (such as subcritical and supercritical alcohols) on the liquefaction yield of lignocellulosic biomass. Critical temperatures and pressures of alcohols are lower than in water and significantly milder reaction conditions could be used. Alcohols are expected to dissolve relatively high MW products derived from cellulose, hemicelluloses, and lignin due to their lower dielectric constants than water. Ethanol and methanol have been widely employed for biomass liquefaction. The mass ratio of biomass/water is considered a vital parameter for the HTL process. Different authors investigated the effect of water density on HTL yield. All solvolytic conversions are benefitted from the dilution of reactants, intermediates, and products during the reaction. This dilution minimizes cross-reactions and produces a more distinct product spectrum. Higher substrate concentrations inevitably lead to cross-reactions leading to undesirable polymerization of the reaction products. Such processes have been observed for HTL of biomasses, promoting the formation of solid fractions. Catalysts are important in the HTL of biomass. A range of homogeneous catalysts (such as mineral acids, organic acids, and bases) and heterogeneous catalysts (such as zirconium dioxide, anatase, and other materials) has been proposed to tailor the reaction toward a specific product and enhance the reaction rates [54–56, 62].

6.3 Hydrothermal gasification (HTG)

HTG operates near or above the critical point of water at 400–600°C and 23–45 MPa. The primary product of HTG is a mixture of non-condensable gases (H_2, CO, CH_4, and CO_2), which can produce syngas enriched with H_2. At the critical point (374°C and 22.1 MPa) of water, the conversion efficiency is improved. Biomass polysaccharides split in the presence of supercritical water (SCW). Due to higher reaction temperatures, HTG reactions progress at a faster rate and complete decomposition of biomass is achieved. This is a distinctive feature of HTG compared to other hydrothermal treatments (HTC and HTL). One of the problems with HTC and HTL is the difficulty in byproduct treatment due to undesirable byproducts being occasionally dissolved in the liquid fraction. The conversion rate of HTG is typically higher than 80% that decomposes biomass into gaseous products. Consequently, post-treatment of liquid fraction is not required or easily carried out because only a small amount of organic compounds remain in the liquid. Conventional gasification can be effectively employed when biomass is not wet, but it is ineffective when biomass has a high moisture content (> 80%). The syngas of conventional gasification is partially diluted with nitrogen (due to partial oxidation using air) and contains tar. Syngas from HTG is not diluted with nitrogen and do not contain tars. Tar, if produced, remains in the liquid fraction [2, 4, 63].

The HTG performance is strongly dependent on the operating conditions, including biomass characteristics, temperature, pressure, residence time, feedstock concentration, and catalyst. The rate of hydrolysis and decomposition is relatively fast in the HTG process; hence, short residence times are expected to degrade biomass successfully. Optimization of residence times is required for the efficient destruction of biomass organic compounds. Pressure helps maintain single-phase media for HTG to avoid large heat inputs required for phase change. Two-phase systems need a large heat supply to maintain the temperature of the system. The rate of hydrolysis and biomass dissolution can be controlled by maintaining pressure higher than the supercritical pressure, which may enhance favorable reaction pathways for bio-oil or gas yield. Pressure imparts minor or negligible influence on bio-oil or gas yield in supercritical conditions. This is because, in the supercritical region, the effect of pressure on the properties of water is minimal [54, 58, 64].

SCW exhibits a unique property; the density, viscosity, ionic product, and dielectric constant change significantly when water changes from ambient conditions (25°C and 0.1 MPa) to the supercritical condition. At ambient conditions, the dielectric constant of water is about 80 F/m and water is a polar solvent due to a high dielectric constant (a large number of hydrogen bonds). At supercritical conditions (400°C and 25 MPa), the dielectric constant is about 6 F/m; because of the decrease in the number of hydrogen bonds, water begins to display the behavior of a nonpolar solvent that can completely dissolve many organic compounds, hydrocarbons, and gases (such as CO_2, CH_4, H_2, and N_2). This results in poor solubility of inorganic polar compounds in SCW. Many rapid homogeneous reactions involving organic compounds occur at supercritical conditions due to the absence of phase boundaries. In subcritical water, inorganic polar compounds (such as NaCl, KCl, and $CaSO_4$) are usually soluble. But these compounds are insoluble in supercritical water and easily separated from the reaction products. SCW exhibits gas-like properties and using SCW as the reaction medium in HTG has several advantages: low viscosity creates a high diffusion coefficient and enhances mass transfer, low density improves the solvation properties, creates a single-phase reaction environment in the reactor by complete miscibility with different organics and gases, enhance mass transfer, prevent poisoning of catalyst (if used) and coke formation and product gas (syngas) does not have tar and has a high heating value. Syngas can be converted to liquid fuels or value-added chemicals via different gas-to-liquid conversions, such as Fischer-Tropsch synthesis or to ethanol and butanol through syngas fermentation using microorganisms [9, 53, 54, 63].

7. Conclusions

Biomass is a sustainable energy source and a promising eco-friendly alternative source of renewable bioenergy. The most abundant biomass, lignocellulose, represents a significant carbon source for bioenergy. Lignocellulosic biomass is a complex mixture of biopolymers. The three major biopolymers are cellulose, hemicellulose, and lignin. Inorganic compounds and organic extractives are among other compounds present in lignocellulosic biomass. The selection of the process to convert biomass to end products depends on several factors, but the desired form of end products and available biomass feedstock are the two key factors usually considered. Thermochemical conversion processes usually offer many advantages over biochemical conversion processes.

Thermochemical conversions convert biomass into liquid, gaseous and solid products. The product distribution depends on the conversion process employed, that is, operating conditions (heating rate, residence time, and temperature). More liquids are produced at moderate temperatures and short residence times. Bio-oil is the desired product in fast pyrolysis and bio-oil yield is maximized at high heating rates, short vapor residence times, and around 500°C. A finely ground dry biomass feed is essential for high heat transfer rates. Due to the higher cellulose and hemicellulose content, woody biomass produces the highest bio-oil yield.

High moisture content is a major barrier in biomass processing for bioenergy. It has a significant impact on the biomass conversion process. High moisture biomass requires a large amount of energy to evaporate moisture to make it suitable for pyrolysis. Hydrothermal processing is useful for biomass feedstocks with high moisture as it does not require drying, thereby reducing energy costs. Hydrothermal processing has been given more attention in recent years and can be classified into HTC, HTL, and HTG based on the reaction temperature, pressure, and residence time. HTC, HTL, and HTG are aimed to maximize the production of solid (hydrochar), liquid (bio-oil/water), and gas (non-condensable) fractions, respectively. More research is required on hydrothermal processing to investigate reaction kinetics and chemistry, heat transfer, energy and heat recovery, combinations with other technologies, such as solar, technical, and economic aspects and the effect of operational parameters.

Author details

Meegalla R. Chandraratne* and Asfaw Gezae Daful
Department of Chemical Engineering, Higher Colleges of Technology, United Arab Emirates

*Address all correspondence to: mchandra@hct.ac.ae

References

[1] Adams P, Bridgwater T, Lea-Langton A, et al. Biomass conversion technologies. In: Thornley P, Adams P, editors. Greenhouse Gas Balance of Bioenergy Systems. London: Elsevier; 2018. pp. 107-139

[2] Daful AG, Chandraratne MR. Biochar production from biomass waste-derived material. In: Hashmi S, Choudhury IA, editors. Encyclopedia of Renewable and Sustainable Materials. Oxford: Elsevier; 2020. pp. 370-378

[3] Daful AG, Chandraratne MR, Loridon M. Recent perspectives in biochar production, characterization and applications. In: Bartoli M, Giorcelli M, editors. Recent Perspectives in Pyrolysis Research. London, UK: IntechOpen; 2022. pp. 327-344

[4] Chandraratne MR, Daful AG. Recent advances in thermochemical conversion of biomass. In: Bartoli M, Giorcelli M, editors. Recent Perspectives in Pyrolysis Research. London, UK: IntechOpen; 2022. pp. 145-176

[5] Lehmann J, Joseph S. Biochar for Environmental Management: Science and Technology. London, UK: Earthscan; 2009

[6] Matsakas L, Gao Q, Jansson S, et al. Green conversion of municipal solid wastes into fuels and chemicals. Electronic Journal of Biotechnology. 2017;**26**:69-83

[7] Bhat AH, Dasan YK, Khan I. Extraction of lignin from biomass for biodiesel production. In: Hakeem KR, Jawaid M, Alothman OY, editors. Agricultural Biomass Based Potential Materials. New York: Springer; 2015. pp. 155-180

[8] Kataki R, Chutia RS, Mishra M, et al. Feedstock suitability for thermochemical processes. In: Pandey A, Bhaskar T, Stöcker M, et al., editors. Recent Advances in Thermochemical Conversion of Biomass. Oxford: Elsevier; 2015. pp. 31-74

[9] Okolie JA, Nanda S, Dalai AK, et al. A review on subcritical and supercritical water gasification of biogenic, polymeric and petroleum wastes to hydrogen-rich synthesis gas. Renewable and Sustainable Energy Reviews. 2020;**119**:109546

[10] Basu P. Biomass Gasification, Pyrolysis and Torrefaction: Practical Design and Theory. Second. Oxford: Elsevier; 2013

[11] Chandra R, Takeuchi H, Hasegawa T. Methane production from lignocellulosic agricultural crop wastes: A review in context to second generation of biofuel production. Renewable and Sustainable Energy Reviews. 2012;**16**:1462-1476

[12] Pilon G, Lavoie JM. Pyrolysis of switchgrass (Panicum virgatum L.) at low temperatures within N_2 and CO_2 environments: Product yield study. ACS Sustainable Chemistry & Engineering. 2013;**1**:198-204

[13] Ruan R, Zhang Y, Chen P, et al. Biofuels: Introduction. In: Pandey A, Larroche C, Dussap C-G, et al., editors. Biofuels: Alternative Feedstocks and Conversion Processes for the Production of Liquid and Gaseous Biofuels. Oxford: Academic Press; 2019. pp. 3-43

[14] Wolf JP. Biomass combustion for power generation: An introduction. In: Rosendahl L, editor. Biomass Combustion Science, Technology and Engineering. Cambridge: Woodhead; 2013. pp. 3-8

[15] Hodge BK. Alternative Energy Systems and Applications. Hoboken, NJ: John Wiley & Sons; 2017

[16] Quader MA, Ahmed S. Bioenergy with carbon capture and storage (BECCS): Future prospects of carbon-negative technologies. In: Rasul M, Azad A, Sharma S, editors. Clean Energy for Sustainable Development Comparisons and Contrasts of New Approaches. Oxford: Elsevier; 2017. pp. 467-481

[17] Mansoori GA, Enayati N, Agyarko LB. Energy (Sources, Utilization, Legislation, Sustainability, Illinois as Model State). Danvers, MA: World Scientific; 2016

[18] Sanchez J, Curt MD, Robert N, et al. Biomass resources. In: Lago C, Caldés N, Lechón Y, editors. The Role of Bioenergy in the Emerging Bioeconomy: Resources, Technologies, Sustainability and Policy. Oxford: Elsevier Inc; 2019. pp. 25-111

[19] Tripathi M, Sahu JN, Ganesan P. Effect of process parameters on production of biochar from biomass waste through pyrolysis: A review. Renewable and Sustainable Energy Reviews. 2016;**55**:467-481

[20] Carpenter NE. Chemistry of Sustainable Energy. Boca Raton, FL: CRC Press; 2014. DOI: 10.1201/b16687

[21] Li R, Chen J. Planning the next-generation biofuel crops based on soil-water constraints. Biomass and Bioenergy. 2018;**115**:19-26

[22] Cowie A, Woolf D, Gaunt J, et al. Biochar, carbon accounting and climate change. In: Biochar for Environmental Management: Science, Technology and Implementation. Oxon: Routledge; 2015. pp. 763-794

[23] Dhyani V, Bhaskar T. Pyrolysis of biomass. In: Pandey A, Larroche C, Dussap C-G, et al., editors. Biofuels: Alternative Feedstocks and Conversion Processes for the Production of Liquid and Gaseous Biofuels. Oxford: Elsevier; 2019. pp. 217-244

[24] Wang S, Dai G, Yang H, et al. Lignocellulosic biomass pyrolysis mechanism: A state-of-the-art review. Progress in Energy and Combustion Science. 2017;**62**:33-86

[25] Basu P. Biomass Gasification, Pyrolysis and Torrefaction: Practical Design and Theory. 2nd ed. London: Elsevier; 2018. DOI: 10.1016/B978-0-12-812992-0.00003-0

[26] Nunes LJR, Matias JCDO, Catalão JPDS. Torrefaction of Biomass for Energy Applications- from Fundamentals to Industrial Scale. Oxford: Elsevier; 2018. DOI: 10.1016/b978-0-12-809462-4.00001-8

[27] Jameel H, Keshwani DR. Thermochemical conversion of biomass to power and fuels. In: Cheng JJ, editor. Biomass to Renewable Energy Processes. Boca Raton, FL: Taylor & Francis; 2018. pp. 375-421

[28] McKendry P. Energy production from biomass (part 1): Overview of biomass. Bioresource Technology. 2002;**83**:37-46

[29] Jafri N, Wong WY, Doshi V, et al. A review on production and characterization of biochars for application in direct carbon fuel cells. Process Safety and Environment Protection. 2018;**118**:152-166

[30] Maniscalco MP, Volpe M, Messineo A. Hydrothermal carbonization as a valuable tool for energy and environmental applications: A review. Energies. 2020;**13**:04098

[31] Collard FX, Blin J. A review on pyrolysis of biomass constituents:

Mechanisms and composition of the products obtained from the conversion of cellulose, hemicelluloses and lignin. Renewable and Sustainable Energy Reviews. 2014;**38**:594-608

[32] Kan T, Strezov V, Evans TJ. Lignocellulosic biomass pyrolysis: A review of product properties and effects of pyrolysis parameters. Renewable and Sustainable Energy Reviews. 2016;**57**:1126-1140

[33] Ranzi E, Faravelli T, Manenti F. Pyrolysis, gasification, and combustion of solid fuels. In: Marin G, West D, Li J, et al., editors. Advances in Chemical Engineering, Volume 49, Thermochemical Process Engineering. Elsevier: Oxford; 2016. pp. 1-94

[34] Nachenius RW, Ronsse F, Venderbosch RH, et al. Biomass Pyrolysis. In: Marin GB, West DH, Li J, et al., editors. Advances in Chemical Engineering, Volume 42. Chemical Engineering for Renewables Conversion. Elsevier: Oxford; 2013. pp. 75-139

[35] Ronsse F, Nachenius RW, Prins W. Carbonization of biomass. In: Pandey A, Bhaskar T, Stöcker M, et al., editors. Recent Advances in Thermochemical Conversion of Biomass. Oxford: Elsevier; 2015. pp. 293-324

[36] Roy P, Dias G. Prospects for pyrolysis technologies in the bioenergy sector: A review. Renewable and Sustainable Energy Reviews. 2017;**77**:59-69

[37] Bridgwater AV. Review of fast pyrolysis of biomass and product upgrading. Biomass and Bioenergy. 2012;**38**:68-94

[38] Demirbas A. Biorefineries: Current activities and future developments. Energy Conversion and Management. 2009;**50**:2782-2801

[39] Bridgwater A. Fast pyrolysis of biomass for the production of liquids. In: Rosendahl L, editor. Biomass Combustion Science, Technology and Engineering. Cambridge: Woodhead; 2013. pp. 130-171

[40] Inayat A, Ahmed A, Tariq R, et al. Techno-economical evaluation of bio-oil production via biomass fast pyrolysis process: A review. Frontiers in Energy Research. 2022;**9**:1-9

[41] Bridgwater T. Challenges and opportunities in fast pyrolysis of biomass: Part II. Johnson Matthey Technology Review. 2018;**62**:150-160

[42] Jahirul MI, Rasul MG, Chowdhury AA, et al. Biofuels production through biomass pyrolysis-a technological review. Energies. 2012;**5**:4952-5001

[43] Rasaq WA, Golonka M, Scholz M, et al. Opportunities and challenges of high-pressure fast pyrolysis of biomass: A review. Energies. 2021;**14**:1-20

[44] Pan X, Lian W, Yang J, et al. Downer reactor simulation and its application on coal pyrolysis: A review. Carbon Resources Conversion. 2022;**5**:35-51

[45] Raza M, Inayat A, Ahmed A, et al. Progress of the pyrolyzer reactors and advanced technologies for biomass pyrolysis processing. Sustain. 2021;**13**:1-42

[46] Heidari M, Dutta A, Acharya B, et al. A review of the current knowledge and challenges of hydrothermal carbonization for biomass conversion. Journal of the Energy Institute. 2019;**92**:1779-1799

[47] Titirici MM, Funke A, Kruse A. Hydrothermal carbonization of biomass. In: Pandey A,

Bhaskar T, Stöcker M, et al., editors. Recent Advances in Thermochemical Conversion of Biomass. Oxford: Elsevier; 2015. pp. 325-352

[48] Lam PS, Tooyserkani Z, Naimi LJ, et al. Pretreatment and Pelletization of Woody biomass. In: Fang Z, editor. Retreatment Techniques for Biofuels and Biorefineries. Berlin: Springer-Verlag; 2013. pp. 93-116

[49] Titirici MM, White RJ, Falco C, et al. Black perspectives for a green future: Hydrothermal carbons for environment protection and energy storage. Energy & Environmental Science. 2012;**5**:6796-6822

[50] Yu KL, Lau BF, Show PL, et al. Recent developments on algal biochar production and characterization. Bioresource Technology. 2017;**246**:2-11

[51] Briongos JV, Taramona S, Gómez-Hernández J, et al. Solar and biomass hybridization through hydrothermal carbonization. Renewable Energy. 2021;**177**:268-279

[52] Ababneh H, Hameed BH. Chitosan-derived hydrothermally carbonized materials and its applications: A review of recent literature. International Journal of Biological Macromolecules. 2021;**186**:314-327

[53] Toor SS, Rosendahl L, Rudolf A. Hydrothermal liquefaction of biomass: A review of subcritical water technologies. Energy. 2011;**36**:2328-2342

[54] Singh R, Prakash A, Balagurumurthy B, et al. Hydrothermal liquefaction of biomass. In: Pandey A, Bhaskar T, Stöcker M, et al., editors. Recent Advances in Thermochemical Conversion of Biomass. Oxford: Elsevier; 2015. pp. 269-291

[55] Biswas B, Kumar J, Bhaskar T. Advanced hydrothermal liquefaction of biomass for bio-oil production. In: Pandey A, Larroche C, Dussap C-G, et al. (eds) Biofuels: Alternative Feedstocks and Conversion Processes for the Production of Liquid and Gaseous Biofuels. Oxford: Elsevier Inc., 2019, pp. 245-266.

[56] Gollakota ARK, Kishore N, Gu S. A review on hydrothermal liquefaction of biomass. Renewable and Sustainable Energy Reviews. 2018;**81**:1378-1392

[57] Bhaskar T, Sera A, Muto A, et al. Hydrothermal upgrading of wood biomass: Influence of the addition of K2CO3 and cellulose/lignin ratio. Fuel. 2008;**87**:2236-2242

[58] Akhtar J, Amin NAS. A review on process conditions for optimum bio-oil yield in hydrothermal liquefaction of biomass. Renewable and Sustainable Energy Reviews. 2011;**15**:1615-1624

[59] Zhong C, Wei X. A comparative experimental study on the liquefaction of wood. Energy. 2004;**29**:1731-1741

[60] Williams PT, Onwudili J. Composition of products from the supercritical water gasification of glucose: A model biomass compound. Industrial and Engineering Chemistry Research. 2005;**44**:8739-8749

[61] Yoshida T, Oshima Y, Matsumura Y. Gasification of biomass model compounds and real biomass in supercritical water. Biomass and Bioenergy. 2004;**26**:71-78

[62] Moller M, Nilges P, Harnisch F, et al. Subcritical water as reaction environment: Fundamentals of hydrothermal biomass transformation. ChemSusChem. 2011;**4**:566-579

[63] Matsumura Y. Hydrothermal gasification of biomass. In: Pandey A,

Bhaskar T, Stöcker M, et al., editors. Recent Advances in Thermochemical Conversion of Biomass. Oxford: Elsevier; 2015. pp. 251-267

[64] Kersten SRA, Potic B, Prins W, et al. Gasification of model compounds and wood in hot compressed water. Industrial and Engineering Chemistry Research. 2006;**45**:4169-4177

Chapter 17

Comparative Analysis of Biodiesel Production from Different Potential Feedstocks in the Philippines

Rona Joyce B. Landoy, Rex B. Demafelis, Bernadette T. Magadia and Anna Elaine D. Matanguihan

Abstract

In response to the worsening crisis on energy security and climate change, the Philippine Biofuels Law (Republic Act 9367) was enacted which mandates the blending of biodiesel to petroleum diesel sold in the country. Primarily, feedstock and pricing concerns led to stagnant growth of the Philippine biodiesel industry. Hence, viability of different potential biodiesel feedstocks such as coconut, oil palm, and soybean (first generation), jatropha and used cooking oil (second generation), and microalgae (third generation) was assessed through extensive research and developments. Among these sources, oil palm is regarded as the best complementary feedstock to coconut due to its high biodiesel productivity of 376 million liters per year. Oil palm biodiesel production in the Philippines was also found to have a low carbon footprint of 1.80 kg CO_2e per liter and a GHG reduction potential of 42%, which corresponds to a GHG savings of about 1.05 million metric tons CO_2e per year for a 5% blending mandate in 2025. Additionally, a low biodiesel selling price of about Php 33.26 per liter can be achieved from using this feedstock for biodiesel production. Hence, use of a low cost and readily available feedstock coupled with established processing technologies and pricing mechanisms will help boost the biodiesel industry in the Philippines.

Keywords: biodiesel feedstocks, biofuels, biomass, transesterification

1. Introduction

The use of renewable energy sources such as biofuels is a major thrust to combat the imminent crisis on energy security and climate change. With diminishing fossil fuel supply and global warming issues, a transition to cleaner and more secure fuel production is necessary. This led to the implementation of Republic Act 9367, otherwise known as the Biofuels Act of 2006. This Act primarily aims to lessen the country's dependence on imported fossil fuels by utilizing renewable and clean energy sources, thereby mitigating climate change while also promoting employment opportunities for the country's economic growth [1].

Pursuant to the Biofuels Law, a mandate was implemented on blending locally sourced biofuels to all petroleum-based fuel sold in the country. After two years since the law took effect last 06 February 2007, the mandated minimum level of bioethanol blending to gasoline was 5% by volume while biodiesel blending to diesel was set to 2% by volume. The Department of Energy (DOE) is mandated to spearhead the implementation of the Act through the creation of the National Biofuel Board (NBB). To further promote the development of biofuels in the country, the Biofuels Act provides incentives to investments related to the production, distribution, and use of locally produced biofuels. These incentives include elimination of specific tax on local or imported biofuels additives, exemption of the sale of raw material used to produce biofuels such as, but not limited to, coconut, jatropha, cassava, sugarcane, corn, and sweet sorghum from the value added tax, exemption of water effluents derived from biofuels production from wastewater charges in accordance with the Republic Act No. 9275 or the Philippine Clean Water Act of 2004, and provision for financial assistance from government financial institutions for activities engaged in the production, storage, handing, and transport of biofuel and biofuel feedstock [2]. Primarily, high selling price of biofuels due to the high domestic cost of production is the main challenge facing the country's biofuels industry. In response to this, development and implementation of various research studies were initiated by the Department of Agriculture (DA) and the Department of Science and Technology (DOST) through the Philippine Council for Industry and Energy Research and Development (PCIEERD) in support to identifying and developing sustainable and viable feedstocks as well as economically feasible conversion technologies for biofuels production and utilization.

At present, the bioethanol blending of 10% remains consistent with the mandate under the Act. From sugarcane as main biomass source for bioethanol fuel, a shift to use of molasses, a byproduct of sugar-making process, has been initiated. On the other hand, biodiesel in the country is solely sourced from coconut. Although NBB has recommended an increase in the biodiesel blend to 5% in 2015, it was indefinitely delayed owing to feedstock and pricing concerns causing the current blending scenario for biodiesel to remain stagnant at 2% [3]. With the plan of further increasing the country's blending targets for biodiesel to 10% by 2020 and eventually to 20% by 2025 onwards, exploration of a more sustainable and economical feedstocks is necessary to meet the increasing biodiesel demand. Some of the feedstocks under study as potential sources for biodiesel production include coconut, oil palm, soybean, jatropha, used cooking oil, and microalgae. Hence, this book chapter provides an information on the suitability of different potential feedstocks in the Philippines that can be utilized for biodiesel production. Appropriate technologies for the conversion of these feedstocks to biodiesel fuel are also discussed. A brief overview of the current situation of the biodiesel industry in the Philippines is also provided in this chapter.

2. The Philippine biodiesel industry

2.1 Biodiesel situation in the Philippines

As the country foresees to become energy self-sufficient, the alarming energy crisis poses challenges caused mainly by heavy reliance on fossil fuels and imported energy as well as the continuously rising energy demand. With the average annual rate of 4.2% increase in energy consumption, the total final energy consumption of the country is expected to rise from 29.8 million metric tons of oil equivalent (Mtoe) in 2015 to about 54.9 Mtoe by 2030. Primarily, transport, industry, residential, commercial, and agriculture are the major energy-intensive sectors [4].

Following the implementation of the Comprehensive Automotive Resurgence Strategy (CARS) Program which aims to strengthen the Philippine automotive industry, local production and domestic sales or market for automotive vehicles are expected to significantly increase. As a result, the transport sector will continue to dominate the Philippines' total final energy consumption with 35.7% average share annually [5]. Consequently, bulk percentage averaging to about 46% of the country's total energy requirement is sourced from petroleum products. Particularly, gasoline and diesel account for average shares of 28.4 and 50.5% of the total oil requirement, respectively [4]. In 2018, it was reported that oil products' consumption reached about 16.9 Mtoe [5]. A slightly lower consumption of 16 Mtoe was recorded in 2020 due to the halted activities especially the public and private transportation brought about by the COVID-19 pandemic restrictions [6]. Nonetheless, with the expected continuous increase in demand for petroleum products as transport fuel, the need for a more sustainable and cleaner alternative fuel such as biofuels is necessary.

Presently, DOE has maintained the implementation of 2% by volume biodiesel blends even though a 10% planned increase in blending must have been imposed for the year 2020 (**Figure 1**). Due to marginally higher pump prices, the recommended increase in blending target has been delayed. With the anticipated implementation of increased blending mandate, a total of 13 biodiesel accredited facilities operate as of December 2020, with a total production capacity of 707.90 million liters biodiesel per year (MLPY) (**Table 1**). With the current scenario, the total local biodiesel production as reported by DOE is 187.67 million liters in 2020 and an overall sale of about 160.42 million liters [6–10]. This volume of local production translates to approximately 26.5% of the total biodiesel production capacity of the country.

Clearly, the local biodiesel production capacity is sufficient to meet the biodiesel demand since 2007 (**Figure 2**). However, amid excess supply of coconut which is the sole feedstock for biodiesel in the country, fluctuating feedstock cost remains a challenge resulting to limitation in feedstock supply for biodiesel. Consequently, higher fuel pump prices at increased blending rate continues to be the main concern impeding the implementation of the recommended increase in biodiesel blending mandates.

As shown on **Figure 3**, the same trend was observed for biodiesel price and the local price of feedstock CNO. An increase in feedstock price results to a rise in the biodiesel selling price since total production cost for biodiesel is largely dictated by the cost of feedstock. On the average, a huge price difference can be observed between diesel and biodiesel prices. This entails that a further increase in the biodiesel blending rate would

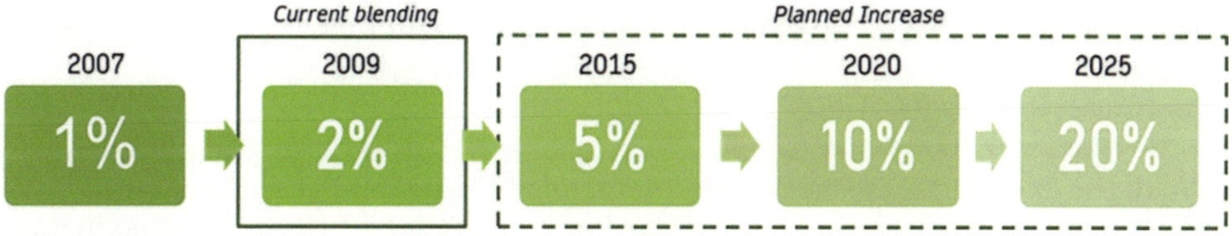

Figure 1.
Mandated biodiesel blending based on the Biofuels Act of 2006.

Biodiesel producers	Location	Plant Capacity (MLPY)
Chemrez Technologies, Inc.	Quezon City	90
Golden Asian Oil International, Inc.	Pasig City	60
Phil. Biochem Products, Inc.	Muntinlupa City	40
Pure Essence International, Inc.	Pasig City	72
JNJ Oleochemicals, Inc.	Lucena City, Quezon	63.3
Mt. Holly Coco Industrial, Inc.	Lucena City, Quezon	60
Tantuco Enterprises, Inc.	Tayabas, Quezon	90
Archemicals Corp.	Tagoloan, Misamis Oriental	33
Bioenergy 8 Corporation	Sasa, Davao City, Davao	30
Ecoenergy Corporation	General Santos City, Cotabato	30
Ecoenergy Corporation	Polomolok, Cotabato	100
Freyvonne Milling Services	Toril, Davao City, Davao	15.6
Phoenix Petroleum Philippines, Inc.	Villanueva, Misamis Oriental	24

Table 1.
List of accredited biodiesel producers in the Philippines as of 31 December 2020.

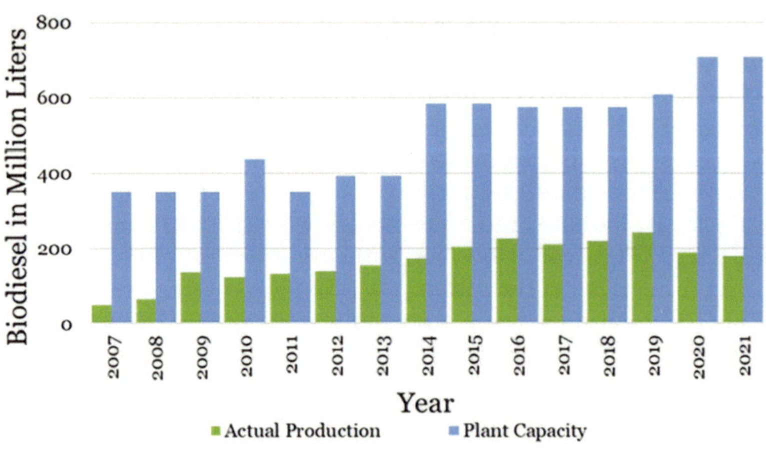

Figure 2.
Biodiesel plant capacity utilization in the Philippines, 2007-2021.

cause a significant rise in diesel fuel pump prices. Perhaps, this remains as the drawback of implementing the increased biodiesel blending. Hence, feedstock diversification is a great advantage to substantially improve the cost savings for higher biodiesel blends.

2.2 Biodiesel industry outlook

With the expected increase in diesel demand in the next 20 years, biodiesel requirement will hike up, more so with the implementation of the impending higher biodiesel blending mandates. At present, the production capacity of the country is about 384% of the biodiesel requirement for a 2% blending [11]. In 2022, the demand

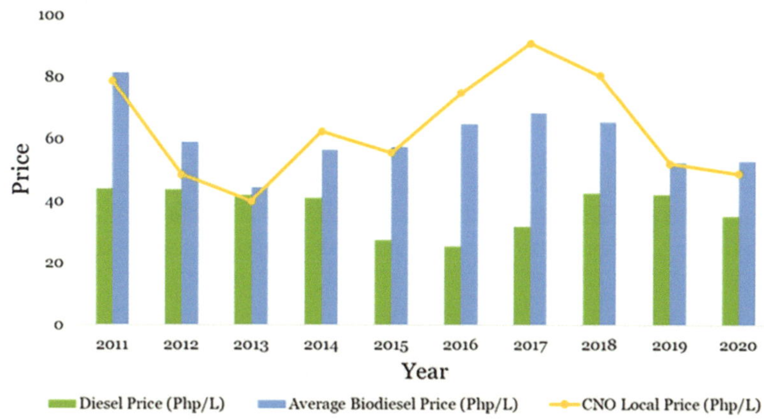

Figure 3.
Comparative prices of diesel, biodiesel, and feedstock CNO, 2011-2020.

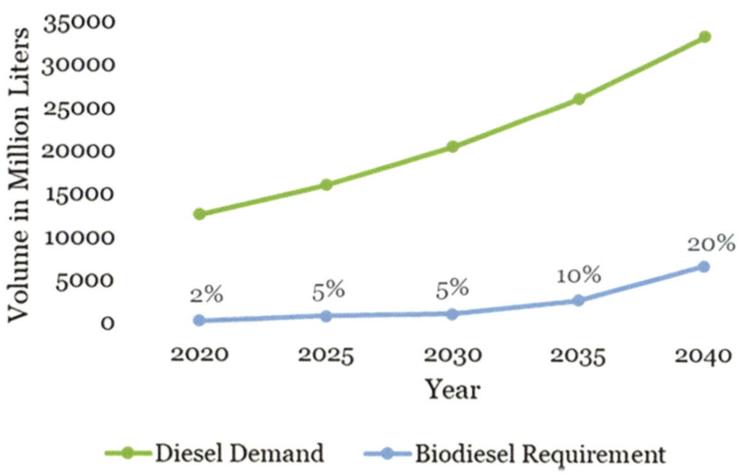

Figure 4.
Biodiesel demand projection, 2020-2040.

for biodiesel is projected to be 690 million liters if the 5% blending mandate will be imposed (**Figure 4**). At an 80% plant utilization rate, additional capacity of nearly 160 million liters is needed to meet this demand. In terms of feedstock availability, the target biodiesel supply even at the increased blending rate by 2022 only requires about 40% of the total coconut oil (CNO) available in the country. By the end of the planning period, further increasing the blending mandate to 20% will require around 6700 million liters biodiesel. This brings the target total production capacity of biodiesel to approximately 8400 million liters by 2040 and a feedstock requirement which is about four times the current local supply of CNO.

3. Conversion technologies for biodiesel production

Biodiesel derived from domestic renewable sources such as animal fats, vegetable oils, and algal oil has considerably similar properties and characteristics to petroleum-based diesel, making it a promising alternative fuel [12]. Edible oils are commonly produced from edible feedstocks such as coconut oil, soybean oil, palm oil, rapeseed oil, olive oil, corn oil, etc. Different non-edible oils including jatropha oil, petroleum nut oil, and castor oil can also be used for biodiesel production. In the case of waste oils, the possible feedstocks are waste cooking oil, fish oil, animal tallow oil, and pyrolysis oil while algal oil is usually sourced from *Chlorella vulgaris* algae [13]. Generally, the process flow for biodiesel production includes feedstock production and harvesting, oil extraction, oil refining, transesterification, and distillation (**Figure 5**).

Oil can be extracted from the raw material using mechanical extraction or solvent/enzyme extraction. Mechanical extraction usually uses a screw type machine to expel the oil through pressing (**Figure 6**). This process is relatively simple and is applicable to almost any kind of nuts and oilseeds, though, oil yield or recovery is oftentimes quite low [14]. Unlike mechanical extraction, solvent/enzyme extraction can result to significantly higher oil yields with oil reduction in meal to less than 1% by weight (**Figure 7**). However, this method has higher energy requirement and takes longer time. Another method that can be used for oil extraction is the enzymatic extraction method which uses suitable enzymes. As compared to other methods such as the

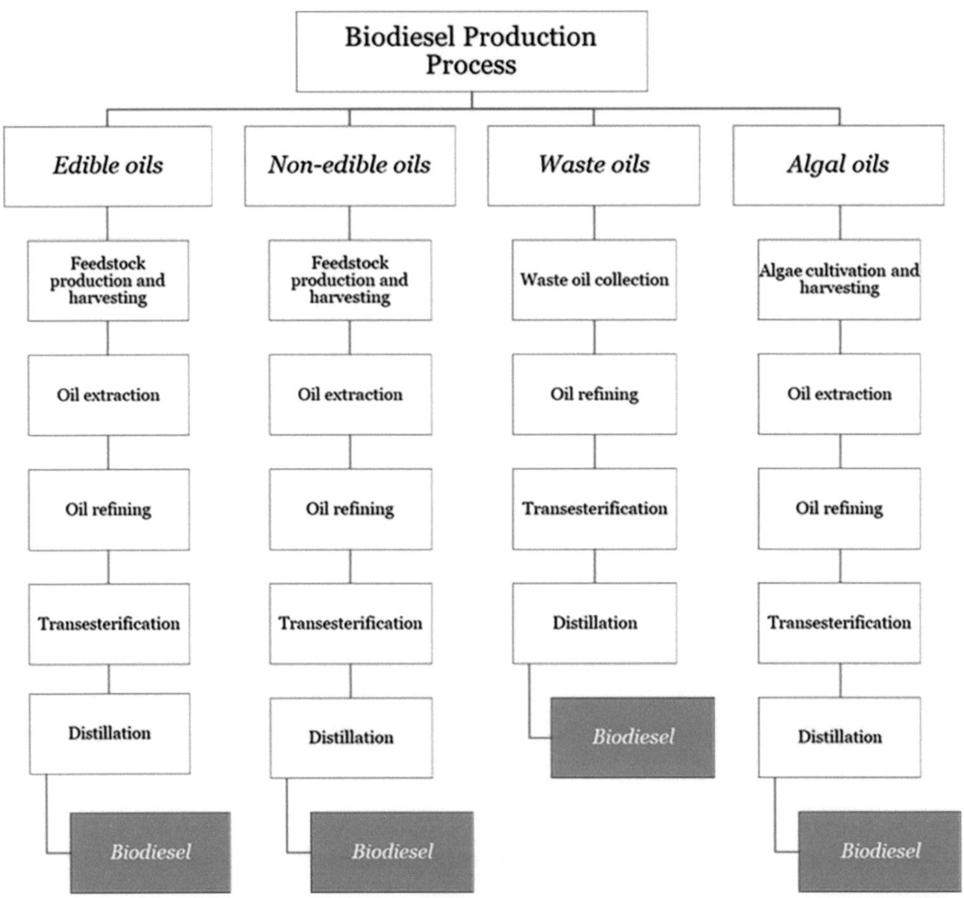

Figure 5.
General process flow for biodiesel production.

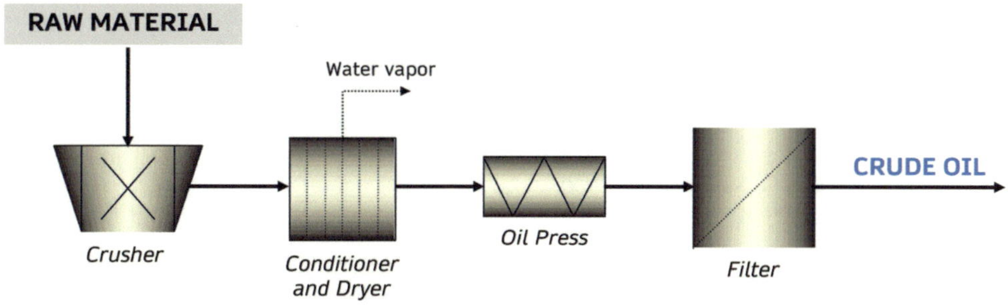

Figure 6.
General process flow of oil extraction via mechanical extraction.

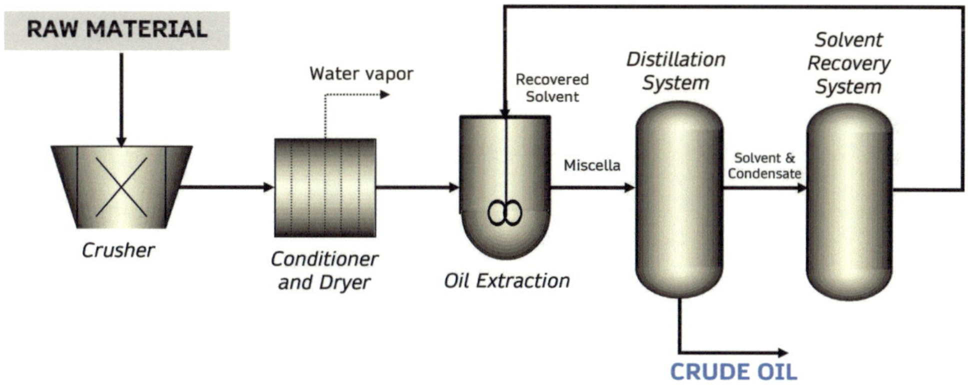

Figure 7.
General process flow of oil extraction via solvent extraction.

solvent extraction method, it is more environment-friendly but disadvantageous in terms of costs and processing time [15].

Crude oil, a product of oil extraction, is then refined to further improve the quality of the oil. Typically, oil refining process consists of several stages such as degumming, centrifugation, neutralization, oil bleaching, filtration, deaeration, and deodorization (**Figure 8**). Phospholipids are commonly removed by acid degumming using concentrated phosphoric acid at a temperature below 100°C. Phospholipids precipitated into gums are separated through centrifugation. Removal of free fatty acids (FFA) is done in the neutralization stage where alkaline solution such as sodium hydroxide is made to react with FFA forming soap stock which is removed again by centrifugation. Bleaching using adsorbents is employed to further improve the quality of the oil through the removal of other impurities and contaminants such as residual soap and gums, chlorophyll, oxidation products, and trace metals causing impurity reduction from 1.2 to 0.84% by mass. The recommended dosage loading of adsorbents used in the bleaching process are 17 kg bleaching earth and 5 kg activated carbon per metric ton of oil fed. These adsorbents are then removed by filtration while the bleached oil undergoes deaeration and deodorization. These last two stages of refining process aid in moisture and FFA removal to attain the desired 0.15% by mass moisture content and 0.025% by mass maximum FFA content of refined oil to be fed for biodiesel production [14, 16].

Transesterification is the main conversion technique for biodiesel production. This process involves the reversible reaction of oil or triglyceride to alcohol in the

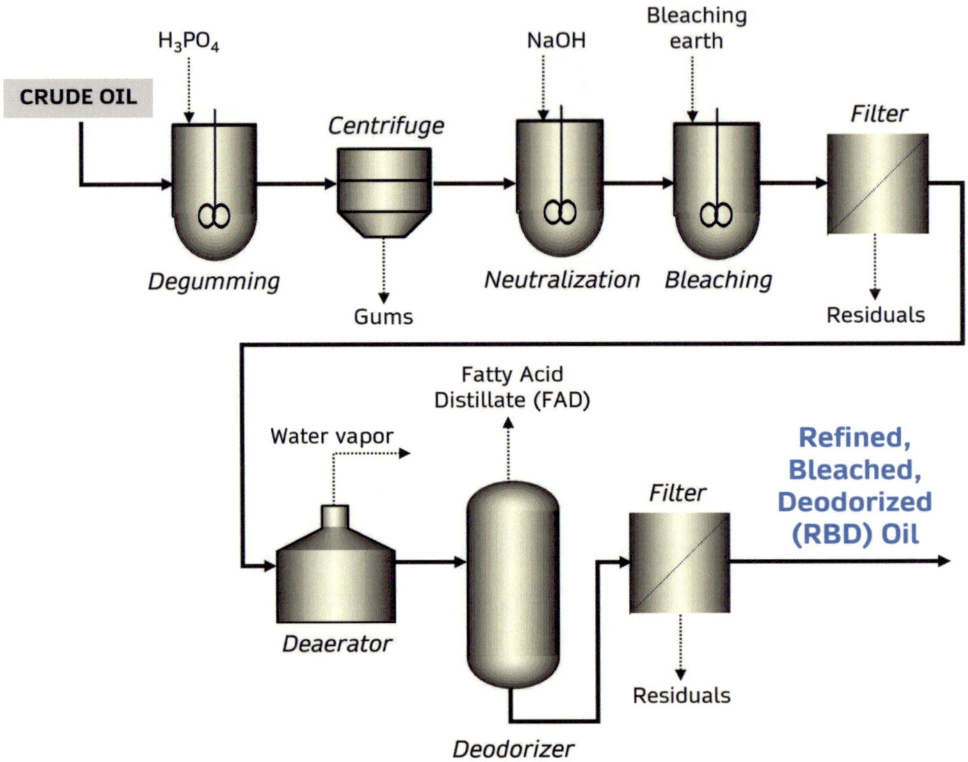

Figure 8.
General process flow of oil refining.

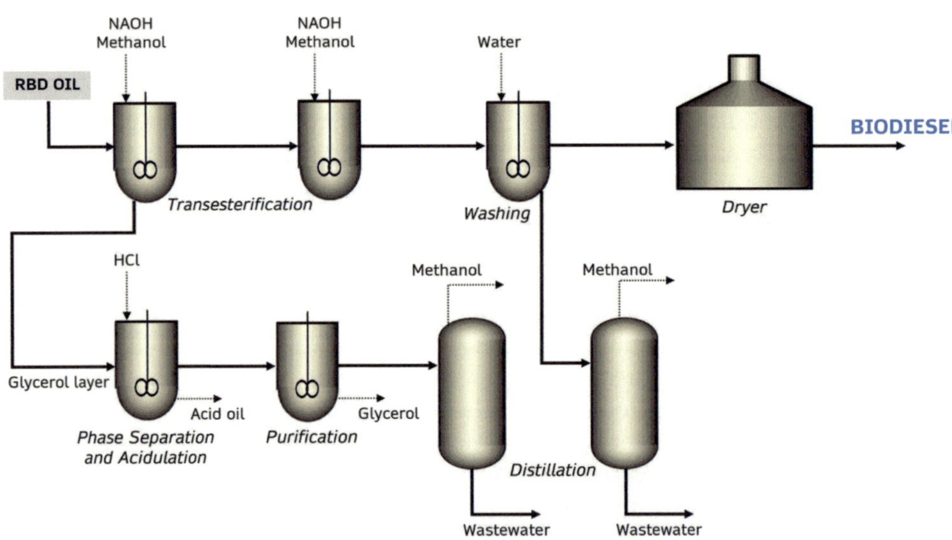

Figure 9.
General process flow of biodiesel production.

presence of a base catalyst forming fatty acid methyl esters (FAME) or biodiesel and glycerol. The process is usually carried out in a series of two batch transesterification reaction at 60°C (**Figure 9**). The initial reaction takes place for two hours causing a

96% conversion of triglycerides to biodiesel. Glycerol, a by-product of the reaction, is immiscible with biodiesel and eventually settles forming a layer below the biodiesel. The glycerol layer along with 60% of the unreacted methanol is allowed to settle for an hour before being withdrawn out of the reactor and processed for purification. The biodiesel layer is then subjected to the second reaction to convert the remaining triglyceride to biodiesel with about 99.95% conversion [14, 16].

Conversion technologies have a significant impact on the competitiveness of biodiesel as alternative fuel since it relates to quality and productivity. Hence, development of advanced processing technologies for biodiesel has been the focus of many researches. More so, selection of a good complementary feedstock is important to bridge the gaps in the Philippine biodiesel industry.

4. Feedstock development

Looking into feedstock development, three generations of biodiesel have been classified. The first-generation biodiesel is generally related to edible biomass sources such as food crops. However, with concerning issues and risks on food security, its implementation appears to have certain restrictions. Drawbacks of first-generation feedstocks led to growing interest on fuels produced from non-edible lignocellulosic biomass sources which are classified as second-generation biodiesel. These include fuels derived from forest and agricultural residues, animal wastes, and municipal solid wastes. Third generation biodiesel, on the other hand, include fuels that are produced from algal biomass or feedstocks which do not compete with food and arable lands [15].

4.1 First-generation biodiesel

4.1.1 Coconut as biodiesel feedstock

The Philippines is known as the world's second largest coconut producer and the top exporter of coconut products such as coconut oil. According to the Philippine Statistics Authority (PSA), 348 million coconut trees can be found in around 70 out of more than 80 provinces in the country in 2019, covering approximately a quarter of the total agricultural lands in the Philippines [17].

Biodiesel from coconut is derived specifically from the extracted oil from *copra*. *Copra* is the dried kernel part of the fruit which can be scooped out of the shell after drying up to a moisture content of about 6%. *Copra* is heated to 104–110°C in a conditioning unit to further improve oil extraction [14]. Crude coconut oil then undergoes oil refining process to increase the efficiency of the transesterification reaction for biodiesel production.

In the Philippines, a hectare of coconut plantation can yield 100 trees with an average nut yield per tree using the tall variety of 70 nuts annually. Equivalently, 1305 kg of *copra* is produced per hectare of coconut plantation per year. For an average yield of 605 liters of coco biodiesel per metric ton of *copra*, about 38,000 ha coconut plantation is needed to supply the nuts requirement of about 266 million per year for a commercial scale 30 million liter per year biodiesel capacity [16].

4.1.2 Soybean as biodiesel feedstock

In the Philippines, soybean is used primarily as a main ingredient in livestock feed because of its high protein content. However, due to insufficient domestic production, the country has been importing huge amounts of soybeans to meet the local demand. In 2019, the country's soybean gross supply was 178,772 metric tons in which only 659 metric tons or about 0.36% of the total supply was produced locally, and the remaining 178,113 metric tons (99.64%) was imported by the country. Domestic production of soybeans was reported to decrease at an average rate of −0.57% growth per year from 2017 to 2019 [18].

Aside from soybean meal, soybean processing also produces soybean oil as secondary product, making it one of the potential alternative feedstocks for biodiesel production. Solvent extraction is usually employed for an integrated soybean meal and biodiesel production system for a higher oil recovery and a more preferred soybean meal grade for animal feeds.

On the average, threshed soybean yield in the Philippines can reach 2.5 metric tons per hectare per cropping with a biodiesel potential of 100–129 liters per metric ton depending on the oil extraction method used. A total of 93,000–121,000 ha of soybean plantation, yielding about 233,000–302,000 metric tons threshed soybean per year is needed to supply the feedstock requirement for a commercial scale 30 million liter per year biodiesel plant [19].

4.1.3 Oil palm as biodiesel feedstock

Oil palm is a tropical tree crop typically grown in areas where rain is abundant. Normally, wild palms have a life span of up to 200 years while commercial palms only have 20–30 years economic life span [20]. Oil palm as a plantation crop is a high-yielding source of two distinct oils such as palm oil and palm kernel oil (lauric oil) which can be obtained from the fibrous mesocarp or flesh of the fruit and kernel of the nut, respectively.

Similar to coconut oil, oil palm is identified as one of the alternative feedstocks for biodiesel production because it contains highly saturated vegetable fats [21]. Processing of oil palm includes bunch reception followed by sterilization and threshing to remove the fruit from the bunch. The fruitlets are then digested and pressed to extract the crude palm oil which undergoes clarification before the oil refining process.

The average yield of oil palm is 135 trees per hectare. About 20 metric tons of fresh fruit bunches (FFB) per hectare is harvested annually with a biodiesel potential of 188 liters per metric ton. For a 30 million liters per year biodiesel capacity, about 8000 ha of oil palm plantation is required to produce 160,000 metric tons of FFB per year [20, 21].

4.2 Second-generation biodiesel

4.2.1 Jatropha curcas as biodiesel feedstock

Jatropha is locally known as tubang-bakod and is considered as a potential source for biodiesel production due to its suitability in tropical and subtropical regions as well as its higher seed productivity and rapid growth [22]. On the average, it has a productive life span ranging from 35 to 50 years. Unlike other crops such as palm and coconut which takes about eight and four years, respectively before the first harvest, jatropha can be harvested in just 14 months [23]. Since this crop is not used for food applications, its potential as a biodiesel feedstock in the Philippines has grown interest. With an oil content of about 20–60%, jatropha is found to have a higher oil content than that of other oilseed crops such as palm oil. However, the high content of free fatty acids (FFA) in jatropha is seen as a disadvantage for biodiesel production since this requires an additional transesterification reaction to improve the biodiesel quality [24].

On the average, the yield of jatropha is 2500 plants per hectare, producing about six to eight metric tons of seeds. With its biodiesel potential yield of 185 liters per metric ton, about 23,000 ha of jatropha plantation to produce approximately 160,000 metric tons of seeds is needed to supply the feedstock requirement for a commercial scale 30 million liter per year biodiesel plant [25, 26].

4.2.2 Used cooking oil as biodiesel feedstock

Used cooking oil has drawn considerable interest as a potential alternative source for biodiesel production due to its low cost and its availability at a huge quantity as waste. Though waste cooking oil has been used in soap production, most of its volume is discarded into the environment. Since feedstock cost is one of the primary concerns in biodiesel production, utilization of used cooking oil as feedstock can significantly contribute to cost savings.

At the optimum conditions of 6.51 mol/mol methanol-to-oil molar ratio, 0.171 mol/mol sodium hydroxide-to-oil molar ratio, 47.0°C, and 30-minute reaction time for the sodium hydroxide-catalyzed transesterification of used cooking oil, the percent mass yield of biodiesel is around 80. This means that approximately 8 kg of biodiesel can be produced from 10 kg of used cooking oil [27]. This results to a biodiesel potential yield of approximately 905 liters per metric ton. Hence, for a commercial scale 30 million liter per year biodiesel plant, about 34,000 metric tons of used cooking oil is required as feedstock annually.

4.3 Third-generation biodiesel

4.3.1 Microalgae as biodiesel feedstock

Microalgae have emerged as a suitable feedstock for biodiesel production due to its high lipid content, rapid biomass growth, and cultivation which does not compete with food crops for arable land [28]. As compared to other crop-based biodiesel feedstocks, microalgae appear to have the highest oil productivity [29].

Parametric studies on microalgae (*C. vulgaris)* as feedstock for biodiesel production revealed that maximum oil extraction efficiency of around 15% can be obtained using a biomass-to-solvent ratio of 1:14 at a 24-hr duration and a 1:2 (v/v) ratio of methanol-to-chloroform as solvent via Soxhlet method. Moreover, the optimum conditions for base-catalyzed transesterification for biodiesel production are 1:6:0.2 oil-to-methanol-sodium hydroxide molar ratio at 55°C reaction temperature and five minutes reaction time [30]. Meanwhile, the biodiesel potential yield of microalgae is 896 liters per metric ton. Hence, a total of 263 ha of cultivation area, yielding an annual biomass production of 34,000 metric tons is needed to supply the feedstock requirement for a commercial scale 30 million liter per year biodiesel plant.

5. Suitability assessment of biodiesel production from different feedstocks

5.1 Feedstock availability and biodiesel potential yield

As shown in **Table 2**, in terms of biodiesel productivity which assumes maximum biomass conversion to biodiesel for the given possible available land area, coconut has the highest potential among the potential feedstocks considering the huge

Feedstock		Maximum biodiesel potential yield (L/ton)	Biomass production yield (ton/ha)	Potential available area (ha)	Biodiesel productivity (L)	Land area needed (ha)	Percent of existing cropping area	Source
First generation								
Coconut (copra)		605	1.30	3.65 M	2.87B	1.02 M	360	[16]
Soybean (grains)	Solvent Extraction	129	2.5	300	0.097 M	2.49 M	0.012	[19]
	Mechanical Extraction	100			0.075 M	3.22 M	0.009	
Oil Palm (fresh fruit bunch)		188	20	0.1 M	376 M	0.21 M	47	[20]
Second generation								
Jatropha (seed)		185	7.5	0.1 M (idle lands suitable for jatropha cultivation)	139 M	0.58 M	17	[26]
Used Cooking Oil		905	0.04 million tons (MT)	—	36.2 M	0.89 MT	4.50	[27]
Third generation								
Microalgae (*Chlorella vulgaris*)		896	128	—	—	6150	—	[30]

Table 2.
Biodiesel potential yield of different biodiesel feedstocks in the Philippines.

plantation area for this crop of about a quarter of the total agricultural lands in the country. Even at a 5% blending mandate by 2025, the existing cropping area for coconut is almost four times greater than the area requirement to produce enough feedstock.

Moreover, oil palm is the second crop-based feedstock with the highest biodiesel productivity. Its utilization for biodiesel production in the Philippines has already been proposed as alternative to coconut oil, however, a more comprehensive study for its viability still needs to be conducted before its implementation as required by the Department of Energy (DOE) [31]. Once allowed as alternative feedstock, the potential available area for this crop can sustain almost half of the biodiesel requirement for a 5% blending rate in 2025.

Looking into the biodiesel potential, used cooking oil and microalgae have the highest maximum yield among the possible feedstocks. However, oil extraction from microalgae is still performed in lab-scale and no technology has been confirmed yet as to its practical application in large scale lipid extraction [15, 32]. Nonetheless, only around 6150 ha will be required as biomass cultivation area to achieve the biodiesel requirement in 2025 if microalgae will be used as feedstock. Similarly, utilization of used cooking oil for biodiesel production still requires further studies specifically on process optimization and raw material quality control [11]. Meanwhile, with the available quantity of used cooking oil, this feedstock can contribute about 4.50% of the total biodiesel requirement in 2025.

	Coconut		Oil Palm		Soybean		Jatropha	
Blending rat (%)e	**Carbon Footprint (kg CO_2e/L)**	**GHG Reduction Potential (%)**	**Carbon Footprint (kg CO_2e/L)**	**GHG Reduction Potential (%)**	**Carbon Footprint (kg CO_2e/L)**	**GHG Reduction Potential (%)**	**Carbon Footprint (kg CO_2e/L)**	**GHG Reduction Potential (%)**
2	3.0839	1.06	3.0908	0.84	3.0933	0.76	3.1014	0.50
5	3.0343	2.65	3.0515	2.10	3.0578	1.90	3.0780	1.25
10	2.9516	5.31	2.9861	4.20	2.9986	3.80	3.0391	2.50
20	2.7863	10.61	2.8552	8.40	2.8801	7.60	2.9612	5.00
100	1.4634	53.05	1.8079	42.00	1.9325	38.00	2.3378	25.00

Table 3.
Carbon footprint and GHG reduction potential of different biodiesel feedstocks at varying blending rates.

Blending rate	GHG Savings (thousand metric tons CO_2e/year)			
	Coconut	Oil Palm	Soybean	Jatropha
2%	529.15	418.92	379.03	249.36
5%	1322.88	1047.31	947.57	623.40
10%	2645.76	2094.62	1895.14	1246.80
20%	5291.52	4189.25	3790.27	2493.60
100%	26,457.60	20,946.24	18,951.36	12,468.00

Table 4.
GHG savings of different biodiesel feedstocks at varying blending rates.

5.2 Carbon footprint and GHG reduction potential

Along with issues on energy security considering the continuously increasing energy demand and diminishing fossil reserves, the alarming impacts of climate change also call for the adoption of sustainable development options. In response to this, the country committed for a 75% greenhouse gas (GHG) emissions reduction by 2030, in which 2.71% is unconditional and 72.29% is conditional based on the 2021 Nationally Determined Contribution (NDC). This is established against the forecasted business-as-usual cumulative emission of 3340.3 metric tons CO_2e for the period 2020–2030 [33]. Hence, use of technologies that can substantially curb emissions, such as biofuels, is targeted. Compared to fossil fuel, biofuels can significantly lower carbon dioxide and carbon monoxide emissions by 78 and 50%, respectively [33].

In the Philippine setting, the biodiesel industry carbon footprint results to 1.4634 kg CO_2e per liter. This was obtained by conducting Life Cycle Assessment (LCA) and taking into account a cradle-to-grave system boundary starting from feedstock cultivation up to biodiesel end-use. In Ref. to the GHG emission of petroleum diesel equal to 3.12 kg CO_2e per liter, a GHG reduction potential of about 53.05% can be achieved upon full displacement of petroleum diesel by pure coconut methyl ester or coco biodiesel [14]. Correspondingly, at varying blending rates of 2, 5, 10, and 20%, the GHG reduction potential that can be attained are 1.06, 2.65, 5.31, and 10.61%, respectively. In 2021, 2% biodiesel blending has a potential GHG savings of 289,380 metric tons CO_2e per year considering the total diesel demand of 8750 million liters. Implementing the 5% blending rate in 2025 will result to a significant hike in the potential avoided GHG emissions to nearly 1.32 million metric tons CO_2e per year from the diesel demand projection of 16,000 million liters.

Table 3 shows the carbon footprint and GHG reduction potential at varying blending percentages of different potential biodiesel feedstocks. Comparing the different feedstocks, biodiesel production from coconut has the lowest carbon footprint and highest GHG reduction potential, followed by oil palm. Oil palm biodiesel has a carbon footprint of 1.80 kg CO_2e per liter and GHG reduction potential of 42% [20, 21]. This corresponds to a GHG savings of about 1.047 million metric tons CO_2e per year for a 5% blending mandate in 2025 (**Table 4**). On the other hand, jatropha biodiesel and biodiesel derived from soybeans using solvent extraction results to a carbon footprint of 2.34 kg CO_2e per liter and 1.93 kg CO_2e per liter, which contributes about 25% and 38% reduction in GHG emissions, respectively [19, 34]. Potential GHG savings of the other feedstocks at varying biodiesel blending rates are also shown in **Table 4.**

5.3 Economic viability

The cost of biodiesel production is highly affected by the feedstock which typically accounts for 70–80% of the total production cost [28, 32]. This led to a usually higher cost of biodiesel than petroleum-based diesel which is a major drawback for biodiesel commercialization in the country. Hence, selection of a more economically viable feedstock is a great advantage to boost the biodiesel industry in the Philippines.

In 2020, the average local price of crude CNO is Php 48.83 per liter. The price of biodiesel in the same year ranges from Php 35.00 to Php 71.00 per liter, whereas the diesel price is only around Php 35.16 per liter [11]. If sourced directly from copra based on farmgate price, a relatively lower biodiesel price can be achieved, ranging from Php 27.67 to Php 52.62 per liter [35]. In the case of oil palm as feedstock, a price equivalent to Php 22.72 per liter of commercially available crude palm oil results to a lower minimum selling price for biodiesel of Php 33.26 per liter, a return on investment of 14.44%, and a payback period of 5.75 years. Assuming the case of an integrated oil palm plantation and biodiesel plant, where the plantation is established from oil palm seeds, the biodiesel selling price is Php 33.53 per liter while the return on investment and payback period are 22.04% and 9.33 years, respectively [20, 21].

For jatropha biodiesel, sensitivity analysis revealed that at a seed price of Php 5.00 per kg, the selling price of biodiesel is Php 35.00 per liter to have a return on investment of 17.26% and a payback period of 3.85 years. However, use of crude jatropha oil as a bunker fuel is found more economically feasible than trans esterified crude Jatropha oil [36]. Similarly, biodiesel production from soybean appears to be economically unattractive as biodiesel price can go as high as Php 87.34 per liter depending on the crop yield and the prices of commodities. Soybean biodiesel production via solvent extraction results to a biodiesel price range of Php 48.49 to Php 84.52 per liter for manual farming and Php 33.36 to Php 67.71 per liter for mechanized farming. Using mechanical extraction, a price range of Php 38.93 to Php 87.34 per liter and Php 19.35 to Php 65.59 per liter can be obtained for manual and mechanized farming, respectively [19].

6. Conclusion

The use of biofuels in the Philippines, in pursuant to Republic Act 9367 (also known as the Biofuels Act of 2006), is a valuable initiative as the country envisions action plans towards energy security and climate change mitigation. However, feedstock availability and pricing concerns remains the primary challenges hampering the growth of the biofuels industry. At present, biodiesel in the country is solely sourced from coconut. The mandated biodiesel blending to petroleum diesel remains stagnant at 2% due to marginally higher pump prices at increased blending of coco biodiesel. Hence, research and development studies on the viability of different potential feedstocks for biodiesel has been initiated.

In this chapter, potential feedstocks for biodiesel such as coconut, oil palm, soybean, jatropha, used cooking oil, and microalgae were assessed in terms of feedstock availability and biodiesel potential yield, carbon footprint and GHG reduction potential, and economic viability. Among the feedstocks, oil palm (first generation), used cooking oil (second generation), and microalgae (third generation) have the highest biodiesel potential yield. Considering the potential available area, oil palm is the most recommended feedstock having the second highest biodiesel productivity of

376 million liters per year, next to coconut. It also has a relatively lower carbon footprint of 1.80 kg CO_2e per liter and a GHG reduction potential of 42% which is higher than the other sources. Moreover, its economic viability makes it a good complementary feedstock to coconut for biodiesel production since it results to a potentially lower biodiesel selling price of Php 33.26 per liter. Although other sources such as used cooking oil and microalgae have emerged as suitable alternative feedstocks, more comprehensive validation studies still need to be conducted for its practical application in biodiesel production.

Hence, ensuring economic and environmental sustainability is the challenge facing the biodiesel industry in the Philippines. It is therefore crucial to develop and establish appropriate and efficient processing technologies and pricing mechanisms, as well as to utilize low cost and readily available feedstocks to sustain the industry's growth.

Acknowledgements

Data presented in this book chapter are from research projects supported by the Philippine Department of Agriculture – Bureau of Agricultural Research (DA-BAR), Department of Energy (DOE), United States Agency for International Development (USAID), and the University of the Philippines. Authors would also like to acknowledge the researchers, collaborators, and stakeholders that contribute to the success of the research projects.

Author details

Rona Joyce B. Landoy*, Rex B. Demafelis, Bernadette T. Magadia
and Anna Elaine D. Matanguihan
Department of Chemical Engineering, University of the Philippines Los Baños,
Los Baños, Laguna, Philippines

*Address all correspondence to: rblandoy@up.edu.ph

References

[1] Official Gazette of the Philippine Government. Republic Act No. 9367: Biofuels Act of 2006. Philippines: Republic of the Philippines; 2007. Available from: https://www.officialgazette.gov.ph/2007/01/12/republic-act-no-9367/. [Accessed: 03 11 2021]

[2] Yap D. Research Brief on Energy: Summary of Biofuels Act [Internet]. 2016. Available from http://wingatchalian.com/policy-category/energy/. [Accessed: 03 11 2021]

[3] Alonzo R. An Economic and Environmental Analysis of the Impact of Higher-Blended Biodiesel on the Philippine Economy [Internet]. 2016. Available from https://mpra.ub.uni-muenchen.de/87717/. [Accessed 03 11 2021]

[4] Department of Energy Philippine Energy Plan 2016-2030 [Internet]. 2016. Available from: https://www.doe.gov.ph/sites/default/files/pdf/pep/2016-2030_pep.pdf. [Accessed: 03 11 2021]

[5] Department of Energy Philippine Energy Plan 2018-2040 [Internet]. 2018. Available from: https://www.doe.gov.ph/sites/default/files/pdf/pep/pep-2018-2040-final.pdf?ckattempt=1/. [Accessed: 03 11 2021]

[6] Department of Energy Philippine Energy Plan 2020-2040 [Internet]. 2020. Available from: https://www.doe.gov.ph/sites/default/files/pdf/pep/pep_2020-2040_signed.pdf. [Accessed: 03 11 2021]

[7] Corpuz P. Philippines Biofuels Annual: Philippine Biofuels Situation and Outlook [Internet]. n.d. Available from: https://apps.fas.usda.gov/newgainapi/api/report/downloadreportbyfilename?filename=Biofuels%20Annual_Manila_Philippines_10-22-2014.pdf. [Accessed: 27 12 2021]

[8] Department of Energy Philippine Energy Plan 2012-2030 [Internet]. 2012. Available from: https://www.doe.gov.ph/sites/default/files/pdf/pep/2012-2030_pep.pdf. [Accessed: 27 12 2021]

[9] Department of Energy. List of Accredited Biodiesel Producers as of 31 December 2020. [Internet]. Available from https://www.doe.gov.ph/renewable-energy?q=renewable-energy/biodiesel&ckattempt=1/. [Accessed 2021-11-03]

[10] Corpuz P Philippines Biofuels Annual: Philippine Biofuels Situation and Outlook [Internet]. 2017. Available from: https://apps.fas.usda.gov/newgainapi/api/report/downloadreportbyfilename?filename=Biofuels%20Annual_Manila_Philippines_10-18-2017.pdf. [Accessed: 27 12 2021]

[11] Corpuz P. Philippines Biofuels Annual: Philippine Biofuels Situation and Outlook [Internet]. 2021. Available from: https://apps.fas.usda.gov/newgainapi/api/Report/DownloadReportByFileName?fileName=Biofuels%20Annual_Manila_Philippines_10-18-2021.pdf. [Accessed: 27 12 2021]

[12] Shereena KM, Thangaraj T. Biodiesel: An alternative fuel produced from vegetable oils by transesterification. Electric Journal of **b**iology. 2009; 5(3):67-74. Available from: https://ejbio.imedpub.com/biodiesel-an-alternative-fuel-produced-from-vegetable-oils-bytransesterification.pdf. [Accessed: 27 12 2021]

[13] Singh D, Sharma D, Soni SL, Sharma S, Sharma PK. A review on

feedstocks, production processes, and yield for different generations of biodiesel. Fuel. 2019;**262**:116553. DOI: 10.1016/j.fuel.2019.116553

[14] University of the Philippines Biofuels Research Team. Environmental Assessment of Higher-Blended Cocobiodiesel [Research Project Final Report]. Philippines: University of the Philippines Los Baños and United States Agency for International Development (USAID); n.d

[15] Sani YM, Daud WMAW, Abdul AR. Biodiesel feedstock and production technologies: successes, challenges and prospects. Biodiesel—Feedstocks, Production and Applications. 2012. DOI:10.5772/5279

[16] University of the Philippines Biofuels Research Team. Life Cycle Assessment in Terms of Carbon Debt and Payback Analyses, Carbon Savings, and Energetics Studies of Biodiesel Production from Coconut Oil in the Philippines [Research Project Final Report]. Philippines: University of the Philippines Los Baños and Department of Energy; 2019. pp. 42-72

[17] Abao L. Oilseeds and Products Annual. United States Department of Agriculture; Foreign Agricultural Service. 2021. Available from https://apps.fas.usda.gov/newgainapi/api/Report/. [Accessed: 03 11 2021]

[18] Philippine Statistics Authority (PSA). Supply Utilization Accounts of Selected Agricultural Commodities: 2017-2019. 2020. Available from https://psa.gov.ph/sites/default/files/SUA_2017-2019_0.pdf /.[Accessed: 03 11 2021]

[19] University of the Philippines Biofuels Research Team. Boosting Farmer's Income through an Integrated Soybean Production for Food and Fuel: An Environmental Assessment, Technical, and Economic Studies [Research Project Final Report]. Philippines: University of the Philippines Los Baños and Department of Agriculture—Bureau of Agricultural Research; 2018

[20] University of the Philippines Biofuels Research Team. Environmental Assessment, Technical, and Economic Study of Biodiesel Production from Palm Oil in the Philippines [Research Project Final Report]. Philippines: University of the Philippines Los Baños and Department of Agriculture—Bureau of Agricultural Research; 2015

[21] Dizon LSH, Pector AA, Demafelis RB, Bataller BG, Bayados RB, Elepaño AR. et al. Environmental and economic viability of biodiesel production from palm oil in the Philippines. PIChE Journal. 2020;**19**(1):38-40. Available from: https://www.researchgate.net/publication/335055308_Environmental_and_Economic_Viability_of_Biodiesel_Production_from_Palm_Oil_in_the_Philippines. [Accessed: 29 12 2021]

[22] Irwan M, Thahir R, Adhiksana A, Marlinda, Ramli. The production of biofuels from jatropha curcas oil using ultrasound energy. In: AIP Conference Proceedings. Vol. 1983, No. 1. AIP Publishing LLC. 2018. DOI: 10.1063/1.5046221

[23] The Philippine National Oil Company-Alternative Fuels Corporation. Cultivation of Jatropha in the Philippines. 2007. Available from: https://jatrophadotpro.files.wordpress.com/2019/03/cultivation-of-jatropha-in-the-philippines.pdf/. [Accessed: 27 12 2021]

[24] Bombo K, Lekgoba T, Azeez O, Muzenda E. The sustainability of biodiesel synthesis from different

feedstocks: a review. Petroleum and Coal 2020; **63**(2):284-291. Available from: https://www.academia.edu/45599204/The_Sustainability_of_Biodiesel_Synthesis_from_Different_Feedstocks_A_Review. [Accessed 29 12 2021]

[25] University of the Philippines Biofuels Research Team. Environmental Assessment of Community-Based and Commercial Scale Biofuels Processing Systems Using Alternative Biofuels Feedstocks: An Initiative Towards Climate Change Mitigation in the Philippines [Research Project Final Report]. Philippines: University of the Philippines Los Baños and Department of Agriculture—Bureau of Agricultural Research; 2014

[26] Demafelis R. Potential of biodiesel production from Jatropha curcas in the Philippines. In: Food and Agriculture Organization of the United Nations. Conference Proceedings. 2007. Available from https://agris.fao.org/agris-search/search.do?recordID=PH2008000635. [Accessed: 03 11 2021]

[27] Cruz MKD. Sodium Hydroxide-Catalyzed Transesterification of Used Cooking Oil: Optimization for Methyl Ester Production. [Manuscript]. 2015

[28] Cruz YR, Aranda DAG, Seidl PR, Diaz GC, Carliz RG, Fortes MM, et al. Cultivation systems of microalgae for the production of biofuels. 2018. DOI: 10.5772/intechopen.74957

[29] Chisti Y Biodiesel from microalgae. Biotechnological Advances. 2007; **25**:294-306. Available from: http://www.tamu.edu/faculty/tpd8/BICH407/AlgaeBiodiesel.pdf. [Accessed 29 12 2021]

[30] University of the Philippines Biofuels Research Team. Technology Piloting of Microalgae as Biodiesel Feedstock [Research Project Final Report]. Philippines: University of the Philippines Los Baños and Department of Agriculture—Bureau of Agricultural Research; 2012

[31] Velasco MM. DOE Seeks Study before Allowing Palm Oil for Biodiesel. 2021. Available from: https://mb.com.ph/2021/12/02/doe-seeks-study-before-allowing-palm-oil-for-biodiesel/. [Accessed: 29 12 2021]

[32] Chen J, Li J, Dong W, Zhang X, Tyagi RD, Drogui P, et al. The potential of microalgae in biodiesel production. Renewable and Sustainable Energy Reviews. 2018;**90**:336-346. DOI: 10.1016/j.rser.2018.03.073

[33] Republic of the Philippines Nationally Determined Contribution Communicated to the UNFCCC on 15 2021. Available from: https://www4.unfccc.int/sites/ndcstaging/PublishedDocuments/Philippines%20First/Philippines%20-%20NDC.pdf. [Accessed 29 12 2021]

[34] Obligado AB, Demafelis RB, Matanguihan AED, Villancio VT, Magadia RV, Manaig LMA Carbon Emission Inventory of a Commercial-Scale *Jatropha (Jatropha curcas* L.) Biodiesel Processing Plant. Journal of Environmental Science and Management Special Issue 1 2017:20-32. Available from: https://ovcre.uplb.edu.ph/journalsuplb/index.php/JESAM/article/view/502 /. [Accessed 27 12 2021]

[35] University of the Philippines Biofuels Research Team. Socio-Economic Assessment of Implementing a Competitive Copra Pricing Mechanism for a Sustainable Philippine Biodiesel Industry [Research Project Report]. Philippines: University of the Philippines Los Baños; 2020

[36] Demafelis RB. Potential of Biodiesel Production from Jatropha Curcas in the Philippines. Laguna (Philippines): SEARCA Professorial Chair Lecture. College; 2007. Available from: https://agris.fao.org/agris-search/search.do?recordID=PH2008000635. [Accessed 29 12 2021]